THE POLITICS OF JOHN W. DAFOE
AND THE *FREE PRESS*

The Politics of
JOHN W. DAFOE
and the *Free Press*

BY

RAMSAY COOK

University of Toronto Press

© UNIVERSITY OF TORONTO PRESS 1963
REPRINTED 1971
PRINTED IN THE NETHERLANDS FOR
UNIVERSITY OF TORONTO PRESS
TORONTO AND BUFFALO

ISBN 0-8020-5119-7

FOR MY PARENTS

Introduction

ON THE OCCASION of the celebration of J. W. Dafoe's sixtieth year as a journalist, Arch Dale, the brilliant cartoonist of the *Free Press*, created a picture of the man who appears in this study. In Dale's cartoon, a shaggy Dafoe peered omnisciently over a scene filled with all the prominent Canadian politicians from Macdonald, Laurier and Roblin to King, Aberhart and Coldwell. In this book about the politics of J. W. Dafoe I have attempted to fill in the details of that picture. Therefore this is not the only book that could be written about Dafoe nor, I hope, the only one that will be written. John Dafoe deserves a full-length biography which should include a more personal picture of his life than I have wanted to create. It should also, perhaps, include rather more about his technique as a journalist and his work with such organizations as the Canadian Institute of International Affairs than I have found possible in this study of politics. There is even at least one aspect of his politics that might bear more detailed discussion—his long war with the Roblin régime in Manitoba. My emphasis has been on politics, and especially national politics. It has also been on Dafoe's years at the *Free Press*. The result is only a preliminary to that complete portrait that may some day be drawn. But I think the study is justified because it attempts to explain the major aspects of Dafoe's career. For after everything is said about the man, one fact remains indisputable: he lived by his mind and his pen.

That mind and that pen were largely devoted to politics, for Dafoe was above all a political animal. He lived in an atmosphere steeped in the discussion of public affairs—prairie, national, and international. The *Free Press* offices constantly hummed with political talk, political ideas and even political action. When there was a lull at the newspaper, or a crisis elsewhere, Dafoe moved to other centres of news, opinion and dispute; he travelled to Ottawa, he ate and talked with his cronies at the Manitoba Club, he consorted with the journalists of the Empire or the members of the Canadian Institute of International Affairs. This is the aspect of Dafoe's life that is analysed here.

JOHN A. MACDONALD LAURIER COLIN CAMPBELL ROBLIN BOB ROGERS BORDEN KING MEIGHEN BENNETT BENNETT ABERHART COLDWELL

Dafoe belonged to a profession that has not lacked honoured names in Canadian history. There have been many influential political editors in the two centuries of Canadian life since the fall of Quebec—Joseph Howe, William Lyon Mackenzie, George Brown, and Henri Bourassa, to name only the more familiar. Dafoe shared with each of these men a desire to serve his country and make it a better place in which to live. According to his lights, he set out day after day in the columns of the *Free Press* his views on Canada, its problems, its shortcomings and its needs. He never fought a famous libel suit like Howe, fomented a rebellion like Mackenzie, led a political party like Brown, or defended a minority culture like Bourassa. But though he did not come into the headlines as these did, his influence was probably no less important. Sometimes he was the most articulate voice of Western Canada, sometimes the propagandist of Liberal nationalism, sometimes the isolated proponent of the League of Nations. Always his views were carefully worked out and worthy of consideration. Whatever one may think about his ideas, few will deny that John W. Dafoe was a distinguished and influential Canadian. Perhaps this essay in Canadian politics will help to explain his reputation and also throw a little light on the dark passages of recent Canadian history.

There is, perhaps, one final word. I have described Dafoe as a "Western Liberal nationalist." These are not, of course, easy concepts to define satisfactorily. In using them I have not intended to suggest that the West was monolithic, nor have I dared to presume that the words "Liberal" and "nationalist" have simple, generally accepted, meanings. Dafoe gave his own content to each of these words, and it is this content, rather than any general definition, that I have attempted to explore. Perhaps this is only to say that I have tried to be a historian, interested in political ideas, rather than a student of political theory.

R.C.

Acknowledgments

LIKE MOST BOOKS, this one has been in the making for a long time. During these years I have been assisted by a great number of people. Not all of them can be thanked individually; nor can any of them be held responsible for the final product. No one has given me more encouragement to complete this work than my teacher and senior colleague, Professor D. G. Creighton, whose own work sets such high standards for all younger Canadian historians. Working for him and with him has been extremely rewarding. All of my other colleagues in Canadian history at Toronto have helped me, but none more than my friends Kenneth McNaught and John T. Saywell. Over the years Dr. A. R. M. Lower and Professor F. W. Gibson of Queen's University have helped me to formulate my ideas. Professor F. H. Underhill read my manuscript and made many friendly suggestions. Mr. George Ferguson of the *Montreal Star*, a former associate and biographer of J. W. Dafoe, read, criticized and corrected my work, and, more important, encouraged me with his kindness and his enthusiasm for my subject. It is probably unnecessary to add that I did not agree with all the suggestions and criticisms of these people. But I did learn something from each of them.

I would like also to thank the people who have placed manuscript collections at the disposal of students of Canadian history. In particular, I must express my gratitude to the Dafoe family, for it was their generosity in making J. W. Dafoe's papers available that made this study possible. I hope they will find that the resulting book justified their action. The staffs of the Public Archives of Canada, the various provincial archives and the library of the *Winnipeg Free Press* gave me the same helpful guidance that has placed so many scholars in their debt. Brigdens of Winnipeg Limited kindly granted permission to use the photograph of J. W. Dafoe in the Arch Dale cartoon which appears in this book.

Numerous individuals and institutions assisted with the financial and technical side of this study. The University of Toronto, through its research funds for staff members, helped to make the costly burden of research possible. My thanks are due also to the Social Science Research Council of Canada and the Canada Council, the former of which, on the latter's behalf, made a grant towards the cost of publication, as did the Publications Fund of the University of Toronto Press. The editors of the Press have been endlessly patient and meticulously careful in their editorial criticisms of my work.

I wish, above all, to thank my wife, Eleanor, to whom most of the credit must go for whatever merit my writing style may have. Indeed, in the course of several years she has become, by force of circumstances, a leading student of J. W. Dafoe. Finally, my affection and gratitude for my parents can only be partly expressed by the dedication of this book to them.

R.C.

Contents

	INTRODUCTION	vii
	ACKNOWLEDGMENTS	xi
I.	Self-Made Man	3
II.	Sifton's Lieutenant, 1901–5	19
III.	Liberalism: Domestic and Imperial, 1906–11	35
IV.	The Luxury of Opposition, 1911–14	50
V.	The War and a New Political Alignment, 1914–17	66
VI.	Ushering in a New World, 1918–20	86
VII.	"In the Lap of the Gods," 1920–3	108
VIII.	The Triumph of Liberal Nationalism, 1921–3	128
IX.	Lord Byng Intervenes, 1924–6	146
X.	Canada, the Commonwealth and the World, 1923–30	170
XI.	Bennett, King and Chaos, 1927–37	187
XII.	Remodelling the Canadian Constitution	214
XIII.	The Whole World in Travail, 1929–39	235
XIV.	Canada Fights, 1939–44	260
XV.	Western Liberal Nationalist	284
	A NOTE ON SOURCES	297
	INDEX	299

THE POLITICS OF JOHN W. DAFOE
AND THE *FREE PRESS*

When, if ever, I am a candidate for Parliament, I shall first give up the editorship of the Free Press; and, as upon the whole I think I would sooner be the editor of the Free Press than Prime Minister of Canada, I don't think I am likely to be a candidate in any constituency for some time to come.

—J. W. DAFOE to J. H. METCALFE
July 27, 1926

Between newspapers which publish news inconvenient to Governments, corporations, interests, etc., and the parties inconvenienced, there are often differences of opinion as to the propriety of these publications; but that the public interest is, as a general rule, better served by the newspaper being the judge in these matters, subject always of course to its responsibility to the law, is a view which I am prepared to defend.

—J. W. DAFOE to SIR EDWARD BEATTY
November 22, 1938

1. Self-Made Man

✦✦✦

IN THE AUTUMN OF 1901 more than ten thousand young men boarded the C.P.R. Harvest Specials in Eastern Canada to travel to the Prairies where another "bumper" crop was being gathered in. At last after the years of stagnation and world depression, the West was growing and prospering. The "wheat boom" had arrived and with it a new, exuberant confidence. "The thrill of life and energy which the garnering of this great harvest will send over the West," hymned the *Manitoba Free Press* on August 8, 1901, "will vibrate all over older Canada." Wheat prices were high, lands cheap and investment flowing more freely. Under the guidance of its energetic young Minister, Clifford Sifton, the Department of the Interior was successfully attracting immigration from all over Europe and the United States to fill up the spacious and unevenly fertile plains of the "last, best West."

But it was not merely settlers and transient harvest help who were moving West in the warm August days of the second year of the new century. On board a Canadian Pacific passenger train heading towards Winnipeg, the burgeoning capital of Western Canada, was John Wesley Dafoe, journalist. This newspaperman had at least one characteristic in common with the harvesters and settlers, apart from his rather farm-boyish appearance. Like them, he had been persuaded to seek his fortunes in the West by Clifford Sifton. At thirty-five, Dafoe was to assume the editor's chair at Sifton's Winnipeg daily, the *Manitoba Free Press*. The growing West had to be instructed in the virtues of Liberalism, and the rest of Canada kept informed of the interests and desires of the Prairies. These were the tasks that had been assigned to Dafoe. Certainly his interests and influence would broaden with the transformation of the West and the nation, but in his forty years at the helm of the Winnipeg paper, Dafoe never lost sight of these main objectives.

At the turn of the century it was perhaps not unusual for a young man to hold a highly responsible position such as the editorship of a newspaper. But it was nevertheless no small honour to have been chosen for this position by so promising a public figure as Clifford Sifton. Certainly in later years, when he had acquired some stature in Canadian life, Dafoe often reflected upon his inauspicious beginnings. Like many prominent men in early twentieth-century Canada, Dafoe was born in the backwoods of Ontario. It was not without irony that this man who came in the inter-war years to occupy a place in the front ranks of the Liberal nationalist shock troops was of United Empire Loyalist stock. At least it was ironic if the typical United Empire Loyalist was the stereotyped conservative imperialist often pictured by Canadian nationalists. Dafoe himself thought otherwise. Only a few of the Loyalists favoured "subordination of the colonies to the central imperial authority as the only possible basis for the Empire." The others favoured "the principle of self-government which was carried unconsciously from the American colonies to the new settlement." Whether Dafoe's great-grandfather subscribed to these frontier liberal sentiments is not known. He had served in the King's army during the American Revolution, and after the British defeat had migrated to Prince Edward County, north of the present-day Belleville. The Dafoes claimed long residence in North America. The family genealogists believed that their origins could be traced to seventeenth-century Flemish Protestants who had settled in New Amsterdam. That the exact origin of the family remained in some obscurity, however, is suggested by a remark made by J. W. Dafoe's sister. "Very reluctantly we have withdrawn our claim . . . to an interest in the Mayflower," she wrote, "and if we have it is only because someone must make the sacrifice lest we all be sunk in an overloaded ship."[1]

Calvin Wesley Dafoe, the editor's father, was born in the new home at the end of Lake Ontario; the conscious Protestantism, if not the doctrinal orthodoxy, of the family is surely evident in his name. While his two brothers turned to the medical profession, Calvin followed his father as a farmer. Though a man of little formal education, he was neither unread nor lacking in civic consciousness. He participated actively in municipal politics and rose to the position of Grand Master of the Orange Lodge. In his early twenties, he married a red-headed English immigrant, Mary Elcome. Shortly afterwards the young couple took up a new homestead in the Ottawa Valley near Combermere, a village not far from the present Arnprior. Here, on March 8, 1866, just a year before the imperial Parliament passed the British North America Act, their second son, John Wesley, was born.

[1]Dafoe, *Canada an American Nation* (New York, 1935), 34. Dafoe Papers, Dafoe to W. A. Dafoe, Jan. 7, 1917; Mrs. E. Emerson to V. Sifton, May 22, 1944.

In backwoods Ontario where farming and lumbering occupied most of the attention of pioneer men and women, mere survival, let alone any thought of advancement, required hard, often back-breaking work. When the summer of agricultural labour failed to provide for all the needs of his small family, Calvin Dafoe went into the bush in the winter, with numerous other struggling farmers, to fell timber for sale to the lumber mills that lay downstream. As John grew up, he sometimes went logging with his father. While he worked he stored up details of lumber camp life that he later used as background for experiments in fiction writing.

The encouragement of his mother, added to a natural dislike of farming, caused young Dafoe to turn his attention increasingly to books and other means of education at hand. Not many years after he started to attend classes at the local one-room school, he began to read the only literature available in his impecunious Protestant home, the Bible, the *Christian Guardian* and the *Belleville Intelligencer*. For high-school education, Dafoe had to leave home and enrol at the school at Arnprior. For some private reason—perhaps lack of money at home—he did not remain long at the little town school, but in 1881 left to take up duties as a teacher himself in a new settlement near his home. Many years later he recalled a woman who "made the entirely just remark to me that I ought to be going to a school instead of trying to teach one."[2]

His education was not extensive, but Dafoe made the most of it. In a pioneer community any education is a luxury, and those who have the opportunity to acquire it are likely to judge it by very pragmatic standards. Education should be useful, for how else can school attendance be justified in a society where every hand is necessary to ensure that the larder is filled against the coming winter? In an address he gave to the Manitoba School Trustees' Association in 1937, Dafoe summed up the conclusions he had drawn from his trials in a rough, rural school:

> Now what that impressed upon my mind was that a school was a place where you equipped people for life. The purpose of the school was to do something for them by which they could improve their position in the world, by which they could acquire some equipment which would fit them better for the difficulties and problems of life. I have never forgotten it and I think all education has got to be judged upon whether in big things as in little things it delivers that particular kind of thing. That is to say I learned what comes first in education. What comes first in education is to equip people to live and to do the things they want to do, and that otherwise they cannot do.

[2] Dafoe Papers, Dafoe to Rev. A. J. Reynolds, May 28, 1943.

Though Dafoe remained in the teaching profession for only two and a half years before moving into a different phase of public enlightenment, he never lost his interest in education. Nor did he ever stop educating himself.

Certainly Dafoe looked upon his education as a tool which would enable him to do what he wanted. And it was becoming clear even before he left school that he was developing political and intellectual interests. His family, like most of the people in the Ottawa Valley, was exempt from the Grit thunderings of the Toronto *Globe*, and clung fast to the Conservative faith of Sir John Macdonald. But as a young schoolteacher, Dafoe began developing some intellectual independence. Soon the first doubts about the infallibility of the family political creed began to creep into his mind. He himself claimed, though it has been denied, that it was through reading a copy of Allison's *History of Europe* that his mind was opened to liberalism. At any rate when he went to Montreal to become a newspaper reporter in March 1883, an interest in politics had already been awakened.[3]

The move from Combermere to Montreal was a huge step in the life of the still teen-aged Dafoe, and it suggests that he had already developed a sturdy independence. There was no place in rural Ontario for him; neither farm nor rural school had won his favour. The serious business of finding a career for life was now to begin. Journalism was one of the few opportunities open to a young man of limited education and means, but with definite intellectual interests. In February 1883, apparently after having returned to high school in Arnprior for a brief time, Dafoe answered an advertisement in the *Family Herald and Weekly Star* published by Hugh Graham in Montreal, which offered employment in the newspaper field. E. G. O'Connor, then the *Star*'s editor, hired him, and a long life in journalism was begun.

At the testimonial dinner given to Dafoe in Winnipeg in October 1943, the old man recounted to his audience, with obvious enjoyment, some of his experiences as a cub reporter in Montreal. It was a story not unlike that told in a variety of ways by Horatio Alger, and it is not without significance that Dafoe viewed his early life in these "country-boy-makes-good" terms. The story began with the text, "Opportunity is half the battle of life." It continued, playing a variation on the theme of the country boy, Dafoe himself, working hand in hand with a reforming newspaper editor in Montreal to outwit a firm of fast-talking clothing merchants who lived on the gullibility of visiting

[3]*Ibid.*, Dafoe to Judge Jackson, Oct. 31, 1943; G. V. Ferguson, *John W. Dafoe* (Toronto, 1948), 9.

farm boys. In this story is the archetypal pattern of Dafoe's career. He never wholly gave up the view that the cities, especially Toronto and Montreal, represented in large the slick suit salesmen of his youth, the Prairies assuming the place of the fleeced country boy. It takes little imagination to cast the *Free Press* in the role of the public-spirited newspaper exposing the dishonesty of the merchant and protecting the innocent yokel.[4]

The abilities of the fledgling journalist apparently impressed O'Connor, for early in 1884 he gave Dafoe the heavy reportorial duty of representing the paper at Ottawa. These were days of great issues in Canadian politics, when the measures which were to shape the nature of the new Confederation were being heatedly discussed by such political giants as Macdonald and Blake, Tupper and Cartwright. In a radio address in 1937 Dafoe recounted some of the impressions that his young mind had received while he was sitting in the Parliamentary Press Gallery. In January 1884, Blake and Macdonald crossed swords in the debate on the Speech from the Throne, and as far as the youthful correspondent was concerned, the only recourse Sir John could find against the carefully ordered arguments of the West Durham advocate was his control of the Conservative majority. To Dafoe, Blake became the "greatest parliamentarian in Canadian history" and "with the desperate seriousness of extreme youth I passed judgment on Sir John's speech as not worthy of the occasion." Whether Dafoe's conversion to liberalism actually took place at this moment, and with the suddenness of a camp meeting testimony, it is impossible to determine. When Blake died, the *Manitoba Free Press* (March 4, 1912) paid the highest compliment to him as an individual, praising his intellectual capacity, his unstained integrity, and the use he made of his natural gifts. But the concluding comment that "the contrast between his qualities and his achievements leaves a haunting feeling of incompleteness and futility" recognized that Blake lacked those qualities which make a successful political leader.

The strength of the impression which Blake made on the eighteen-year-old Dafoe may have been due in part to the similarities in their background and aspiration. Both men were the product of unpretentious rural Ontario homes, and both chose to seek their fortune by the exercise of mind rather than muscle. Blake's interminable, fact-packed criticisms of Macdonald's seemingly over-confident policies provided a pattern for the heavily documented editorials that the later Dafoe was to write on tariffs, freight rates and other matters close to the hearts

[4]Dafoe, *Sixty Years in Journalism* (Winnipeg, 1943), 2.

of Western Canadians. Moreover, Blake's frequent demand for clearer definition of Canadian powers of self-government foreshadowed Dafoe's later preachments on this subject. More important, the Liberal party which first gained the adherence of the young Dafoe was a party with banners unstained and principles uncompromised by the corrupting influence of power. Blake's intellectual brilliance stimulated Dafoe's instinct to rebel against the traditional Conservatism of his family, and he moved naturally into the party of pristine purity—a party that in large measure represented the virtues of rural Canada's Anglo-Saxon Protestant population. In the happy phrase of Sir John Willison, the Liberals prior to 1896 were the party of "voluble virtue." In the late 1880's many young men, inspired by a touch of idealism, were magnetized by the eloquence of Blake and his lieutenants as they summoned the hosts to support their principled criticisms of Macdonald's opportunism. Theirs was a righteousness becoming to politicians free from the cares of office. The doctrine of the Blake Liberals also had a strong appeal for a youth of Dafoe's background. Their support of freer trade in opposition to the Conservatives' protectionist National Policy and their criticisms of the Canadian Pacific Railway both rang true in the ears of a person of his antecedents. His rural upbringing had imbued him with that distrust of city life and big business which often characterizes the farmer.[5]

Dafoe was a gregarious youth and an aggressive reporter. While increasing his knowledge of Canadian politics and history in the Parliamentary Library, he struck up new friendships with the younger politicians. Charles Hibbert Tupper was there, a man whom Dafoe grew to admire. There also he began a friendship and an alliance with young Wilfrid Laurier, a man whom Dafoe perhaps never completely understood, but with whom there would be years of co-operation before the bitter break of 1917.

Railways and Riel, tariff and trade questions: these were the public issues which excited Canadians in the 1880's when John Dafoe was growing to manhood. The greatest political issue during his first years in the Parliamentary Press Gallery was the Northwest Rebellion, and the subsequent conflict over the fate of Louis Riel. For the first time, Dafoe was introduced to the problems presented to the Canadian Government and to the nation by the vast empty expanse of territory that lay between the dirty little city of Winnipeg and the foothills of the Rockies. Twice in fifteen years the restless and unprotected Métis had taken up

[5]F. H. Underhill, "Edward Blake and Canadian Liberal Nationalism" in R. Flenley, ed., *Essays in Canadian History* (Toronto, 1939), 132–54.

arms to defend themselves against the encroachments of Eastern civilization. Twice they had failed, and now their leader, Louis Riel, had been captured, tried and sentenced to hang. Unfortunately, but nevertheless truly, there was centred on this enigmatic Métis the whole problem of the relations between the French and the English in Canada. Dafoe watched eagerly when the issue of Riel's fate and the Government's responsibility for the Western trouble came before Parliament. That he had not yet become a partisan Liberal is shown by his later admission that he supported the decision of the Macdonald Government to allow the court's sentence to be carried out. He could not understand Quebec's attachment to Riel and felt a "resentment at the disturbances which were staged in Montreal by the French at the time of the execution."[6]

The self-assurance which characterized Dafoe's entire life was evident in his decision in December 1885 to accept the editorship of the newly established *Ottawa Evening Journal*. The paper, published by A. S. Woodburn, was independent in politics. During Dafoe's five months as editor it followed a completely non-partisan line, sometimes criticizing the Liberals, often berating the Tories, frequently scrapping with party-line newspapers, always praising its own independence. Discussing the esoteric subject of "Mugwumps" on January 27, 1886, the paper implicitly defined and commended its own position: "Great is the mugwump and his mission is to teach the divine right of bolting. May his shadow never grow less."

There were many issues for the *Journal* to discuss in these months, and the editor attempted to cope with them all. In domestic politics he was vigorously opposed to the defenders of Riel who led a "treasonable agitation." While his admiration for Edward Blake was obviously strong, he could not bring himself to defend Blake's attempt to lay the whole blame for the 1885 Rebellion in the Northwest at the feet of the Conservative Government. His attitude to the Tories was only lukewarm, but he did have laudatory words for Macdonald's defence of Canadian fishing rights on the East Coast. He attacked socialism in Chicago and supported Home Rule for Ireland, though he had room to praise Joseph Chamberlain for leaving Gladstone's party on the Irish question. Neither the proponents of Imperial Federation nor of Commercial Union with the United States won any favourable comment from the *Journal*. But it did show a sympathetic interest in the Canadian Northwest, though it expressed doubts about the practicability of the

---

[6]Dafoe Papers, Dafoe to Hon. J. T. Brown, Oct. 22, 1943. By this time Dafoe believed that Riel's hanging had been carried out because of "political necessity."

proposed railway to Hudson Bay—a view which brought down the wrath of the *Manitoba Free Press* upon it. Few French Canadians would have found the *Journal* an attractive paper to read; on March 6, 1886, it argued that it would be best for Quebec politicians if they "abandoned forever the use of their language in Parliament, and regarded themselves not as a distinct race...."

Undoubtedly the paper was directed by a bright, studious, young mind anxious to promote, as one editorial was headed, "The Science and Study of Politics." The editor was full of self-confidence and not inclined to serve any master. Obviously he was writing about himself when he remarked on one occasion that "The most striking characteristic of young men is a repugnance to being led by the nose." Indeed, the quality of the whole paper, during Dafoe's term of office, was that of a very good undergraduate production. And why not? But for his lack of means Dafoe would probably have been at a university during these years instead of attempting to run a struggling newspaper. He was not yet twenty-one when the *Journal* ran an editorial entitled "To Young Men," which remarked on the purifying effect that the young men just reaching political maturity should have on Canadian public life. Without this cleansing influence,

there is but little hope for Canada, for our present hole-in-corner politics, the senseless strife over issues not worth ten minutes' consideration, the unpatriotic and demagogic appeals to prejudices of race and creed and section are preventing far more effectually than the natural obstacles of which we hear so much from pessimists, the welding together of the different provinces, and the unification of our Confederation into a stable and strong nation.[7]

But self-confidence and even obvious promise were not enough to overcome youth and inexperience in the rough world of Canadian political journalism. Moreover, the *Journal*, like the country at large, was experiencing economic difficulties. By May 1886, young Dafoe was thinking that perhaps the United States would provide opportunities for an ambitious youth that were apparently lacking in a stagnating Canada. Many Canadians had despairingly succumbed to this temptation but Dafoe was saved from it by the offer of a position with the *Manitoba Free Press*. At least the West would be a change from a city dominated by the civil service.[8]

But Dafoe's decision was not made on such entirely negative grounds. The West was a vigorous young country just opening up, an agrarian

[7]*Ottawa Evening Journal*, March 15, Feb. 15, 1886.
[8]Dafoe, *Sixty Years in Journalism*, 5; P. D. Ross, *Retrospects of a Newspaper Person* (Toronto, 1931), 32–7.

community which reproduced many of the conditions and situations he had experienced during his boyhood days in the Ottawa Valley. But the Prairie lands were more fertile, and a farmer had a better opportunity to earn a decent living from the soil than could be had from the inevitable back-breaking toil of the farmer-lumberman existence of eastern Ontario. Dafoe decided to go West, and his parents went too. They would make a new start in the productive, rolling wheatlands near beautiful Lake Killarney in the southwestern corner of the province.

The *Manitoba Free Press* had been established in 1872 by W. F. Luxton. The founder was still editing the paper when Dafoe joined it, and his partisan Liberal sympathies may have helped to confirm Dafoe's opinions about the Tories. In Manitoba important issues were being debated and Dafoe's interest was soon sparked. He was assigned the task of reporting the activities of the local legislature where proposals for railway construction provided the staple of controversy. The Greenway Government, a Liberal régime, was attempting to circumvent the C.P.R. "monopoly" clause in order to build a railway to the United States boundary. At every turn their efforts were being blocked by Macdonald's readiness to exercise the federal power of disallowance in order to ensure the success of the East–West transportation system. In this issue lay the roots of Western sectionalism, arising from the feeling that the East wished to keep its Western hinterland in a state of permanent inferiority. Dafoe enthusiastically identified himself with the Western cause, even going so far as to take part in an organized attempt to help one of the local railways build its line directly across the C.P.R. tracks near Fort Whyte, just south of Winnipeg. He no doubt shared the satisfaction of Westerners when the Macdonald Government decided to terminate the C.P.R.'s monopoly in the spring of 1888.[9]

But Thomas Greenway's Government was not out of trouble yet. It continued to be embroiled in railway problems, but by 1889 the attention of politically conscious Westerners was turning more and more to the growing racial tensions in the East, which were beginning to spill over into Manitoba. Dafoe, who had witnessed at first hand the strains that the Riel crisis had placed on French-English relations in Eastern Canada, must have felt some foreboding when Premier Greenway's volatile colleague, Joseph Martin, joined hands with the Francophobe D'Alton McCarthy at Portage la Prairie in August 1889, to attack the French school and language rights in the province. In fact, even before this meeting Dafoe had reason to believe that the Govern-

[9] Dafoe Papers, Dafoe to G. de T. Glazebrook, Aug. 8, 1935.

ment was going to move against the rights of the French-speaking Manitobans. Now he saw the legislature sweep away all that the Roman Catholics thought they had secured in the 1870 Manitoba Act, amidst cries of betrayal from Archbishop Taché and his flock. What was just as important, he saw the rise of his future employer, Clifford Sifton, to the position of Attorney General of the province, and chief defender of the "national" school system.[10]

The Manitoba school question had only just begun its long and involved history of litigation and political repercussion when an opportunity for advancement called Dafoe back to Montreal in 1892. He liked the West, but no ambitious journalist could afford to turn down an opportunity to move up the scale from reporter to the editorial desk.[11]

His new position was with the editorial staff of the Montreal *Herald*, a paper which was now in the hands of the Liberal party and under the management of his old friend E. G. O'Connor. If he thought that he was leaving the Manitoba school controversy behind when he left Winnipeg, he was soon disabused of the notion, for it was gradually becoming the leading issue of federal politics, and one that was of primary interest to the electorate in the province of Quebec. From his new vantage point Dafoe had an opportunity to observe the disintegration of the old Macdonald Conservative party in Quebec and the gradual forging of a powerful Liberal machine in the hands of Laurier and Israël Tarte. Working for a Liberal newspaper he was in close touch with these events.

But the position with the *Herald* was of short duration, for the ownership changed hands again in August 1895. So Dafoe moved once more, this time back to the *Montreal Star*. Evidently he had established himself as such a qualified journalist that Hugh Graham, who was a Conservative, did not mind harbouring a Liberal viper in his bosom.

Of course most of Dafoe's time was consumed in managing the operations of Graham's *Family Herald and Weekly Star*, but in what spare time he had he tried to add his mite to the Liberal cause. As the last days of the legal existence of the Parliament elected in 1891 drew to a close and Mackenzie Bowell floundered in his attempts to find a solution to the Manitoba school crisis and thus save the Tory party, Dafoe turned his pen to a defence of the Liberals.[12] In February 1896

[10]W. L. Morton, *Manitoba: A History* (Toronto, 1957), 244; Dafoe, *Clifford Sifton in Relation to His Times* (Toronto, 1931), 43.
[11]Dafoe, *Sixty Years in Journalism*, 9.
[12]H. J. Morgan, *Canadian Men and Women of the Time: A Handbook of Canadian Biography* (Toronto, 1898), 236–7.

he wrote a long letter to the editor of the *Week*, expounding the course that he felt should be followed in settling the school question. While admitting the right of the federal government to review provincial educational legislation he declared that the approach being taken by Bowell and Company could only lead to religious and racial strife in Canada. Laurier's policy, the policy of conciliation, was the only answer "which every man in Canada, Catholic or Protestant, can follow with honour." It represented the solution which the people wanted "despite the efforts now being made at Ottawa to perpetrate a high crime against the peace of this nation by the passage of a premature, mischievous, futile law."

Laurier was pleased with this defence of his position. He wrote to tell the young journalist that he was "more than satisfied that sooner or later that plan will have to be resorted to." In the bitter campaign which followed the dissolution of Parliament, Dafoe played an important role. He saw to it that a letter from a Western priest, Father Lacombe, threatening Laurier with the wrath of the clergy, found its way into the English-Canadian press. Whatever effect this action had on the final outcome of the election, the clerical campaign against the Liberals in Quebec had an impact on Dafoe. His Orange, Protestant upbringing and his growing liberalism left no doubt in his mind about the need for a complete separation of church and state, but the election campaign of 1896 further confirmed his belief that there was no place in politics for priests. Throughout his life he regarded clerical power with suspicion and always responded with forthright opposition to any suggestion that the influence of the Roman Catholic Church in education should be increased.[13]

After the election campaign of 1896, Dafoe settled down to the serious task of establishing a home. He was now thirty and held a good position as editor of the Montreal weekly. Moreover, his marriage to Miss Alice Parmelee, whom he had met in the offices of the newspaper, brought domestic responsibilities. The five years after 1896 were apparently a quiet time in his life, and he never spoke much of them in later years. No doubt he was not entirely happy working for a man of Hugh Graham's politics, especially with a Liberal Government in office at last. Perhaps, too, he was uneasy about the great campaign of the *Montreal Star* to force the hand of Laurier in the matter of Canadian participation in the Boer War. But if the policy of the *Free Press* after he assumed its editorship is a trustworthy guide, Dafoe, like

---

[13]Dafoe Papers, Laurier to Dafoe, Feb. 17, 1896; Dafoe, *Laurier: A Study in Canadian Politics* (Toronto, 1922), 47.

most English Canadians, must have agreed that Canada's duty lay in lending assistance to Great Britain in South Africa. At any rate, the Boer War opened his eyes to the importance of the imperial question, a subject which was never far from his attention in later years.

Of course there were other matters to absorb him. He had already tried his hand at poetry, producing some surprisingly sentimental verse for a man later to become renowned for his political realism. The theme of unrequited love, which appeared in at least one of these poems, was also central in a tale of tragic romance in the Canadian backwoods, "A Call from the Gorge," which he published in the *Canadian Magazine* in November 1901. Yet even during these quiet years, Dafoe did not forget politics or Western Canada. No doubt he was watching for an opportunity of employment with a newspaper where he could satisfy both his financial requirements and his political convictions. If such a position could be found in Western Canada, so much the better, for then he would be reunited with his parents who were still farming in Manitoba.

Just such a position was gradually developing in Winnipeg. During the years immediately after 1896, a certain amount of political dissatisfaction and unrest developed in Clifford Sifton's bailiwick. A working agreement on the school difficulties had been reached between the Liberal governments in Ottawa and Winnipeg, but there were other troubles that demanded the attention of the new Minister of the Interior and Liberal chief of Western Canada. The first difficulties arose within the Liberal party itself. Joseph Martin had been disgruntled when Laurier overlooked his talents and took Sifton into the cabinet. Then there was the independent R. L. Richardson who was not easily kept within the bounds of Liberal orthodoxy and, as owner of the Winnipeg *Tribune*, was capable of causing considerable trouble. These people were attempting to undermine Sifton's position and for not entirely laudable reasons, according to his account. "They are unfriendly to me because, to put it shortly, they are all for boodling, and they do not see any chance of success so long as I am here," he told the editor of the Toronto *Globe*. This internal strife could only aid the Conservatives. With a provincial election in the offing, the party ranks had to be closed.[14]

When the provincial election campaign ended in the summer of 1898, Sifton's fears were fulfilled. The Liberals suffered defeat despite his efforts on their behalf. As the time for the federal elections approached, the situation in Manitoba was no more promising. The

[14]Willison Papers, Sifton to Willison, Oct. 24, 1898.

Tories were full of life and vigour, the Liberals divided and listless. Sifton was to be deposed. Hugh John Macdonald resigned his recently won provincial premiership to contest the Brandon seat that was held by the Minister of the Interior. Perhaps the main bright spot was the fact that Sifton's acquisition of the *Manitoba Free Press* could offset the damage done by the defection of Richardson's *Tribune*.

When and how the sphinx-like Sifton acquired the *Free Press* is a matter of considerable interest. Sometime early in 1898 Sifton, in cooperation with a man named John Mather, a wealthy business man with extensive interests in lumber and power developments, obtained control of the journal which seems to have been somehow connected with the Canadian Pacific Railway. According to Sifton, the paper, apart from its news franchises—and there was difficulty over these—was not at first a very valuable property. He soon set about making it a profitable business enterprise as well as a powerful organ of the Liberal party. His first step in reorganizing the paper was to hire a new business manager. The position was filled by E. H. Macklin, who was then a bookkeeper on the staff of the Toronto *Globe*.[15]

It took a rather longer time to solve the difficulties in the editorial department. Not long after the change of ownership, friction arose between Sifton, who was in charge of the newspaper's policy, and his chief editor, A. J. Magurn. Several times Sifton had to correct his editor on policy questions, once complaining that Magurn was failing to live up to his contracted obligation of "holding yourself to the advancement of the interest of the property."[16]

Clifford Sifton had very definite ideas about the methods of operating a party newspaper. He was a hard-headed realist who subscribed to very few liberal sentiments about the nature of man. He doubted if many electors read editorials or were influenced by them. It was the news articles that counted, and these had to be written and arranged so as best to influence the reader. If this was done properly, "The simple-minded farmer will swallow it, and a great many people who are not farmers and who ought to know better." At election time especi-

---

[15]Sifton Papers, Sifton to Sir William Van Horne, July 23, 1900; Sifton to A. J. Magurn, Jan. 23, 1900; Sifton to John Mather, April 1, 1898. Mather's obituary in the *Ottawa Free Press* on June 11, 1907, listed among his business interests the Keewatin Lumber and Power Company, the Lake of the Woods Milling Company, the Bank of Ottawa and a variety of other enterprises. I know of no contemporary source for the story that Sifton obtained the *Manitoba Free Press* as part of a bargain which resulted in the Crow's Nest Pass Agreement. See Blair Fraser, "The Many, Mighty Siftons," *Maclean's Magazine*, Dec. 19, 1959, 54.

[16]Sifton Papers, Sifton to A. J. Magurn, July 13, 1899.

ally, he thought the end justified the means in a newspaper's campaign tactics. The objective of a party newspaper was to "get the public mind saturated with its views and ideas." The Opposition views had to be kept constantly in the background, for party leaders preferred that "the people did not read the Opposition literature." To Sifton an election was a propaganda war, not a great national debate. "The theory that you want the elector to read both sides and trust to him that you are right is not practical politics," he claimed. Dafoe was never more acute in his judgment than when he wrote that Sifton "had not in any marked degree the disposition of the social or political reformer." He was perhaps even understating the case.[17]

The appointment of Macklin was only a beginning of the complete reorganization that Sifton planned for the *Free Press*. Once its financial affairs were straightened out a new editor had to be found, for Magurn was definitely unsatisfactory. In January 1901, Sifton approached John Dafoe with a tentative offer of the Winnipeg position. After three months of waiting for a more definite proposal, Dafoe, who was obviously anxious for the position, took the initiative. The lease on his house in Montreal was running out, and since it was an annual arrangement, his position was growing a bit awkward. Could Sifton give him any definite information about the Winnipeg opening? Sifton was encouraging, but still indefinite. He was not yet in a position to make an offer, but he assured Dafoe that the Liberal party needed his talents. "I do not think we can afford to let you work for the Tories any longer," he remarked in his business-like way.[18]

By mid-June the Board of Directors of the *Free Press* had determined to make a change in the paper's editorship. A month later Sifton offered the position to Dafoe, who accepted immediately. It would take a month to wind up his affairs in Montreal, he explained, and then he would go to Ottawa for a conference with his new employer before leaving for the West. He had kept in fairly close touch with Western affairs, but he felt that "a little coaching will not be out of place." Sifton was now able to write to his party lieutenants in Manitoba that the policies of the *Free Press* would soon be in capable hands. Dafoe, Sifton explained, "is well and thoroughly known to the leading Liberals of Ontario and Quebec, and in respect of his ability and character there is no journalist in Canada who stands higher. It is a good deal to say that the Liberals so regard him

[17]*Ibid.*, Sifton to E. H. Macklin, July 27, 1900; Willison Papers, Sifton to Willison, Feb. 7, 1901; Dafoe, *Sifton*, xiii.
[18]Sifton Papers, Dafoe to Sifton, March 27, 1901; Sifton to Dafoe, March 29, 1901.

notwithstanding the fact that he has been for many years on the Montreal *Star*." This was indeed a letter of recommendation.[19]

Dafoe must have been elated at his new appointment. He and his growing family would now be able to rejoin his parents, and this time he was returning to the Prairies as editor of the largest daily newspaper in Winnipeg. Nor was it just any newspaper; it was the organ of the man who, next to Sir Wilfrid Laurier, was probably the most important Liberal politician in Canada, certainly in Western Canada. Furthermore the *Free Press* was already a newspaper with a reputation. In the cosmopolitan atmosphere of Winnipeg it was "not merely a sharp-tongued organ of Liberal party views but the most representative voice of the Northwest."[20]

Though there was no formal contract between Dafoe and the publisher of the *Free Press*, it had been generally agreed that within understood limits Dafoe would have a free hand in formulating the policies of the newspaper. He was hired as a known Liberal party supporter, and it was assumed that he would support the Laurier Government. Naturally he was expected to be mindful of the fact that a newspaper was an expensive enterprise and its editorial policy had to be such as to ensure its financial viability. This was not a difficult requirement, for the paper was to speak for its constituency, Western Canada, as well as to inform Western voters of the merits of the Liberal party. Near the end of his life Dafoe remarked that Sifton took a "self-denying ordinance" with respect to the policy of the *Free Press*, but by this he did not mean that the paper's owner abdicated all responsibility for the paper's views. On the contrary, by "suggestion and consultation," Sifton played a large part in establishing general lines of policy. Generally speaking there were few policy disagreements among the triumvirate of Dafoe, Sifton and Macklin. The relation was not as easy as Dafoe, in mock-serious mood, once described it:

> That two men of Irish descent, one from Drogheda and the other with Tipperary in his blood, and a Sassenach without a drop of Irish blood, should for nearly thirty years have worked together with nothing but an occasional high word, no shillelaghs or anything of that sort, certainly means something—perhaps that after all the millennium is attainable.[21]

It was nevertheless a fruitful partnership that began in 1901, and one that was to build the *Free Press* into a highly influential national news-

[19]*Ibid.*, Dafoe to Sifton, July 20, 1901; Sifton to J. D. Cameron, July 15, 1901.
[20]Morton, *Manitoba*, 170.
[21]Dafoe, *Sixty Years in Journal.*, 11; Dafoe, *Sifton*, xxv; *Winnipeg Free Press* Library, MS of speech delivered by Dafoe on his seventieth birthday, 4.

paper. Dafoe was anxious to take up his post that autumn, and it must have cheered Sifton to hear that his new editor thought it "necessary to get to work on the fall campaign for the weekly if we are to capture some of the wealth that is going to be poured into the pockets of the farmers this fall."[22]

Until 1901 Dafoe had moved frequently from one newspaper to another. He had acquired much valuable experience and acquainted himself with the problems of various parts of the country. Now he was ready to send down some permanent roots. He had been given the opportunity for which he had waited, and he quickly settled into the task of studying Western conditions and formulating the policies that his paper would follow.

[22]Sifton Papers, Dafoe to Sifton, July 17, 1901.

II. Sifton's Lieutenant

1901-5

NINETEEN HUNDRED AND ONE was an important year in the history of the city of Winnipeg. It was the year that the Winnipeg Grain Exchange—"a combine" with "a gambling hell thrown in," a Western radical called it—was reorganized. This institution was the symbol of Winnipeg's importance in the Western economy. Through Winnipeg for the next twenty years was to flow much of the rich, golden grain grown on the Prairies. At the turn of the century the wheat boom had begun and its dynamic influence provided a stimulus for the entire economic structure of the Dominion. Moreover the West's growing pains were to have important political repercussions on Canadian life.

There was an irritable sensitivity about the new growth. The chief reason was that the West occupied a position of inferiority in the broad scheme of the national development policies. Not only had the federal government maintained control of Western lands, but Dominion fiscal and transportation policies frequently seemed to be framed without much reference to Prairie needs. Already in 1901 there were complaints about inadequate grain-loading facilities, congested autumn rail traffic and unfair tariff policies. In the following years these murmurs would grow louder, and the numbers of people brought in by the Dominion Government's immigration policies would add new voices to swell the chorus.

Just as the turn of the century saw the relation of the West to the Dominion changing, so the same period saw the beginning of a change in the relation of Canada to the outside world. The Boer War, which symbolized the transition at the British Colonial Office from the policies of Manchester to those of Birmingham, was also the occasion for a display of developing Dominion nationalism. Canada's autonomy would have to be defended and perhaps advanced in the face of a well-intentioned but ill-conceived desire on the part of Joseph Chamberlain and his followers to give the Empire some type of central directing authority. To the south, Canada's nearest neighbour was now led by Theodore Roosevelt, a man just as truculent, if less suave, than the British Colonial Secretary. Here, too, Canada's interests would require forthright defence. The Dominion was growing up in a world where international relations, if cloaked in democratic nostrums, were still conducted on Hobbesian precepts.

If the West was to receive what it considered fair treatment from Dominion policy-makers, and if Canada's status in the Empire was to be successfully defended, strong voices would be needed to give form to otherwise amorphous feelings. Probably few Westerners realized that the small, black-faced type at the head of the *Manitoba Free Press* editorial page on August 19, 1901, announced the arrival of just such a voice. This, of course, is to overdramatize the role of John W. Dafoe. Editing a daily journal, a Liberal journal, involved decisions and actions on more mundane affairs than these. Nevertheless, from his first arrival in Winnipeg Dafoe showed a broader vision and interest than might normally be demanded from the editor of a provincial newspaper. He was soon speaking not only for and about the Liberal party, but also for his Western constituency. And his concerns encompassed the affairs of Canada as a whole, domestic and international, for he was anxious to fight for those policies which he thought would best serve the interests of all the country.

On the day that Dafoe assumed his new position the paper carried an editorial that was both a Western manifesto and the confident expression of the views of the self-made man. The West appealed to Dafoe, for here he saw evolving an equalitarian society where a man could win the top prize through sheer hard work, a society based on rugged individualism. Commenting on the causes of the rapid progress of Western economic development, the new editor pointed to the fluid social structure where "more than anywhere else on the globe, large rewards can be earned by individual energy." Of course these circumstances, so important for the ambitious, had to be carefully preserved. The conditions could only be guaranteed by the presence of a large contingent of Western Liberals in Ottawa. The West, following the directing hand of the Liberal party and stimulated by the general moral and material progress of the world, could provide the basis for the development of a society as nearly perfect as man could conceive.[1]

Matters of more immediate concern than speculation about the future

[1] *M.F.P.*, Aug. 19, 1901; Feb. 3, 1902.

of the West and the moral progress of mankind soon demanded Dafoe's attention and involved him in an important controversy. In mid-October, he decided, apparently on Sifton's prompting, to launch an attack on the Governor General, Lord Minto. The *Free Press* did not trust Lord Minto. Dafoe apparently thought of him as Chamberlain's imperial proconsul—"a combination of country squire and heavy dragoon," as he later wrote quite unfairly. The Governor General was looked upon as a meddler, and worse, a man lacking sufficient prestige to warrant his having the position of Governor General of Canada, "the premier dependency of Great Britain." That it was not just Minto's imperial views that were suspect is clear from the newspaper's suggestion that Lord Curzon or Lord Milner were men of the calibre that were required at Rideau Hall.[2]

The enthusiasm which surrounded the visit to Canada of the Duke and Duchess of Cornwall and York in the autumn of 1901 offered an occasion to discuss imperial affairs and again to attack the Governor General. The *Free Press* extended a warm welcome to the royal party, but soon turned to interpreting the welcome given by Canadians, which, it pointed out on October 19, should not be mistaken for "any disposition to undervalue the constitutional rights" that Canada had acquired. Then, in close consultation with Sifton, Dafoe turned his heavy artillery on Lord Minto, charging on October 22 that the Crown's representative suffered from "a radical misconception" of the powers of his office. The misconception was rooted in the belief that as the imperial representative he could strike out on an independent line and even override the advice of his ministers. This state of affairs was wholly of Minto's making, for no previous incumbent had attempted to overstep the bounds of constitutional convention. It might well be necessary to obtain a precise definition of the Governor General's powers in order to avert any recurrence of this unfortunate situation.

Dafoe knew that such an open attack would invite declamations of disloyalty, and therefore he determined to follow up with an editorial which would deflect any such criticism. He had already developed his line of defence, which would be that "the best interests of the Empire are served by the Colonies jealously preserving their self-governing powers...."[3] This defence, entitled "Building the Empire," appeared on October 23 and set forth a full-blown colonial nationalist theory of the British Empire. It argued that the Empire, composed of free and autonomous nations, was in the main a monument to liberalism, for the

[2]Dafoe Papers, Dafoe to Harry Sifton, Feb. 28, 1931; Dafoe, *Laurier*, 77; *M.F.P.*, Oct. 14, 1901. [3]Sifton Papers, Dafoe to Sifton, Oct. 18, 1901.

Tories had failed to read the lesson of the American Revolution. Now a new phase of imperial development had arrived which required liberalism to be imperialistic, but sanely so. Sane imperialism meant opposition to all schemes of imperial centralization for either military or fiscal purposes, because centralization could only lead to disruption. Any imperial reorganization must follow the well-trodden paths of the past

along lines not of less freedom to the Colonies, but of more. The great Colonies must rise in the scale until they are recognized as full partners with the Motherland.... Every attempt to depart from these safe paths should meet with unyielding opposition; and he is the best servant of the Empire who is quick to challenge any innovation the effect of which must be to sow the seeds of decay and distintegration.

This declaration of faith in the liberal theory of Empire was not, however, meant to suggest any withdrawal of the charges against the Empire's representative in Canada. A parting shot was fired on November 4 when *Free Press* readers were informed that the Governor General had "no personal powers whatever," and should Downing Street, "a name which does not sound well in Canadian ears," attempt to increase this officer's powers to the detriment of the colonies, the Empire would be strangled beyond any possible resuscitation.

Dafoe had not been mistaken in thinking that his attacks on Minto would bring quick rejoinders. The Governor General was extremely perturbed that such unjust criticism should come from a newspaper known to have close connections with the Government. He perceived that this was an attack not only on himself but on the office and told Sir Wilfrid Laurier that it was "absolutely untrue from beginning to end," and a complete misrepresentation of the view which he took of his position. Sir Wilfrid agreed with Minto's complaint and immediately sent off a letter to Winnipeg taking up in detail each of the criticisms which the *Free Press* had launched against the Governor General. The Prime Minister concluded by noting that it was a wholly erroneous impression that bad relations existed between the Governor General and his advisers. Lord Minto had always shown himself anxious to "discharge his duties" and any differences which had arisen "had always been honourably and satisfactorily adjusted between us." He asked that the earliest opportunity be taken to correct quietly the inaccurate impression that the articles had created.[4]

Though Dafoe disclaimed any desire to embarrass the Government,

[4]Laurier Papers, Minto to Laurier, Oct. 31, 1901; Minto Papers, Laurier to Dafoe, Nov. 5, 1901 (copy).

he refused to alter his assessment of Lord Minto. When Minto was appointed Viceroy of India in 1905, the *Free Press* took the opportunity to repeat its view that he had been entirely unfit for his position in Canada. Dafoe never changed this opinion; in fact, for him Minto became a set image of the imperial proconsul, and he harboured a continuing suspicion that the office of Governor General before 1926 was an instrument by which schemes of imperial centralization could be promoted. Twenty-five years after this skirmish with Minto, when another soldier occupied Rideau Hall, Dafoe saw the completion of the attack which he had begun on the office of Governor General in 1901.[5]

In the tilt with Minto, Dafoe entered the lists for a competition from which he never withdrew. Imperial relations was one of the areas of controversy that interested him most intensely. During the first four years of his editorship of the *Free Press*, he devoted much space to a consideration of this problem, and established the main lines of his thought about Canada's relation to the Empire. Freedom and flexibility were the touchstones of Dafoe's attitude: Canada should co-operate in imperial activities, but on its own initiative, not on the direction of any central executive acting for the Empire as a whole. Freedom of action meant flexibility and an empirical approach; Canada would decide its attitude to each imperial question in the light of the surrounding circumstances. At least in the *Free Press*, Dafoe frequently used the Boer War as an example of successful voluntary co-operation.[6] The preferential treatment which Canada gave to British goods under the Fielding tariff of 1897 was another example of the voluntary co-operation that had resulted in a smooth working of imperial relations. But the campaign of the British tariff reformers to transform the Empire into a closed preferential trade area received no support in the *Free Press*.

As the Colonial Conference of 1902 approached, the paper in its issue of May 12 preached what it called sane, Liberal imperialism, which was simply a defence of the imperial status quo. Canada's representatives should hold fast to Dominion autonomy, and strike out sharply at any innovations that smacked of centralization. This, of course, was Laurier's view. It was the view which *Free Press* readers were told was the property of the Liberal party, whereas the Tories were anxious to promote the establishment of a central imperial authority.

Fundamentally, Canadian autonomy meant that the Canadian Parliament decided all issues which affected the Canadian people, and Dafoe

[5]Laurier Papers, Dafoe to Laurier, Nov. 9, 1901; *M.F.P.*, Aug. 26, 1905.
[6]Sept. 3, 1901; Jan. 1, 16, 1902.

attacked any suggestion that this right be limited. This did not mean that the unity of the Empire was shattered but that "the bond of union of the Empire is the Crown, not the authority of the British parliament." Under the authority of its own Parliament, Canada had a great contribution to make to the strength of the Empire, but it was a contribution which could be made only if Canadians concentrated on the development of their own potential. The *Free Press* explained its view on June 7, 1902: "Let us develop our own resources, defend our own interests, and build up here a puissant Commonwealth which, in times of peril, will voluntarily place at the disposal of the Motherland her entire available resources. To ask for more than this is to risk the chance of getting less."

This doctrine, labelled Liberal imperialism by Dafoe, was really colonial nationalism. It was a Canadian policy, not a Liberal one, promoted by Macdonald and Laurier alike. What made Liberal imperialism, or colonial nationalism, different from later nationalism was that the strengthening of the autonomy and the internal development of Canada was not an end in itself. The ultimate objective was the strengthening of the Empire, which was conceived of as a unity, though an undefined unity, based on sentiment rather than legal ties and political commitments. Canadian imperial sentiment was, in reality, often nationalism in an immature form.

This sentiment, as expounded by Dafoe, was not merely a negative reaction to every proposal for imperial federation, or a demand that British officials in Canada be replaced by Canadian ones. It was this, but it was also more. Its objective was a recognition of the equality of the self-governing members of the Empire, and it found expression in terms reminiscent of Sir John Macdonald's Kingdom of Canada in permanent alliance with Britain. A formal agreement entered into between Canada and Britain could not be looked upon as a limitation of Canadian self-government, but rather a vindication of it. "We demonstrate our freedom by binding ourselves; but no one else has the power to bind us," the *Free Press* noted on September 5, 1903. This was no scholastic distinction; to enter into a formal, specific agreement with Britain was an expression of sovereignty, whereas to relinquish control over any aspect of Canadian affairs to an external body, whether it was the Admiralty or an imperial executive council, was a limitation of that sovereignty.

The refusal to grapple with the problem of defining more strictly the relations of the dominions and the mother country, and of reducing to concrete rules their rights and responsibilities, may be written off as Liberal casuistry. Of course Dafoe was aware that much of what he said about imperial relations, as about other matters, was an apology for the course followed by the Laurier Government. But there was more to it than that. A basic element in Dafoe's liberalism was a firm conviction that institutions in themselves were useless unless supported by public opinion. Given a strong enough public sentiment, institutions and laws were frequently unnecessary. In an organization such as the Empire, with its wide geographic dispersion and individual differences, a laissez-faire policy which left room for the development of colonial nationalism could only rest on sentiment, and any attempt to channel it into institutions would increase the possibility of friction and lead to eventual disruption. Thus the strength of the Empire, in this view, rested not on a unity guaranteed by institutions or binding commitments, but on the strength of the components. The contribution of the dominions to imperial strength and unity lay in the cultivation of their own gardens. "National duty and Imperial duty . . . go hand in hand," the *Free Press* noted on Dominion Day, 1905, "because the strength of the Empire depends upon the strength and unity of its parts."

By 1905, of course, the threat to the autonomy of the dominions which Joseph Chamberlain and his followers represented had disappeared, and the British Liberal party once more held office. No matter what the future held, Dafoe felt that an important stage had been passed. The *Free Press* outlined this feeling on December 9 when it remarked: "The Imperial ideals to which the British statesmen in office during the past ten years have been wedded looked to a centralization of power in the capital—the Roman plan modified to meet twentieth-century requirements." The garland for successfully defeating this renovated Roman plan was awarded to Sir Wilfrid Laurier, and the reward was doubly deserved because the victory meant a strengthened Empire:

> Canada under the Laurier regime has taken steps which have strengthened the Empire, not by consenting to the appointment of some fussy bureaucrats dominated by some fads, to meddle with Colonial affairs, but by enormously increasing the power and resources of this country. Canada, in taking over the entire responsibility of her defence, in modifying her Militia system, in making a start in the establishment of a Canadian navy, makes it very clear that she intends to be a factor in world politics in alliance with the Motherland. But it will be an alliance, not a merger.

Though this claim was based as much on hope as on fact, its healthy optimism was obviously rooted in the belief that if the hardy snake of centralization had not been killed, it had at least been scotched. Perhaps now the golden age of imperial co-operation, based on the equal partnership of the British nations, was opening up. A Liberal Government in the motherland seemed to support this project, and it would be ensured if Canadians continued to give their support to Laurier.

Dafoe's thinking in this period on Canada's relations with the United States serves both to underscore and complement his imperial views. His basic assumption was that Canada's goal was to develop on the northern half of the continent a new nationality, "working in and through British institutions" and forming part of the British Empire. An undeniable axiom of Canadian life was that union with the United States was not a possible answer to the Canadian question. Yet there was a certain uneasiness that the United States, under the voluble leadership of Theodore Roosevelt, might not allow Canada to design its destiny unhampered. Particularly irritating were the extensive claims made by self-assertive Americans for the application of the Monroe Doctrine. These were looked upon as "exhibitions of the highly original methods which it has sought to introduce into diplomacy and international law to serve the purpose of the United States."[7]

The dispute over the settlement of the Alaska boundary was the chief irritant in Canadian-American relations. The United States treated Canada's claims in this matter in a singularly cavalier fashion, and Dafoe was annoyed. Sifton had realistically appraised the situation early in 1903, remarking that Canada was caught between the upper and nether millstones of British and American interests. The British had cold-bloodedly decided to abandon Canadian claims in favour of the friendship of the United States. "The United States would not recede and England would not take any chances of a quarrel," he reported.[8]

While the tribunal established to negotiate the boundary dispute was in session (in September of that same year), the *Free Press* emphasized the determination of Canada, as a nation, to remain within the British Empire. Should the Empire disappear then Canada would take its stand as an independent nation. The alternatives were no longer what they had been in Sir John Macdonald's day—either remaining in the Empire or joining the United States. The country was now strong enough in both wealth and national sentiment to stand alone should the calamitous day arrive when the British connection could no longer be continued. Canada could not in "any circumstances consider for a moment the suggestion that it should throw in its lot with the United States."

When the boundary award unfavourable to Canada was announced, the *Free Press*, like the Liberal Government in Ottawa, was in an awkward position. It did not want to stir up a protest that might prove

[7]*M.F.P.*, Dec. 9, 1905; Oct. 21, 1901; July 23, 1902.
[8]Sifton Papers, Sifton to Dafoe, Feb. 4, 1903.

detrimental to the Laurier administration, and it therefore accepted the decision stoically. The next move was to try to undercut Conservative criticisms. The simple fact was that "Great Britain could not for Canada's sake afford to go to war with the United States, and Canada was powerless in the matter." There was, however, an object lesson to be learned from the Alaskan experience: Canada should prepare itself against a repetition of these events by assuming control over negotiations of this character. This demand was limited by a qualification which is of interest in showing the important part the maintenance of the imperial tie played in Dafoe's thinking. In matters which affected Canada alone, "the Canadian Government should have full charge of all the negotiations subject, of course, to the ultimate possibility of an Imperial veto." Clearly there was no desire here to sever the umbilical cord. Any frank analysis of the realities of power in the world in which Canada lived showed that the imperial connection was an absolute necessity. Dafoe did not relish the thought of losing this source of strength, though it was possible to speak of Canadian independence. But it was also perfectly clear that Canada would have to defend its own interests against the United States. "The Yankees," Sifton told Dafoe, "have simply got a lust for power, territory & expenditure & they are going to be the biggest bully the world has ever seen." The Alaska boundary award was a sharp stimulant to Canadian nationalism, for it resulted not only in resentment against Britain's betrayal of Canada's interests, but also in a realization that Canada would have to be strong if it wished to maintain its integrity against the United States. The lesson of Alaska was not soon forgotten.[9]

ii

It would be a serious error to suggest that Dafoe's thoughts were exclusively, or even largely, concerned with such matters of high politics as imperial relations and international affairs during his first years in the Western newspaper world. Actually domestic politics were the greatest preoccupation of the Canadian electorate, and as Dafoe was directing a Liberal party newspaper, domestic questions provided the bulk of the fuel for his editorial furnace. In practice, of course, there was no real division between domestic and external questions; one depended on the other, and both depended on preserving the Liberals' hold on office. Therefore Dafoe's first objective was to strengthen the position of the Liberals by explaining and justifying party policies to his

[9] *M.F.P.*, Oct. 18, 1903; Jan. 13, 1904. Sifton Papers, Sifton to Dafoe, Dec. 9, 1903.

Western readers, though not without an interpretation which warned the Liberal Government of the needs of the West. In short, an ideal situation would be one in which the needs of the West and the policies of the party were indistinguishable. Moreover this harmony would simplify the task of formulating *Free Press* policy, and ensure the paper's financial success.[10]

But since there was not complete identification of Western demands and Liberal policy, Dafoe frequently had to exhibit some intricate footwork. One of the first lessons he learned about editing a Liberal newspaper in the West was the necessity of walking carefully in the heavily mined no man's land between the Liberal Government's national policies and the increasingly blunt agrarian attack upon them. The providential agent which saved him from blundering was the Conservative party. *Free Press* readers were not only instructed in the virtues of Liberalism but also sternly warned of the vices of Conservatism. Indeed, the mortal sins of the Tories made it possible, on occasion, to admit that the Liberals, too, had their weaknesses. These weaknesses, of course, paled into insignificance when measured against the black record of their rivals "whose policy has always been, as it is now, a policy of sacrificing Western interests," an editorial on November 12, 1901, pointed out.

The issue which was at the centre of most farm discontent in Western Canada was the tariff. It was therefore one of the chief subjects on Dafoe's editorial page. The position which he would repeat and defend many times was set out soon after his arrival in Winnipeg:

> The present tariff is the outcome of an attempt by the Liberal government to cope with the state of affairs as they existed in Canada at the end of a long term of office by the Conservatives; and though it has been subjected to its fair share of criticism there is a general agreement that it has met the situation in a manner fairly satisfactory.

This was hardly an anthem of praise, but neither was it a battle hymn. The tariff was not perfect but it was the best available at the moment. Dafoe knew it was a difficult tariff to defend, but even more, he worried about the possibility of its being raised. One of his earliest complaints to Sifton was that "it is a tough enough job to defend the tariff as it stands up here; and an increase would have a tendency to put us out of business in a political sense." His long suit on this question, as on others, was the argument that the West should send more Liberals to Ottawa to influence party counsels.[11]

[10]Sifton Papers, Dafoe to Sifton, April 12, 1902.
[11]*M.F.P.*, Nov. 2, 1901; Sifton Papers, Dafoe to Sifton, Nov. 7, 1901; *M.F.P.*, April 1, 1902.

Sifton was never anxious that the tariff be given much publicity in the West. Personally he did not sympathize with the farmers' demand for lower tariff rates; indeed he favoured an increase on many items. His chief interest was in maintaining the party equilibrium on this issue, and he felt that this feat could best be managed if the question was not too frequently in the public eye. Dafoe argued with his chief that the paper should pay closer attention to the tariff and its effect upon agrarian political sentiment. He believed that sentiment for low tariffs was very strong; perhaps it did not carry enough support to elect a government, but certainly enough to turn one out. What favoured the Liberals, he believed, was the fact that the Conservatives had declared themselves definitely in favour of increased tariff rates and had thus strait-jacketed themselves. The secret of success was a flexible policy, that is, a tariff policy not rigidly enough defined to disturb any element in the country. This policy would allow the Liberals "if they are discreet" to "consolidate the low tariff men and the moderate protectionists into a working alliance." The position that Dafoe thought safest to follow in his newspaper was to attack the high tariff views of the Tories and the Canadian Manufacturers' Association without saying much about the Liberal policy. Of course it was impossible to hide the fact that there was a high tariff wing in the Liberal organization. The best tactic would be to admit this fact and then draw the moral that "if the West does not leaven the party with a strong contingent of Liberal members, it need not be surprised if it gets a tariff that it does not like."[12]

Dafoe's personal views about fiscal policy are difficult to determine with assurance. His chief concern seems to have been to protect the Liberal lifelines in the West. In addition, however, he made every effort possible to postpone tariff changes in the hope that increased representation of the West at Ottawa would be able to block any weakening of the Liberal Government's determination to maintain a moderate tariff.

The moderation which characterized Dafoe's public statements on the tariff question was indicative of the general tone of his presentation of Prairie problems. "The policy of the F.P., it seems to me," he explained to Sifton, "should be to be critical but not to become an encourager of the kickers. There are too many of that kidney here already, and they are just as ready to use their boot-toes on the Liberal party as on anything else." This remark summed up the attitude of the *Free Press* on nearly every issue. Its desire was to represent Western Canada but without damaging the Laurier Government. Therefore the

[12]Sifton Papers, Sifton to Dafoe, Nov. 21, Nov. 23 and Dec. 7, 1903; Dafoe to Sifton, Nov. 28, 1903.

achievements of the Government which were most beneficial to the West, such as the strengthening of the Manitoba Grain Act, the success of the immigration policy and the decision to assist in constructing additional railway facilities, were played up. While Dafoe was personally opposed to government ownership of existing railway facilities, he nevertheless gave strong support to the plan for a publicly owned line to Hudson Bay. In its attitude to large-scale business, the *Free Press* refused to take part in "the vast amount of cheap and insincere talk against corporations."[13]

The frequently unstated major premise of almost every editorial that appeared in the *Free Press* on domestic policy was that the prosperity and development of the nation as a whole depended upon the welfare of the West. At the turn of the century this was an economically sound argument. Numerous were the variations on this theme. "The future of Canada is bound up with the development of this Western country; and in the long run that policy which will conduce most to the rapid settlement of Manitoba and the territories will be the best for the East," an editorial on March 15, 1905, claimed. And there was only one way in which the West could ensure that Western development would be a major consideration of the Government at Ottawa—send strong delegations of members united by this common purpose to Parliament. On April 10, 1902, the *Free Press* portrayed the results that could be achieved by a united Western bloc:

> If the West could poll a solid vote in Parliament against every proposition looking to a higher tariff we should hear much less protection talk from Eastern politicians; for the spectre of an ever-growing West, hostile to the last voter to all their elaborate proposals for higher taxation, would make them hesitate about embarking on a course that would be sure to lead to disaster in time, if not immediately.

Obviously the moral was that the electors of the West should throw their entire weight behind the Liberal party, and transform it into an instrument for the expression of ideas with a Western flavour. On the whole the Liberals' record was good, but the party could be made more sensitive to Prairie needs if all the Western representatives sat on the Government benches. Certainly the Conservatives were unregenerate beyond salvation, and the idea of a third party was simply absurd.

Thus during his first four years at the *Free Press* Dafoe developed into a vital cog in the Liberal party's Western machine. His primary function was that of an editor, but he also assisted in efforts to herd the

[13]Sifton Papers, Dafoe to Sifton, Nov. 27, 1901 and Feb. 18, 1902; *M.F.P.*, Aug. 5 and June 26, 1905.

masses of new immigrants into the Liberal fold, and occasionally advised Sifton on patronage. At one point he found himself at serious odds with Laurier over a question of organization. Dafoe wanted the Dominion Government to assume control of the voters' lists, for in Manitoba Roblin's Conservative Government was suspected of using its jurisdiction in this area unfairly. Much to Dafoe's chagrin, Laurier refused to interfere in this area of provincial power.[14]

In 1905 a more explosive issue arose to range Dafoe and Sifton against Sir Wilfrid. This was the Northwest school question. The school question always lay close to the surface in Manitoba politics, and it was a dangerous issue because it raised a fundamental question about the nature of Canada: the relations between the two predominant cultures. Shortly after Dafoe arrived in Winnipeg, the *Free Press* made a statement on "The Race Question" which suggested that, though it would "in some respects be a convenience" if the French lost their cultural heritage, this was impossible, hence tolerance and understanding between the races was necessary. One of the chief objectives of Canadian politicians, the editorial of January 29, 1902, remarked, should be the promotion of this co-operation: "Only by compromise, by giving and taking, by seeking to unite on essentials and by agreeing to differ on matters of less moment can we keep the peace. Coercion of one race by the other is out of the question; separation is equally impossible."

The problem of schools was the most important point of dispute between the races in the Western provinces, where the French Canadians hoped to establish a dual school system such as existed in Quebec and Ontario, and the English Canadians, for the most part, supported a secular, state educational system. The first round of this struggle had been fought in Manitoba, a province where French-Canadian rights seemed to be securely established, in the 1890's. It ended in a split decision which satisfied no one. The guiding principle of this settlement had been the abjuration by the Laurier Government of federal legislative interference in educational matters. Dafoe and the *Free Press* accepted this as a principle enshrined permanently in Liberal dogma. As far as the federal authorities were concerned then, in Dafoe's view the Manitoba school question was settled.

Dafoe, of course, was fully aware that the school question was not settled in Manitoba. The Roman Catholics, especially those of French origin, were very dissatisfied with the Laurier-Greenway agreement of 1897, while the Protestants seemed determined to prevent the granting

---

[14]Laurier Papers, Dafoe to Laurier, June 20, 1904; Laurier to Dafoe, June 28, 1904.

of any special privileges to their religious opponents. Thus the question was a politically dangerous one. Laurier made several attempts to work through the Manitoba Liberal party to have some modifications made in favour of his co-religionists, but the local Liberals were reluctant to make any commitment that might be used against them by the Conservatives. Dafoe's attitude was one of cautious co-operation; he showed a willingness to aid any negotiations, but agreed with the Manitoba Liberals that Roman Catholic educational grievances should not be allowed to endanger the party's fortunes. Furthermore, his willingness to see small adjustments made in the provincial school system stopped far short of any deviation from the principle of state-controlled schools.

Though it was possible to temporize over the unsettled state of the school question in Manitoba, by 1905 it was no longer possible for the federal Government to delay the granting of provincial status to the Northwest Territories. Laurier had promised a settlement in the election campaign of 1904 and the people in the territories were impatient. Dafoe had long been aware that the Government might find itself in difficulty over this problem, for the question of separate schools was bound to complicate the matter. But despite his anticipation of trouble, he was caught completely off guard by the magnitude of the crisis which developed. He certainly had no premonition of his employer's decision to leave the Laurier administration over the matter.

The autonomy bills came before the House of Commons on February 21, 1905. Four days later Dafoe received the shocking announcement of Sifton's resignation. Sifton feared that the clauses relating to schools in the two new provinces were vague and open to misinterpretation. He felt that this ambiguity was calculated and suspected the fine hand of the Minister of Justice, Charles Fitzpatrick, who was a Roman Catholic. Moreover he was annoyed at Laurier's failure to consult him on the matter. This information struck Dafoe like a "bolt from the blue," for the *Free Press* had already declared itself in favour of the proposed legislation on the assumption that the school clauses were designed to retain the existing school system. A quick reversal of this position was now necessary and Dafoe found himself "put in a very difficult position in order to bring the Free Press through without any injury."[15]

The subsequent course followed by Dafoe was governed by the action taken by Sifton. Though opposed in principle to all separate schools, Sifton was prepared to agree to an arrangement whereby the new pro-

[15]Sifton Papers, Sifton to Dafoe, Feb. 25, 1905, and wire of same date; *M.F.P.*, Feb. 24, 1905; Sifton Papers, Dafoe to Sifton, Feb. 26, 1905.

vinces would be left both with their existing educational arrangements and with complete control over education. Even after Laurier satisfied him that this dual objective would be achieved, Sifton refused to withdraw his resignation, though the fact that he discouraged his colleague, W. S. Fielding, from joining him indicates that he had no desire to destroy the Government. Once Sifton's determination to resign was made known, the *Free Press* attacked the autonomy bills head on. "The first thing for the Government to do," it declared, "is certainly to get on firm ground by recasting the educational clauses." This was precisely what the Government did, and by the end of March a settlement had been reached which the *Free Press* could praise as "a wise and statesmanlike solution." The school agitation did not drop into obscurity immediately, but once the new provinces held elections, both of which were won by the Liberals, the storm rapidly abated. In Manitoba the school controversy was briefly enlivened by Roblin's cabinet colleague, Robert Rogers, who charged that the Apostolic Delegate, Mgr Sbaretti, and Sir Wilfrid were planning to force separate schools on Manitoba in return for an extension of the province's boundary. Both the Prelate and the Prime Minister denied the charge to the satisfaction of the *Free Press*, and the matter ended there temporarily.[16]

Dafoe's final assessment of the events of 1905 is difficult to judge. His later view was that the crisis over the autonomy bills was caused by the surrender, the first of a series, made by Laurier to the demands of his own Quebec people. The Northwest school question certainly caused Dafoe to suspect Laurier's intentions, but it must be remembered that his later judgments of Laurier were all coloured by the events of the Great War, which brought a complete break between the two men. Certainly in 1905 Dafoe did not think that the autonomy bills dispute changed his relation with the Liberal party. "The Path to National Peace" was the Liberal path of moderation, the *Free Press* advised.[17]

Thus when Dafoe's anniversary as Sifton's lieutenant arrived in the autumn of 1905, he had acquainted himself with most of the issues of Prairie politics, and handled them with facility. The immediate prospects seemed promising. Certainly Sifton's retirement from the Laurier ministry would make the editor's task easier, and leave more room for the exercise of his powerful critical faculties. The *Free Press* would still be a Liberal journal, of course, but now it would be able to identify

[16]Sifton Papers, Sifton to Laurier, Feb. 24, 1905; Sifton to W. S. Fielding, Feb. 27, 1905. *M.F.P.*, March 1, March 22 and April 5, 1905.
[17]Dafoe, *Laurier*, 124; *M.F.P.*, May 13, 1905.

itself even more closely with Western interests. Then there was imperial and international policy. Here Laurier could be completely trusted, especially with a Liberal Government in power in the United Kingdom. Already aware of the unpredictability of political life, Dafoe probably did not expect complete tranquillity, but certainly the future carried little suggestion of serious problems, nor of the great events that were to have such a marked effect on Dafoe and on Canadian development in the next nine years.[18]

[18]For a shrewd estimate of Dafoe in 1903 see Frank C. Steele, *Prairie Editor: The Life and Times of Buchanan of Lethbridge* (Toronto, 1961), 17.

III. Liberalism: Domestic and Imperial
1906-11

++

THOUGH THE VIEWS OF THE *Manitoba Free Press* during Dafoe's apprenticeship may not have been radical enough for some members of the agrarian population, its moderate approach had apparently succeeded in winning the confidence of a large segment of the Prairie farmers. The maintenance of this confidence, of course, depended upon the ability of the newspaper to continue to express the needs and convince the minds of its readers. The five years that elapsed between Sifton's departure from the Laurier Government and the emergence of the great reciprocity issue were pregnant with questions that called for tactful consideration by the *Free Press*. In these five years, besides the perennial problems of Canadian politics and economics, and the day-to-day fight with the Roblin Government in Manitoba, two issues of fundamental importance arose. The first was the problem of naval defence, which in fact evoked a discussion of the wider question of imperial organization. It remained unsettled. The second was that of trade with the United States. This thorny question implied a host of other problems, such as the position of agriculture in the national economy, the farmer's place in national politics, Canada's relations with the United States, and even the country's future within the British Empire.

Though the rejection by the Canadian electorate of the proposed reciprocity agreement was decisive enough, it would be wrong to conclude that this set of related questions was definitely answered. Indeed there is a certain indecisiveness and lack of unanimity about the decisions made by Canadians on the great national issues that they faced in the decade before the outbreak of the Great War. It was a period of furious debate, but the national mind remained equivocal. At the same time, however, individual minds were hardening into firm conclusions about the nature of Canada's future. Dafoe was one of those whose opinions evolved into articles of faith in these years of national uncertainty. On a more personal level, these years encompassed the most serious conflict that Dafoe ever experienced in his relations with Sifton. This crisis was solved in a manner that left no doubt that Dafoe had completed his apprenticeship.

ii

Although reciprocity and the naval question coalesced into a combined issue in 1911, they began as separate problems. For Dafoe the discussion of imperial relations, of which the naval issue was part, was a continuing dialogue. Even when there were no particular incidents to discuss, the *Free Press* kept its readers acquainted with its views on the nature of the relations among the members of the Empire. "A foundation principle of Imperial unity," the paper noted on November 5, 1906, "will have to be that each partner will have to mind its own business." This was the foundation principle of Dafoe's thoughts about the Empire.

No doubt the Winnipeg editor's consciousness of the Empire had been quickened by his first trip to Britain in the summer of 1906, a trip which he made as a member of the Canadian delegation to the meeting of the Chambers of Commerce of the Empire. Here he had an opportunity to see the mother country as well as to meet delegates from other parts of the Empire and listen to their views on questions affecting the well-being of the organization. He took an active part in the debate, seconding a resolution declaring the meeting's concern that British emigrants should settle in British countries. No doubt he was more impressed with Prime Minister Asquith's praise for self-government as the best guarantee of imperial unity than with Sir Charles Tupper's anti-American tirade. He returned home more convinced than ever that the Liberals, both at home and in Britain, could best be trusted with the keys of Empire.[1]

The general discussion of imperial relations was brought into closer focus in March 1909 when, on Conservative initiative, the Canadian House of Commons unanimously adopted a resolution calling for the establishment of a Canadian naval force. The move received the full approval of the *Free Press*. It represented the proposal as the logical

[1] *The Times,* July 11, 12, 13, 1906; *C.A.R.* (Toronto, 1906), 618–21.

consequence of the country's national development and the acceptance of the proper responsibilities as a self-governing member of the Empire. In fact the *Free Press* was prepared to go even further than the adopted resolution. Not only was the immediate construction of a Canadian navy desirable, but "it would nevertheless have been a good thing, all things considered, if the offer of a couple of Dreadnoughts had been made to the British Government. It would have been one of those spectacular things which have an instantaneous moral effect more important in its meaning than the thing in itself." German truculence constituted a real threat to British naval supremacy, the *Free Press* believed, and the Empire had to show its determination to defy intimidation. An increasing number of Canadians came to agree with this view.[2]

While the Laurier Government set about finding the best means of implementing the March resolution, Dafoe had an opportunity to study the situation at close quarters. In July 1909 the first meeting of the Imperial Press Conference was held in London. This affair was called together on the suggestion of an English newspaperman, Harry E. Brittain. He had conceived the idea during a visit to Winnipeg in 1907, and looked upon Dafoe as one of its originators. Its purpose was to discuss imperial problems especially as they related to journalism. When the conference finally convened, the problems of Empire had seemingly been reduced to the single question of naval defence.[3]

Besides hearing speeches from most of the leading figures in British political life and engaging in wide-ranging discussions, the delegates travelled throughout the United Kingdom. As an added attraction, not offered to ordinary tourists, the journalists were treated to a mock battle performed by the British Army at Aldershot, followed by a display of 140 vessels of the Royal Navy flashing past Spithead. Such a display was enough to take a colonial journalist's breath away and, it was probably hoped, strengthen his imperial loyalties.[4]

Dafoe was enthusiastic about the activities of the meeting. Though he spoke only infrequently, he was a member of the important committee on the wire services that linked the various parts of the Empire. With his fellow delegates he inspected many of the industrial areas of Britain. At Sheffield, where he toured the Vickers armaments plant, he spoke on behalf of his colleagues at the Lord Mayor's dinner. He told the assembly that the conference had done much to strengthen imperial

[2]*M.F.P.*, March 31, April 6, April 21, 1909.
[3]*The Times*, June 28, 1909; Sir Harry Brittain to *The Times*, Jan. 12, 1944; Dafoe, *The Imperial Press Conference* (Winnipeg, 1909), 4.
[4]T. H. Hardman, *The Parliament of the Press* (London, 1909), 70.

unity. It had done so because he and the other delegates had discovered that no responsible statesman in British public life accepted the views of the people "who believed that they could sit in a library in London and formulate a constitution, or a working programme, in which they could compress the life of the nation overseas." The sweet wines of imperialism had obviously not turned this nationalist's head. Dafoe always abstained from imperial as well as alcoholic intoxicants.[5]

As a good reporter, Dafoe made certain that the readers of the *Free Press* were kept informed on the conference. He told them that any suspicion that the conference was manipulated in the "interest of one set of imperialistic theories" was totally unfounded. The conference had convinced him that the old conflict in imperial affairs between centralizers and autonomists was a dispute of the past. The Empire was now accepted as an association of equals in which a new loyalty had grown up to replace the old subservience. "In the sense in which loyalty implies the devotion of a subject race," he wrote, "the Colonies are not loyal to England, nor are the Colonials loyal to Englishmen; but in the other sense—the loyalty of brother to brother, of friend to friend, of ally to ally—our loyalty is unbreakable and imperishable." This was the basis of the newly emerged league of free nations which would "continue to grow in strength and solidarity as a confederation of democracies."[6]

It is important to stress that Dafoe believed that the struggle against a centralized Empire had been won by 1909. He believed it had been won because he heard assurance given by politicians from both parties in Great Britain at the gathering of the journalists of the Empire. He also believed that there was no longer any significant conflict of views on this subject between the political parties in Canada. He had reached this conclusion because of the unanimity which had been expressed in the acceptance of the naval resolution in March. Now that the nature of the Empire was settled, one could even begin to discuss its ultimate objectives. After all, this was no temporary Empire like those of the ancient world, which had been based on conquest, oppression and exploitation. The British Empire was enlivened by a liberal spirit. As an association of "free and enlightened democracies dedicated to the cause of peace and to the service of humanity," it could command the devotion of all British peoples, and "perhaps in some far-off time, the support of all Anglo-Saxondom." Neither the imperialist Sir Charles Dilke nor the anti-imperialist Goldwin Smith would have found this statement of

[5]*Ibid.*, 85.
[6]Dafoe, *Imperial Press Conference*, 6, 32; *M.F.P.*, March 18, 1910.

Anglo-Saxon idealism objectionable. But there were Canadians of French origin who could be expected to shudder at its implications.[7]

When Dafoe returned from overseas he discovered that Canadian politics were once more in a state of turbulence over the imperial question. The unanimity of the previous March was in process of disintegrating. Some Conservatives and their newspaper allies were now dissenting from the declared policy of their leader and demanding a Canadian contribution of Dreadnoughts to the British Admiralty. The *Free Press* immediately took up the challenge, pointing out that although it had at one time favoured a direct contribution, the emergency which had inspired that suggestion had now passed. The proper course for Canada to follow was to establish its own navy on lines that would be standard for the entire Empire.[8]

As the Conservative clamour for a direct contribution to the Admiralty grew, so did the vehemence of the *Free Press*'s attack upon the suggestion. In the furious debate over naval policy Dafoe saw the revival of the discussion of the nature of the Empire which he had so recently pronounced dead. The supporters of the policy of contribution were anathematized as "Bourbons" who never learned and never forgot. Their suggested policy proved that they did not want an Empire of equal nations, but rather one of colonial subjection to Britain. There had always been Bourbons in Canada, usually centred in Toronto, who had opposed every advance towards Canadian self-government since Lord Durham's day. Now, despite the unanimous support shown by the Canadian House of Commons, the majority of the people, the British government and naval authorities for the proposed Canadian navy, the Bourbons had begun their "frantic, fatuous and futile agitation." It could not be allowed to succeed, the *Free Press* insisted on September 10, 1909.

Repeatedly the paper exhorted the parliamentary Conservatives to hold fast to their position of March, and assailed both the groups that were attempting to undermine Borden's approval of a Canadian navy. On the right there were the fire-eating imperialists, led by Premier Roblin, demanding a direct contribution; on the left, the French-Canadian nationalists, led by F. D. Monk, demanding a policy of isolation. Both groups failed to realize that Canada had outgrown its colonial status and was now an equal in the Empire. The *Free Press* declared scornfully: "they cannot get away from the idea that Great Britain is the Empire in a sense in which Canada is not; that Canada is,

[7] Dafoe, *Imperial Press Conference*, 43.
[8] *M.F.P.*, Aug. 13, 1909.

in a sense, external to the Empire and owes allegiance and subjection to Great Britain. This idea is a relic surviving from the Colonial era." For Dafoe, the evolution of the Empire made the founding of a Canadian navy a natural step. There could be no doubt that Canada was an equal member of the imperial partnership; this position demanded that it shoulder its share of imperial defence. In the event of a threat to imperial security the Canadian navy would be "placed at the disposal of the British government as rapidly as the cable can flash the message under the seas." Though this action would take place only after Parliament had decided to transfer the navy to Admiralty control, no one with any faith in Canada's attachment to the Empire would dare to suggest that there would be any other decision.[9]

Thus the imperial question which Dafoe had thought settled in the summer of 1909 had gained a new lease on life within twelve months. Though Laurier's Naval Service Act, establishing a Canadian navy, was finally made law after long and acrimonious debate, it had reopened all the old questions of imperial relations. When Sir Joseph Ward, at the Imperial Conference of 1911, proposed the establishment of an Imperial Council, the *Free Press* remarked (May 8), "Thus we find ourselves on the old abandoned ground of a centralized Empire with the Dominions in subordination to the central power." Moreover, the naval debate had injected a new element into Canadian politics. Not only had the old division between Liberals and Conservatives been emphasized, but a new group had appeared in Quebec under the guidance of the passionate Henri Bourassa. This new group had proved its strength in a by-election in Drummond-Arthabaska in November 1910. It was a disturbing situation, for Dafoe knew that Bourassa's appeals to race would result in similar appeals being made in English Canada.[10]

At the end of the naval debate in 1910, Dafoe's own views about the Empire remained unchanged, though they were perhaps clarified. While rejecting outright the proposal for an Imperial Council, he found the isolationist viewpoint of the French-Canadian nationalist equally distasteful. "Between the contemptible policy of doing nothing," the *Free Press* pointed out on May 19, 1911, "and the absurd programme of the militarists, a proper mean must be found." In determining this "proper mean," consultation and co-operation with the other members of the Empire was both necessary and proper, but the final decision rested with Canada. Dafoe looked on the Empire as a unit of equals with a common foreign policy, each Dominion deciding upon the action to be taken in

[9]*Ibid.*, Nov. 19, 1909; Feb. 19, 1910.
[10]Dafoe Papers, Dafoe to William Maxwell, Dec. 29, 1910.

implementing that policy. There was, as yet, no suggestion of the idea of independent foreign policies for the dominions. In the terms of the *Free Press*, Dafoe was a "sane imperialist" which, of course, was also a "sane autonomist." This equivocal position is probably best described as liberal imperialism.

By the summer of 1911 Dafoe had seen the passage of the naval service bill and the defeat of the proposed Imperial Council. The liberal imperialist view of the Empire seemed once more safely enshrined in the Canadian experience. But the discussion stimulated by the naval debate was carried over into the argument about reciprocity with the United States, where the real question was once more Canada's status and destiny.

iii

When he wrote on domestic politics Dafoe's Western viewpoint was always far more apparent than when he turned to issues of international concern. He had a nearly boundless confidence in the West and looked upon it as his special preserve. His efforts as a political editor were designed to promote those causes which he thought were necessary for the full development of the Western potential. To him, supporting the Liberal party was the best means of winning favourable attention for Prairie problems. Furthermore, he believed that unless the West sent Liberal members to Ottawa, its complaints would not receive a sympathetic hearing. This was one of the main reasons for his bitter and prolonged fight against the Roblin Conservatives in Manitoba. To defeat Roblin, he argued, "would break the power of the Conservative party West of the Lakes for a decade because the motive power for the entire political machinery in this territory has come from the Government buildings on Kennedy street."[11]

Two aspects of local politics particularly concerned Dafoe in his unending struggle to evict the Tories from the West. First there was the danger that the school question might flare up again, especially since the rumour persisted that Laurier was anxious to trade the extension of Manitoba's boundaries for changes in the educational system which would give Roman Catholics more equitable treatment. Whatever truth there was in this rumour, and there was very little, it served the Roblin Government's purposes to keep it alive as part of its successful technique of laying Manitoba's problems at the feet of the Ottawa Government. Dafoe was extremely reluctant to see the school question

[11]Dafoe, "Western Canada: Its Resources and Possibilities," *American Monthly Review of Reviews*, XXXV (June 1907), 697–709; Sifton Papers, Dafoe to Sifton, Feb. 8, 1907.

raised again, both for political reasons and because of his own opposition to separate schools. Moreover, his mind was never quite free of the suspicion that Laurier might take some action on the matter which would jeopardize the position of the Manitoba Liberals. "He is a Latin mind of extreme subtlety; and the Anglo-Saxon is simply confused in attempting to follow its workings," he wrote of Sir Wilfrid in 1908. But as long as Laurier was in office, Dafoe's apprehensions remained unfulfilled.[12]

Dafoe believed that the Liberals' disadvantages in Manitoba could be at least partly offset if Laurier would agree to some federal action to limit Roblin's control of the voters' lists. Dafoe kept at this problem with the persistence of a terrier. It even appeared for a brief period in 1908 as though some action might be forthcoming, but in the end Laurier gave in to pressures from other provinces and let the matter drop. Dafoe saw in this retreat an unwillingness on Laurier's part to support his Western allies. In a burst of impatience, he told Sifton that "We are not Liberals because we support Laurier, but we support him because we are Liberals; he is a mere incident while the party goes on." Here was an attitude which in a more serious crisis could lead to a complete rupture. But in the meantime, Dafoe went on fighting for the Liberal party in the West, and for the West in the Liberal party.[13]

As usual, in fulfilling his task Dafoe had to contend not only with the reluctance of the Liberal party to accept Western demands, but also with the growing radicalism of Westerners. They had given their support to Laurier in 1904, but various questions affecting the farmers' welfare were causing increasing restiveness. Already in 1905 many farmers had reached the conclusion, according to a Winnipeg grain buyer, that "all grain buyers are thieves, and hell's divided equally between the railways and the milling companies." The farmers were not yet ready to enter politics independently but there were certain problems upon which their demands for prompt government action were becoming insistent. The *Free Press* had to pay close attention to these demands.[14]

The staples of Western discontent were railway services and fiscal policy. On the former the *Free Press* was a consistent supporter of increased railway facilities and reduced freight rates. Increased railway facilities, for the newspaper, included the construction of at least one more transcontinental system to compete with the C.P.R. In 1904 the *Free Press* condemned the proposal made by the Conservatives for

[12]G. R. Cook, "Church, Schools and Politics in Manitoba, 1903–1912," *C.H.R.*, XXXIX, no. 1 (March 1958), 1–23; Sifton Papers, Dafoe to Sifton, July 7, 1908.
[13]Sifton Papers, Dafoe to Sifton, June 15, 1908.
[14]H. Moorehouse, *Deep Furrows* (Toronto and Winnipeg, 1918), 72.

public ownership of the Grand Trunk Pacific as a "Socialistic fad," but this did not prevent Dafoe from supporting the agitation for a government constructed and operated railroad to Hudson Bay. He put special emphasis on this latter project. If the Government failed to settle this "outstanding question," the farmers would press their more radical proposals, and perhaps even desert the Liberals. The West finally had its way. Though the completion of this contentious project required another two decades, the Laurier Government did begin construction in a desultory fashion late in 1910.[15]

Far more important than any of these peripheral issues was the delicate question of the tariff. Here the position taken by Dafoe and the *Free Press* was more opportunist than consistent. Until almost the day when the announcement was made that the reciprocity negotiations with the United States had proved successful, the *Free Press* preached moderation to Western tariff reformers. The newspaper argued that the best the West could hope for was the maintenance of the existing tariff, and persistently attempted to dampen any hope for reciprocity with the United States. At the same time the *Free Press* had a watchdog's instinct for any attempted tariff increases, and objected vigorously to every suggestion that the existing tariff failed to meet the needs of the country. The Liberals were being praised with faint damnation when the paper observed on August 7, 1909, "The tariff as it stands shows that the Government has not been so much protectionist as opportunist."

Shortly after this sigh of resignation, the Taft administration in Washington decided to send two representatives to Ottawa to discuss trade relations. The chief problem was that the new American tariff, the Payne-Aldrich measure, called for the application of maximum duties to Canadian products. President Taft, harried by domestic problems, hoped to avoid a tariff war with Canada. The *Free Press* interpreted the American move as a direct threat to Canadian fiscal independence, and warned the Government not to give in to American pressures. But the resolution of the Winnipeg newspaper was firmer than that of the Laurier Government. In return for a promise that the retaliatory provisions of the new tariff would not be implemented against Canada, the tariff was reduced on a few American imports. The *Free Press* back-pedalled, but with evident distaste.[16]

Perhaps Dafoe's attitude to the 1910 tariff negotiations was based on his belief that the tariff was not the most pressing political issue in Western Canada. He felt sure that a railway to Hudson Bay was of far

[15] *M.F.P.*, April 27, 1904; Sifton Papers, Dafoe to Sifton, Aug. 16, 1910.
[16] *M.F.P.*, March 16, 31, 1910.

more significance. And he admitted to Sifton that "the West, in view of its political strength, cannot reasonably hope to be more than a modifying influence in determining the tariff policy of the dominion." Moreover he did not believe that the tariff would become a pressing political issue because the farmers "all recognize that free trade is out of the question in Canada." Small concessions, such as the reduction of the duty on agricultural implements, would be enough to placate the restive. The real danger, he felt, lay in the possibility that if the Government went "wrong on other questions, the tariff might easily be the last straw."[17]

Thus Dafoe saw no reason for making the *Free Press* an advocate of reciprocity with the United States. In fact on May 27, 1910, an editorial appeared which took a highly critical approach to the question. In the first place, it was pointed out, it would likely be impossible to obtain a satisfactory agreement for the exchange of farm products and raw material with the United States. And secondly, even if an agreement could be reached there was no way to ensure its permanency "against such a sudden and violent reversal as the reciprocity arrangement of half a century ago suffered in 1866." In sum, reciprocity was an idle dream not to be taken seriously by practical political advocates.

When in the autumn of 1910 negotiations were set in motion to explore the possibility of a reciprocal trading agreement between Canada and the United States, the *Free Press* offered only infrequent comment. It took sharp issue with the claims of alarmists that closer trading relations with the United States would force Canada into the political orbit of the Republic. If this were so, all that the American Congress had to do was to lower the trade barriers and Canada would be swallowed up. The other side of the question, it pointed out, was that any American who believed that Canada would accept a bargain detrimental to its political integrity was deluding himself. "If a fair bargain can be made, Canadians will be pleased, but they have no intention of becoming partners to a bad bargain."[18]

When the terms of the concluded agreement were announced in January 1911, "its scope astonished the public." Probably not the least astonished was the editor of the *Free Press*. The fact that the agreement's main feature, apart from the novel method devised for bringing it into operation, was the provision for freer trade in natural products made it popular in the West. Though the *Free Press* immediately admitted (January 27) "that the people of Canada as a whole will be well

[17]Sifton Papers, Dafoe to Sifton, Aug. 16, 1910.
[18]*M.F.P.*, Oct. 4, Nov. 5, 1910.

satisfied with the conclusions that have been reached," a couple of weeks were needed before it really warmed to the subject.

The reciprocity agreement posed two immediate problems for Dafoe. The first was to manœuvre his paper into support of the agreement. This was easily enough done, for the paper had not opposed reciprocity; it had merely taken the view that it could not be achieved. The second problem was more serious, for it involved the relation between editor and owner. Sifton early decided that he could not personally support the trade agreement. He had some discussion with Dafoe and E. H. Macklin, the business manager of the *Free Press*, but remained unmoved. Yet he seems to have made no attempt to impose his views on the *Free Press*.[19]

From March until September 1911, the *Free Press* organization exhibited an acute case of schizophrenia. While editor Dafoe took the newspaper into the camp of the supporters of reciprocity, the owner of the journal, Clifford Sifton, became one of the leading spirits in the powerful opposition to the agreement. The precise facts of the *modus vivendi* between the two men cannot be reconstructed with absolute certainty, but it is possible to determine the main outlines by inference. Since Dafoe's task as editor of the newspaper was to represent the Western viewpoint and to protect the valuable business interests of the property, he no doubt pointed out to his employer that neither of these functions could be served unless the paper supported the reciprocity agreement, which had widespread Western support. The ardour with which Dafoe pressed these points was no doubt increased by a personal predilection for freer trade. At any rate, by the beginning of March Sifton was prepared to accept Dafoe's view of the situation, a fact which supports the suggestion that Dafoe did not argue in favour of the trade agreement, but rather put the case in terms of the paper's interests. Dafoe now went his way, and Sifton another. Dafoe was always convinced that his employer had no other motives for opposing the agreement than those which he publicly and forcefully stated, and there seems no reason to doubt his judgment. It is true, however, that the two men kept their own counsel after their agreement to disagree. Many years later, Dafoe remarked of the attitude to reciprocity taken by his employer that there was "an inside story as to all important political developments, but I do not know the ground well enough to venture on speculation."[20]

[19]Dafoe Papers, Sifton to Dafoe, Feb. 24, 1911.
[20]*Ibid.*, Sifton to Dafoe, March 2, 1911; Dafoe to A. K. Cameron, Jan. 2, 1932; Dafoe to Harry Sifton, May 28, 1931.

The *Free Press*, in supporting the reciprocity agreement, investigated every line of argument both before the election was called and with increased enthusiasm after the campaign had begun. In addition to stressing the benefits which the agreement would bring to the Western farmer, the paper maintained that it was a means of unifying the various sections of the country. If business men and financiers consistently and successfully prevented the satisfaction of the needs of the Western farmers, the traditional political parties would disintegrate and be reformed on class and sectional lines. A farmers' party demanding the complete abolition of tariffs would spring up, and would have to be resisted by all people whose thinking was national rather than sectional. The reciprocity agreement, with its provision for moderate free trade, was put forward as the best means of preventing national disruption. The violent opposition of the "organized interests" was the real cause of growing class and sectional conflict. To those who claimed that the acceptance of reciprocity was the first step towards political union with the United States, the *Free Press* replied that this morose prediction failed to recognize the strength of national sentiment.[21]

Dafoe did not confine himself to statements about the actual trade agreement in the election of 1911. Despite Sifton's admonition to keep to principles, the *Free Press* found the co-operation between the Conservatives and the Quebec Nationalists too obvious a target to be bypassed. With other Liberal campaigners the paper emphasized the possibility that a victory for Borden would really be a triumph for Henri Bourassa. This result, it was predicted, would mean Conservative acceptance of the Nationalists' views on schools and the navy. "Was there ever in Canada so cynical, so sinister, so unprincipled an alliance?" the *Free Press* asked righteously.[22]

A month before the conclusion of the heated campaign the *Free Press* offered a summary of its optimistic predictions on the effect of accepting reciprocity. It claimed on August 22:

Reciprocity means prosperity to every section of Canada. It means increased population; more trade; larger traffic for our railways; higher values for every foot of land in Canada; enlarged orders for our factories; bigger cities—in short an advance all along the line. Nor will the more populous and more prosperous Canada of the near future lose any of its present national characteristics. It will remain a distinct country, vibrant with national feeling, proud of its position as an integral part of the British Empire; and ready to meet every obligation, national or Imperial, that may arise.

---

[21]*M.F.P.*, March 6, Aug. 4, March 9, 1911.
[22]Dafoe Papers, Sifton to Dafoe, March 2, 1911; *M.F.P.*, Sept. 20, Aug. 9, 1911.

Even in Manitoba this attractive picture was not convincing enough. Though two of the Prairie provinces gave their approval to the Liberal programme, Dafoe's province agreed with the national verdict in favour of the Tories. Robert Borden, with valuable assistance from Clifford Sifton and Henri Bourassa, had vanquished the apparently invincible Liberal machine.

On election day the *Free Press* published some very interesting reflections on what it described as the "political revolution" which had taken place during the campaign. A new alignment had taken place in Canadian politics, dividing radicals from conservatives. The policies of the Liberal Government since its victory in 1896 had been moderate and even conservative, since it had relied for its support upon the great body of moderate opinion in the country. But it had only succeeded at the price of increasing the size of the body of dissatisfied voters. Laurier had envisaged the reciprocity agreement as part of his programme of moderation, but he had enormously under-estimated the vigour with which the protectionist interests would fight the proposal. Once the opposition made its position clear, however, Laurier had not failed to accept the challenge, recognizing that "the era of compromise was over and that he must draw his sword and lead the hosts back to the abandoned battleground of long ago." The reciprocity debate had thus transformed the Liberal party into a party of the left. Quite apart from the outcome of the election it was now clear that the party's future lay in the direction of radical and progressive policies. The editor's conclusion of September 21 was:

> We are thus certain to have henceforth in Canada a real Liberal and a real Tory party. We believe the change will operate to the public good. Parties with real policies and real principles, for which they will fight and face defeat, are factors of great value in the moral and material development of a nation. There is no need to regret that the truce between the conflicting economic ideas in Canada, which has persisted now for fifteen years, has come to a definite close.

This was fairly radical talk for the *Manitoba Free Press*. Did Dafoe really mean it or was he merely trying to ensure that the West, where third-party ideas were already in the air, would be kept with the Liberal party? Some of the radicalism may be written off as journalistic flourish, but in fact Dafoe was not profoundly sorry when the Liberals were defeated. And perhaps it is wrong to describe the views presented as radical, since the writer emphasized the necessity for the party to go "back to the abandoned battleground of long ago." This meant that the party had to return to the policies of its principled, but unsuccessful days before its vision had been blurred by the powerful intoxicants of office.

Dafoe pursued this same theme in a letter to an old journalistic acquaintance. He told his friend that he had long believed that the Liberal party was dying a natural death; its arteries had hardened and it had grown unreceptive to new ideas. The decision to champion reciprocity had really been a resolve to forestall the indignity of a lingering death by facing destruction in battle for a meaningful cause. Apart from the fact that he felt the Canadian people had been idiotic in rejecting the agreement, he personally was not mourning the defeated Government. Canada was really a conservative country, or at least had been for a decade because it had fallen under the control of corporation and moneyed interests. Laurier, who had achieved power in 1896 largely because of the blunders of the leaderless Conservatives, had managed to hold office "by placating various powerful interests at the expense of the general public. The moment he showed signs of putting real Liberal doctrine into effect the interests combined and crushed him." With the party at last out of office, there was an opportunity for a genuine reformation. After a period in Opposition, perhaps shorter than many observers anticipated, the Liberals would be able to regain power and effect a truly progressive programme "without regard to the desires and feelings of the privileged classes." The entire Anglo-Saxon world was on the eve of an upsurge of reformist spirit which in Canada would make possible "a reforming and radical government at Ottawa." Dafoe hoped to play a personal role in the reformation of the Liberals and therefore believed that it was an advantage to have the party in Opposition. He would thus be able to advocate "reforms and innovations which would have proved embarrassing had the Liberal government remained in power." Faced with a Conservative administration he felt free to take a "pretty radical and independent line without much regard to their immediate political consequences." Thus in 1911 Dafoe began to consider the ideas which after a decade of unavoidable delay were to flower into his own variety of progressivism.[23]

Dafoe had yet another reason which prevented him from shedding any tears at the Liberal defeat. It was this reason that he expressed to Sifton shortly after the dust of the campaign had cleared. The letter is most revealing and helps to explain Sifton's decision to allow Dafoe to use the *Free Press* as a propaganda organ for reciprocity. Dafoe wrote:

Re the elections—I wrote you months ago that from the viewpoint of the Free Press interests alone the best thing that could happen would be for the govt. to be beaten provided the Free Press did not help to beat them. This has now come to pass, and I am quite satisfied with the situation. Had we

[23]Dafoe Papers, Dafoe to George Iles, Sept. 27, 1911.

fought the govt. we would have greatly injured this property, whereas as things are, the F.P. is, I shd. say in better shape than ever before.[24]

Dafoe had apparently convinced his employer that to have fought against the trade agreement would have seriously damaged the prestige of the *Free Press* in the farming community. This argument naturally appealed to Sifton's business instinct. The election and the trade agreement had been lost, but this was in no way damaging to the *Free Press*. Indeed the fact that the farmers' fight had been fought unsuccessfully placed the *Free Press* on the martyrs' pedestal beside the cause of reciprocity. Dafoe no doubt knew that some farmers were already suspicious of the large newspapers. The *Grain Growers' Guide* had voiced this sentiment when it declared (October 11, 1910): "The ownership of newspapers in Canada has become a sideline with politicians and with capitalists and it is to suit the views of these people that the wells of truth have been defiled. The freedom of the press is a myth and, with the exception of a few bright examples, in Canada the freedom of the press is gone completely." The *Free Press*'s defence of the farmers' interest in the reciprocity election left it free from these suspicions and won it new prestige in the agrarian community.

In the autumn of 1911 Dafoe had passed his forty-fifth year and completed more than a decade as editor of the *Free Press*. He had become well known in the West and in journalistic circles as an effective Liberal party editor. His national reputation was yet to be made. A Toronto professor, Edward Kylie, surveying the Western scene on behalf of the Round Table movement in the summer of 1912, met the Winnipeg editor and was not especially impressed. He offered his judgment to a friend: "Of newspaper men I met only Dafoe (*Free Press*) and Healy, his first lieutenant. Dafoe is strong, rugged, large, with plenty of dark red hair—a really big character, reserved, but emphatic at times—with probably no more imagination than most journalists."[25] The description, though curt and hasty, was not altogether unfair. There were few occasions during his first ten years in Winnipeg when Dafoe had moved outside the confines of the orthodox Liberal programme. He was a Liberal journalist and used his considerable talents in the cause of his party. But now that his political friends were in Opposition, he was left with more room to feel his way, and perhaps even assume a position of leadership in formulating the criticisms of the Borden régime. Dafoe had not tasted the luxury of opposition before, but he soon found it gave new scope to his wide-ranging intelligence.

[24]Sifton Papers, Dafoe to Sifton, Sept. 23, 1911.
[25]Walker Papers, Edward Kylie to A. J. Glazebrook, June 2, 1912.

iv. The Luxury of Opposition
1911-14

THE DEFEAT OF THE LAURIER GOVERNMENT in September 1911 marked the end of an era in Canadian politics. But few Canadians realized how near they were to the end of an era in the history of the Western world when Robert Borden and his colleagues assumed office. There were, of course, signs of the approaching calamity—the threatening arms race, bitter disputes over colonial possessions, national unrest in Eastern Europe, and even suggestions that the glowing economic prosperity of the early twentieth century was nearing an end. But few observers in 1911 recognized that the cataclysmic confluence of these forces would, in a few short years, lead to a war of global proportions.

In the *Free Press* Dafoe wrote in the vein of the popular liberal optimism that characterized the period. "The human race," the paper's readers were told on New Year's Day, 1913, "is moving upward, not by leaps and bounds in spite of the speed of science, but slowly as knowledge grows more to more, with wisdom keeping pace." Dafoe was a liberal in religion who accepted what he took to be the ethical side of Christianity, but had no use for the doctrines that emphasized man's weak and sinful nature. In his public writings before the Great War, he often spoke of man's moral progress, and, coupling this with the spread of democracy, seemed to foresee the eventual coming of the liberal millennium. Of course democracy had its shortcomings, but these rarely justified the criticism of reactionaries, since they could easily be overcome by the application of the simple dictum that "the cure for the evils of democracy is more democracy."[1]

Some of this unbounded optimism may be written off as journalistic flourish or the need to fill newspaper space, but its frequent repetition

[1] M. S. Donnelly, "J. W. Dafoe" in Robt. L. McDougall, ed., *Our Living Tradition*, Fourth Series (Toronto, 1962), 96–7; *M.F.P.*, Aug. 20, 1913.

suggests that it was the characteristic tone of the period. It was an attempt to express the spirit of reform which Dafoe thought was leavening the entire Anglo-Saxon world—especially in the United States where the election of Woodrow Wilson on his New Freedom platform brought expressions of envious admiration from the *Manitoba Free Press*. While this spirit ensured the triumph of progress, it did not make its spokesmen complacent. Progress might be virtually inevitable, but it could be accelerated by a push. At any rate there were no signs of complacency in the liberal optimism of John Dafoe while the Tories reigned supreme at Ottawa and Winnipeg. The problems of government were not changed by the election upset of 1911; it remained to be seen whether the Conservatives had any answers that differed from those of the previous Liberal administration. But the change was important to Dafoe, for he no longer had to defend the party in power.

ii

In the West the Liberal party remained strong after 1911 because it had gone down fighting for a popular cause. In reality, however, the Liberals, and especially the national leaders, had grown too staid and conservative for the progressive Western temper. Perhaps if reciprocity had been accepted, Western grain growers would have been temporarily appeased, but there were other aspects of their programme which the aging Laurier found too radical. After his Western tour of 1910 he was convinced that the farmers' demands were unreasonable. The rest of the country would no doubt have agreed. The attitude of an Eastern business man to Western demands was summed up in a single, unfriendly sentence. "The attitude of the West regarding elevators, freight rates, free trade, etc., etc.," wrote Sir Edmund Walker sourly, "is quite natural when one remembers that agricultural people are both selfish and ignorant." But whether unreasonable or merely selfish, the Prairie farmer was convinced that the acceptance of his demands for reform was necessary for the country's well-being, and thus self-evidently just. If necessary they would be achieved through direct, and perhaps independent, political action.[2]

Western protest might prove beneficial to the Liberals in Opposition, but it could only be a headache to the freshman Prime Minister, Robert Borden. For Dafoe, it necessitated a modification of *Free Press* policies in an effort to turn the situation to the advantage of the West, the

[2]Laurier Papers, Laurier to E. W. Nesbitt, Dec. 23, 1910; Walker Papers, Walker to C. F. Hamilton, July 29, 1910.

Liberals and the *Free Press*. In his view the first requisite was a recognition that the Conservative victory was a complete triumph for protectionism. The Liberals should therefore face the future with a clear-cut programme of tariff reform, but Dafoe was very much afraid that they would not see this necessity. Despite Sifton's confident claim that the only fiscal policy that could ensure a party success was one of moderate protection, and his advice to "forget the reciprocity episode," Dafoe continued to believe otherwise. He knew that Laurier was being "urged on many sides in Quebec and Ontario to drop reciprocity," and he was quick to admonish the Liberal leader about the perils of relenting to these pressures. Certainly caution was necessary. But he did not believe that a rejection of past policy would expedite the Liberal return to power. "There are some issues which a political party can manufacture, try out on the electorate, and quietly shelve if they don't work," he explained somewhat condescendingly to Laurier. "The issue of a larger measure of trade with the United States is not one of these." The 1911 proposition had excited furious opposition, to be sure, but it had also attracted ardent support. The moral effect on a Liberal party which admitted it had been wrong in supporting reciprocity would be disastrous. It would undoubtedly result in the rapid development of a "Western Liberal group which would formulate a very radical fiscal policy." To avoid this possibility, and to transform the West into a "Gibraltar of Liberalism," the party leadership would have to agree to a platform which would include such progressive planks as low tariff, anti-combines legislation, and the regulation of such large enterprises as railways and banks. The division of the two parties on questions of fundamental principle had to be made self-evident to the electorate:

> The Conservative party in Canada, though it made a bluff of being radical when in opposition, is of necessity the party of the interests and of privilege. These characteristics have shown themselves strongly already, and they will become more marked with every passing year. The Conservative government at Ottawa, though I have no doubt it will be very generous with its sops in the way of public works, etc., will get more and more out of touch with Western sentiment and desires; and this must accrue to the advantage of the Liberals, particularly if their attitude is one of aggressive advocacy of popular rights.

Dafoe believed that if Laurier could keep his followers in tune with the reform sentiments of the Prairies, sentiments which he thought were shared by all progressive-minded Canadians, a party that was truly Liberal could be returned to power. He did not include urban labour in the progressive category, for this group was thought to be protectionist.

In fact Dafoe's prescription for Liberalism was one whose tonic effect was limited to agrarian application. Both in his advice to the Liberal Opposition and in his criticism of the Conservatives' domestic policy, he distinctly pronounced his Western Liberal views.[3]

When Dafoe turned to direct his editorial shafts against the Borden Government his criticisms found wider appeal because of the declining prosperity of the West and the resulting growth of political discontent. Laurier's successive administrations had owed much to the prosperous climate of the world economy. Robert Borden's Government was afflicted with less fortunate circumstances which, though largely beyond its control, nevertheless played into the hands of its critics. Western Canada particularly was sharply affected by the shrinkage of world prosperity which began shortly after the Conservatives had settled into office. The great wheat boom which had lasted through the first decade of the twentieth century was gradually subsiding. Moreover, freight rates were moving upward, and the uncertainty of European affairs was a large factor in drying up the flow of British investments to Canada. Most serious of all for Prairie farmers was the contraction of the world market for wheat, their staple product. Without large, lucrative markets the autumn harvests were little better than fool's gold.

Naturally not only agricultural but also urban classes were squeezed by the economic recession. The growing labouring population, particularly in Winnipeg, did not quickly forget the austerity of these last years of peace. But it was the farming community, because of its importance and numbers, that first made itself heard. Dafoe was quick to note the pleading of his chief constituents.

The failure to provide new markets and cheap transportation, the two pivots of Western prosperity, was the feature of Conservative policy that most often provoked editorial comment in the *Free Press*. It is doubtful if any of Borden's supporters needed to be reminded that

> the problem before the Borden government is as easy to define as it is difficult to solve. It must secure markets for the Western farmers as profitable and as readily available as those to the south from which they have been debarred in the supposed interests of the Dominion at large, under penalty in the case of failure of having the Western farmers persist in their hostility to it.

Dafoe continued to believe that the obvious market for Western Canada's products was the United States. He had little expectation that there would be any lowering of the North American trade barriers so long as the Conservatives were in power in Ottawa. In fact, quite the

[3]*M.F.P.*, Sept. 23, 1911. Dafoe Papers, Sifton to Dafoe, Sept. 26, Oct. 18, 1911; Laurier to Dafoe, Nov. 5, 1911; Dafoe to Laurier, Nov. 18, 1911.

contrary; for it had been the high tariff interests who had made the Conservative victory possible, and their demands would now have a sympathetic hearing in the capital. That Eastern members should oppose tariff reductions was understandable, though unenlightened, but that a Western member of either party should do so was a grievous sin. And the chief of sinners, now as later, was Arthur Meighen, the young Conservative member for the agriculturally rich Portage plains constituency in Manitoba. Here was a man who while in Opposition had called upon the Liberal Government to lower the tariff on farm equipment, but having moved to the Government side of the House had become a tongue-tied party slave.[4]

Dafoe represented the demands of the Western farmer for the promotion of wider markets through tariff reductions as a national necessity; the advocates of high tariffs were accused of sectional selfishness. Surely any fair-minded Easterner could understand that

the great need of Canada today is the encouragement of production. Manufacturers may think they need higher protection. What they actually need is more orders from prosperous producers. The way to increase production and ensure these orders is to lighten the producer's burdens and increase his rewards. Judicious tariff revision will help on this movement.

"Judicious tariff revision"—these ambiguous words are indicative of Dafoe's views on the tariff. He was not a free trader in the classical sense, nor did he expect any Canadian government to implement a policy of complete free trade. Tariff reductions had to be relative, for in the realm of politics there were no absolutes. Both parties were opportunist on the tariff, though Conservative opportunism was directed towards protectionism, Liberal towards freer trade. "The Conservative party is as protectionist as it dares to be; the Liberal party as 'low tariff' as it thinks it discreet to be," the *Free Press* explained.[5]

Of no less importance to the West was the matter of cheap transportation. The Laurier Government had attempted to meet this need by supporting the construction of new railways. By the time that Borden had been in office for a few years the difficult economic situation, combined with the loose financial practices of the Mackenzie and Mann interests, brought the Canadian Northern to the door of the government for further assistance from the public treasury. In this situation, the view of the *Free Press* was that the railway was still necessary and its financial stability should be ensured even if this required government ownership. But increased rail facilities were not the only problem. As the margin of

[4]*M.F.P.*, Jan. 29, Sept. 30, 1912.
[5]*M.F.P.*, May 7, April 25, 1914.

profit in farming began to shrink, freight rates became an increasingly heavy burden. Here was a case where the Western farmers could not have had a stronger advocate than the *Manitoba Free Press*. Nor could the Borden Government have had a more persistent critic. The central point of the newspaper's argument was that freight rates would have to be based on the principle of equal charges in every section of the country. The justice of this demand seemed undeniable for it was part "of the fight against the selfishness that seeks to have this country organized on the basis of injustice, with a limited number of millionaires in control," the paper noted on November 4, 1912. The railways existed to serve trade and agriculture, not to profit from these activities. In the spring of 1914 the Railway Commission ordered a few concessions to the Western producers, but rejected the case for equalization of rates. "Sops instead of justice," the *Free Press* branded the changes, and the fight was to go on for many more years.

The defeat of the Liberals in 1911 made Dafoe's task easier in his own province as well as in the federal field, for it was no longer possible for Roblin to blame Ottawa for the problems of Manitoba. In the hope of driving a wedge into the political façade of the local Government Dafoe attacked it on every count with partisan vigour. Of particular interest was the school system. With no further fear of embarrassing Laurier, the *Free Press* began a concerted attack to end mutilingual schools in the province. These schools were not limited to the French-Canadian minority; every national group was permitted to use its own language as well as being required to learn English. In practice Manitoba school children spoke a babel of tongues, often to the exclusion of English. To the *Free Press* the situation was intolerable. "We must Canadianize this generation of foreign-born settlers, or this will cease to be a Canadian country in any real sense of the term," the paper argued on December 1, 1913. But on this, as on many other issues, the Roblin Government remained unmoved.

So bitter had Dafoe's partisanship become by 1913 that Sifton found it necessary to suggest that a halt be called to the vitriolic campaign.[6] Dafoe found this advice difficult to accept. He had nothing but scorn and distrust for the local Conservatives, no doubt in part because of his failure to blast them from their apparently secure position inside the walls of the graceful new legislative building which they had begun to construct in 1913. But as the last days of peace were slipping away in 1914 the Manitoba electors went to the polls and the returns showed that confidence in the Roblin administration had been badly shaken.

[6]Sifton Papers, Sifton to Dafoe, Nov. 17, 1913.

While the storm clouds gathered in Europe Dafoe saw some sunshine in Manitoba, and pronounced, too early as events proved, that "the day of machine politics, of liquor domination, of Boss rule, of contemptuous disregard for progressive movements is about over." Certainly the constant stream of abuse that the *Free Press* had directed at the record of the Roblin Government in Winnipeg and at the domestic policies of the Conservatives in Ottawa had produced some of the desired results by 1914. Dafoe proved just as unsympathetic to the Conservative party's programme in the more complicated field of imperial relations.[7]

iii

Perhaps the most pressing necessity which Borden faced when he took office was to find a solution to the naval controversy. It was crucial not only because of the increasingly serious state of world affairs, but also because it was the source of a deep division in the Conservative party and the nation. Certainly the new Government was expected to act with celerity, for the ground upon which it had opposed the Laurier plan for the construction of a Canadian navy was that the critical international situation faced by the Empire demanded an immediate contribution of Dreadnoughts to the Admiralty. This emergency contribution, the Conservatives contended, was to be a temporary expedient to fill quickly the gap in the Empire's naval strength until the people could be consulted on a permanent policy. But there was at least one obvious difficulty in the way of an easy solution to the naval issue. Borden's French-Canadian supporters, especially those who had followed the line laid down by the Nationalist mentor, Henri Bourassa, were strongly anti-imperialist and apparently committed to oppose any Canadian involvement in imperial affairs until Canada was given a voice in the determination of imperial policy. To compound this difficulty, Borden had received the support of many Canadians whose opposition to reciprocity was coupled with a desire for closer co-operation with Great Britain and the other members of the Empire. Obviously conditions within the Conservative party contained the seeds of discord.

Borden showed himself prepared to face conflicting views within his party by including in his cabinet both shades of opinion. The French-Canadian cabinet members drew from the *Free Press* on October 11, 1911, the comment that "all three, Monk, Nantel and Pelletier, are Nationalists. They are all on record as being opposed to naval contributions to the British Admiralty or to a Canadian navy. Their presence in

[7]*M.F.P.*, July 11, 1914.

the Government must be interpreted as meaning that the naval question must remain an open one until the decision of the people of Canada is obtained by a referendum." For the moment the paper refrained from attempting to make capital out of the tenuous Conservative-Nationalist alliance. While the Government was searching for a solution to its dilemma over naval policy, Dafoe was giving some serious thought to the same problem. He was convinced that despite, or even because of, the election results of 1911 a "reasonable and sane nationalism" was developing in Canada. This nationalism was not the Bourassa variety, which Dafoe characterized as "tribalism," but a healthy growth which would encompass the whole nation and stifle "the shoddy Imperialism which finds its most congenial field in Toronto." This spirit would prevent the Conservative Government from launching the country on any imperial adventures even if the Unionists won office in Britain. "Face to face with the necessities of the case," he told a friend in Toronto, "Conservative governments there and here will find that progress is only possible along the lines laid down by their Liberal predecessors, and that if they try to carry out their ideas of a centralized Empire, perpetuating military and caste ideas, the result will simply be to blow the Empire up."[8] Here Dafoe was giving expression to a fundamental antithesis in his mind which characterized the struggle for Dominion autonomy as a conflict between the virtues of liberalism, democracy and national self-government and the vices of conservatism, aristocratic militarism and imperial centralization. Dafoe applied this antithesis to every problem of imperial relations. A striking illustration was his treatment of Borden's naval policy.

Dafoe had never tied himself to the letter of the Liberal naval plan and thus left himself room to manœuvre. In June 1912, when Borden announced his intention of travelling to England for consultations on the naval situation, Dafoe maintained an open mind, though he still held firmly to the principle of ultimate Canadian control. The *Free Press* of June 7 greeted Borden's announcement with the comment that

> No solution to the problem will be acceptable to the Canadian people which does not recognize the necessity of a Canadian fleet, made in Canada and officered by Canadians. Canadians are not necessarily wedded to the Laurier scheme, though they are in sympathy with its root ideas, and no doubt will be prepared to consider favourably any proposition by the Borden government which is an improvement upon it.

Borden claimed that prior to his consultations with the Admiralty in 1912 he had not discussed naval policy with his colleagues. But he did

[8] Dafoe Papers, Dafoe to J. T. Clark, March 22, 1912.

make at least one inquiry about possible schemes in the form of an exchange of letters with Premier Whitney of Ontario, whose opinions carried a good deal of weight in the party. Whitney made it quite clear to him that he favoured an immediate financial contribution to the Admiralty, and also suggested exploring the possibility of obtaining a voice for Canada in the direction of imperial policy. What effect this suggestion had on Borden's final policy, which closely paralleled it, is open to speculation. It did, however, bear some similarity to another plan which was put forward, and which involved Dafoe.[9]

In the summer of 1912, under the general direction of the Canadian section of the Round Table movement, a plan was devised to remove the naval question from the realm of political controversy. "To show you how far the movement is genuine," Philip Kerr wrote to his fellow Round Tabler, Lionel Curtis, "I may say that Sir Edmund Walker on the one side and Dafoe on the other have agreed to further the scheme." That Dafoe was sympathetic to a plan that would harmonize the Liberal and Conservative viewpoints is clear from the fact that when Borden, in England, suggested that Canada would make a contribution to the British Admiralty, the *Free Press* treated the suggestion favourably. But in tentatively supporting the proposal the paper was careful to add that Canadians would support a contribution "provided it is distinctly understood that it is not be regarded as establishing a policy of contribution, but it is to be merely precedent to the formulation of a Canadian naval policy embodying ... the principle of a local navy, as efficient and as powerful as the resources of the Dominion will permit." Nor was a Canadian contribution to become part of a plan to reorganize the Empire on "the basis of a highly centralized military organization." Only an undoubted emergency would justify a direct payment to the Admiralty, in which case "nothing must be allowed to stand in the way of coming to the assistance of the Motherland."[10]

Thus, when Dafoe was asked to assist in the formulation of a non-partisan naval policy, he was firmly committed to the principle of Canadian control, a position that was to conflict with some of the suggestions being put forward in Toronto. Dafoe even admitted that he had joined

[9]H. Borden, ed., *Sir Robert Laird Borden: His Memoirs* (2 vols., Toronto, 1938), I, 355. Whitney Papers, Borden to James Whitney, June 1, and reply June 14, 1912.

[10]Borden Papers, Philip Kerr to Lionel Curtis, July 31, 1912. (It is noteworthy that for his part Lionel Curtis was not inactive. Discussing Borden's visit to England he wrote, "We got Borden, Mrs. Borden and Foster to a quiet country house for one night on Saturday and had the most instructive talk with them." Wrong Papers, Lionel Curtis to G. M. Wrong, July 24, 1912. Curtis did not say who did the instructing.) *M.F.P.*, July 25, July 27, Aug. 10, 1912.

the movement "for the purpose of seeing that it did not express the Toronto jingo view." By forcing a compromise which reaffirmed the Liberal principle of Canadian control but allowed for further action if it was proved necessary, he believed that he had defeated the jingo designs. He thought that the suggested compromise was one that should be acceptable to the leadership of the Liberal party, and pressed Laurier with the necessity of adopting a flexible policy. He argued that although the party should adhere to the principle of a Canadian navy, it was true that "a contribution, if the terms of the gift are carefully defined, need not constitute any infringement on Canadian autonomy." The Liberals should avoid pressing the autonomist argument to extremes, for it would leave them open to the charge of refusing to aid the motherland in a time of crisis. Laurier admitted the strength of Dafoe's argument, though his isolationist, even colonial, viewpoint was evident when he admitted a fear that Borden's talk of a voice for Canada in imperial policy would "bring us into the intricacies of European diplomacy with all its consequences."[11]

Dafoe was not daunted at the prospect of Canada moving into "the intricacies of European diplomacy," though he was as suspicious as Laurier of any talk that smacked of imperial centralization. He was also aware that the debate over naval defence involved such fundamental issues that it could be destructive of Canadian unity. The problem involved Canada's first real venture into world politics and would naturally stimulate deep differences of opinion. The *Free Press*, discussing the subject on September 3, 1912, warned that "in the matter of naval defence, with its imperial involvements, we are dealing with issues that reach the fundamentals of national life. We cannot afford to make a mistake." The parties in the debate were once more forming. Dafoe's paper made it clear that it stood with those who subscribed to the "Canadian-Imperial ideal which looks forward to Canada as a British nation in perpetual alliance, upon terms of absolute equality with the other British nations, carrying out concerted policies determined upon in free Conference." Here again Dafoe provided evidence that he had not yet moved beyond the conception of a common imperial foreign policy to the acceptance of the view that the dominions should have the right to formulate independent foreign policies. In 1912 he had not seriously considered the possibility that the nations of the Empire might disagree fundamentally on a matter of common concern. But his insistence upon equality, coupled with his resistance to every attempt at

[11]Dafoe Papers, J. E. Atkinson to Dafoe, Aug. 19, 1912; Dafoe to Atkinson, Aug. 22, 1912; Dafoe to Laurier, Sept. 23, and reply Sept. 26, 1912.

devising machinery to formulate a common policy, made the next step in his thinking inevitable.

By September 1912, Dafoe had grown disillusioned with the prospects of winning acceptance for a non-partisan naval policy. He told Hamar Greenwood, a Canadian-born member of the British Liberal party, that the difficulty with the non-partisan scheme was that "the Canadian politicians of both camps are as busily engaged in playing politics with the navy as they were a year ago. Both sides are manoeuvring to put their enemies in the wrong, with a view to rousing the country against them." His assessment of the situation led him to the conclusion that in a party fight the Liberals would be victorious, provided Laurier did not fall under the influence of the Quebec Nationalists. Laurier knew that "the real feeling in French Canada, Conservative and Liberal alike, is one of deep hostility to the establishment of a navy of any kind," but his recent speeches had indicated that he would not give in to this isolationism. What Canadians wanted, Dafoe insisted, was a Canadian navy, though a direct contribution to the Royal Navy would also be approved if an emergency could be proved beyond doubt. Nor would the promise of a voice in an imperial body which exercised control over imperial defence and foreign policy find approval among Canadians. Finally, Dafoe told Greenwood, the effort of the Canadian Tories to force the Liberals into an anti-imperial position, in order to go to the country with a flag-waving campaign, was bound to fail. Laurier was too adroit to fall for this ruse, and even if he did the Conservatives might find their expectations disappointed.[12]

By October the *Free Press* was moving rapidly away from its earlier dalliance with non-partisanship. It was becoming increasingly clear, the newspaper's readers were told, that "great influences, both in Canada and the Motherland, which have the ear of Mr. Borden, are inveterately opposed to Canada doing anything in the way of building her own fleet." During his trip to England, the Prime Minister had fallen prey to the schemes of the centralizers. The warning flag was up, and Canadians interested in the free development of their country as a member of the Empire were called upon to be vigilant "that nothing is done which

[12]Dafoe Papers, Dafoe to Hamar Greenwood, Sept. 21, 1912. Dafoe was not just guessing when he claimed that the parties were playing politics with the naval question. Commenting on the proposal to take the question out of politics Premier Whitney observed: "There are two considerations, however, which occur to me. First, if the two parties in Parliament agree on action with regard to the navy our people will lose the benefit of that question when they go to the country, and secondly, I believe that whatever he may do on the surface, Sir Wilfrid will intrigue against such an understanding whenever he has an opportunity to do so." Whitney Papers, James Whitney to Borden, Aug. 15, 1912.

may establish a precedent in any way detrimental to the integrity of the principle of Canadian self-government." Once more the stalking horse of imperial centralization was being groomed and sent into the fray.[13]

Dafoe was not satisfied that the Liberals should simply stand on their 1910 proposals. In the face of what he expected would be a "halting, partial, temporary" policy put forward by the Government, he urged Laurier to offer a counter-proposal which would be "a full and complete policy, fitted to the needs of the occasion." On the principle, he said, "that it is as well to be hanged for a sheep as for a lamb" the Liberals should propose the construction of a Pacific as well as an Atlantic fleet. In addition they should call for the immediate placing of an order for two Dreadnoughts, which could either become Canadian flagships or, if an emergency arose, could be placed at the temporary disposal of the Admiralty. In comparison with this generous proposal, the Conservative policy would look "cheap and trivial."[14] Laurier apparently found the plan too grandiose. Or perhaps he thought it was better to be hanged for a lamb in English Canada than for a sheep in Quebec.

On the eve of the Government's announcement on naval policy, perhaps because Sifton had warned that he did not want any "hairsplitting" on the issue, the *Free Press* again pointed out that it was absurd to suggest that a contribution to the British Navy infringed upon Canadian autonomy. "It is not beyond the power of statesmanship," the paper pontificated, "to draft a programme which will be acceptable to both sides of the House." But Borden's temporary policy was unacceptable, no less so because it was coupled with a suggestion that a permanent policy would be part of an imperial reorganization which would give Canada a voice in the determination of imperial affairs.[15]

By the beginning of 1913 Dafoe had the *Free Press* arrayed in full national armour, prepared to battle the Conservative proposal that Canada contribute thirty-five million dollars to the Admiralty for the immediate construction of Dreadnoughts. The country's self-respect was at stake, and could only be protected by a large contribution to imperial security in the form of a powerful national navy, the Winnipeg newspaper held. Anyone who suggested that Canada should abstain entirely from imperial defence was contemptible. As a member of an Empire which carried obligations as well as honours, abstention was impossible.

[13]*M.F.P.*, Oct. 3, 30, 1912.
[14]Dafoe Papers, Dafoe to Laurier, Nov. 18, 1912.
[15]Sifton Papers, Sifton to Dafoe, Nov. 21, 1912; *M.F.P.*, Dec. 5, 1912; Dafoe Papers, Dafoe to Arthur Hawkes, Jan. 28, 1913.

Canadians had to face the reality that "the primary obligation is to make such preparations as will enable us, in the event of war, to contribute our share to the defence of the whole Empire." This obligation could not be fulfilled merely by voting funds to the British Navy; in fact, this payment would be an evasion of duty. "We must offer something more substantial than our pocket-books to the assaults of the enemy," the *Free Press* declared. "Not to give ourselves is to be disgraced to a degree falling but little short of the shame of refusing to do anything." Borden was now denounced as a full-blooded imperialist prepared to sell the nation's birthright for the promised pottage of a voice in imperial affairs. Once he had been a Liberal, but now he had given in to "that little junta of pushful Imperialists who are led on this side of the water by our friend Hugh Graham," Dafoe told a friend. By yielding to this pressure, Borden had brought into conflict the powerful forces of nationalism and imperialism, and in the end nationalism would emerge the victor. There could be no other result, for when properly controlled, the two sentiments were in reality "only two forms of the same strong race feeling." As was often the case, Dafoe forgot the French Canadians when he made this revealing remark.[16]

Dafoe refused to see any force in Borden's argument that the threat of Germany to British naval supremacy justified a Canadian contribution to the Royal Navy. Under the pretence of loyalty the Prime Minister was attempting "to commit the people of Canada to a policy which is a complete negation of our whole national development to date." This dishonest action, Dafoe remarked, substantiated the conviction "which I have long held, that the Tories are not to be trusted." Moreover the true explanation of Tory policy was to be found in the unscrupulous alliance which had been arranged with the Bourassa Nationalists in 1911. In an attempt to ride both the imperialist and Nationalist horses, Borden had branded the contribution as temporary and promised a future, permanent policy which would include a voice for Canada in the direction of imperial affairs. Here Dafoe was expressing the orthodox, and probably accurate, Liberal explanation of Borden's naval policy. W. S. Fielding had stated it crisply when he wrote that "the 'emergency' is not that of the Empire, not that of the Imperial government, but only that of Mr. Borden, who apparently has begged the Imperial government to give him some excuse for a new line."[17]

Using these two arguments, Dafoe struck out at the Conservative

[16]*M.F.P.*, Jan. 3, 1913; Dafoe Papers, Dafoe to Arthur Hawkes, Jan. 28, 1913.
[17]Sifton Papers, Dafoe to Sifton, March 1, 1913; *M.F.P.*, Feb. 27, 1913; Laurier Papers, Fielding to Laurier, Dec. 3, 1912.

proposal with all the unfairness of a polemicist. With impassioned fervour he denounced the Conservative naval plan as an attempt to destroy Canada's independence and turn the country into a "satrapy of Great Britain." When the Conservatives, exasperated by the delaying tactics of the Opposition, decided to introduce closure, the *Free Press* compared the decision to Pride's Purge, though it had suggested the use of similar procedure two years earlier during the debate on reciprocity. An election, wrote the editor, was the only just method of settling the dispute.[18]

The Conservative argument that the policy of temporary contribution would be followed by a permanent scheme which would give Canada direct influence in imperial affairs brought from Dafoe the reply that this thinly disguised plan for imperial federation would take away the last Canadian rights. "Canadians will not be left even with the right to make contributions. Their business will be to pay the levies made upon them by a body meeting in Westminster," the *Free Press* announced on May 7, 1913. As an alternative Dafoe offered the traditional Canadian policy of autonomy, which allowed the Canadian Parliament to decide on all matters touching the country's interests. "Self-government in regard to defence, as in regard to all else, is the vital, fundamental British principle. On no other foundation can the Empire exist." This statement of May 9, 1913, was for Dafoe and the *Free Press* the ark of the imperial covenant.

After its protracted journey through the House of Commons the Conservative naval aid bill met defeat at the hands of the Senate, where the Liberals had a majority. The deadlock should be broken, the *Free Press* maintained, by taking the issue to the people. The Liberal leaders, Dafoe believed, were entitled to a warm vote of gratitude from the Canadian people for the courageous stand they had taken against the Government's naval plan. Though regretting the furore that the dispute had aroused, he felt that in the long run it would be recognized that Canada had been saved from a policy that eventually might have had to be retracted "at the cost of separation from the Empire."[19]

Dafoe never relinquished his view that the only acceptable principle upon which naval policy could be founded was one which met the necessity of Canadian control. To him Canadian control meant control through the Dominion Parliament alone. He could see nothing but the old, discredited theory of a centralized Empire in Borden's suggestion that there might be a unified imperial policy which each member of

[18]*M.F.P.*, April 7, 14, 1913; April 27, 1911; March 13, 18, 28, 1913.
[19]Dafoe Papers, Dafoe to Arthur Hawkes, July 12, 1913.

the Empire would share in formulating. Though he had frequently repeated his willingness to see Canada assist the British Navy by direct contribution in time of stress, he was unconvinced by Borden's contention that an international crisis existed in 1912-13. The only crisis he allowed himself to see was the one in the Conservative party. Even as late as May 1914, when European tensions were drawing rapidly to a climax, Dafoe refused to alter his conviction that only a navy built, manned and controlled by Canadians would satisfy the desire of the nation.[20]

Naval policy had been the specific issue of debate for almost five years, but in fact the question was really that of Canada's relation to the Empire. Behind each successive proposal for naval defence lurked the emotion-packed problem of imperial organization. Instead of a cool, rational consideration of the national interest, the debate repeatedly developed into a series of passionate, unedifying declarations on the subjects of nationalism, colonialism and imperialism. This result was perhaps inevitable, given the bicultural composition of the country and the immaturity of its national consciousness. Nevertheless, the emotions aroused by the naval question meant that the issue did not receive the calm discussion which it merited. During the naval debate, Liberals and Conservatives alike frequently seemed more concerned about gaining a political advantage than serving the national interest. In the eyes of most politicians, of course, the national and party interests are usually divided by an almost invisible line which disappears entirely in the heat of debate.

It is difficult to calculate what part the naval policy of the dominions played in the strategy of the Kaiser's naval advisers. In December 1912 a highly placed German official noted that the impending grant of Dreadnoughts by Canada "seemed to be excellent material for agitation." This observation suggests that a Canadian contribution to the British fleet would have further inflamed Anglo-German relations. Yet when it became apparent that Canada's contribution would not be forthcoming the German Naval Attaché in London reported: "The naval policy of the self-governing colonies tends . . . more and more in the direction of establishing small fleets for themselves. This development is a very slow one and will take place outside of European waters, and in comparing England's naval strength in Europe with that of Germany it may be ignored." Whether the direct contribution of financial assistance by Canada would have provided ships in time to affect these calculations is a subject best left to the speculation of naval experts.

[20]*M.F.P.*, May 7, 1914.

But it seems fair to suggest that any policy would have been more valuable than the complete stalemate which Canadians had reached by the summer of 1913.[21]

Yet one thing had resulted from this apparently endless and fruitless debate, and that was a sharper definition of positions and objectives. Dafoe misrepresented the Borden ideal when he defined it as a centralized Empire taking orders from London. He made his own position clear, however, when he declared that the only possible alternative was Canada's "rapid development to complete nationhood in perpetual alliance with the other British nations, on terms of equality, under a common crown and with a common white citizenship." In suggesting this goal for imperial development, Dafoe was not interested merely in status. Throughout the naval debate he had emphasized that Canada's national self-respect demanded that the country assume those obligations which membership in an Empire of equal partners necessitated. As the naval controversy drew to a tortuous and inconclusive close the time was rapidly nearing when Canada would be called upon to fulfil those obligations to a degree that Dafoe certainly never imagined.[22]

[21]*Die grosse Politik der Europäischen Kabinette, 1871–1914* (Berlin, 1926), XXXIX, 6–7, Zimmermann, Memo of the Undersecretary of State, Berlin, Dec. 12, 1912; *ibid.*, 65, report of Von Müller, Naval Attaché in London, Nov. 30, 1913.

[22]*M.F.P.*, June 24, 1913.

v. The War and
a New Political Alignment
1914-17

╌╌╌

THE QUARRELS OF FARAWAY EUROPE were somewhat unreal to people living in a provincial society isolated in the centre of the North American Continent. The assassination of the Archduke Ferdinand of Austria may have excited the attention of some members of the polyglot population of Manitoba, but most residents of that province had their eyes on the battle which was being waged with white-hot fury in the local political arena. For the provincial election was just drawing to a close while the major European powers were preparing to test their armed strength.

Dafoe was no exception. For months he had been concentrating his attention on driving Roblin from power, and though he had always prided himself in a more than provincial interest in international affairs, he was caught off balance when he learned that a war involving the British Empire was virtually inevitable. At first he warned his readers to remain calm and wait upon events. But he left no doubt where he stood. On August 3, 1914, the paper stated firmly, "If Great Britain is involved in war either by her own decision that circumstances leave no option, or through the aggression of an outside party, it is quite certain that Canada will come to her assistance with all the power at her disposal." Two days later, the issues of the war were defined: "Upon the issue of the conflict depends the future of the Empire and the freedom of the world." And on August 6, the morning edition carried the terrible message on the front page: "Canada in State of War for first Time Since Becoming a Nation." Thus, from the outset, the Great War was Canada's war.

That August 6 headline may not have been written by Dafoe, but it certainly expressed his view about Canada's role in the war. To him Canadian participation was not a case of colony assisting the mother country, but rather of partner nations united together in defence of a cause which was greater than, though indistinguishable from, the Empire—the cause of freedom and democracy. Since Canada was a full-fledged participant in the struggle to preserve these values and not a mere supporting actor, the country had to be willing to offer its blood and treasure without stint. At the beginning of the war, of course, few Canadians stopped to make subtle distinctions about Canada's status in the struggle; it was a measure of Dafoe's nationalism that he did so. The country, for whatever reasons, was united in its acceptance of Canadian participation in the war, and few suspected the demands that would be made before victory was accomplished. Without asking for exact definitions the vast majority of Canadians must have accepted the claim of the *Free Press* that the co-operation of the dominions in the war effort fully justified the shape the Empire had taken: "All the world knows that Canada, like the other self-governing Dominions, has gone into this war with the determination to fight shoulder to shoulder with Great Britain to the finish, under no compulsion save that of conscience and duty and devotion to the ideals of civilization of which the British flag is the symbol." This was an expression of responsible nationalism, not of sycophantic colonialism or crude jingoism. Canada was not fighting for Great Britain; she was fighting "shoulder to shoulder" with Britain and the other self-governing members of the Empire.[1]

ii

Since Canada was engaged in a war abroad, it seemed reasonable to Dafoe that a political truce should be signed at home. He hoped it could be achieved, but his scepticism was apparent when he wrote in the first days of the war that "Sir Robert Borden at this juncture is entitled to the co-operation, sympathy and support of the Liberal party in Parliament. This he will get if he can keep Mr. Rogers and his newspaper echoes in hand." Rogers, of course, was Dafoe's old enemy who had moved in 1911 from Roblin's cabinet in Winnipeg to Borden's Government in Ottawa. The Liberals were warned that their first duty lay in giving unflinching support to the war effort. Nevertheless Dafoe was quite aware that there were political stirrings, especially in the Tory party, to keep controversy alive and bring on an election in the tense war atmosphere. The Minister of Public Works, Robert Rogers,

[1] *M.F.P.*, Aug. 8, Sept. 19, 7, 1914.

was the leading suspect. The *Free Press* argued that there should be a complete retreat from party government in the normal sense during the crisis and roundly attacked anyone suspected of fomenting political dissension.[2]

Both Liberals and Conservatives were conscious of the election possibilities created by the war. In December 1914 Laurier wrote to Dafoe warning him that although the first wartime session of Parliament had not ended in the expected dissolution, an early session in 1915 might be followed by an appeal to the country. He underlined the importance of "going ahead with our preparations." Similar thoughts were running through the minds of prominent Conservatives. Dafoe genuinely wanted to prevent both parties from disrupting the war effort for political ends. Throughout 1915 the *Free Press* repeatedly warned about the perils of partisanship. In mid-1915 a somewhat vague proposal for coalition government was made. As the constitutional limit of Parliament's duration drew nearer, the fear increased in Dafoe's mind that the Liberals, seeing their advantage in the growing weaknesses of the Conservatives, might force an election. The *Free Press* argued that the life of the existing Parliament should be extended, and expressed enthusiastic approval when this step was agreed upon.[3]

That the *Free Press* advocated a political truce during the first two years of the war did not mean that the paper was uncritical of the Government's military programme. It did criticize the Borden administration, but usually for not doing enough. Dafoe's paper repeatedly demanded a more active recruiting campaign, for instance, but politics in the partisan sense were largely banished from its comments on the federal Government. In Manitoba a different situation obtained. The *Free Press* had long been the bitterest critic of the local Conservative Government. Therefore the cessation of political asperities on the national level never tempted Dafoe to adopt a similar line in his own province. This fact promised future trouble for the continuance of national political peace because of the close connection between the Manitoba Premier and his former colleague, Robert Rogers.

It is thus somewhat ironic that the demission of the Roblin Government in May 1915, rather than strengthening the political truce, stimulated new controversies that spilled over into federal politics. These led directly to renewed political strife and the division of the Liberal

[2]*Ibid.*, Aug. 6, Nov. 16, Oct. 10, 12, 20, 1914.
[3]Dafoe Papers, Laurier to Dafoe, Dec. 16, 1914; Willison Papers, Sir John Willison to Sir Edward Kemp, May 5, 1915; *M.F.P.*, May 12, Dec. 6, Dec. 30, 1915, and Feb. 10, 1916.

party. The source of this friction was the ever irritable school question, which cut across party lines and threatened national unity. With the Liberal party finally in power in Manitoba, Dafoe grasped the opportunity to press for long-advocated educational reforms. These reforms demanded the removal of the multiplicity of languages from Manitoba schools, and their replacement by English. For Dafoe, this was necessary not simply for educational reasons, but also for national ones. The common school was to be made the effective agency of the Canadian *Kulturkampf*. "Our gates are open to the oppressed of Europe," the *Free Press* wrote on August 19, 1914, "but when they come here they must forget their feuds, forswear their racial aspirations, and become Canadians not only in name but in fact." The new Liberal administration agreed essentially with the paper's view that the privilege of using languages other than English, including the meagre rights that had been allowed to the French Canadians after 1897, should be removed from the Manitoba educational structure. In 1916 Premier Norris' Government took action which, after a quarter of a century of heated debate, transformed the province's schools into exclusively English language institutions. But the controversy was by no means concluded.

The educational reforms in Manitoba coincided with the growing agitation being carried on by the French-Canadian leaders in Ontario against less radical changes brought about by the famous Regulation 17. Clearly there was a serious racial fracas boiling up in the early months of 1916. The question of bilingual schools was not one that could easily be kept within the confines of Manitoba and Ontario, for the province of Quebec naturally felt that its interests were at stake. The eruption of the problem into national politics was thus all but inevitable. That this should happen when the war was entering a new and serious phase, and the manpower situation was beginning to evoke accusing glances at the French Canadians, only increased the explosiveness of the language issue.

In the early months of 1916 Laurier consulted his provincial leaders in both Manitoba and Ontario in an effort to encourage their opposition to limitations that might be placed on his people's privileges. The Conservative party was also feeling the pressure of racial tensions. Prime Minister Borden was faced with a revolt on the part of his French-Canadian ministers, who wanted the federal Government to take action that would ensure French language privileges in the provinces. While Borden was able to adopt the defensible position that educational matters rested solely with the provinces, Laurier was faced with a more threatening situation. His claim to the leadership of his people was at stake. He therefore agreed to the introduction in the House of Commons of a resolution requesting the province of Ontario to respect French language rights in the schools. Despite the opposition of some leading Liberals, the carefully phrased Lapointe Resolution was moved on May 9, 1916. Moderate though the resolution was, the intensity of feeling evoked by the war was allowed full vent in the subsequent debate. Though the resolution referred specifically to Ontario it interested Canadians everywhere, especially in Manitoba.[4]

The question raised by the Lapointe Resolution was of that rare category which may cause even the most ardent partisan to break his allegiance. John Dafoe was convinced that Laurier had committed the gravest error in allowing the language question to be discussed at the federal level. Naturally his conviction was strengthened by the belief that Ontario and Manitoba had acted correctly in their educational reforms. He was therefore prepared to place his convictions above his loyalty to Laurier—a loyalty which had never been blind.

Dafoe expressed his attitude in his reply to an old French-Canadian friend who accused him of fathering the new Manitoba legislation and warned him that he had "brought into the world a child who has all the appearances of a monster." Dafoe's rejoinder was that he was only one of a number of parents who had come to see that the "absurd arrangement of 1897" could no longer be tolerated "if the province of Manitoba was not to be transformed into middle Europe on a small scale." Of course the French might have been given special consideration, but the obvious fact was that their leaders, especially the clergy, intended to use their privileges to transform the schools into clerical institutions. Therefore French privileges had to be abolished too. If the French acted in a reasonable manner they would probably be given fair treatment, Dafoe asserted, but the province had no intention of being intimidated by the people of Quebec "who appear to think they have a right to impose their will throughout the length and breadth of Canada." This delusion was the belief of Henri Bourassa, and the Quebec Liberals had succumbed to his influence. He continued with evident heat:

> I know that you boast that you have beaten Bourassa and put him out of business; but as a matter of fact he has conquered you. He may not command your allegiance but he controls your minds. You all think his thoughts, talk his language, echo his threats; and I should suspect that when Sir Wilfrid

[4]Laurier Papers, Laurier to T. C. Norris, Feb. 22, 1916; Laurier to N. W. Rowell, March 1, 1916. Borden Papers, T. C. Casgrain, P. E. Blondin, E. L. Patenaude to Borden, April 20, 1916, and reply April 24, 1916. Laurier Papers, N. W. Rowell to Laurier, April 15, 1916; W. S. Fielding to Laurier, April 23, 1916.

Laurier passes away—may the day be long distant—that you will accept him as your chief.

The suggestion that French Canadians were entitled to equal rights throughout the Dominion sparked from Dafoe a further exposition of his growing suspicion that the Liberal party in Quebec was falling under the long shadow of Bourassa. Its acceptance of Bourassa's views could only lead to the formation of political parties along racial lines. "I should be sorry to see anything like this happen," Dafoe told Côté, "but I have no doubt that this will happen if the Nationalist movement in Quebec becomes more formidable than it is, and swallows up both the Liberal and Conservative parties as it gives promise of doing."[5]

Prior to the Lapointe Resolution Dafoe had publicly warned the Liberal party of the danger of countenancing any federal interference in the provinces' educational affairs. Early in May he travelled to Ottawa to exert his personal influence direct with the party leaders. He talked with Laurier and found him "stubborn as an army mule." As Dafoe saw the situation, the party was inextricably impaled on the horns of a dilemma: "If the whole party follows Laurier, the party is gone; if only the French follow him, Laurier is gone as a national leader." Sifton was outraged at Laurier's attitude; in his characteristic, forthright way he described him as acting "the part of a boy who has just been elected for a back concession and thinks that he will not be elected again unless he shouts for his county." The sooner the party was rid of him, the better for everyone. But where Dafoe was unsuccessful in influencing Laurier, he was in a stronger position with the Western Liberal members. Apart from their personal views they were fully aware of the weight that the *Manitoba Free Press* carried in *their* back concessions. Dafoe's influence was therefore important in producing the split in the Liberal ranks when the roll call on the Lapointe Resolution was taken. Eleven Western Liberals and one from Ontario kicked over the party traces in the division. The rupture of national unity and the loosening of the West's ties of loyalty to the Liberal party were thus two of the most important consequences of the debate on the school controversy in the spring of 1916. Both Laurier and Dafoe, in their separate ways, were responsible for these developments—Laurier because he had approved the tactics of the Lapointe Resolution, Dafoe because he had encouraged the Western Liberals to break with their leader.[6]

[5]Dafoe Papers, Thomas Côté to Dafoe, March 27, 1916, and replies of April 6 and 17, 1916.
[6]*M.F.P.*, April 15, 1916; Sifton Papers, Dafoe to Sifton, May 7, 1916; Dafoe Papers, Sifton to Dafoe, May 11, 1916; Dafoe, *Laurier: A Study in Canadian Politics* (Toronto, 1922), 161–2.

Even before the Lapointe Resolution, Dafoe had reached the conclusion that the majority of the Quebec leaders had fallen under the spell of Bourassa, but he had not included Laurier among them. By May 1916, however, he was no longer certain of Laurier either. In the *Free Press* he placed the responsibility for the debate on the language question squarely on the Liberal leader's shoulders. Moreover, writing on May 12, he made it clear that "there will be no yielding at any point to these Nationalist demands, which have so unaccountably received the blessing of the French Liberal chiefs." Everywhere but in Quebec, where the Liberals were already too strong, the result of the Lapointe Resolution would be to weaken the party. But in the West, only the Laurier Liberals would suffer, for the Prairie Liberals had issued their declaration of independence. This action should be followed by the formation of a radical, progressive, Liberal party, the *Free Press* advised the next day. In contrast to the existing parties the members of the new group "will be far more interested in furthering their programme than in office-holding and will be indifferent to the time-servers and opportunists to whom the enjoyment of office is the be-all and end-all of political existence. 'To Your Tents, O Israel.' " Thus the language debate had greatly increased Dafoe's distrust of Laurier. Though he was not yet ready to break completely with the old man, the bond between them was now extremely fragile.

Dafoe's doubts about Laurier increased his anxiety to prevent an election. The country was in a state of turmoil, and growing opposition to the Borden Government was everywhere apparent. It was possible that the benefit of this discontent might not accrue to the Liberals, but even if it did Dafoe was not certain that he wanted to see them returned to office. If Laurier, back in power, surrounded himself with the old guard, no advance on the existing Government's hesitant leadership could be expected. Reflecting on these matters in the autumn of 1916, Dafoe warned Sifton that there was one possibility that would bear careful watching. He wrote:

> I have some reason to believe that some very daring spirits in the Conservative party are trying to induce the Government to adopt conscription for the purpose of bringing the trouble in Quebec to a head with a view to a dissolution at that particular moment. So daring a stroke might save the Government, with the consequences that the domestic peace of Canada might be seriously threatened.

Perhaps this was just another of those rumours that frequently circulated in political smoking rooms, but it suggested that Canadian politics were entering a profoundly unsettled state. The disruption created by the

French language problem and the increasingly frequent criticisms that were being directed at the Borden administration were edging open the floodgates through which the currents of renewed political strife soon began to flow.[7]

iii

Dafoe's declining confidence in Laurier's leadership in mid-1916 was not accompanied by increased sympathy for the existing Conservative Government. He was disturbed by the repeated charges of corruption in the Government's handling of the war effort and felt justified in encouraging a vigilant opposition. But more disquieting than this charge was the crisis in manpower. Two of Dafoe's sons had gone to the war, so that he had personal as well as public reasons for keeping a sharp eye on recruiting. If the war was to be brought to a decisive conclusion, Canada and the Allies had to keep their military strength at full capacity. Borden recognized that necessity when, in January 1916, he called for an increase in Canada's forces to 500 thousand men. This objective, which was to be achieved by voluntary enlistment, had the full support of the *Free Press*. But before the end of 1916 it was becoming obvious to anyone with eyes to see that the men could not be obtained by voluntary means. For a variety of reasons, including the Government's blundering, the stream of enlistments had dwindled to a trickle. What could be done to meet this critical situation? On April 17, 1916, the *Free Press* expressed the view that conscription, at least under a party government, would lack the necessary support of a united public. But was there any alternative to conscription?

During the summer of 1916 Dafoe began to move towards a possible solution to the combined political and manpower problem. One thing was patently clear—the existing leadership had failed. On December 20 the *Free Press* offered its readers a depressing appraisal of the country's political state:

> We have had during the war a mean-spirited, selfish, far from competent, patronage-dispensing Government, made up in large part of inveterate and embittered partisans whose first thought is for themselves and their positions and the jobs and patronage they can deliver to their supporters....
>
> The Liberal opposition has retaliated, as was inevitable, with the consequence that we have not a united people intent upon the greatest task that ever fell to our nation, but a country distracted by partisan strife, drifting surely and steadily into a General Election campaign which will still further divide the people into warring factions.

But even as he was writing these lines, Dafoe was working out a solution

[7] Sifton Papers, Dafoe to Sifton, Oct. 17, 1916.

which he hoped would save the country from renewed political conflict and provide the leadership necessary to prevent the war effort from slowing to a halt. He was convinced that the chief members of the Borden cabinet were corruptionists. The Prime Minister himself was a "well-meaning incompetent." But the Liberals were no better. "No Liberal Government made up of the public men in sight could give the people of Canada what they want: a leadership so plainly disinterested and competent as to command their whole-hearted support," he told G. M. Wrong. Since an election contest between the existing party leaders could produce no satisfactory result and would only divide the country, it had to be avoided. One possibility would be to replace half the existing cabinet with Conservative business men like Augustus Nanton, the two Galts and Joseph Flavelle. The other possibility was a coalition. Canadian history offered an encouraging parallel. Dafoe hardly needed to remind Wrong that "if Brown and Macdonald could sink their differences—personal and political—to bring about Confederation, Sir Wilfrid and Sir Robert (between whom there is a personal friendship) might be able to loyally combine for a far greater purpose." Such a coalition seemed the obvious course to promote.[8]

As the year 1917 opened Dafoe began his campaign for union government. He admitted that the arrangement would not be easily achieved: "It will require a united effort of the nation," the *Free Press* remarked on January 13, "to substitute a National Government for blind partisan leadership of the blind." Dafoe was one of many people who were prepared to make the effort. One of his first tasks was to make a new assessment of the available political leaders. He visited Borden late in January, and discussed a wide variety of imperial and domestic topics with him. After Dafoe had left, the Prime Minister wrote in his diary that he was "a very able man and evidently far above the class which our Western newspapers command." This was the beginning of a long and mutually beneficial friendship between the liberal Conservative Prime Minister and the conservative Liberal journalist. At this time, Dafoe did not find the situation in Ottawa encouraging. "Both sides," he wrote, "are bent on playing the old party game with all its vigour, just as though we were not in the third year of the greatest war that has ever been seen." However, he found support for union government growing in the East.[9]

Dafoe had not been home from Ottawa long when he had further evidence that preparations were being made for an early election. In

[8]Dafoe Papers, Dafoe to G. M. Wrong, Dec. 12, 1916.
[9]Borden Diaries, Jan. 21, 1917; Sifton Papers, Dafoe to Sifton, Feb. 12, 1917.

April Laurier sent George Graham and E. M. Macdonald out west to scout the situation. He then consulted Dafoe by mail on the advisability of forcing an election. Dafoe replied that although the Government was obviously in trouble, the Liberals would be put on the defensive if they made dissolution necessary. A Conservative defeat seemed inevitable "unless some new factor enters the contest and gives them a good battle cry," he admitted, but there were other considerations. The Conservatives could use Quebec as a whipping horse, capitalizing on the indiscretions of some Liberal speakers. Such an appeal would find a sympathetic audience in English Canada. Perhaps hoping to discourage Laurier, he concluded with an eye to the future:

> I think it very necessary in the interests of the whole country that a Liberal Government should be in office for the period immediately following the war. I don't think anything can prevent this coming about unless in some way the Liberals throw the control of the situation into the hands of the Government. They might do this by forcing an election. They ought, therefore, to be very sure that they are right before going forward.[10]

On his return from the meetings of the Imperial War Cabinet and visits to the front early in May, Sir Robert Borden threw the confused political situation into further disorder by announcing that the Government would ask Parliament to adopt military conscription. The *Free Press* immediately agreed that the measure was necessary, but insisted that it could not be carried out by a party government. On May 29, Borden proposed to Laurier that a coalition should be formed to enforce the new manpower policy. On the following day Dafoe wrote the Liberal leader, telling him that "I think that public opinion is very strongly in favor of the formation of a National Government and the adoption of whatever policy is necessary to secure such reinforcements for our troops at the front as will prevent the gradual disappearance of our armies by wastage." Laurier, however, clung to his long-standing promise to oppose conscription and refused to enter a coalition pledged to its implementation.[11]

Thus in the spring of 1917 conscription came to Canada, and a political revolution was soon to follow. That revolution came partly because Laurier chose to honour his pledge to oppose compulsory enlistment. He summed up his position in a letter to a supporter in May:

> In the Province of Quebec I have been accused by the Nationalists of being a conscious or unconscious Jingoist and of leading the country to conscription. This was on account of the truth which I often proclaimed

[10]Laurier Papers, Laurier to Dafoe, April 10, 1917, and reply April 26, 1917.
[11]*M.F.P.*, May 21, 1917; Laurier Papers, Dafoe to Laurier, May 30, 1917.

that our position in the British Empire might make it imperative for us to participate in wars in which Britain might be engaged. At the same time I asserted that this did not lead to conscription, and that I was opposed to conscription. That statement was never objected to by either friend or foe, the Nationalists excepted. If I were now to take a different attitude, I would simply hand over the Province to the Nationalists, and the consequences might be very serious.

Two points should be emphasized about Laurier's attitude, for they help to explain the position taken by Dafoe. First, Laurier had always held that Canada might be called upon to assist in British wars. Dafoe, and those of his stripe, saw the matter in a different light—Canada was fighting her own war in co-operation with the other members of the Empire. Secondly, Laurier clearly expressed his fear that if he supported conscription he would lose the leadership of Quebec to Bourassa. Dafoe, in his study of Laurier, argued that Laurier's career after 1911 could best be understood in terms of two objectives: "to win back, if he could, the Prime Ministership of Canada; but in any event to establish his position forever as the unquestioned, unchallenged leader of his own people." When the two objectives conflicted, Dafoe believed that Laurier invariably chose the second. In the case of conscription, Laurier's letter makes it obvious that his most acute fear was that he would lose Quebec to the Nationalists. Of course he argued that such an eventuality would jeopardize national unity. The fear was entirely justified, but it failed to take account of the fact that English Canadians supported conscription nearly as enthusiastically as the French Canadians opposed it. Whatever choice Laurier, or any other politician made, national unity was threatened. Laurier quite naturally made the choice which placed him in agreement with his compatriots. Dafoe believed that by this decision Laurier had given up his title to national leadership; indeed he had held Quebec only by adopting Bourassa's platform.[12]

Conscription made coalition impossible for Laurier, but in the long run the measure made coalition almost inevitable for the Liberals in English Canada. In the spring of 1917 the road to union government was by no means clear of pitfalls, however. With conscription about to be enacted, Dafoe's main objective was to keep it from becoming a partisan issue. In mid-June he journeyed to Ottawa where he had a brief, inconclusive interview with Laurier who was now suggesting that conscription should be preceded by a referendum. Dafoe also consulted with the Western Liberal members with a view to having them form an

[12]Laurier Papers, Laurier to A. C. Hardy, May 29, 1917; Dafoe, *Laurier*, 156–7. See also A. Laurendeau, "Henri Bourassa" in R. L. McDougall, ed., *Our Living Tradition*, Fourth Series (Toronto, 1962), 139.

independent group which could force both parties to accept a further extension of the parliamentary term. He still believed that an election was the most serious threat to national unity. Back in Winnipeg, Dafoe conducted some further tests of the political atmosphere. T. A. Crerar, "the big man in the farmers' movement," believed that a Western bloc of Liberals and farmers should be sent to Ottawa. Certainly there was little sympathy for Laurier's viewpoint. Dafoe decided that the time had now come to break completely from the Liberal leadership. Perhaps the Quebec situation would have been better if Laurier had been taken into the Government at the beginning of the war, but the opportunity had been missed and the time had come to face the realities of Quebec politics.[13] The *Free Press* made its candid assessment on June 25:

> The authentic voice of Quebec today is that of Bourassa. He has been stating his views with perfect frankness. He says Quebec is against the war. Laurier is at best a moderating, not a controlling power in Quebec. If he came into a coalition government he would leave Quebec behind him. This is why the problem now before the people of Canada must be solved, if there is any solution, without the assistance of Laurier or of Quebec.

The only solution, as Dafoe saw it, was a coalition without the support of Laurier and Quebec. "Even majorities have rights in this country," the *Free Press* snapped. By mid-July the Winnipeg newspaper had read all the anti-conscriptionists out of the Liberal party.

During much of the early part of July, Dafoe was in Ottawa, where he worked hand in hand with Sifton to get the coalition movement speeded up. At first there was some suspicion of him in the Conservative camp, where he was thought to be helping Laurier prepare for an election. But this was not Dafoe's intention; after apparently being convinced by Arthur Meighen as well as by his own experiences that there was no hope in his scheme to form a Western bloc that would hold the balance of power, he turned all his energies to the cause of union. If Borden ever had any doubts about Dafoe, these were banished by a conversation on July 18, after which the Prime Minister recorded that Dafoe "seems intensely in earnest." Dafoe now saw that what was necessary was to unite all the conscriptionist forces in order to smother the Laurier Liberals. "If we can prevent a party fight in the West we shall have no trouble with the foreigners," Dafoe wrote Borden after his return home. But the Western Liberals were fully aware of their importance and were reluctant to throw their weight behind Borden.

[13]Laurier Papers, Laurier to Dafoe, June 20, 1917; Dafoe, *Clifford Sifton in Relation to His Times* (Toronto, 1931), 405; Dafoe Papers, Dafoe to Sifton, June 27, 1917.

Dafoe saw that the Westerners, while favouring coalition, wanted to show their strength in an election first.[14]

The future of the coalition movement seemed to rest with the Western Liberal convention that was scheduled for Winnipeg during the second week in August to draw up a platform for the increasingly independent Western wing of the party. The *Free Press* gauged Western sentiment fairly accurately when it announced on June 28 that the West

> has no confidence in the present Dominion Government as a whole or in any member of it as an individual. It admits no allegiance either to the leaders on the other side of the House.
>
> The Canadian West is in the mood to break away from past affiliations and traditions and inaugurate a new political era of sturdy support for advanced and radical programmes. The break-up of the parties has given the West its opportunity; and there is no doubt but that it will take advantage of it.

But even in the radical West, war policies were of primary concern, especially the question of conscription and coalition.

Laurier hoped that the Winnipeg meeting would confine itself to the questions of domestic politics which affected the West, but he suspected that Sifton was using his influence to have the delegates commit themselves to conscription. He advised his supporters to avoid the conscription issue and follow the course he was advocating—that of leaving conscription a matter to be settled by individuals. Both the conscriptionist and anti-conscriptionist forces were manœuvring for control of the Western convention. The Laurier Liberals feared that the Siftons, Dafoe and Calder of Saskatchewan were organizing conscriptionist delegations. The proponents of conscription, on the other hand, were suspicious that the men who controlled the party machine and especially the large foreign vote were attempting to pack the gathering with their minions.[15]

Dafoe himself harboured doubts about the outcome of the convention. Though he realized that a large step towards a union government would be taken if the convention could be won to the cause, he feared that was too much to expect. One of the danger signals had been the Liberal convention in Toronto on July 20 which had expressed its full confidence in Laurier. Dafoe believed that the most important problem was to see that the Western delegates were kept straight on the issue of winning the war. One thing he was certain of—the time for paying deference to the wishes of Quebec was passed. He told George P. Graham angrily:

[14]Borden Diaries, July 3, 4, 7, 18, 1917; Borden Papers, Dafoe to Borden, July 18, 1917; Dafoe Papers, Dafoe to N. W. Rowell, July 25, 1917.
[15]Laurier Papers, Laurier to A. W. McLeod, July 31, 1917, and A. W. McLeod to Laurier, July 27, 1917; Dafoe Papers, G. H. Barr to Dafoe, July 27, 1917.

I hope most Westerners are as tired as I am of being told that we must not do this because Quebec would not like it, or that the party must do that because otherwise Quebec will rally to Bourassa. After one has been told twenty-five times in succession, as I was at Ottawa, that our national course on the war must be determined by the consideration that it is preferable that Laurier instead of Bourassa should control Quebec the dose becomes nauseating. I did for a while think this myself, but now I believe this is the wrong view.

Already, he continued, Bourassa controlled Laurier because of the latter's fear that he would lose the leadership of his people. Should Laurier become Prime Minister again, Bourassa would be the power behind the throne. Such a situation would be completely intolerable. Laurier, Dafoe judged, was now playing exclusively for the benefit of Quebec, claiming at the same time that, if the English-Canadian Liberals suppressed their views, victory would be won. Had Laurier joined a coalition on the condition that one last appeal for voluntary enlistment should be made, he "would have closed his career secure in the confidence and affection of the English Canadians, and I believe also the better half of his own people." Since he had not done so, Dafoe could no longer follow the old man's leadership. Clearly there was no longer any question of subordinating the issue of conscription to the exigencies of Liberal party unity.[16]

But when the Western Liberal convention met, Dafoe found himself in a minority with these strong views. Right from the outset, it was clear that a majority of the delegates favoured continued support for a party led by Laurier. Main Johnson, who had gone West to watch the proceedings for N. W. Rowell, the Ontario Liberal leader, found Dafoe convinced that the meeting was a Laurier gathering. Having reached this conclusion, Dafoe apparently decided to salvage something from a desperate situation. After many hours of labour in the resolutions committee, a compromise "Win-the-War" resolution, written by Dafoe, was reported to the plenary session. It called for a maximum war effort but eschewed any mention of conscription. Perhaps it was thought that such a resolution could be later interpreted as implying the necessity of both conscription and coalition. Unfortunately for those who hoped to profit from ambiguity, J. G. Turriff, a conscriptionist Liberal, remained unsatisfied and attempted to have the convention add a rider calling for compulsory military service if it became necessary. Not only was his effort a failure, but the debate revealed the sharp division within the

[16]Dafoe Papers, Dafoe to N. W. Rowell, July 25, 1917; Dafoe to George P. Graham, July 30, 1917.

Western Liberal camp and the strength of the anti-conscriptionist delegates.[17]

Having refused to support conscription, the convention turned to an enthusiastic endorsation of Laurier's leadership. Nevertheless, in confining itself largely to the Liberal leader's past record, the resolution illustrated that it, too, was the result of a struggle in committee. Thus, on all major points respecting the war the convention rejected the views that Dafoe supported. As he wrote later, the meeting developed into "a bomb that went off in the hands of its makers." Perhaps Dafoe accepted this result as substantiation of the rumour he had heard earlier of a bargain that had been struck between some Western Liberals and the Quebec leadership; in return for Western acceptance of Quebec's attitude to the war effort, the French-Canadian Liberals would support tariff reductions. Certainly the convention was a serious defeat for the unionist cause, and a personal defeat for Dafoe and his newspaper, which had almost been openly condemned by the delegates.[18]

The machine politicians had won, the *Free Press* announced on August 10. The West's true aspirations had been thwarted by a group of scheming politicians who cared little for the vigorous prosecution of the war. But plans for a coalition government were by no means defeated. Sifton, his ardour little dampened, proceeded to Ottawa, leaving Dafoe to handle the Western negotiations. It was well that Sifton had gone East, for Dafoe was aware that his employer's business connections had made him suspect on the Prairies, and this unpopularity had contributed to the result of the convention. For a month negotiations continued, important Western leaders shuttling back and forth to Ottawa after being briefed by Dafoe. The editor-politician's task was to persuade the Western leaders—T. A. Crerar, H. W. Wood, A. B. Hudson and J. A. Calder, among others—that the success of a coalition depended upon their inclusion in it. He assured them that it was simply a war government in which no one would be expected to compromise his views on domestic policy.[19]

In mid-September, the Borden Government took a step which no doubt helped to convince the Western politicians of the advantages of

[17]Main Johnson Papers, Diary, Main Johnson to N. W. Rowell, Aug. 7 and Aug. 9, 1917 (morning).

[18]Main Johnson Papers, Main Johnson to N. W. Rowell, Aug. 9, 1917 (afternoon); Dafoe Papers, Dafoe to A. Bridle, June 14, 1921; Main Johnson Papers, Diary, Main Johnson to N. W. Rowell, Aug. 7, 1917; Laurier Papers, J. K. Barrett to Laurier, Aug. 9, 1917.

[19]Dafoe Papers, Dafoe to Borden, Sept. 29, 1917; Sifton to Dafoe, Aug. 12, 1917.

union government. This step was the adoption of two new and unusual electoral laws: the Military Voters' Act and the War-time Election Act. The clauses of the latter act which disfranchised "enemy aliens" were particularly important to the Western politicians, for a large section of their constituents fell into this category. How much of a fillip this legislation gave to the unionist cause is impossible to determine exactly; it certainly did not bring the protests from the West that some people expected. At any rate, by the first week in October the Westerners were ready to throw in their lot with the coalition. On October 12 the successful result of months of critical negotiations was announced. Prime Minister Borden was now to lead a cabinet divided between Liberals and Conservatives, pledged to enforce conscription. An election was announced for December 17.[20]

Dafoe was naturally greatly relieved and elated. Though he claimed for himself only a minor role in this success of the coalition movement, others gave him a much higher place. Sifton maintained that the "principal credit" was due his editor. The Prime Minister wrote of the "great debt of gratitude for the splendid aid which you have brought to a great purpose." N. W. Rowell, nineteen years later, claimed that Dafoe made union government possible by his success in persuading the Western leaders to join the movement. Certainly Dafoe threw whatever skill he possessed in the arts of political management into the struggle. More important, he turned his influential editorial page into a propaganda machine for the cause. He did so because he was convinced that the winning of the war demanded a government that could enforce conscription. Naturally there were other matters that required the attention of a strong government, and the increasingly critical railway problem stood near the head of the list. But above all, Dafoe was convinced that only under union government could Canada fulfil the responsibilities that nationhood entailed.[21]

The final act in the drama of union government and the break-up of the Liberal party was the wartime election. For the first time since he had joined the *Free Press*, Dafoe and his newspaper were arrayed against the Liberals. Many of his lifelong political friends were now bitter foes. He told his correspondent in Ottawa in October 1917 that although he had no intention of making the *Free Press* the handmaiden of the new government, he did intend to give it strong independent support. No

---

[20] Rowell Papers, N. W. Rowell to F. Pardee, Sept. 9, 1917.
[21] Dafoe Papers, Sifton to G. W. Allen, Feb. 6, 1918; Borden to Dafoe, Oct. 13, 1917; MS speech of N. W. Rowell at Dafoe's seventieth birthday celebration, April 10, 1936.

longer should Sir Wilfrid be treated as the gallant knight, for he had to be made to realize the "shameful mess" he had made of things. Dafoe's view was that it would be best for the old warrior to resign, for his continued leadership could only mean the ruin of the Liberal party.[22]

Laurier, of course, persisted courageously in the course he believed was right despite the signs that the ground was crumbling under him. On November 5, the *Free Press* outlined the alternatives before the electorate, leaving no doubt about its own decision:

> The choice is between the Government which represents, so far as the complex conditions of Canadian political life in the past have made it possible for it to represent, every section of the community which is in favor of winning the war, and a party just as definitely pledged against the measures by which alone this Dominion's obligations and given word can be fulfilled, and which will be supported by all the elements opposed, from various motives, to the pursuit of an active war policy.

In the heat of partisan strife, Dafoe identified the views of the Laurier Liberals and the Bourassa Nationalists, and misrepresented them both.

The result was never in serious doubt. The Government, campaigning on the issue of conscription and aided by the extraordinary electoral machinery it had devised, far outclassed the truncated Liberal party. At last, on December 17, the unequal but bitterly fought winter campaign ended. The result showed the Laurier Liberals reduced to little more than a party of French Canadians, while the Unionist roster sagged under the weight of its enormous English-Canadian representation. Ignoring the country's serious racial division, the *Free Press* proclaimed on December 18 that "Canada was saved yesterday—from shame, from national futility, from treachery to her Allies, from treason to the holiest cause for which men have ever fought and died."

Dafoe was not unaware of the critical situation caused by the racial rupture of the country. The day after the election he appealed to a French-Canadian friend to counsel the Quebec Liberals against any action that might increase the gravity of the condition. "I do not think," he concluded, somewhat condescendingly, "[that] the situation which is full of peril to Canada, can be changed except upon the initiative of Quebec herself." His friend replied coldly that the crisis resulted from the fact that Dafoe himself, who knew Quebec and knew it was not disloyal, had "made racial appeals to the Anglo-Saxon element in the West against the Province of Quebec." The charge was just. In his anxiety to ensure the success of the war effort Dafoe had contributed his share to the grim disunity which faced Canadians at Christmas 1917. But that

[22]Dafoe Papers, Dafoe to H. E. M. Chisholm, Oct. 14, 1917.

disunity had not been created *ex nihilo* by conscription. Disunity is always a potential danger in Canada. Racial friction had been aggravated into an ugly sore by the years of debate over imperial policy and the naval question; the language controversy and the Lapointe Resolution brought it to a head and in the heat of the conscription crisis it burst. At each stage of this development Dafoe had played his part. By 1917 he had reached the conclusion that the national interest was so critically at stake that, though racial disharmony might result, a greater cause had to be served: the cause of winning the war. He deliberately chose his side and fought for it passionately as an honest, though sometimes unfair, partisan.[23]

iv

As the New Year approached, the Canadian political scene was freer of confusion than it had been for many months. But the confusion had only been resolved at the price of a bitter, though peaceful, political revolution. Dafoe, like many thousands of Western Canadians, had cut the Gordian knot which for years had tied him to the Liberal party. Why had this radical step been taken? Laurier offered a paradoxical explanation when he wrote of Dafoe that "on many things he has the most advanced ideas of Liberalism and even Radicalism; on others his horizon is the horizon of the sixteenth century." There was certainly truth in this temperate judgment. Since 1911, Dafoe had been growing increasingly uneasy about the conservatism of the Liberal party, especially on tariff policy. His sympathies were with the Western farmers, while Laurier, hoping to rebuild a national party, refused to accept the full measure of Western demands which conflicted with the views of the Eastern Liberals. Moreover Dafoe and Laurier differed completely on the French language question. By characterizing him as "sixteenth century," Laurier meant that Dafoe was militantly Protestant in his attitude to the Roman Catholic Church. Certainly Dafoe had a Protestant's suspicion of "clerical influence," though it was more of a nineteenth- than a sixteenth-century variety. Besides, he had, perhaps unconsciously, an Anglo-Saxon's belief in the innate superiority of his culture over that of the French Canadians. He believed that, with the exception of Quebec, Canada was an English-speaking nation. Therefore his genuine concern to reform the Manitoba school system, and his belief that outside Quebec the French Canadians were without legal rights to their language, brought him into conflict with the French-Canadian Liberals. In theory he admitted a historic claim to special

[23]*Ibid.*, Dafoe to Thomas Côté, Dec. 18, 1917, and reply Dec. 27, 1917.

treatment for the French Canadians, but in practice he allowed almost none. His suspicion of the French Canadians, aroused by the Lapointe Resolution, was confirmed by Quebec's opposition to conscription.[24]

But the source of the conflict between Dafoe and Laurier over conscription and union government went deeper than the Liberal leader was prepared to recognize. It stemmed from a fundamental difference over the nature of the Great War and the role Canada should play in it. From the very outbreak of the conflict, Dafoe had taken the view that it was Canada's war and that the country's interests and aspirations were wagered upon its outcome. Of course, Canada was fighting on the side of Great Britain, but that was not because Canada was a colony, but because the interests of the two countries in the cause of "freedom and democracy" were identical. Since it was Canada's war, Dafoe placed no limitations on the extent of the country's participation. When voluntary recruiting failed to provide the men necessary for a maximum war effort, Dafoe immediately agreed that compulsory enlistment would have to be put into effect. Union government was the best available means of achieving this end.

Laurier viewed the war as Britain's war, and Canada's contribution to it as the assistance given by a colony to the mother country. This was the central theme of his speech on the declaration of war in the Canadian House of Commons on August 19, 1914. Again and again he emphasized that it was "the duty of Canada to assist the Motherland to the utmost of Canada's ability," and that Canadians "stood behind the Mother Country, conscious and proud that she was engaged in this war." Legally he took the correct position expressed in the maxim, "When Britain is at war, Canada is at war." But since Canada was fighting for Britain, it would not be called upon to make the same sacrifices as the principal participants. For Laurier, that sacrifice fell just short of conscription. Searching for the cause of his disagreement with Laurier, Dafoe perceptively placed his finger on this crucial point. Characterizing Laurier's viewpoint, Dafoe wrote in his *Sifton*, "The war was England's; Canada was to assist; her assistance, humble as it might be, would be appreciated both for its material value and its moral help." Here Dafoe was giving a telescoped paraphrase of Laurier's peroration. In words that must have stuck in the mind of the Tory member for Portage la Prairie, Arthur Meighen, and caused Henri Bourassa to shudder, Laurier had declared exultantly:

It is the opinion of the British government ... that the assistance of our troops, humble as it might be, will be appreciated, either for its material

---

[24]Laurier Papers, Laurier to A. W. McLeod, Jan. 24, 1918.

value, or for the greater moral help which will be rendered. It will be seen by the world that Canada, a daughter of old England, intends to stand by her in this great conflict. When the call goes out, our answer goes at once, and it goes in the classical answer of the British call to duty: "Ready, Aye Ready."[25]

When the conscription issue was raised, Laurier, not for the first time, had more sober thoughts, though his later conclusions were implicit in the attitude which he had taken to the war from the outset. Certainly he had a multiplicity of reasons for opposing conscription—a desire to preserve national unity, fear of the reaction in Quebec, doubts about the ability of the measure to produce the promised reinforcements, as well as his pledge to oppose it. But also there was the assumption that Canada was engaged in the war not in its own interests, but merely to assist Britain. Perhaps nothing was more indicative of Laurier's attitude than his suspicion that conscription and union government were merely aspects of an imperialistic plot to centralize the Empire according to the plan of the Round Table. Like every other scheme for imperial reorganization, this one had to be resisted.[26]

Laurier's explanation for Canada's entry into the war was undoubtedly correct legally, and perhaps most Canadians would have agreed that Canada was at war to assist Britain. But Dafoe was not one of those Canadians. Regardless of legal technicalities, he believed that Canada was a nation which had entered the war because its interests were at stake, and that it had to employ every available means to protect them. As he wrote on August 26, 1917, "Canada is in the war as a principal, not a colony." This had been his position since the day the *Free Press* announced the country's involvement in the war.

The nationalism of Dafoe and the nationalism of Laurier were at fundamental variance at this precise point. Dafoe viewed Canada, even in 1914, as part of a wider world in which it had international interests and responsibilities. Laurier saw Canada isolated from the world and, as far as possible, concerned only with its own pressing problems. These conflicting assumptions brought the rupture of 1917. At the close of the turbulent events which had filled 1917, Dafoe at last felt confident that the country had a government that was prepared to assume the full measure of its international responsibilities.

[25]A. B. Keith, ed., *Select Documents and Speeches on British Colonial Policy, 1763–1917* (Toronto, 1953), 360, 358; Dafoe, *Sifton*, 395; Keith, ed., *Documents and Speeches*, 362-3.
[26]O. D. Skelton, *The Life and Letters of Sir Wilfrid Laurier* (2 vols., Toronto, 1921), II, 508–9. Laurier Papers, Laurier to Sir Allen Aylesworth, May 15, 1917.

VI. Ushering in a New World
1918-20

✦✦

THE POLITICAL TRUCE achieved by the formation of the Union Government was one which had serious limitations. The most obvious one, of course, was the fact that the administration was not really national. The accepted leaders of Quebec remained opposed to it, smarting under the bitterness of the wartime election. Yet even where the Unionist appeal had seemed most successful—in the West—its roots were not deep. In fact the election of 1917 had merely completed a process which had begun in the West in 1911 and had been gaining velocity ever since. That process was the destruction of the two old national parties. The thin topsoil of non-partisanship which the movement for union government had spread over unsettled Prairie political conditions only served as ideal germinating ground for the seeds of political independence which the farmers' movements had been scattering over the West.

Nevertheless in 1918 the Union Government had a great cause to serve—military victory and diplomatic settlement. Until these objectives were reached, domestic politics could be kept in the background. But the ardour which the campaign for the Unionists had stimulated in Dafoe was not easily quelled. He felt that there were still some necessary remarks to be made, and perhaps a few scores to settle, before the campaign was forgotten. In the *Free Press* he was prepared to remain quiet about the French Canadians, but privately, to Thomas Côté, he let his strong views be known. The French Canadians, he suggested, would have to admit that they had been wrong before there could be any real basis for reconciliation. He continued,

> The trouble between the English and the French Canadians has become acute because the French Canadians have refused to play their part in this war—being the only known race of white men to quit. They try to excuse themselves by alleging that they have domestic grievances which should first

be righted. The excuse, if true, would be contemptible. In the face of an emergency like this domestic questions have to stand.

A solution would soon work itself out, for once it was demonstrated that a sulky Quebec phalanx was without influence "there may be a return to reason along the banks of the St. Lawrence."[1]

As for the Liberal party, part of which had been the instrument of the French-Canadian betrayal, it was damned. Its organization was gone, and its true leaders had become Unionists. The rumour that the party was to be reorganized under Mackenzie King drew scorn from the *Free Press* on January 8, 1918; King would do well to go back to working for John D. Rockefeller. "There is no future for him in Canada."

Dafoe had become a thoroughgoing supporter of the new Borden Government. The bitterness of the 1917 campaign and his desire to see the war brought to a successful conclusion combined to convince him that he should support the Unionists with a vigour he had rarely shown for any government. Indeed in the spring of 1918 Sifton complained that no government had ever had "a more entirely docile and apologetic supporter."[2] It was true, for Dafoe had grown very close to the Unionist leaders, especially Borden, Rowell, Arthur Sifton and Crerar. He refused to desert them while there were still victories to be won. Like many Canadians he still had sons on active service and he believed that the uncompromising war policy of the Government deserved his support. Furthermore, as the end of the conflict approached, he was beginning to think about a peace settlement, and he realized that only a strong government at home could insist upon peace terms that recognized Canada's contribution to victory.

It was not until the autumn of 1918 that the *Free Press* began to discuss the questions involved in peacemaking. These discussions were always prefaced by the condition that peace could only follow the total defeat of the enemy, and by November it was pretty clear that this objective was near at hand. Post-war plans now demanded increased attention. Dafoe admitted that "in many cases there is no obvious solution."[3] But the kind of peace that he would approve was implicit in the Wilsonian spirit that infused his announcement that the war had been won. "Feudal Germany and predatory Austria," the *Free Press* said on November 12, "have struck their flag to democracy; their armies are defeated."

Whether Dafoe ever thought that the end of the war would bring

---

[1] Dafoe Papers, Dafoe to Thomas Côté, Jan. 1, 1918.
[2] *Ibid.*, Sifton to Dafoe, April 27, 1918.
[3] Sifton Papers, Dafoe to Sifton, Nov. 5, 1918.

his connections with the Unionists to a conclusion is doubtful. But if he did, his intention was rapidly dropped when he found himself brought even closer to his colleagues during the peacemaking than he had been during the war. Even before the war ended, N. W. Rowell, concerned that the Canadian electorate should be kept apprised of the activities of the Government's representatives at the Peace Conference, suggested that Dafoe accompany the Canadian delegation as the representative of the Department of Public Information. Dafoe apparently needed little encouragement, for a week after the Armistice was signed Rowell was able to tell the Prime Minister that the Prairie editor had accepted the assignment. Borden was delighted; he would now have the assistance of a journalist who had no superior in Canada.[4]

ii

At the end of November Dafoe embarked on his first trip to Europe in a decade. It was an important experience for him. At Paris he saw the great wartime leaders disputing over the spoils of war and attempting to devise a permanent peace settlement. He was in daily contact with the Canadian delegation, and especially with his good friend Sir Robert Borden. The Prime Minister had risen greatly in Dafoe's estimation since 1917. His fight to have the Dominion represented naturally won the full approval of the nationalist editor. Dafoe later judged that the Peace Conference was the "catalytic agent which broke up the traditional Empire and replaced it with a brotherhood of nations." In 1919 the situation seemed less clear-cut.[5]

Like Borden, Dafoe was concerned about the extensive evidence of national selfishness which he saw at Paris. Early in January a disillusioned Borden concluded that "the methods and aims of nations at a Peace Conference are not much higher than or superior to those of an ordinary Town Council." To be sure, the conference had opened in an atmosphere of hopefulness. Its aim was to secure a just and enduring peace which would provide guarantees against future blood-letting. But quarrels among the victors soon obscured these aspirations. Dafoe was drawn to a little group of leaders who he thought were making a genuine attempt to fulfil their wartime promises of a better world. Lloyd George, Lord Cecil, General Smuts, Sir Robert Borden and Philip Kerr along

[4]Rowell Papers, N. W. Rowell to Borden, Nov. 7, 1918; Rowell to Borden, Nov. 19, and Borden to Rowell, Nov. 20, 1918 (cables).

[5]Dafoe, "Canada and the Peace Conference of 1919," *C.H.R.*, XXIV, no. 3 (Sept. 1943), 235; Dafoe, "Canada at the Peace Conference," *Maclean's Magazine* (May 1919), 76.

with President Wilson won Dafoe's admiration. He realized, however, at least after he returned to Canada, that Wilson had erred in failing to include any representatives of the Republican party in his entourage.[6]

Though it was largely for his journalistic talents that Dafoe had been invited to Paris, there were many occasions when he was consulted on policy. Borden kept him well informed about the inner workings of the conference. When the League Covenant was given to the delegates, Borden passed a copy on to Dafoe for comment. What Dafoe thought of Borden's criticism of Article X, the heart of the collective security provisions of the Covenant, is impossible to discover. As a stalwart autonomist Dafoe was occasionally approached by his employer's brother on matters where Canada's status was involved, and these discussions with Arthur Sifton about British opposition to Canadian representation in the International Labour Organisation helped to convince him of the need for a clearer definition of Canadian status.[7]

Even during the exciting days of treaty-making, Dafoe was able to slip off for a brief visit to the scenes where Canadians had given their lives during the war. Here were a few days to reflect upon the meaning of the Great War for a country like Canada. To a nationalist, its primary significance was clear. "Canada's participation in the war," Dafoe wrote in *Over the Canadian Battlefields*, "is a fountain from which succeeding generations can drink deep, learning thereby the lessons in valor, sacrifice, patriotism and national pride. . . ." He would not succumb to the disillusionment which followed the war. The victory of democracy and freedom over the agents of tyranny and enslavement only assured him further of man's progress:

> Thus the human heart, unconquerable by adversity, resolutely sets about repairing the ravages of time and war. Man re-builds his ruined home, sets up again the family altars, renews the sweet amenities of life, re-tills the fields. . . . Behind lies the wreckage, the pain, the terrors of those impossible, those unimaginable years of war—ahead stretches the future of clean and fruitful work, the dear reward of love and affection, the blessings of a healing and fruitful peace never to be broken again—else these millions have died in vain—by the trumpets of the Lords of War.

Could such optimism remain unimpaired by the obvious refusal of the statesmen gathered at Paris to accept the idealistic preachments of the American President? The statesmen might fail to secure the peace, Dafoe

---

[6] Rowell Papers, Borden to Rowell, Jan. 25, 1919. Dafoe Papers, Dafoe to Nichols, Jan. 19, 1919; Dafoe to Dr. Holgate, Dec. 22, 1919.
[7] Borden Diaries, Dec. 1918 to Feb. 1919. Dafoe Papers, Borden to Dafoe, March 21, 1919; Arthur Sifton to Dafoe, April 11, May 10, 1919; Dafoe to H. Duncan Hall, June 13, 1921.

realized, but then theirs would be a horrible responsibility. "It rests with the statesmen of Paris to keep faith with the aspirations which turned millions of peace-loving men into militant crusaders. If they succeed only in patching up the old order under a pretentious false front, it will be only too true that much of the sacrifice will have been in vain."[8]

At the beginning of March 1919, Dafoe had to leave for Canada. The conference was not over, but he had been away from his editorial desk and his family for over three months. Paris had been a wonderful experience, and he had stored up much knowledge gathered from secret documents that would help in interpreting future events. Moreover, he had developed a great affection for the city of Paris where in company with Borden and others he had spent many spare hours walking and sightseeing. It was on these walks that his friendship with Borden had grown very close. On March 6 Sir Robert, who was practising his French, recorded in his diary, "Sir G. Foster & M. Dafoe partiront pour Londres d'où M. Dafoe commençera son voyage au Canada mercredi prochain. Celui-ci est un homme de grande valeur et il nous a donné beaucoup d'assistance dans nos travaux à Paris."

Dafoe returned home from Paris tired and ill. He had worked hard to keep the news flowing to the papers at home. Perhaps, too, he was sick at heart. His North Americanism was rarely more vocal than in the months after his return. He claimed that the most lasting impression of his visit to Europe was the renewed conviction that "the North American Continent is a good place to live." Europe was too bound by the past, and not willing enough to scrap past enmities for future peace. This was evident in the peace treaties, which had done little more than patch up the old order. But the seemingly pretentious front, the new-born League of Nations, was not false, and offered an opportunity for a change in structure. Both the old and reactionary, the new and progressive, had been present at Paris. Each had won its victories. "In the secret councils of the Peace Conference," Dafoe told a North American audience, "Idealism and what the Germans call Realpolitik, fought out their duels; and they each won something from the struggle. The Treaty was made by the Past; the League of Nations is the charter of the Future, the one star of hope shining in the overcast sky."[9]

Dafoe assumed the personal responsibility of popularizing the cause of the League in Canada. In addition to supporting the idea in the editorial columns of the *Free Press*, he accepted numerous speaking

---

[8]Dafoe, *Over the Canadian Battlefields* (Toronto, 1919), 17, 51–2, 82.
[9]Dafoe, "The Sister Nations of North America" in *The Free Press Prairie Farmer*, Aug. 27, 1919.

engagements throughout the West. Frequently his high-pitched, rasping voice was heard in passionate advocacy of the League's mission. Typical was his address to the Canadian Club in his own city shortly after his arrival home from overseas. He told his listeners that on the whole the defeated Central Powers had received their just deserts at the Peace Conference. Germany especially had to be taught the cost of launching the world into war. But the Peace Conference had done more than punish the guilty nations; it had drawn up an outline for an organ of international co-operation. Through the League, democracy would be brought to politically "barbarous" Europe. The ultimate success of the League depended upon the willingness of every nation to assume its obligations and share the burden of a world in travail. No nation, certainly not Canada, could hope to find safety by retreating behind its national frontiers. "There are 60,000 graves in France and Flanders, every one of which tells us that, for good or ill, we are in the world and must bear our part in the solution of its troubles."[10]

The primary task in 1919, as Dafoe saw it, was to win acceptance for the idea of the League. Thus he gave only slight attention to the responsibilities that the member nations assumed in the new institution. The obligations were light compared with the returns offered by a successful League. Article X of the Covenant, guaranteeing the territorial integrity and political independence of member nations, was the object of much criticism in English-speaking countries, including Canada. Prime Minister Borden had felt that the Covenant would be improved by its omission. The *Free Press*, in 1919, did not flinch at the obligations that the article implied; in fact it rightly saw them as the cornerstone of the League.[11]

Dafoe knew that the League would be weakened by the absence of any of the great powers. It was particularly important to Canada that the United States should accept the Covenant. The campaign against the League in the latter country infuriated Dafoe both because its success would leave the League emasculated, and also because part of the American opposition was based on a misinterpretation of Canada's newly won status. The *Free Press* replied to the isolationists indignantly by asserting that Canada had a complete right to its position in the League because of the part it had played in winning the war and because of its "place in the world." There could be no thought of relinquishing this position "to help one political party in the United States to play its

---

[10]Dafoe, "Canada at the Peace Conference" in *Addresses of the Year* (Winnipeg: Canadian Club, 1919), 104.
[11]Rowell Papers, Borden to N. W. Rowell, April 21, 1919; *M.F.P.*, Sept. 4, 1919.

game for office. Canada will be equal in status to the other members of the League or she will not be a member." When the United States Senate failed to give the Treaty of Versailles the necessary two-thirds majority, the *Free Press* saw the act as a "world tragedy" which placed the League idea in serious jeopardy.[12]

The war and the Peace Conference had given Dafoe the faith of an internationalist. This faith made his position as editor of the *Free Press* somewhat awkward, for Sir Clifford Sifton did not have much enthusiasm for the League, claiming that if he had been in office he would have rejected the Treaty of Versailles. The League, in Sifton's judgment, was a "preposterous and expensive farce," which would involve Canada in "European and Imperialistic complications." Thus Dafoe had to chose his ground carefully when he discussed the League in the *Free Press* while Sir Clifford was alive.[13]

Nevertheless Dafoe was convinced that Canada could not shirk its international responsibilities if it expected to be recognized as a nation. When in 1919 the Liberal Opposition in Parliament rejected the Borden Government's claims that Canada had achieved a new status by signing the peace treaties and joining the League, the *Free Press* showed them no sympathy. They refused to face the fact that the old pre-war days had passed and they were abdicating the traditional Liberal position on the Empire by accepting "the old abandoned formulas of colonial subordination and impotence," the paper argued on September 13.

Dafoe's difference with the Liberal party over the question of Canada's place in the new world order indicated that he had grown and had accepted the forward steps taken by the Union Government while some of his former friends had not. Dafoe had always shown more awareness of Canada's international interests than many Liberals. The war convinced him finally that the years of sheltered national development were over, and that Canada had emerged on the world stage as a nation. But political reality had far outstripped legal fact. Canada's claims to nationhood had gone beyond the understood legal framework of the British Empire and there was to be much acrimonious debate before fact and theory were brought into agreement.

iii

The war sharpened Dafoe's views on imperial relations. This was owing in part to the heightened sense of patriotism which gripped much

[12]*M.F.P.*, July 26, 1919; March 22, 1920.
[13]Dafoe Papers, Sifton to Dafoe, Aug. 14, 1919; Dafoe, *Clifford Sifton in Relation to His Times* (Toronto, 1931), 487.

of the country as a natural concomitant of the struggle, but also to a realization that the war necessitated a clearer definition of Canada's status. During the first two years there had been a tenuous truce in Canada on the discussion of imperial relations, but Dafoe occasionally reminded his readers of his views on the subject. Shortly after the outbreak of the war, the *Free Press* suggested that it might be desirable to hold an immediate imperial conference as a demonstration of the common purpose of the members of the association. But if the suggestion was taken up, the paper warned, the centralizers should not be allowed to use the circumstance of war to forward their plans for a politically unified or federated Empire. On the whole, however, Dafoe refrained from commenting on the subject of imperial organization until the other side, "the centralizers," opened the offensive.

Dafoe welcomed the publication of Lionel Curtis' *The Problem of the Commonwealth* in 1916. It provided an opportunity for serious discussion of the imperial question. Curtis' main contention was that the Empire was at the parting of the ways; would the dominions become independent, or could a plan be devised to unite and preserve the imperial association? Curtis' view was that the Empire had either to be given a federated structure which would give the dominions a voice in foreign policy or allow the self-governing colonies to become independent nations following separate foreign policies. For the hard core of Round Table members, federation was the only answer; Curtis worked out the plan in great detail. Dafoe answered by claiming that Curtis did not offer the only possible alternatives. In addition to federation and independence there was the more nebulous, but so far satisfactory, theory of the free association of equals. This was the lesson of the past that should guide the future.[14]

The appearance of the Round Table study caused Dafoe to worry that an effort would be made at the end of the war to drive the Empire into an integrated union. Such a project he denounced as "entirely mad, and it will have to be rejected with sufficient vigor to ensure its rejection." To a Canadian member of the Round Table movement, G. M. Wrong, who had tried to convince him that the movement was not made up of people who had accepted Curtis' views, but only of people who wanted to study the imperial question thoroughly, Dafoe replied that he was suspicious of the whole association. He felt that behind the organization was some powerful financial interest dedicated to a plan of imperial centralization. The Canadian members were being led unknowing down

[14] Lionel Curtis, *The Problem of the Commonwealth* (Toronto, 1916), vii; *M.F.P.*, Aug. 28, 1916.

the path blazed by the British centralizers. Turning to Curtis' plan, Dafoe pronounced it entirely unsatisfactory.

> I cannot see that there is any satisfactory solution to this problem other than that of the co-operation of all the British dominions on the basis of nations and not of provinces. This is the vital point at issue. We cannot be a nation in Canada if we are simply a province of the Empire, and if we are not a nation with a high national spirit we can never solve the problems which are before us. A permanent alliance of British nations dedicated to the cause of civilization and progress appears to me to be a sublime conception, but this project of a centralized Empire, adjusted to a symmetrical pattern, with a strong probability that it would become militarized, not only leaves me cold, but actually fills me with deep apprehensions that this proposition, if carried out, would ruin the race.

Thus while Dafoe denied the antithesis suggested by Curtis—federation or independence—he thought in terms of an antithesis himself—imperialism or nationalism. He failed to recognize, or refused to admit, that the followers of Curtis had no wish to stunt the growth of freedom in the dominions. Like Dafoe these men were looking for the solution to the problem encountered by nations which had no real control over their own foreign policy. Of course the solution of the Round Tablers was wholly unacceptable to those of Dafoe's way of thinking, but he misrepresented them when he charged that they wanted to keep the dominions in the status of "provinces."[15]

Perhaps Dafoe would have been less concerned about the implications of the Round Table movement if the Liberal party had been in office in Canada. He never trusted the Conservatives on imperial policy, and tarred them with the brush of centralization. His fears were laid at rest, however, after a discussion with Borden just prior to the Prime Minister's departure for London to attend the Imperial War Conference in 1917. The two men discussed the Curtis scheme and Dafoe was relieved to learn that "our views were in great measure in agreement." Borden's first speech on imperial problems delivered in England received high commendation from the *Free Press*. The most interesting feature of the 1917 conference was the acceptance of Resolution IX on the structure of the Empire. Though the resolution postponed the final determination of imperial constitutional questions, it did state that the dominions were "autonomous nations of an Imperial Commonwealth" whose right to a voice in the determination of foreign policy had to be recognized. It concluded by recommending the establishment of machinery for "continuous consultation in all important matters of common Imperial con-

[15]Dafoe Papers, Dafoe to J. Obed. Smith, Sept. 12, 1916; Dafoe to G. M. Wrong, Oct. 16, 1916.

cern and for such necessary concerted action founded on consultation as the several Governments may determine." The *Free Press*, on May 5, 1917, praised the resolution, declaring, "The language is discreet; but the reasonable interpretation of the resolution is that it is a declaration in favor of a future for the Empire far removed from the highly colored dreams of the centralizers." The editor might have described the language of the resolution as ambiguous rather than discreet. Borden actually told Sir John Willison that the resolution was in essential agreement with the views of the Round Table. This difference in interpretation, of course, may only be a measure of Dafoe's misunderstanding of the views of the Round Table. The important point, however, is that Dafoe was fully satisfied with the general tone of Borden's ideas on imperial relations. For the remainder of the war, therefore, he did not worry much about the question.[16]

But when the war ended, Dafoe again turned his mind to the implications of Resolution IX. The time was at hand when the rather ambiguous sentiments of 1917 would have to be transformed into specific realities. Though he was becoming increasingly anxious to obtain a clear-cut definition of the imperial tie, Dafoe was never a strict legalist. He believed in the pragmatic approach whereby Canada claimed the full powers of nationhood without awaiting legal enactments; this had been his position at the outbreak of war in 1914. In short Canada should assume the full power to decide all issues which touched its interests. This was the test by which every scheme of imperial organization had to be measured. The war, Dafoe told the Imperial Press Conference in 1920, had worked to "permanently reinforce the foundations upon which the Commonwealth rests." That foundation was composed of a permanent alliance of self-governing nations under a common Crown.

This seemingly simple definition of imperial partnership was unsatisfactory to many Canadians in 1919. To those who believed that a united Empire demanded an imperial parliament or council, Dafoe's view was "nonsense," as Sir John Willison branded it. Others, like John S. Ewart, were of the opinion that the only solution to the imperial question was independence, a solution which would make Canada's status legally definite. In fact the discussion of imperial relations was carried on in a virtual babel of tongues, and much of the dispute's bitterness was caused by its very indefiniteness. This anomalous situation should not be allowed to continue, Dafoe believed. The position which the dominions had assumed at Paris "reinforced powerfully the necessity for a new defini-

[16]Borden Diaries, Jan. 21, 1917; Dafoe Papers, Dafoe to Sifton, Feb. 12, 1917; *M.F.P.*, April 4, 1917; Willison Papers, Borden to Willison, May 13, 1917.

tion of our status." Canada had assumed the powers of a nation, but it was clear from the debate over the League of Nations in the United States that in international legal practice this status remained unrecognized. Canada's position had to be clarified to prevent future confusion.[17]

Dafoe argued that the best manner of approaching the problem of constitutional definition of the Commonwealth was "to assume that our national status is all that is claimed for it and put it in strong contrast with our legal position as set out in the constitutional documents." He felt that to cling to the legalistic view that Canada had no more powers than the written documents showed would only serve to promote a grievance against Great Britain. This latter situation was to be avoided at all costs; the movement for full recognition of Canadian status must not be open to the charge of being either republican or anti-British.[18]

His close agreement with Prime Minister Borden on the imperial question led Dafoe to hope that the post-war discussion could be carried on in an atmosphere of political non-partisanship. His first doubts were aroused when the National Liberal convention in August 1919 passed what he considered a singularly ambiguous resolution on the subject of imperial relations. Then, when Borden relinquished the leadership of the Unionists, he feared that the old-line Tories would find the new medicine which Sir Robert had prescribed for the party too potent. He re-emphasized his view that if the nationalists were to see their cause triumph they had to avoid antagonizing those Canadians who had strong sentimental attachments to Britain. This, he felt, could best be achieved by adopting a programme which recognized the Crown as the symbol of the Britannic alliance, and the "further recognition that facilities for Conference between the various British nations looking conceivably to common action in certain respects will be provided." He was already groping towards the idea of Canada as a separate kingdom with a viceroy as the representative of a common Commonwealth Crown.[19]

Thus Dafoe had a programme for the definition of imperial relations worked out in rough form by 1920. As the *Free Press* put it on March 25, "Our status of equality must become a matter of right, not of grace,

[17]Dafoe, "Our Future in the Empire: Alliance under the Crown" in J. O. Miller, ed., *The New Era in Canada* (Toronto, 1917), 290–1. R. Donald, *The Imperial Press Conference in Canada* (London, n.d.), 208. Willison Papers, Sir John Willison to J. G. Harvey, Dec. 30, 1919. Dafoe Papers, J. S. Ewart to Dafoe, Dec. 6, 1919; Dafoe to Sifton, Aug. 26, 1919.
[18]Dafoe Papers, Dafoe to Sifton, April 3, 1920.
[19]*M.F.P.*, Aug. 7, 1919; Dafoe Papers, Dafoe to Sifton, April 28, 1920.

as speedily as circumstances will permit." Though his views were the natural evolution of the position he had taken in the pre-war days, the experience of the Great War and the distinction that the country had won in the peacemaking had strengthened Dafoe's nationalism. He now felt that the nation's sovereignty should be fully defined. Of course these views had been developed under some pressure, for he had expected that an imperial conference on constitutional problems would be convened immediately after the signing of the peace treaties. For Canada, the early post-war years were a time of deep uncertainty and it was perhaps well that the expected conference was postponed. Such a conference might have done serious harm, especially, as the *Free Press* warned, if it were held before "the people affected had clear ideas of what they want." By 1920 it was evident that there were many problems in Canada, particularly in the domestic field, that required consideration before the decisive imperial question could be settled with any hope of permanence.[20]

iv

When Dafoe arrived home from Paris in the spring of 1919 he found Canadian politics and society in a state of turmoil. Already the Union Government was showing signs of separating into its constituent parts. It had been an uncomfortable alliance from the start and a single year too short a period for it to set firmly. Less than a month after the Armistice was signed, signs of political uneasiness began to appear. One shrewd observer noted that the "die-hard Conservatives" who had never been especially favourable to the coalition were anxious for a return to party lines. At the same time many Liberals were beginning to look forward to the time when their broken party could be reunited. "There is," wrote Sir Joseph Flavelle, "... enough loose powder lying around that any loose spark may set up a conflagration that may easily get out of hand."[21]

The most disturbing element was the farmers' movement. The enthusiasm of the farmers for the Union Government was dampened rather quickly when the Government cancelled the military exemptions which had been promised to farmers' sons. By the end of the war most farmers were entirely disgusted with the coalition and with the old parties. In less than three weeks after the shooting in Europe ended, the Canadian Council of Agriculture, a body claiming to speak for all the provincial and local farm organizations, issued a manifesto under the revealing

[20]*M.F.P.*, Oct. 2, 1920.
[21]Flavelle Papers, Sir Joseph Flavelle to R. H. Brand, Dec. 7, 1918.

title, "The New National Policy." It was a platform for a political movement which envisaged a radical alteration in the country's economic and political structure. Its underlying theme was that, while the country had since 1867 been run according to the needs of Eastern business men, in the future it should be run in accordance with the needs of the agrarian community. The *Manitoba Free Press*, its editor absent in Paris, greeted the new programme on December 4 in a friendly but unenthusiastic manner, remarking that whatever government held power in the near future it would have to consider the farmers' demands.

Dafoe himself was still unwilling to revoke his support of the Union Government and was apparently interested in suggestions made in government circles that the coalition be given a permanent basis. In Paris he frequently discussed Canadian domestic politics with Borden, but he was unable to commit himself to any position for the future until he was able to survey the situation at home for himself. When he arrived in Winnipeg he found conditions far more disturbed than he had believed possible. The cause of disquiet was not the farmers, though they were restive enough, but rather the labouring classes.[22]

Labour disturbances at the end of the Great War were most acute west of the Great Lakes, though there was unrest in the working class throughout the country as well. As early as January 1919, some members of the Union Government were on the verge of hysteria, having received reports of revolutionary activities on the Pacific Coast. So severe were the jitters in Ottawa that the cabinet asked Borden to request the use of a British cruiser to be sent to Vancouver to warn the fomenters of discontent. Borden, of course, rejected the suggestion.[23] Still, the reports about the seriousness of labour unrest could not be denied. Pressed by post-war inflation on one hand and a glutted labour market caused by demobilization on the other, working people all over the country were searching for solutions to their difficulties. No doubt they were encouraged by the early idealism of the Russian Revolution and by the charter of working class liberties embodied in the newly founded International Labour Organisation. But there was no organized revolutionary movement. Even the efforts to form the One Big Union at Calgary in March 1919 had ended in little more than highflown radical nostrums and somewhat inchoate plans for organization. But if the Russian Revolution and international labour unrest had inspired working class

[22] Borden Papers, Borden to Arthur Meighen, Feb. 26, 1919; Borden Diaries, Feb. 9, 1919.
[23] Borden Papers, Borden to Sir Thomas White, Jan. 1, 1919; Sir Thomas White to Borden, April 16, 1919.

leaders in Canada, these same events had made the beneficiaries of the established order uneasy and susceptible to hysteria. The times were ripe for a "big Red scare." Moreover, the presence in Winnipeg of a large mixed immigrant population easily made charges of foreign-inspired "Bolshevism" ring true in the ears of the nervous, usually Anglo-Saxon, middle class. Given the instability of the political and economic situation in post-war Canada, it was perhaps impossible to avoid the bitterness which arose out of Canada's most publicized labour disturbance—the Winnipeg General Strike.

In brief, the general sympathetic strike which began in Winnipeg on May 15, 1919, resulted from an appeal by the local Trades and Labour Council, after the failure of protracted efforts by the workers in the metal and building trades to win better wages and the right of collective bargaining. In the face of the refusal of the iron masters to recognize the union, a general sympathetic strike was called. The call met with great success, some thirty thousand workers leaving their jobs. It also stirred the employers and other conservative elements in the community to react by forming the Citizens' Committee of One Thousand to oppose the Strike Committee. The strike lasted for six weeks, bringing with it deprivation, bloodshed and deep-seated bitterness.

When the first signs of disturbance arose in Winnipeg, Sifton advised that the *Free Press* should not take sides in the dispute, but rather provide a forum where both parties could present their arguments. For a few days the editor followed this advice. Indeed on the second day of the strike, May 16, the paper carried a reasonable set of proposals for the guarantee of industrial peace, in the hope that both sides could be brought around to the discussion of concrete proposals. The paper suggested that pre-strike arbitration should be accepted, though arbitration boards should not consider questions of principle, such as the right of collective bargaining, which had to be accepted before arbitration could be practised. Sympathetic strikes should be recognized as a rightful weapon of the working class, but public utilities would have to be exempted. Such proposals, however, received little consideration in the heated Winnipeg atmosphere. The workers were showing unexpected strength and determination and soon most activities in Winnipeg were at a standstill. By the fifth day, the *Free Press* itself had been reduced to a single page. In the face of this situation a new spirit gripped the paper's editorial writers. On May 24, *Free Press* readers were told that the strike had developed into a potential social revolution, whose Bolshevik leaders intended to "divide the country among themselves and their following." Thus the paper gave up every pretence of objectivity and became the virtual mouthpiece of the Citizens' Committee whose aim was the unconditional surrender of the strikers and the punishment of their leaders.[24]

Even though the *Free Press* had supported the view that the right of collective bargaining should be recognized, it was soon arguing that this problem had been superseded by the question of the Strike Committee's right to act as the government of the city. This was a revolutionary act. The supposed stoppage of such public services as the delivery of bread and milk was condemned in inflammatory terms. "Between the German Zeppelin policy and the cutting off of the food of infants and children through the sympathetic strike there is no perceptible difference," the paper pronounced on June 7. The remark was more emotional than accurate, for bread and milk were delivered as arranged by the Strike Committee, the Citizens' Committee and the City Council.[25]

During the first three weeks of the strike, Dafoe was evidently less worried about the possibilities of open violence than were some of the members of the Citizens' Committee. On June 5 he was reported to have thought that "the existing crisis could come to an end with but slight outbreaks, if any, but he looked forward to a long period of unrest." But the tension in the city, created at least in part by the *Free Press*'s vitriolic denunciations of the "Bolsheviks," naturally erupted in some violence. One riot resulted in the injury of a special constable, and Dafoe's newspaper described the rioters as "bohunks," "aliens" and "foreigners." This extreme language, and an earlier demand that the government take action to "deport the aliens," displays Dafoe's growing conviction that the strike had to be broken.[26]

On June 6, action was forthcoming from Parliament. Two measures, an amendment to the Immigration Act and an amendment to the Criminal Code, gave the Government authority to deal with people thought to be subversive. While these illiberal enactments brought no protest from the *Free Press*, which carried in its masthead the motto, "Equality of Civil Rights," the paper did oppose the arrest of the strike leaders on the ground that it would "enable them to pose as martyrs in the cause of the workingmen."[27]

Dafoe's lack of sympathy for the leaders of the General Strike was based upon the unfounded assumption that the strike was the first step

[24]Sifton Papers, Sifton to Dafoe, May 12, 1919.
[25]*M.F.P.*, May 24, 1919; K. W. McNaught, *A Prophet in Politics: A Biography of J. S. Woodsworth* (Toronto, 1959), 107.
[26]Borden Papers, O. M. Biggar to the Adjutant General, June 5, 1919; *M.F.P.*, June 11, 7, 1919.
[27]*M.F.P.*, June 18, 1919.

in a planned social revolution. Two years after the strike had collapsed, Dafoe explained to a friend that there was a simple key to understanding the purposes of the strike leaders:

> ... it was a made-to-order strike for revolutionary or semi-revolutionary purposes by the Reds who had captured control of the Trades and Labor Council of Winnipeg during the war. They realized that there was an extraordinary sense of solidarity among the labor elements in the city and they were obsessed by a desire to pull off a general strike and see what would happen. Some really thought it would start something that would bring about actual revolution as in Russia.

Dafoe never gave up this view. Of course it is possible to argue that a general strike is revolutionary by definition. But for such an argument to be valid the term "general strike" would have to be defined in such a way as to exclude the Winnipeg affair about which a careful historian has concluded that there was "no seditious conspiracy and that the strike was what it purported to be, an effort to secure the principle of collective bargaining." Dafoe refused to accept this conclusion, and for years continued to oppose the reinstatement of members of the police force and postal service who had joined the strike. Characteristically, however, he was willing to make exceptions for individual cases. In 1943 he appealed to Prime Minister King to find a job for one of the strike leaders, John Queen, who had lost his seat in the legislature and was left without an income. Queen, who had been one of the "Reds" who led the strike in 1919, was now seen as "an honest soul of the Clydeside type."[28]

The opinions of the *Free Press* during the Winnipeg General Strike reflected Dafoe's views accurately. He was certainly not a social radical, and had no sympathy for a movement which he considered, in too hasty a judgment, to be bent on revolution. As the product of an agrarian community and as the spokesman for Western agricultural life, Dafoe knew little of the working man and his problems. When labour's demands were dramatically underscored in the sympathetic strike, Dafoe read them in the extremest terms. But while he was unable to sympathize with, or even to understand, the strikers, he was not a blind reactionary. He realized that the post-war years were a period of social dislocation and change, and that the working classes had just demands that would have to be met. Two months after the strike was broken, he told a leading Winnipeg business man that the world was "in the opening

---

[28]Dafoe Papers, Dafoe to A. Bridle, June 14, 1921; D. C. Masters, *The Winnipeg General Strike* (Toronto, 1950), 134; Dafoe Papers, Dafoe to W. L. M. King, March 8, 1943.

phase of a new stage in the development of the social system under which we live; its characteristics are not yet defined, but the new spirit is best indicated by the declaration by the Peace Conference in the Labor Charter that henceforth labor is not to be regarded as a commodity." He saw this concept as a radical doctrine which entirely upset the traditional view of the relations of capital and labour. "It proposes to make business considerations subordinate to human necessities; and whether this can be done or not must be established by experimentation." To refuse to co-operate in the fulfilment of labour's desire for a fuller share of the profits of industry would be to court disaster, he warned.[29] Not very radical sentiments, to be sure, but Dafoe never considered himself a spokesman for labour in any special sense. His liberalism was closely connected with the agricultural economy and the free enterprise system. The general prosperity of Canada depended upon the well-being of the agricultural economy, and thus the labourer's welfare depended upon a stable and prosperous agricultural trade. But the end of the war brought economic depression and social dislocation to the farming community as well as to labour. It was to the farmers' problems that Dafoe turned a sympathetic ear as the last echoes of the Winnipeg General Strike were dying away.

v

Signs that the West was drawing away from the Union Government multiplied during the spring of 1919. Probably no government would have been satisfactory to the farmers in the post-war period, but one that was drifting indecisively could not satisfy their demands for measures to ameliorate their straitened conditions. On June 6, 1919, T. A. Crerar took his cue from the growing farm discontent and submitted his resignation to the Borden cabinet. The *Free Press*, whose editor probably was not surprised by the action, declared the next day that the resignation of Crerar marked the final stage in a long-foreseen political evolution. "There will emerge, sooner or later, a Western Progressive party under its own leadership which will either sit in opposition or co-operate in the government of the country on the basis of alliances that will make possible, wholly or in part, the enactment of its policies." The ambiguity of the statement reflected not only the indecision of the paper's editor about the course he would follow in the unstable political weather, but also the fact that the farmers' organizations had not yet reached a firm decision about political action.

[29]Dafoe Papers, Dafoe to J. W. W. Stewart, Aug. 12, 1919.

Sifton, who was watching political developments in the East, again warned Dafoe not to tie himself down to the continuance of the Union Government. Dafoe replied that he had no intention of committing the paper to the Unionist, Liberal, or any other party, "at least under existing circumstances." He had been carefully canvassing the situation and, though its confused state allowed few conclusions, he found some interesting material. He was certain that a concerted effort was being made to maintain the Unionist party on a permanent basis, even though it would become a thinly disguised Conservative organization. The movement might meet with success, particularly if it evolved a policy that would appeal to Quebec. There seemed little chance that it could offer a programme satisfactory to the West. In fact, Dafoe feared that regardless of what was done by either of the parties, there was little chance of stable government in Canada during the years of reconstruction. This danger worried him for Dafoe believed that "a government not strong enough to do unpopular things will be a menace."

If the Union Government succeeded in prolonging its stay in office, it would be faced by a formidable but disunited opposition. The Liberals would be split into three groups representing Eastern industrial and protectionist interests, Quebec clericalism and Western radicalism. If the Liberal convention announced for August successfully welded these disparate elements together, Dafoe questioned whether the resulting party would be anything but "an organized hypocrisy dedicated to getting and holding office." Of course the whole situation was confused by the enigma of the undeclared intentions of the organized farmers. Throughout the Prairies the farmers had already held conventions which had expressed the intention of placing candidates in the field at the coming election. But nominations had not yet been made.

Crerar had informed Dafoe that he had no confidence in the ability of the Unionists to win the West. But the former cabinet minister had said it was very possible that the leaders of the province of Quebec might be brought into the Union Government. Dafoe agreed that this was a possibility, for there was a serious division in the Quebec Liberal ranks on the tariff question. Sir Lomer Gouin and Rodolphe Lemieux might join the protectionist government forces, leaving Ernest Lapointe to lead the rump of low tariff *rouges*. "There is, I am told, a contest going on in the French Liberal party between Lapointe who represents the rouge tradition and Lemieux who is pretty tender to the 'interests'; and ... Lemieux realizes that he is going to be dislodged from his position of leadership," Dafoe told Sifton. This situation obviously opened up possibilities for a new party alignment by offering a chance for the farmers to work with part of the Liberal party. Crerar had suggested that, if the Liberals chose W. S. Fielding as their new leader and built the party on a radical platform, the West could be corralled by the Liberals. But an anti-conscriptionist leader, such as Mackenzie King, supported by the stand-pat element, would lose the Prairies. Dafoe judged that Crerar's estimation of the situation was based upon what the agrarian leader desired—a Liberal-farmer alliance. Dafoe himself was more sceptical, believing that, no matter what happened at the Liberal convention, there was a movement afoot among the farmers which neither the Liberals nor the Unionists could control. The Alberta farmers particularly seemed fully intent upon independent political action.

Dafoe thought that before any definite conclusions could be drawn, the events of the last months of the year would have to be patiently awaited. His tentative prediction, however, was that an election would result in a new House of Commons divided among a number of minority parties, some of which would have to coalesce to provide a government "strong enough to initiate and carry through policies of retrenchment and reform that will be necessary for the country if it is going to be saved from economic prostration." For his own part, the only group which attracted his whole-hearted sympathy was the Unionist-Liberals, who, having made a real sacrifice in entering the coalition, were now without a party machine and faced electoral slaughter. His chief fear was an alliance between the Roman Catholics of Quebec and their Western co-religionists.[30]

Two features of the Canadian political scene in the autumn of 1919 caused Dafoe special anxiety. The first (which has already been mentioned) was the possibility that the chaotic political conditions would produce a House of Commons unable to support a strong, stable government. He thought that the moderate farm leaders—Crerar, Langley and Dunning—hoped to make a deal with the Liberals. But, Dafoe suspected, they had started something they could not control. "I think from what I hear," he told Sifton, "that any attempt to tie the farmers' movement with the official Liberals will blow both ends out of the barrel." It seemed more probable that the farmers' representatives would be divided between those who would continue to support the Unionists and those whose radicalism would lead them to independent action. It was these radicals whom Dafoe feared and distrusted. Especially disquieting was the prospect of a union between the radical

[30]Sifton Papers, Sifton to Dafoe, July 16, 1919. Dafoe Papers, Dafoe to Sifton, July 24, 1919; Dafoe to Sifton, July 21, 1919.

farmers and the labour movement. His own wish was to see the moderates of all parties get together in a movement that would not harken to the siren calls either of extreme radicalism or of reactionary big business:

> My judgment is that after we shoot the chutes, bump the rocks, set fire to the ship, etc., we'll have to come to this union—if there's anything left to save. Much of this current "playing politics" is like people playing on sand bars while the tides rise between them and the shore. Anyone who doesn't realize how serious the possibilities are should have been in Winnipeg from May 15th to July 1st. That was an experience that confirmed all my fears for the future.

This was an expression of the very real concern of a man who had seen the ugly head of radicalism raised among the working classes in the summer of 1919 and had been thoroughly shaken. It was fine to talk about the end of the old political parties and the formation of new political alignments, but when political forces appeared that demanded fundamental social changes the old pre-war days of moderate political parties gained a new lustre. It was men of the Unionist-Liberal stripe, traditional Liberals whose plans for reform went little beyond tariff reductions, perhaps a moderate income tax, and retrenchment in government spending, that met with Dafoe's approval. The modifications in the economic system proposed by J. S. Woodsworth, or the changes in the political structure suggested by Henry Wise Wood, could hope for little support from the editor of the *Manitoba Free Press*.[31]

The Unionist-Liberals did not quickly lose hope that Dafoe might throw his support behind a revamped Unionist Government. In July 1919 Premier Borden went East in search of new pillars of strength, while N. W. Rowell journeyed West on a similar mission. Borden negotiated with Gouin, Lemieux and Lapointe in Quebec, while Rowell talked with Western moderates. Neither achieved much success, for everywhere politicians were awaiting the results of the Liberal convention. Dafoe expressed interest in the proposed Unionist reorganization, but refused to commit himself, at least until its policy statement was made public.[32]

In the late summer of 1919 the Liberals' August convention represented the primary constellation in the Canadian political universe. Everyone awaited its appearance, not least of all John Dafoe. Since the convention was dominated by Laurier Liberals, Dafoe, like many Westerners, kept a healthy distance from it. From his Winnipeg editorial

---

[31] Dafoe Papers, Dafoe to Sifton, July 24, 1919.
[32] Rowell Papers, Borden to Rowell, July 20, 1919, and Rowell to Borden, July 17, 1919; Rowell to Borden, July 15, 1919.

pedestal he saw little that attracted him arising out of the Ottawa gathering. The resolution on imperial affairs lacked the clarity that the Canadian electorate had a right to expect from a party ambitious for office. The tariff resolution was a weak child compared with the sturdy offspring that the Canadian Council of Agriculture had urged upon the convention. The *Free Press* commented sarcastically that "a remodelling of the tariff on the basis of a mathematical calculation of the resulting harvest of votes is not an adequate solution of this particular problem." Mackenzie King must have received cold comfort from the editorial that marked his giant stride to eminence as the chosen leader. Fielding, the defeated candidate, would have been the better choice, though King had the advantages of youth, experience and familiarity with industrial problems. But he suffered a serious handicap, his "record on the war; or rather his lack of record." Still, the future offered him an opportunity to prove his mettle.[33]

Dafoe believed that the selection of King greatly increased the Liberal party's difficulties in the West. Nor did he now see his own future with any added clarity. In the West, King's election had done nothing to heal the breach between Laurier Liberals and Liberal-Unionists. "It looks more and more like a strong independent farmers' movement throughout the West," Dafoe predicted shortly after the Liberal meeting. But he was not prepared to support the movement himself. That left the possibility of supporting the Unionists.[34]

In December, Dafoe's Unionist friend, N. W. Rowell, asked him to come East to discuss Unionist problems and policy. Dafoe, who was ill, declined the invitation. He explained, however, that not even good health would have allowed him to attend the meeting because the directors of the *Free Press* had decided to keep the paper in a position of "detached, watchful waiting." He admitted personal feelings of sympathy towards the Unionist administration. It had done an admirable job, but now it was drifting aimlessly. The programme which was most attractive to the *Free Press* was that of the farmers' movement, he acknowledged, but support would not be given the movement "unless it sheds its class characteristics." As for the Liberal party, Dafoe expressed no pleasure in the prospect of an increase in its parliamentary membership. A moderate centre party was the medicine that the Canadian political system required. Dafoe told Rowell that a reformed Unionist party might be able to fulfil these requirements:

I think there is a future in Canada for a moderate party, a centre party; if the govt. following can be turned into such a party, & if it will get out and

[33]*M.F.P.*, Aug. 7, 8, 9, 1919.
[34]Sifton Papers, Dafoe to Sifton, Aug. 26, 1919.

do some hard fighting it may save itself from ruin. The load it carries is the public obsession that it is the creature of the "interests". Unless in its programme it can tend to shake this deep-set belief it will carry a heavy handicap. Personally I think a declaration in favor of a tariff-for-revenue wd. do more in the way of checking this correction [sic] than anything else.[35]

Dafoe was obviously withdrawing his support from the Union Government with reluctance; he had fought for its formation and many of his closest political friends had joined it. But its purpose had been served, and its former friends, especially in the West were turning against it. Perhaps when it appeared evident in December 1919 that Sir Robert Borden would soon be retiring from the prime ministership it became easier for Dafoe to cut his last ties with the wartime Government. Dafoe had watched the Prime Minister's declining health with growing concern and agreed with his decision to retire. It was a warm friend who wrote:

Nothing can detract from the position which you will hold in history as the war premier; but I shd. be sorry to see it followed by an anti-climax in wh. with decreasing strength you struggle against increasing & multiplying difficulties. You have earned an honorable discharge; do not go in for a new campaign unless this is your real desire. We are bound to have years of political turmoil in Canada; no man, nor combination of men, can in my judgment, control or direct developments: we are in the lap of the gods.[36]

Borden's retirement marked the real conclusion of the war period in Canadian politics. Both the old leaders, Sir Wilfrid and Sir Robert, had now gone. The Liberals had found a new champion, and the Conservatives had only a short wait before Borden's mantle was passed on to Arthur Meighen. But it was not merely the old leaders that had taken their leave. The old parties were gone too. King and Meighen were soon to be joined by T. A. Crerar, leader of a new movement just entering the lists. Each of these young political leaders faced a future filled with uncertainty. Both at home and abroad the new world had been ushered in. Dafoe judged with more acuteness than he perhaps realized when he wrote, "we are in the lap of the gods."

[35]Dafoe Papers, Rowell to Dafoe, Dec. 11, 1919; Rowell Papers, Dafoe to Rowell, Dec. 13, 1919.
[36]Borden Papers, Dafoe to Borden, Dec. 21, 1919.

VII. "In the Lap of the Gods"
1920-3

++

DURING THE LAST MONTHS OF 1920 the pieces of the Canadian political puzzle gradually began to fall into place. Dafoe was both observer and participant in the events which brought a solution. He was an observer because he thought it was necessary to have a sure grasp of the direction in which political trends were moving before committing the *Free Press* to the support of any one party. He was a participant because he held considered views about the needs of post-war Canada, though he was less certain of the means to the desired objective. He was clear on one point: he could not return to a Liberal party dominated by the Liberals who had opposed conscription.[1]

The Liberal party had been destroyed in the West and this situation gave the Union Government an opportunity to revive its fortunes. Actually Dafoe had little hope, and perhaps less desire, to see the Unionists take advantage of this opportunity unless they were prepared to take over a large part of the farmers' programme. Already he was considering the possibility of a new Liberal movement based on the farmers' organizations but broadened out to include other like-minded individuals and groups. The farmers' movement, he admitted, was a class organization which had grown up in reaction to the class-dominated governments that had ruled Canada since the inception of the National Policy. "But there is no reason why it [the farmers' movement] should retain these characteristics; to the extent that it does it will weaken its opportunities for usefulness," the *Free Press* argued on January 9, 1920.

Dafoe had no sympathy with the farmers' organization as a class movement. The radical agrarians like Henry Wise Wood of Alberta who advocated "group government" based on class were condemned as the promoters of a "soviet system." But he did see in the agrarian protest movement a distinct possibility of forcing a new alignment in Canadian

[1] Rowell Papers, Dafoe to Rowell, Jan. 11, 1920.

politics which would unite all those people who opposed government by the "interests." In the post-war political flux he thought he could perceive this realignment taking shape. He had talked with several men from various parts of the nation and all the signs seemed to point in the right direction. T. A. Crerar had been especially enlightening. The coming election, Crerar reported early in 1920, would result in the return of a large number of Progressives; he hoped for about seventy, as he had no wish to become Prime Minister. Of course there would be some trouble in Ontario, where there was a high tariff interest among the farmers, but this group could be appeased. More important, the agrarian leader had maintained that the Liberals were so divided on the tariff issue that it was quite possible an election would be followed by the departure of the protectionist Liberals, probably led by Sir Lomer Gouin, from the party of King in favour of the Unionist camp. The low tariff Liberals would then be free to coalesce with the farmers.

This opinion seemed to have a good deal to recommend it, for Dafoe had corroborative information from other sources. C. F. Crandall of the *Montreal Star* had told him that the Liberal party was seething with discontent. Even those elements in the party which had combined to give King the leadership were having second thoughts about their new captain. Dafoe was by no means in despair when he drew his conclusions from these facts:

> I see nothing before the Liberal party but disintegration even though it should come back to the next House with a considerable group. Sooner or later one wing of the Liberals is bound to unite with the farmers to form a new party which will be in effect a Liberal party, although it will probably bear some other name. The other wing of the Liberal party is bound to be forced by common economic interests into a merger with the other groups which now are loosely tied together to form the Unionist party.

The result would be a stand-pat government faced by a truly Liberal opposition led by Crerar, who would likely be associated with Mackenzie King. Dafoe saw only one possible weakness in this prediction. Strangely, perhaps, the weakness was not a fear that King would be able to hold the warring factions of his party together. Rather Dafoe saw the real danger within the Western forces, for there were already signs of friction between the radicals who were "men ingrained with class feeling who feel that the country is theirs & that they are invincible," and the moderates like Crerar who believed that the movement should be broadened out. Dafoe wished at all costs to prevent a division within the Western ranks.[2]

Thus early in 1920 Dafoe had begun to see his task in the strange

[2]*M.F.P.*, Nov. 5, 1919; Dafoe Papers, Memo re political situation, Jan. 20, 1920; Sifton Papers, Dafoe to Sifton, Jan. 22, 1920.

conditions of the post-war political scene. The Western political forces had to be kept united, or at the very least, the radicals had to be prevented from gaining ascendancy in the movement. If this aim were achieved, then a new alignment could be organized which would provide a realistic division of the parties into progressive and conservative. This assessment of Dafoe's provides the clue to his view of the purpose of the Progressive movement. To him the Progressives were nothing more than Liberals, perhaps not even "Liberals in a hurry," but simply Liberals stripped of all the reactionary barnacles that they had acquired during Laurier's years of leadership. The worst of these were the Eastern business interests which had kept the tariff at a level detrimental to the interests of Western Canada. The tariff was the prime issue, the test which separated the reactionary from the progressive elements. In 1927 Dafoe defined Progressive as "a word used to describe candidates pledged to bring about tariff reduction in the interests of agricultural production." The Progressives might promote other policies, especially those deemed necessary to Western prosperity, but the tariff was the primary concern. Dafoe believed that a low tariff party could be established on a national scale with supporters from all sections of the country. The Western agrarians would form the nucleus of the party and, until it could attract national support, it would act as a powerful sectional bloc which would prevent the business-dominated parties from taking steps that would jeopardize Western interests.[3]

In the columns of his newspaper Dafoe set out the economic policy which he believed would best serve the West, and therefore the whole nation. His basic assumption was that the economic well-being of the country depended upon a thriving agricultural industry. The *Free Press* made this point clearly when it stated on October 18, 1920:

> To state the divergence of outlook in the broadest terms the Western tariff reformers indict the policy which has been adhered to for forty years as consciously tending to encourage the development of manufacturing and the growth of cities as the greatest factor in national development; and they advance the alternative of a policy devoted primarily to the encouragement of basic industries, with special reference to agriculture, urging that upon this basis, once obtained, a diversified and thriving economic structure can profitably rest.

Though tariff reform was his projected panacea for Canada's economic problems, Dafoe was by no means a classical free trader. He did not need Sifton to warn him of the "disastrous conditions" which would

[3]Dafoe, "The Problems of Canada" in Sir Cecil J. B. Hurst *et al.*, *Great Britain and the Dominions* (Chicago, 1928), 169.

result from "a crusade to revolutionize the tariff and put taxes on income and business." He was in favour of lowering the tariff, but not of abolishing it. The best tariff "at present," he assured his employer, was one "designed primarily to produce revenue." Nor did Dafoe favour any other radical changes in the National Policy, even when these might have bettered the position of the farmer. Government control of grain sales was not a policy which he fancied. Indeed he found it best to avoid the issue because opposition might damage the *Free Press*'s reputation. In fact he hoped to avoid all radical proposals which might limit the ability of the Progressive movement to become a national party.[4]

As Dafoe watched the three new political leaders, King, Meighen and Crerar, manœuvre for position with the electorate, and especially with the Western voters, he became more strongly convinced that a political realignment was in the making. Various informants led him to believe that the new Prime Minister, Arthur Meighen, was making a concerted effort to bring all the protectionist interests, including those in the Liberal party, into the Government ranks in preparation for an assault on the Western farmers' stronghold. This report helped to confirm certain conclusions that Dafoe had reached about the course of Canadian politics at the end of 1920. Mackenzie King had visited the West and the reception he had received convinced Dafoe that there was no possibility of a pre-election marriage between Liberals and Progressives. Any attempt to force a wedding would be met by a revolt on the part of two segments of the farmers' movement. In the first place, former Conservative farmers would never agree to it. Secondly, the radical wing of the movement would interpret the move as a betrayal to the "interests." Therefore, it was certain that Crerar would lead a group of Progressives in the next House of Commons.

Crerar's main conviction, Dafoe believed, was that the country required free trade, "though he recognizes that it must be reached in Canada by a series of successive steps." This firm conviction did not preclude the possibility of close Liberal-Progressive co-operation after an election. Indeed Dafoe believed that a post-election coalition between Crerar and 75 per cent of the Liberals on the basis of the Progressive tariff policy was a virtual certainty. "I think this tariff factor is going to be the determining factor in the alignment of the parties, which is now in process throughout Canada," he told Sifton, "and that in essence Mr. Meighen has got the matter correctly sized up." On the

[4]Dafoe Papers, Sifton to Dafoe, Feb. 10, 1920; Dafoe to Sifton, April 3, 1920; Dafoe to Sifton, Oct. 11, 1920.

whole, Crerar was a pretty safe Liberal, Dafoe thought. He had a good deal of practical business and political experience and showed little interest in the more radical proposals made by the farmers, such as public ownership of utilities and land taxes. "In fact," Dafoe summed up shrewdly, ". . . Crerar is nothing more or less than a Liberal of the type with which you and I were quite familiar prior to 1896."[5]

Dafoe found himself very much in sympathy with Crerar's brand of Progressivism, a Progressivism which was in fact hardly progressive at all. In essence it involved looking backward rather than forward. Canada had taken a wrong turning in 1879 in adopting a protective tariff. At least this was the view that many of Macdonald's Liberal critics had held before 1896. Once in office, however, the Laurier Liberals had followed virtually the same policy. Now was the time to retrace those steps, the Dafoe-Crerar Progressives maintained, and return to the golden age of free trade, or at least the bronze age of freer trade. That is what Dafoe meant when he described Crerar and the National Progressives as "the real inheritors of the Liberal economic tradition. . . ." What in fact the Dafoe-Crerar Progressives desired was a radical modification of the national policies for a conservative purpose. They believed that a decrease in the tariff, and one or two other measures to protect Western interests, would ensure the importance of agriculture in Canada and save it from the dominance of those business interests which had been nurtured by the tariff and stimulated by the war. If the tariff was kept high the agricultural population would be seriously depleted by urbanization, a shift which, the *Free Press* remarked on October 18, 1920, would lead to "social and economic convulsion." Dafoe's enthusiasm for the Progressive movement, or at least the section of it that followed Crerar, was based on a realization that it was not a socially radical movement.[6]

Dafoe's view of the nature of Canadian politics was a realistic one. Interests, sections, groups—though curiously not classes—struggle for control of the state in order that policies which best serve their needs will be put into effect. He once wrote that politics is "war in which nothing is foul if it furthers the end of attaining or holding power—for the purpose, as is always avowed, of putting into force policies which will save the state, or of preventing the application of policies destructive of the Commonwealth." Thus, if the West was to protect its interests by breaking the protectionist hold over the nation's policies, it had to sound forth at Ottawa with one voice. Dafoe hoped and believed that

[5]Sifton Papers, Dafoe to Sifton, Oct. 11, Nov. 10, 1920.
[6]Dafoe Papers, Dafoe to A. Bridle, June 14, 1921.

this would not be a class or sectional voice, but rather a national one, made up of all the primary producers of the country singing for a lower tariff.[7]

Dafoe watched like a hawk, a hungry hawk, for every sign of disintegration in the Liberal party. Late in 1920 he remarked to Sifton, "My 'hunch' that there is bound to be a break-up of the French group with the city Libs. going to the Govt. is stronger than ever. I have heard a hint that the replacing of Meighen by some compromise leader may be a condition." The observation was not without an element of wishful thinking. He and Crerar hoped to see the rapid splintering off of the protectionist Liberals so that all the truly progressive, low tariff elements in the country could be absorbed into a single movement, headed in all probability by Crerar and E. C. Drury of Ontario. King, it was agreed, was a Liberal, but he was also a hopeless leader. Dafoe had the impression that, although Crerar was prepared to work with King, he was not prepared to work for him.[8]

Apart from failure to drive the protectionist elements from the Liberal party, Dafoe realized that his hopes for a broadly based progressive party could be jeopardized by at least two other dangers. Most serious, perhaps, was the internal division within the Western movement. The class-conscious agrarians, Dafoe realized, "antagonize the very element which Crerar is trying, by broadening out, to add to his party." It was no time for rejoicing when Henry Wise Wood's followers, after virtually defying Crerar, won a by-election in Medicine Hat in the summer of 1921. Equally distressing was the fact that the Western Liberal party was unwilling to abdicate its position in favour of the Progressives. To divide the vote between Liberals and Progressives would only add to the advantages of the Unionist enemy. "I am more and more convinced," Dafoe wrote in February 1921, "that the tactics for King are to make a virtue of necessity and renounce his right to contest the prairie constituencies with a fine gesture of apparent disinterestedness." King apparently agreed with this view, although he could not always control the local organization.[9]

Though Dafoe hoped for co-operation rather than conflict between the Liberals and Progressives in Western constituencies, he was not anxious to promote a hasty, ill-considered alliance. Alliance after the Progressives had been given an opportunity to show their electoral

[7]Dafoe, *Clifford Sifton in Relation to His Times* (Toronto, 1931), 172-3; M.F.P., Dec. 13, 1920.
[8]Sifton Papers, Dafoe to Sifton, Dec. 18, 1920; Dafoe Papers, Dafoe to Sifton, Feb. 14, 1921.
[9]Dafoe Papers, Dafoe to Sifton, Jan. 26, June 30, Feb. 26, 1921.

strength, rather than a pre-election agreement, seemed the best course to follow. Dafoe expressed no regret when combined Liberal and Progressive forces in the House of Commons failed to bring down the Government on a want-of-confidence motion in the spring of 1921. Had the motion carried, he thought, the Progressives might have been obliged to aid in the formation of a government whose policies would be unattractive to the farmers. As the day of the inevitable election approached, Dafoe grew increasingly convinced that Mackenzie King was the Liberal's poorest asset and if the Progressives played their cards carefully they might not only win control of the Liberal party, but also take over its leadership.[10]

By the summer of 1921 Dafoe was moving his newspaper into a position to fight an election. He was not in a hurry for the contest, especially as there had not yet been a redistribution of seats which would give the West some additional strength. Equally important was the need to establish the *Free Press* as the farmers' spokesman. As always Dafoe was conscious that the newspaper business was a commercial as well as an educational and political enterprise. Other papers such as the *Regina Leader* only did themselves injury by attempting to "tie the farmers' movement in Western Canada to the Liberal chariot"; the *Free Press* would serve both its own and Western interests better by remaining independent. As the 1921 election campaign opened, Dafoe told his employer that "our real objective in this campaign ought to be to confirm and reinforce the position of the *Free Press* as the great independent newspaper of Western Canada."[11]

With this objective in view, the *Free Press* began a series of campaign editorials which, rather than recommending any one political party, presented a statement of policies attuned to the needs of the West. The tariff naturally played a leading part in the campaign. Here Dafoe defended Crerar and the moderate Progressives and their policy of a tariff for revenue. When the critics of the Progressives attempted to brand them as free traders, the *Free Press* (July 30, 1921) flatly denied the charge: "Hon. T. A. Crerar and the other leaders of the Progressives have stated repeatedly that they have no intention whatever of revolutionary changes in the tariff if they are made responsible for the government of the country."

Another important question which was frequently brought to the

[10]Dafoe Papers, Dafoe to T. A. Crerar, March 7, 1921; Dafoe to Sifton, May 2, 1921.
[11]*Ibid.*, Dafoe to Sifton, Dec. 7, 1920; Sifton Papers, Dafoe to Sifton, Oct. 1, 1921.

attention of *Free Press* readers was that of the railways. Dafoe had given serious attention to the railway problem which had harassed successive governments. In 1917 he suggested a plan to Prime Minister Borden for the amalgamation of the Grand Trunk and the Canadian Northern under government control but, he hoped, beyond political interference. His chief concern was to ensure that an efficient and competitive system was maintained. During the campaign of 1921 the so-called Shaughnessy plan for the amalgamation of the two national systems was the subject of much discussion. Dafoe, who was suspicious of the influence of the Canadian Pacific Railway, especially in the Liberal party, recognized in the Shaughnessy plan a distinct threat to Western interests. Writing to Sir Joseph Flavelle, he emphasized Western objections to railway monopoly:

> I see that down East a good many people are flirting with the Shaughnessy plan. I would say that Western opinion would be almost solidly against any such solution to the problem. The West knew once upon a time the effects of a railroad monopoly and the tradition of disservice and insolence is still very strong. I don't think anybody in the West wants a repetition of the dose.

The same line was followed on the editorial page where the Montreal Liberals came in for particularly sharp criticism. To accept the Shaughnessy plan, it was argued, would be for the Canadian people to put on "the collar of servitude to the great corporation interests which centre in Montreal and Toronto."[12]

Similarly, the question of Western natural resources came up for discussion. Before the war the *Free Press* had repeatedly berated Prime Minister Borden for failing to fulfil his promise to return the West's natural resources. Shortly after the war Dafoe again turned to this problem. "The present condition is wholly indefensible and simply adds to the bad feeling between East and West which is already altogether too strong," he told Sir John Willison. During the 1921 campaign, the *Free Press* emphasized the claim that one of the West's major demands was for the return of the remaining lands and compensation for those already alienated.[13]

In sum, though claiming independence, the *Free Press* presented a programme during the 1921 election which was closely parallel to that of the Progressives. A month before the contest closed, Dafoe remained uncertain of the outcome. Nevertheless he ventured the prediction that

[12]Borden Papers, Dafoe to Borden, n.d. 1917; Flavelle Papers, Dafoe to Sir Joseph Flavelle, Oct. 21, 1921; *M.F.P.*, Oct. 6, 1921.
[13]*M.F.P.*, Oct. 29, 1913; Willison Papers, Dafoe to Sir John Willison, Dec. 10, 1920; *M.F.P.*, Oct. 7, 1921.

anti-Government candidates would sweep the country. This, he suggested, would mean the return of from thirty to thirty-five followers for Crerar from the Prairies.[14]

Dafoe was not far wrong in his calculation, though even he had to admit that the stinging defeat of the Government and the election of sixty-five Progressives in the West and Ontario "exceeded my expectations." Even with King and the Liberals back in office, the West could expect to have its problems sympathetically considered with this united representation in Ottawa. The *Free Press* announced the election returns in confident tones on December 7, but at the same time underlined its particular assessment of Progressive strength as "a genuine and sincere movement of Liberalism and as such worthy of support."[15]

On the same day Dafoe let Sifton know that Crerar was going to assume an attitude of "watchful waiting," giving the new Government scope to develop its policies. He was speaking for himself as well as for Crerar when he observed that the Progressive leader did not have very much confidence in the new administration.[16] On December 8 the *Free Press* explained at length the nature and purpose of the Progressive movement. It is no accident that these views reflected the confused and paradoxical position of the Progressive politicians in the Canadian political scene. The editorial explained:

The Progressive movement as we have understood it is not a political enterprise looking to office. It is a movement of opinion intended to determine the strength of a programme of proposed reforms with the electors....

The Progressives, we take it, will not regard themselves as a political party out of office, and therefore bound to bring about, if possible, the downfall of the government of the day. Rather they will regard themselves as holding a watching brief for the public to see that the promises of better government and wiser policies made in the campaign are fulfilled. If the Liberal government proves worthy of its name and lives up to the engagements made on behalf of his party by Mr. Mackenzie King, the Progressives will pursue, we have no doubt, a course of sympathetic and useful co-operation with the new administration. There are, it is very clear, strong reactionary elements in the Liberal party as returned to power. The presence in the House of sixty-odd Progressive may be useful to Mr. King in making it possible for him to hold them in check....

The future of the Progressive party will take care of itself. If the Liberal party devotes itself to Progressive policies and shows itself in office devoted to the public interests, there may be little need in the future for a Progressive party. But if the great and powerful influences, to whom all governments look alike, succeed in making the Liberal government the instrument of their

[14]Sifton Papers, Dafoe to Sifton, Nov. 5, 1921.
[15]Dafoe Papers, Dafoe to Sifton, Dec. 7, 1921.
[16]*Ibid.*, Dec. 7, 1921.

policy, as they will most certainly attempt to do, the public will have in Parliament, in the Progressives, champions of their interests.

The question which Dafoe, like the Progressives, faced at the close of 1921 was whether to be or not to be a Liberal. There was a good deal of Danish uncertainty in Dafoe's mind when he discovered the movement which he had supported holding second place in the parliamentary standing. He had not really expected events to take this sharp a turn. The anomalous, illogical structure of the Canadian party system had survived his pre-election analysis. The expected realignment had not taken place. Now his Progressive friends found themselves associated in opposition with the worst sinners, the Conservative protectionists, facing the more attractive, though many-faced, Liberal Government. Or was there still an opportunity for a truly liberal administration of Liberals and Progressives? Mackenzie King was prepared, indeed forced, to explore this possibility; Dafoe hoped to assist in moulding just such an alliance.

ii

During the last weeks of the 1921 election campaign, Mackenzie King's attitude to the Progressives had hardened. On their side the Progressives had shown a wariness of King, or more particularly of his Eastern associates. King may have seen the farmers' attitude as "the irresponsible actions of a group of naive reformers," but it would have been more just to have judged them political realists who saw, or thought they saw, that the inexperienced Liberal leader would be unable to control people like Sir Lomer Gouin. At any rate, during November King had cast some harsh words at the Western movement, warning the farmers that he would not lead a coalition. In other words he would accept them into the Liberal fold only on his own terms—terms which meant absorption into the Liberal party. Once the election returns had been calculated, King had to face the fact that he had only a plurality, not a majority of seats. The Liberal leader now began his long courtship of the Progressives. In the negotiations King took the understandable position that supporters already in his hand—the Eastern members whom the Progressives found unpalatable—were safer than agrarian members who remained figuratively in the bush. He therefore offered the Westerners very little in the way of concessions. The shrewd Westerners, brought up in familiarity with horse-trading, remained unconvinced by Liberal promises.[17]

[17]R. MacG. Dawson, *William Lyon Mackenzie King, I, 1874-1923* (Toronto, 1958), 335.

In the weeks of negotiations which followed the election, Dafoe played the role of a very interested observer. Essentially he agreed with Crerar, though at times he felt it necessary to encourage the Progressive leader to maintain his independence in the face of Liberal blandishments. Dafoe and Sifton were both anxious to prevent power falling into the hands of the old guard of the Liberal party. Sir Clifford had warned King not to take a definite stand against coalition and now felt that the Liberal leader was regretting his adamant pre-election pose. Sifton argued that the Progressives should only join the Liberals if they were offered half the cabinet posts. He told Dafoe to warn the Progressive leaders to avoid the fate of the Unionist-Liberals who, having entered Union Government without a written agreement, had been swallowed up. If the Progressive leaders were too easily seduced by the Liberals, their followers would turn on them with the wrath of the betrayed.[18]

There was no need to warn Dafoe of these pitfalls. Andrew Haydon, the Liberal organizer, had already arrived in Winnipeg to assist King in his ambition of "shewing the 'interests' that wise conservative leadership of radical forces is better than reactionary Toryism." It remained to be seen whether the Progressives could be satisfied with "wise conservative leadership." Dafoe took no direct part in the talks between Haydon and the Progressive leaders, though Crerar kept him apprised of all the developments. He was well satisfied when he found that the farm politicians were reluctant to commit themselves to the King administration without a written agreement that would guarantee the implementation of the policies desired by the West. Nor was he optimistic about the prospect of King's accepting such a stipulation; King had not yet realized the profound nature of Western unrest and therefore would not make the concession necessary to win Crerar. Without the Progressives, Dafoe wrote, "it will not be very much of a government, and I should not be surprised if its life should be brief and far from merry." Any coalition that was arranged, he held, should be the result of the political realignment that he so desired. Throughout the tense period of negotiations, the *Free Press* continued to hammer home its editor's view that a truly liberal government should result from any Liberal-Progressive agreement. "The compromise and skilled evasions of the Laurier regime will no longer serve," it declared, and demanded that "those Montreal Tories who call themselves Liberals" should be driven from the party.[19]

During the negotiations, Dafoe's powerful paper was voicing what was

---

[18]Dafoe Papers, Sifton to Dafoe, Dec. 8, 1921; Sifton Papers, Sifton to T. A. Crerar, Dec. 12, 1921; Dafoe Papers, Sifton to Dafoe, Dec. 14, 1921.

[19]Dawson, *Mackenzie King*, 316; Dafoe Papers, Dafoe to Sifton, Dec. 19, 1921; *M.F.P.*, Dec. 21, 22, 1921.

essentially the Progressive line. Or at least, the line of the Manitoba moderates led by Crerar. The radical Progressives, always suspicious of any alliance with the sinful Easterners, were greatly troubled by the influence which the *Free Press* was thought to exert over Crerar. During the period of negotiation between the Liberals and Progressives, the *Farmers' Advocate* complained bitterly that "the *Manitoba Free Press* is telling Mr. Crerar what to do. And Mr. Crerar listens to the *Free Press*." There was a good deal of justification for this complaint. Though Dafoe and Crerar agreed basically about the purposes of the farmers' movement, Dafoe thought that the Progressive leader had a "boyish and trustful nature" and could easily be misled by nebulous Liberal promises. "I think it was his friends who saved him from putting his neck in the noose," the worldly-wise Dafoe remarked after the negotiations had failed. For his own part, Dafoe was wary of committing the *Free Press* to any political combination, and so attempted to avoid the appearance of being the mouthpiece of the Progressives rather than an independent Western spokesman. In this sense Dafoe wished to exercise the luxury, open to journalists and intellectuals, of telling the politicians what to do without accepting any of the responsibility or risk of implementing policy.[20]

By the end of December the negotiations had proved fruitless. Perhaps the reason was that the Progressives would not "relinquish their propensity for coyness and unreliability." But the Westerners did have a thorny path to tread. On the one hand the Liberals offered no specific guarantees about policy, and the suspicious Progressives thought that unexplained changes in the proposed cabinet slate confirmed their view of the nefarious influence of the Eastern interests. On the other hand Crerar was faced with the fractious criticism of his more radical followers. The very nature of the movement made it virtually impossible for a leader to speak for all the members. Many farmers, according to Dafoe, regarded the coalition negotiations as "one of the old-fashioned manoeuvers by which they were to be buncoed in the interests of the big corporations." Whether this is evidence of a "narrow" outlook and "incredibly naive minds," as Professor Dawson suggested, is at least debatable. However much King's later course of action was necessitated by the absence of the farm leaders from his cabinet, he certainly showed himself reluctant to annoy the "interests" by implementing policies which met the Progressives' demands.[21]

[20]P. F. Sharp, *The Agrarian Revolt in Western Canada* (St. Paul, 1948), 157; Dafoe Papers, Dafoe to Sifton, Dec. 31, 19, 1921.
[21]Dawson, *Mackenzie King*, 368; Dafoe Papers, Dafoe to Sifton, Dec. 31, 1921; Dawson, *Mackenzie King*, 371.

After the failure of the negotiations King went ahead and announced an entirely Liberal cabinet on December 29, 1921. The next day, the *Free Press* carefully commented on the new administration, pointing out that it should be given an opportunity to display its wares. The fact that Gouin rather than Lapointe was awarded the important portfolio of Justice did not pass without critical comment. Privately, Dafoe was much more severe. He claimed that "the Montreal interests have never been so well satisfied with a Government as with this one & regard themselves as definitely in charge of Canada." Mackenzie King, Dafoe had heard from a friend, was being put in his place "as per programme."[22]

The first opportunity to shape a realignment in Canadian politics had been missed, but Dafoe did not drop the idea. For the moment he merely retired to his editorial office to watch the activities of the new Government. Even though the Progressives had not entered the Liberal inner sanctum, they were strong enough in Parliament to prevent the fledgling Government from falling wholly under the influence of the scheming Eastern business interests. But the Progressives, too, had to be watched, prompted and generally kept on their toes or the whole movement might collapse in ridicule. Not least of all they had to remain united and the shrill agrarian radicalism of the left wing muted.

iii

After the dust had settled following the inconclusive cabinet negotiations of December 1921, Dafoe travelled down to the nation's capital to survey the scene. On the whole he was satisfied with what he saw. The atmosphere seemed quiet and he believed that, unless the Government allowed the railway question to explode, the opening session of the new Parliament would be a peaceful one. The Progressives needed a session to get their sea-legs, but were already making a good public impression. Barring the unforeseen, Dafoe still felt that all signs seemed to point in the direction of political developments that would make the Progressives the real Liberal party after a splintering-off of right-wing Liberals. He judged that the prospects for the existing Tory party were bleak. "All the powerful interests upon whom they rely for support," he told Sifton, "are really enlisted behind the Government and they have as a leader a man who is never likely to develop in strength either in Western Canada or in the Province of Quebec."[23]

But even in the first session, which had begun so quietly, problems developed which demanded Dafoe's constant attention. One of the first

[22]Sifton Papers, Dafoe to Sifton, Feb. 15, 1922.
[23]Dafoe Papers, Dafoe to Sifton, March 30, 1922.

to arise was one which directly affected the grain growers' interests and also illustrated the division in the Progressive movement. This was the problem of marketing grain. In 1916 the Borden Government had established a board to control the sale of wheat. At the conclusion of the war, the Unionists allowed the forces of the free market to come back into play. In the face of the post-war depression some farmers came to the conclusion that government-control grain sales were the best guarantee of just prices. In 1922 the King Government offered legislation to re-establish the board through Dominion-provincial co-operation; the measure was dependent upon passage of concurrent legislation by the three Prairie legislatures. The Progressives were by no means agreed in their attitude to the proposal. Crerar was opposed to it, while some of his more radical followers, especially those who represented Saskatchewan and Alberta, where wheat was predominant in the economy, favoured it. As Sifton put it, the Progressives made "a complete mess of the Wheat Board business at Ottawa." Neither Dafoe nor Sifton favoured the idea, but both were concerned about the rift which the issue caused in the farmers' ranks. Ultimately the proposal was destroyed when Manitoba failed by a narrow margin to pass the necessary enabling legislation. But the effect of the debate on the question was to divide the Progressive forces. The centre of the discontent was occupied by Wood of Alberta who was unhappy about Crerar's moderate leadership. Wood believed that Crerar's influence had destroyed the wheat board. He was reported to have remarked after an interview with the national leader that "he never knew a dog which had been killing sheep which did not have a perfectly guileless look upon its face after the deed was done." Clearly the Western bloc was anything but monolithic![24]

Dafoe had more reason for satisfaction with his Progressive protégés' achievements when the freight rates question was discussed. During the war increases in the rates had been necessitated by rising labour and operational costs. Not only had over-all increases been granted by the Board of Railway Commissioners, but the Government, in July 1918, had suspended the Crow's Nest Pass Agreement. By this agreement special rates on the Canadian Pacific Railway had been granted to Western wheat and flour moving East and to certain agricultural necessities moving West. At the conclusion of the war the Union Government decided to continue the suspension for an additional three years. Thus the question came up for reconsideration in the session of 1922. At the end of March the *Free Press* stated its position bluntly. The West, it claimed, "regards the Crow's Nest Pass Agreement as its freight rate charter and will certainly never forego it for something less satisfactory."

[24]*Ibid.*, Sifton to Dafoe, April 22, 1922; Dafoe to Sifton, May 6, 1922.

Dafoe kept up the barrage throughout the sessions of the special parliamentary committee which the King Government established to consider freight rates. On this question the Progressives were able to present a united front while the Government struggled with its internal divisions. The result was a compromise which gave the West part of its demand. Though the agreement was suspended for an additional two years on westbound commodities, the special rates for eastbound wheat and flour were immediately re-established. The *Free Press* interpreted this as a victory for a "united and defiant West." But even this partial triumph for the Progressives was the exception rather than the rule during their first parliamentary session, and it was only accomplished because of the difficult position in which the Liberals found themselves. Moreover, the concession on freight rates was probably offered as bait with which to catch Western support for the budget.[25]

Certainly the 1922 budget contained little to recommend it to the Progressives. Other than offering some slight reductions on the duty on imported farm implements, the Liberals were satisfied to leave the tariff as they had inherited it from Meighen. This was a sharp disappointment to Dafoe, and he interpreted it as another sign of the continued influence of the Montreal "Tories" in King's cabinet. In fact he believed that King and Fielding had originally planned more sweeping tariff changes, but had been forced to relent to the threats of "Gouin and his crowd." At any rate, on the issue which had been of first importance to the Progressives—the tariff—their first session in Parliament brought little cause for rejoicing.[26]

When the session concluded, Dafoe's feelings were mixed. Certainly his hope for a new political alignment seemed no nearer fruition. At times during the session, as in the debate on freight rates, he had almost despaired of its ever being achieved. "I expect the Crow's Nest Pass business to put a chasm between the Liberals and the Progressives which will never be bridged," he complained to Sifton. Still, it had turned out all right in the end. At home in Manitoba, there were reassuring signs that the Liberals and Progressives were moving together at least on the provincial level. This development was much to be desired, for Dafoe believed that after an inconclusive election, a Liberal-Progressive fusion would prevent a "Farmer-Labor combination which would be very unfortunate." Dafoe believed that the independent Labour party of Manitoba was "theoretically, at any rate, identified with the communist political philosophy," and he had earlier remarked that J. S. Woodsworth

[25]*M.F.P.*, March 31, July 4, 1922.
[26]Dafoe Papers, Dafoe to Sifton, June 8, 1922.

was "almost mentally unbalanced with respect to Social and Labor questions." Dafoe realized that there were enough troublemakers in the farmers' movement without adding difficulties by allowing the farmers to fall into an alliance with labour.[27]

Crerar had experienced serious difficulties with the radicals during the parliamentary session, but fortunately he had done some plain talking to them in caucus, and almost the whole group had lined up behind him by the end of the session. On the credit side, balanced against the left-wing snipers, there were signs that the moderate Progressives had found many friendly associates among Liberals in Ottawa. Here was an optimistic sign that some of the low tariff Liberals from Western Ontario and Quebec were growing restive in a party which seemed to be under the muscular thumb of the Montreal business interests. Especially promising was the growing division in the Quebec Liberal group. Though Lapointe was still not in a position to raise the standard of revolt against the Gouin forces, his strength was important. What was needed most of all, Dafoe believed, was for King to make some obvious demonstration of goodwill towards the Western members. If only King could manage to rid his Government of such reactionaries as Gouin, J. A. Robb and George Graham, then an alliance or coalition with the Progressives would be virtually assured. But to Dafoe, it was obvious that the real weakness was the Prime Minister. "Personally, I might say, I doubt whether anything will happen during the parliamentary recess," he wrote disconsolately. "I don't think King has the courage to 'bell the cat'. Matters will probably drift along until the next session of parliament when a crisis may develop." Dafoe had no doubt that King's heart was in the right place, that he was basically a progressive Liberal. But, he said, in a judgment that must have haunted him later, "his political amateurishness in view of the position he holds is almost unbelieveable."[28]

At the end of 1922 Dafoe had to do some fresh thinking about the Progressive movement. The situation which caused this reassessment was T. A. Crerar's decision to retire from the leadership. In Dafoe's estimation Crerar's decision was a temporary blow to "the prospect of fusion between the Liberals and Progressives." But he was still convinced that the movement was necessary. As the Progressives were preparing for the opening of their convention in Winnipeg in November 1922, the

[27]*Ibid.*, May 6, July 7, July 29, 1922; Sifton Papers, Dafoe to Sifton, Oct. 1, 1921.
[28]Dafoe Papers, Dafoe to Sifton, July 29, 11, 1922; Dafoe to W. F. Maclean, Sept. 9, 1922.

Free Press advanced its reasons for believing that the farmers' movement should persist in its political activity. The Western voter, the paper declared on November 1,

can find no home in the Conservative party under a leadership which is becoming constantly more reactionary upon the very questions upon which such an elector is primarily interested. The Liberal party affords a likelier refuge, but while Sir Lomer Gouin assumes the airs and exercises the functions of a joint leader with Mr. King, there will be decided reluctance by tens of thousands of voters in Western Canada and elsewhere to enroll in that army.

Ultimately, the *Free Press* made plain, the Progressives and Liberals would form a single party, but the time had not yet arrived. Despite initial doubts, Dafoe was soon suggesting that Crerar's retirement might even help the coalition movement, for now the Manitoba politician would have a free hand to deal with the left-wingers and he could "make things pretty warm for Mr. H. W. Wood." And while Crerar was pursuing this objective the movement would continue to follow a moderate policy. This future was assured by the choice of Robert Forke as Crerar's successor. He would not "be trapped by Mr. Meighen into upsetting the government and forcing an election prematurely."[29]

At the close of the year Dafoe was not completely without a feeling of satisfaction about the achievements and future of the farmers' political movement. It had made some impression in Parliament, and though it had not been able to force a political realignment, at least the moderates had maintained their pre-eminence in the party councils. Most promising of all, perhaps, were the renewed rumours of party convulsions in the East. King was reported to have made a move to get rid of Gouin by appointing him Canadian Minister in Washington. Moreover, there was again talk of a coalition of Gouin Liberals and the Conservative party. Plans for party realignment were by no means hopeless, Dafoe thought.[30]

But these harbingers of political developments did nothing to abate the temper that had produced the Western uprising. In fact at the beginning of 1923 Dafoe thought that, despite some signs of improving economic conditions, the farmers were more rebellious than ever. The bountiful harvest of 1922 had failed to raise them from their position as debtors. Now new and disturbing proposals were being voiced to rectify the situation. Dafoe had very little sympathy for suggestions that the government should step in and assist the farmer in his financial plight.

[29]*Ibid.*, Dafoe to Sifton, Nov. 2, 1922; *M.F.P.*, Nov. 10, 1922; Dafoe Papers, Dafoe to Sifton, Nov. 9, 1922; Sifton Papers, Dafoe to Sifton, Nov. 13, 1922.
[30]Dafoe Papers, Dafoe to Sifton, Nov. 2, 1922.

He saw farm credit and debt problems through the eyes of a laissez-faire liberal. It would have to be solved, he argued, "upon the basis of the individual farmer who is hopelessly involved, dealing with his own set of creditors and securing adjustments upon lines which will permit him to stay upon the farm."[31]

For Dafoe, the solution to the farmers' difficulties was still to be found in fiscal policy: the tariff had to be lowered. And the tariff was the key not only to Western economic problems, but also to an understanding of the political confusion that reigned on the Canadian scene. When the 1923 session of Parliament began, the *Free Press* warmly praised the Progressives for moving a low tariff amendment which displayed to all that on this question the Liberals and Conservatives were "merely wings of the same party." As long as the Liberals maintained this reactionary position there would be no chance of the Progressives' joining the Government.[32]

The budget of 1923 was once more a stand-pat measure, and again indicated that the remaking of the major political parties was no nearer to realization. Crerar had again been approached by King, but he remained shy of the Montreal-dominated cabinet. Believing that their strength would be further increased in a new election, the Progressives had now decided that it was best to wait until a final showdown with the Liberals could be forced. Dafoe, too, was moving towards this opinion, though he was plagued by fears that the Progressive strength would be seriously sapped by internal divisions. And the parliamentary session of 1923 only served to underline the difficulties which beset every effort to unite the moderates in both Liberal and Progressive parties in a low tariff coalition. As the budget had illustrated, the protectionist interests seemed to have unbridled control of King's cabinet. And what of the doughty Progressives? There were increasing signs that they too were splitting into factions.[33]

Throughout the spring of 1923, the *Free Press* published a series of

[31]*Ibid.*, Dafoe to Sifton, Jan. 2, 1923. Sifton's reply is interesting, especially when it is recalled that he, like Dafoe, gave some support and advice to the Progressives. He wrote: "I have received your letter of January 2 which I have read with great interest. I am not alarmed about the unrest. I have no confidence whatever in any of the schemes propounded for relief. I never accomplished anything myself except by hard work, frugality and self-denial, and I don't believe anybody else ever did. This is the road that Western Canada, in common with the rest of humanity, has to travel." *Ibid.*, Sifton to Dafoe, Jan. 5, 1923. See also Sir Clifford Sifton, "Immigration" in *Proceedings of the Canadian Club of Toronto for the Years 1921–22*, XIX (Toronto, 1923), 182–91.

[32]*M.F.P.*, Feb. 10, 1923.

[33]Dafoe Papers, Dafoe to Sifton, March 12, 1923; Dafoe to Sir Alfred Zimmern, Feb. 22, 1923.

editorials outlining the needs of Western Canada—lower tariffs, settlement of the Western natural resources question, lower rail and ocean freight rates. But there were few signs from Ottawa that these demands were receiving any sympathetic consideration. Even the Progressives were falling below expectation. Sifton was greatly annoyed at the Government's evident lethargy. He told Dafoe that he should get down to the capital and line up the Western members in an effort to build a fire under the King administration. Dafoe agreed. He had to speak at his daughter's graduation at the University of Manitoba first, but he was sure that there was no rush to get to Ottawa, as the important report on freight rates had not yet been published.[34]

The most immediately pressing problem, Dafoe believed, was the necessity of finding a means to break the power of the Great Lakes shipping monopoly. A mere statutory prohibition was not enough; there had to be machinery established to ensure that Western producers would not be forced to pay outrageous rates. But was Mackenzie King ingenious enough to devise the machinery and force it through the Commons against the opposition of the shipping interests? Dafoe doubted it, despite the fact that the Prime Minister's views on the subject differed little from his own. "King appears to have no capacity for giving effect to his views," Dafoe wrote. "When it comes to action, the older and more resourceful members of his cabinet decide what is to be done."[35]

By early June Dafoe was in Ottawa. He was relieved to find that on the issue of ocean and lake freight rates the Progressives were a fairly united group. But the Government was a different matter. It apparently had no collective plan, but rather seemed on all matters "to drift until action can be no longer postponed & then the individual minister concerned does something." Dafoe spent a fortnight in Ottawa during which time he kept watching for evidence of an improvement. He had hoped that King would gradually pull himself together, but as the days passed and no action on freight rates was taken, his pessimism grew. "I am extremely sorry," he confided, "because I had hoped for better things from King and Robb. They will never have a better chance to show their mettle than on this occasion, and if they entirely fail, there is little to be hoped for in the future."[36]

Dafoe went home filled with pessimism about more than just the rates question. Perhaps if the Progressives fought strenuously they could force the Government to take action. But these open disagreements be-

[34]Sifton Papers, Sifton to Dafoe, May 4, 1923; Dafoe to Sifton, May 7, 1923.
[35]*Ibid.*, Dafoe to Sifton, May 12, 1923.
[36]*Ibid.*, June 4, 5, 1923.

tween the farmers and the Liberals seriously widened the breach between the two groups which he had hoped would grow together. In the end King did pull himself together and an attempt was made to deal at least with the question of lake freight rates by giving their control to the Board of Grain Commissioners. Perhaps this renewed Dafoe's hopes for King. But in the midst of his worries about the relations between the Liberals and the Progressives something more important happened to draw him closer to the Liberal Prime Minister. King invited him to accompany the Canadian delegation to the Imperial Conference in London in the autumn of 1923.

VIII. The Triumph of Liberal Nationalism

1921-3

IT WAS NO MERE REPORTER that Mackenzie King invited to accompany the Canadian delegation to the Imperial Conference in 1923. Dafoe had given much thought to the question of imperial relations throughout his mature years, and had reached a set of very firmly held conclusions. Since the war he had frequently turned his pen to the subject, underlining every expression of Canadian autonomy, striking at any suggestion that Canada's right to independent action should be limited, vociferously advocating the definition of Dominion status. His attendance at the conference would offer an opportunity to act as reporter, watchdog, consultant and even advocate of those principles which he had been working out for so long.

In the years since Borden's retirement and Dafoe's final break with the Unionists, the Winnipeg editor had worked to smooth off the rough edges of his plan for a settlement of the imperial question. The events of the war, the Imperial Conference of 1917 and the Peace Conference had convinced him that a new day had dawned for Canadian nationhood. But he believed that before that day reached its fullness, Canada's status would have to be fully worked out and defined. It had to be declared to the world at large that Canada could act with the same independence as other nations. Canada had to be recognized in the eyes of the world, the *Free Press* noted on February 12, 1921, as "a sovereign independent state, the equal in status of Great Britain itself; and, like Great Britain, one of the family of British nations."

The process of achieving this end, Dafoe knew, was twofold. The last vestiges of British authority over Canada had to be removed. In this area the final test was Canada's right to express its independent judgment in international affairs. No longer could the British Empire automatically sing in unison, though it was hoped that it would voluntarily sing in harmony. The Empire had worked in co-operation during the war and had even found in the Imperial War Cabinet an instrument through which this spirit could be expressed. But by 1920 Dafoe had come to look upon the war cabinet as a purely wartime expedient whose importance had been overrated. Indeed its activities had strengthened his conviction "that it is very difficult for Imperial boards of any kind to function in the atmosphere of Whitehall." Thus control of matters affecting Canada would have to be in the hands of Canadians in Canada.[1]

But merely to end imperial limitations on Canadian sovereignty was not enough. It was also of the highest importance that Canadians be educated in the need to exercise their own independent powers. Certainly Canadians would not accept sacrifices demanded for the purpose of reviving the lost ascendancy of the British Empire. If such demands were made, the Empire would be destroyed. "I know, of course," Dafoe wrote in 1921, "that the difficulty is more with Canadians than with the British authorities, but I do not know that this mitigates the dangers of the situation."[2]

Dafoe had very definite ideas about the means to be used in educating his countrymen in the matter of national status. The educating had to be done by people whose loyalty to Britain was unimpeachable, and it had to be represented as the logical application of the old, respectable doctrine of responsible government to the new field of foreign affairs. John S. Ewart was an old friend of Dafoe's and his writings were usually sympathetically received in the offices of the *Free Press*. Still, Dafoe believed that Ewart might be a dangerous adherent to the nationalist cause. Shortly after the Great War, Ewart formed a "Canada First" movement, which interested Dafoe but also disturbed him. He wrote to his friend explaining his fears. The greatest danger was that such an organization might fall under the influence of people whose chief wish was to express anti-British sentiments. "I am afraid of the professional Sinn Feiner and the French Canadian with a marked anti-British racial bias," Dafoe cautioned. If these people gained control of the nationalist movement it would be discredited and destroyed. "My own hope," he continued,

is that the leadership of this movement will fall, as it should fall, into the hands of the people of unquestioned British stock and of known devotion to British constitutional principles. As you and I realize, the movement is in

---
[1] Wrong Papers, Dafoe to G. M. Wrong, Jan. 9, 1920.
[2] Dafoe Papers, Dafoe to J. A. Cooper, Jan. 26, 1921.

no respect a break with the spirit of British traditions however much it may conflict with the past machinery of government, and its success is essential to the continuance of the brotherly relationships which at present exist between the British nations.

Ewart's shortcoming was that he was obsessed with the idea that every British move was directed towards preventing the dominions from assuming full powers of nationhood. "There is not nearly as much design in the movements of the British government as he thinks," Dafoe commented in 1921.[3]

Ewart was the one extreme—the nationalist. And there was another extreme—the imperialist. Dafoe had less sympathy with the latter, but he felt that the imperialist position could be undermined by education. "Most of this sentiment is . . . due to lack of knowledge of the question and the work before us is very largely educational. It will have to be done with discretion and persistence," he pointed out. With a post-war Imperial Conference to deal with the constitutional problems of the Empire in the offing, Dafoe wanted to get his educational campaign into immediate operation.[4]

His objective was simple. Canada and the other dominions should be recognized to have the right to exercise the sovereign powers of nations, that is, powers equal to those of Great Britain. Anticipating an imperial constitutional conference in 1921, the *Free Press* announced on February 19 that "NATIONHOOD and EQUALITY are the twin foundation stones of the British Commonwealth as it will hereafter exist." The duty of the conference was to declare this self-evident truth. Dafoe had no desire to see Canada sunder the imperial bond. On the contrary, he saw great virtue in the continued co-operation of the British nations. But his hope was to see the well-tested principle of responsible government extended to the last remaining area of Dominion subordination to Britain—foreign policy. He did not consider this a radical proposal. In fact, it was the means of preserving the traditional bonds of unity between Canada and Great Britain by applying a traditional formula of imperial relations. From Dafoe's point of view the real radicals were the followers of Ewart on the one hand, who demanded complete independence, and the Round Tablers on the other, who wanted to limit the application of responsible government by establishing machinery for the formulation of a common imperial foreign policy. Dafoe's position was the conservative one.[5]

[3]Ewart Papers, Dafoe to J. S. Ewart, Jan. 7, 1921; Dafoe Papers, Dafoe to Sifton, April 25, 1921.
[4]Dafoe Papers, Dafoe to Sifton, Feb. 14, 1921.
[5]*Ibid.*, May 18, 1921.

His traditionalism is further underlined by his frequent claim that the development of full Canadian autonomy was not merely in keeping with the British tradition, but was also part of a Canadian tradition which transcended party lines. When Prime Minister Meighen publicly expressed opposition to an imperial executive, the *Free Press* on April 4, 1921, noted that in doing so he had "inherited from his predecessors in high office, Sir Wilfrid Laurier and Sir Robert Borden, what might be called the traditional Canadian attitude on these questions." Writing to an Australian historian, Dafoe pointed to the same conclusion; each generation in Canada had produced political leaders who contributed to the growth of Canada's self-governing powers. "Perhaps of all this distinguished succession," he suggested, "Sir Robert Borden deserves the highest place." Dafoe argued persuasively that his objective was the one that had been in the minds of the Fathers of Confederation in 1866. Sir John Macdonald had suggested that Canada be called a kingdom with all the authority that such a title would suggest; a clearly defined alliance would govern the relations between Great Britain and the auxiliary Kingdom of Canada. Speaking of his own attitude, Dafoe wrote, "There is nothing new in this, it was Sir John Macdonald's idea 50 years ago." The immediate objective in Dafoe's view was to win the status of "kingdom" for Canada. The idea of a treaty defining mutual obligations always remained a somewhat nebulous ideal to which he paid lip service. The important point, however, is that Dafoe believed that his views were conservative because they were quite in keeping with the past history of imperial and Canadian development. He never asked himself if that tradition was as applicable in the 1920's as it had been in the days of Macdonald and Laurier. He simply assumed that it was.[6]

In the early twenties the problem facing imperial statesmen, as Dafoe saw it, was to carry to fruition the promise of the 1917 Imperial War Conference. Resolution IX of the conference had admitted the equality of the British nations but had refrained from defining it. As long as the relation remained ambiguous there was room for disagreement, and it was possible for the British government to act without regard for the independent interests of the dominions. The lack of definition could be the source of friction between the dominions and the mother country, and those who rejected the idea that the situation should be clarified were merely laying up store for the day when an outburst of Canadianism might damage the relation beyond repair. "After all, our status is one of subordination," Dafoe told a sympathetic English friend, "&

[6]Dafoe Papers, Dafoe to Sir Alfred Zimmern, April 28, 1922; Dafoe to Borden, Jan. 24, 1923.

once it gets into the Canadian consciousness that they can only be British at the cost of permanent subordination, there will be something doing."[7]

The only possible way to end this confusion was to give each Dominion full control over all matters domestic and foreign. A common foreign policy for the Empire was an impossibility in Dafoe's estimation, unless the dominions were denied some of the attributes of orthodox nationhood. "To attempt to reconcile these conflicting conceptions of Canada as a nation, and at the same time an integral part of a unit which in itself has the characteristics and powers of a nation, is to find oneself in a fog," he argued. Only a resort to the Athanasian creed of the incomprehensible one and many, accepted on faith, could provide a reconciliation. Dafoe confessed that his faith was weak. A common foreign policy would either mean that Canada was subject to the decisions of Britain, which meant that the country remained a colony, or that foreign policy was determined by a common imperial body to which dissenting members must bow. The latter solution was nothing more than the old centralist concept of the Empire. "I am thoroughly convinced that no solution which leaves Canada either a colony or the province of a centralized empire will be acceptable even to Canadians of this generation, to say nothing of the future," he argued confidently. A continuation of the imperial partnership depended on the right of the individual members to make their own decisions. A moral unity would hold the association together in critical times, but the whole association would be destroyed by an attempt to commit Canadians to obligations before they were acquainted with the circumstances surrounding any given crisis.

The rock upon which all schemes for a common foreign policy were wrecked was national interest. Each member of the Commonwealth had individual interests with which it alone was competent to deal. Britain could never allow her hands to be tied by the dominions where her interests were vitally at stake. British interests might be threatened in an area where Canada had neither interests nor knowledge and therefore lacked the basis for an intelligent judgment. Britain would have to deal with the problem as she saw best in the light of her own interests and accept full responsibility for her action. The idea of a common foreign policy, then, was a dream fraught with dangers and unmanageable complications. Dafoe concluded this long exposition of his views to Sir Robert Borden by saying,

I can see no way out of the difficulty but a frank recognition that each British nation must look after its own foreign policy, with facilities for

---
[7]Dafoe Papers, Dafoe to Sir Alfred Zimmern, April 28, 1922.

adjustment where a conflict of interest promises to arise; and facilities also for common action where it is the wish of the various nations to pool their interests and their strength as in the case of the Great War.[8]

Dafoe's conclusions are difficult to escape if his premises are accepted. Even Sir Robert Borden, who had looked towards a continuation in peacetime of the common imperial policy which had been operative during the war, was prepared to accept "most" of Dafoe's claims. He added, though, "I am inclined to think that you attach too much importance to the formal, technical, legalistic aspect of the problem."[9] In arguing as he did, Dafoe made a twofold assumption. First, he accepted the orthodox political definition of the nation-state: a political organization capable of acting without outside restraint in both domestic and international affairs. If Canada was to be a nation it must fall within this definition. Secondly, Dafoe assumed that Canada's interests in foreign affairs were largely, though not wholly, independent of the interests of the other members of the Empire. Where the interests of the member nations of the Commonwealth were similar, he hoped there would be co-operation; where they conflicted, he hoped there would be conciliation. But in each case the individual dominions would decide upon their own interests and formulate policies in keeping with them. Dafoe did not view the imperial connection as a counterweight for Canada against any other nation which might threaten Canadian independence. He saw the national task as one of winning full independence from Britain. He did not foresee the possibility that close connection with the Commonwealth might be necessary to protect that independence. He failed to calculate this contingency because he did not think of the Commonwealth, or world politics, in terms of power. The Commonwealth was a moral unit; world politics had to be governed by principles of voluntary co-operation as in the League of Nations.

In Dafoe's view there were two groups of Canadians who opposed the effort to clarify Dominion status. In the first group there were the "imperialists" and "colonials," who for widely different reasons opposed definition. "Imperialist" was a term which Dafoe conveniently left ambiguous. In effect, it applied to anyone who disagreed with his view of the direction in which the Empire should develop. For a variety of reasons, some Canadians opposed the idea that Canada should assume independent powers in international affairs. This attitude was not always based on the belief that Britain should continue to assert full control over the foreign policy of the Empire. Dafoe tended to assume that it was so

[8]*Ibid.*, Dafoe to Borden, Jan. 24, 1923.
[9]Borden Papers, Borden to Dafoe, Feb. 22, 1923.

based, and therefore could collect men of such varied views as Arthur Meighen, Sir John Willison, and Sir Allen Aylesworth into a single, mixed bag labelled "imperialists." But some of these men thought a common foreign policy was a means through which Canada could assert a more powerful influence on the affairs of the world. This was an expression of one form of Canadian nationalism. In the same group were the "colonials." This category included in particular French Canadians who differed from the "imperialists" in that their objection to full Canadian autonomy was based on the fear that once Canada had full control over its constitution, their minority rights would be less secure.[10]

The second group which was an obstacle in the way of final definition of status was the great mass of people who opposed any change because of apathy and inertia. "They block the Imperialists when they try to commit Canada to schemes of organic union or to foreign adventures; and they also resist any attempt to advance along the only other road to the future. They are mentally lazy and timid," Dafoe complained in 1923. This was the group that allowed the Liberals to wallow in indecision. These were the people to whom the educational process had to be applied most severely, though in a mood of pessimism Dafoe admitted that "there appears to be no greater illusion than to assume that an unanswerable argument is conclusive with the public; it gets nowhere unless it is agreeable to them on other counts."[11]

These were the views which Dafoe had worked out on the background of the events which took place before the Imperial Conference of 1923. In these years both the Meighen and King governments were faced with decisions which affected the course of imperial development. Dafoe watched these decisions carefully in an effort to find support for his views, to aid in guiding the Empire along the lines he desired, and to educate the public in the gospel of Liberal nationalism.

ii

Dafoe had expected that the first Imperial Conference that would be held after the war would devote its attention to the promised revision of the imperial constitution. In fact, of course, the first post-war Imperial Conference which met in 1921 did not choose to deal with the constitutional problem explicitly. Rather it devoted its attention largely to a consideration of international affairs and particularly the question of the renewal of the Anglo-Japanese alliance. The conference quickly revealed that there was a wide divergence of views about the desirability of

[10]Dafoe Papers, Dafoe to Sifton, Jan. 29, 1923.
[11]*Ibid.*, Feb. 12, 1923.

renewing the alliance. Canada's representative, Arthur Meighen, stalwartly upheld the position that in view of the hostility of the United States to the alliance, it should be allowed to lapse. American friendship was of vital importance to Canada, and therefore had to be carefully weighed in formulating a common imperial foreign policy for the Pacific. In the end Meighen's view that the Americans should be consulted won acceptance, though not until the opposition of the Australasian delegates had been overcome.

Liberal nationalists like Dafoe mistrusted Meighen's views on imperial affairs. The Prime Minister had never shown any great interest in imperial or international problems, but was generally considered to favour a common imperial foreign policy. To Dafoe, this meant that he was an imperialist, and needed to be watched closely. The *Free Press* on June 8, 1921, emphasized its viewpoint in commenting on the Prime Minister's task in London. "The governing principle of Canadian policy is easy to understand and not difficult to apply, given the necessary resolution. It is that no decision binding upon Canada can be made by any other body than the Canadian parliament." Dafoe believed that the Anglo-Japanese alliance should be terminated for the sake of amicable relations between the United States and the Commonwealth. The alliance was an undesirable hindrance to the necessary and natural association of the English-speaking peoples.

Dafoe was sure that Meighen, in opposing the Anglo-Japanese alliance, was faced by a dilemma that could only be escaped if he accepted the liberal nationalist idea that each Dominion should make its own foreign policy. He was pleased to see the Canadian Prime Minister succeeding in his effort to have the Canadian view of the Japanese treaty accepted by the delegates in London. But surely this was an attempt to square the circle. Canada's view could hardly be accepted without destroying the idea of a common policy. He explained his notion of Meighen's dilemma to Sifton:

> I have been particularly interested in Meighen's attempt to provide at one and the same time a voice for the Dominions in foreign policy and a theoretical diplomatic union for the Empire. His plan appears to be that the Canadian view as to Imperial policy would predominate in matters which Canada is particularly interested in and that the Imperial government shall execute this policy upon the advice of the Canadian government.

Such a scheme, Dafoe thought, was unworkable, and it would not likely even be given a test. At any rate foreign policy control was a constitutional question and the conference could not deal with it in any conclusive fashion. "Meanwhile," Dafoe observed, "the discussion is of value, and the credit must go to Mr. Meighen that he has had the courage to insist upon Canada's right to determine her foreign policies in matters of prime importance to her."[12]

Newspaper reports of the acrimonious proceedings at London in 1921 convinced Dafoe, if any further proof was necessary, that the attempt to achieve a common foreign policy was futile. The British Government, he surmised, had tried to trap the Dominion delegates into accepting the renewal of the Japanese treaty and the result was an explosion. To Dafoe the explosion was "enlightening" as one more proof "of how difficult it will be to carry out the plans suggested in the 1917 resolution of securing a common foreign policy for the Empire through the agency of continuous consultation."[13]

The outcome of the conference of 1921 must have both pleased and annoyed Dafoe, for in fact a common imperial foreign policy was formulated. But it was a common policy which in essence accepted the Canadian view of the Japanese treaty. The decision of the conference was to meet with the United States, Japan and other nations with Far Eastern interests in an effort to arrange a general agreement on Pacific affairs. This proposal reopened the whole knotty problem of Dominion representation, which had been fought out in 1919. Would the Empire attend as a single delegation or would separate invitations be extended to each Dominion? Dafoe's view, quite naturally, was that each Dominion had a right to an invitation. He was informed, however, that while the American State Department had intended to invite the dominions separately, the idea had been coldly received at the British Foreign Office. As a result invitations did not go to the separate Dominion governments. Here was another indication that until the definition of status was put on paper, the British would continue to act as though the Empire was a single unit. Moreover, the *Free Press* interpreted this situation as a failure on the part of Prime Minister Meighen who "by ignorance, by weakness, or by design has destroyed much of the great work that was done for Canada by his predecessors." General Smuts, who protested against the Washington procedure, received glowing praise from the *Free Press* while Meighen was condemned as unfit for the office of Prime Minister.[14]

Before the Washington Conference met, the Government was transferred from Unionist to Liberal hands—on December 6, 1921. But this change had no immediate effect on the question of status. In fact, one week later the British Prime Minister, David Lloyd George, made a statement in the British Parliament which increased Dafoe's anxiety. The

[12]*Ibid.*, June 30, 1921.
[13]Sifton Papers, Dafoe to Sifton, July 5, 1921.
[14]Dafoe Papers, Dafoe to Sifton, Oct. 14, 1921; *M.F.P.*, Nov. 4, 1921.

British Prime Minister made it clear that Britain no longer either solely controlled or assumed sole responsibility for the foreign policy of the Empire. Both control and responsibility were now shared with the other members of the self-governing Empire. Here was an official pronouncement that substantiated all Dafoe's suspicions that Meighen had agreed to the centralizing policy. "Lloyd George's formal declaration of Dominion responsibility for foreign affairs really precipitates the issue and makes it necessary for the new Canadian Government to face it without further evasion," Dafoe exclaimed. But could King be relied upon? "I may say that I have little confidence in King with respect to those questions," Dafoe wrote unhappily.[15]

Dafoe's mistrust of King on the imperial question was an important aspect of his over-all attitude to the new Liberal Prime Minister. He did not doubt that King's heart was that of a nationalist, but the political balance was so delicate that he was afraid the Liberal leader would not raise the imperial issue lest it "disturb the equilibrium of political forces." Dafoe himself was anxious to see this equilibrium disturbed. He thought that the settlement of the imperial problem would assist in bringing about the political realignment he so desired. So long as the imperial question remained unsettled, the French Canadians would cling to the Liberal party, for the Tories were too prone "to wave the flag and pound the big Imperial drum, particularly when they are in opposition," to be able to win the trust of Quebec. But if Dominion status were given final definition, Dafoe thought that the way would be cleared for the bulk of the French Canadians to join the Conservative party—their natural home—making it possible for the Liberals to become a sincerely progressive party.[16]

The hopes which Dafoe had that the imperial issue would be disposed of quietly, rather than in an atmosphere of crisis, were dashed in September 1922 when the dispute over the Chanak episode stirred Canadian politics. Naturally the *Free Press* offered no support for the British Government's request for an expression of imperial solidarity in the face of the crisis in Asia Minor. The request was condemned as another of the persistent attempts to use every opportunity to commit the dominions to a "moral responsibility" for the actions of the British Government, the *Free Press* charged on September 20. Meighen's famous "Ready,

[15] A. B. Keith, ed., *Speeches and Documents on the British Dominions, 1918–1931* (London, 1948), 86; Dafoe Papers, Dafoe to Sifton, Dec. 19, 1921.
[16] Dafoe Papers, Dafoe to W. C. Good, April 17, 1922; Dafoe to Sir Alfred Zimmern, Feb. 22, 1923. It is interesting to note that King saw the possibility of Liberal-Progressive unity on the basis of common views on imperial policy. See R. MacG. Dawson, *William Lyon Mackenzie King*, I, *1874–1923* (Toronto, 1958), 413.

Aye, Ready," suggested as the only proper reply, brought thunderbolts flashing out of Winnipeg. And the whole incident was taken as further proof that the Empire was in danger so long as the status of the Dominions remained undefined. "It ought to be impossible for anything of this sort to happen," the *Free Press* declared tartly on September 30, "and the way to make it impossible is to define in black and white the actual constitutional status of Canadian equality with Great Britain under the Crown." Privately Dafoe feared that another crisis of this kind might force the Canadian Government to take matters into its own hands and define its status unilaterally. "This would be the worst possible way of settling the question," Dafoe observed, "but it may prove the only way of doing it."[17]

Prime Minister King had acted with unexpected determination in the Chanak episode, and he was enthusiastically praised by the *Free Press* for this action and for his stated opposition to a common imperial foreign policy. Dafoe was less impressed with the Government's action in the signing of the Halibut Treaty with Washington in March 1923. It was true that Canada had signed for itself, but the glory was limited by the fact that the Canadian plenipotentiary had been appointed on the advice of British ministers, not of Canadian. But despite this scepticism about the importance of the treaty-signing, Dafoe was beginning to feel that perhaps his initial impression of Mackenzie King had been mistaken. King had given evidence of his willingness to stand up for his nationalist beliefs. Though there was no sign that the much desired definition of status was any closer to achievement, perhaps King was the man who would get it. In April 1923 Dafoe admitted to the Canadian High Commissioner in London that "Mr. King is very much interested in the matter of imperial relationships and his views, I think, are both advanced and sound."[18]

iii

During the early autumn of 1923 Prime Minister King began devoting his attention to the arrangements connected with the forthcoming Imperial Conference. One of the problems was to ensure that the Canadian public received the correct slant on his activities in London. King feared that unless he took some Liberal journalists with him the Canadian Press would be choked with "despatches from Tory imperialist sources." About the same time Sir Clifford Sifton was wondering how King could

---

[17]*Ibid.*, Dafoe to Sifton, Jan. 29, 1923.
[18]*M.F.P.*, March 3, 22, 1923; Dafoe Papers, Dafoe to P. C. Larkin, April 20, 1923.

be kept on the right track at the conference. O. D. Skelton of Queen's University was going with the Prime Minister, but Sifton was "not impressed by the profoundness of his grasp of the subject." Perhaps Dafoe should go. "You can undoubtedly have great influence with King and might conceivably exert a determining influence on vital matters," Sifton told his editor. "It is most important that no principle should be compromised, and equally important that no rupture of friendly relations should take place." For different reasons, then, both King and Sifton thought that Dafoe's presence at the conference might prove useful.[19]

Dafoe, too, had already given some thought to the possibility of travelling to London to watch the proceedings. But the fact that his personal relations with King were somewhat cool had discouraged him. Now that King had taken the initiative in inviting him, the whole complexion of the matter was altered. Perhaps now he could expect to be taken into the new Prime Minister's confidence as he had been by Borden at Paris in 1919. If this were assured, he could provide interpretative dispatches for the Canadian Press and also gain knowledge and experience that would be invaluable in later discussions of imperial affairs. "It is also quite possible," he told Sifton, "that I may be able at some opportune moment to render some such service as that which you suggested in your letter." But he did not want to be put in a position which might imply responsibilities which "I should not care to assume either personally or on behalf of the Free Press." When Sifton informed King that Dafoe would accept the invitation, the Prime Minister was pleased. "I confess," he wrote, "this has given me a feeling of security with respect to a fair and just representation of Canada's position, which I have not thus far wholly enjoyed."[20]

Dafoe, of course, had firm views about the matters that should be the main concern of the conference. Of fundamental importance was the need to clarify, once and for all, the position of the dominions in matters of foreign policy. It should be obvious, the *Free Press* wrote on September 10,

> that the only system that will work is one by which each British nation will attend to its own foreign affairs and accept the responsibility therefor; reserving for a common policy only those questions—comparatively few—in which we are all interested. When those questions arise there will be no difficulty about securing common action, as in war.

This objective was clear enough, but Dafoe knew that it was easier to

[19]Dawson, *Mackenzie King*, 453; Dafoe Papers, Sifton to Dafoe, n.d., 1923.
[20]Sifton Papers, Dafoe to Sifton, Aug. 28, 1923; L. M. King to Sifton, Aug. 30, 1923.

define than to achieve. First, there was the question of the Prime Minister himself. His views were probably sound enough, but his ability to put them into practice was still in question. "I must say I have little confidence in King," Dafoe admitted. "I am afraid his conceit in his ability to take care of himself is equalled only by his ignorance and I should not be surprised if he should find himself trapped." And even if King was equal to the occasion, there were many pot-holes to be avoided. The distinction between policy and status had too often been successfully blurred. If the conference was prevented from examining and clarifying the subject of status, it could easily result in the formulation of commitments to a policy which might "qualify or destroy the present status of the Dominions." Surely the safest tactic would be for the Prime Minister to approach the conference with a demand for a clear-cut definition of status. "He should take the position stoutly that he is not prepared to discuss policies or machinery till the question of our constitutional position is definitely cleared up." So much depended on King, and Dafoe's greatest fear was that the conference would be the scene of a planned effort to side-track the issue of definition. As for himself, Dafoe denied any desire to become an "unofficial member of a board of strategy," but his gnawing suspicion that King would need assistance was indicative of the position he was to assume in London.[21]

As events turned out, the Imperial Conference of 1923 was one of the most important meetings in the history of the British Empire. Here the idea of a common imperial foreign policy was given a decent burial, and for practical purposes the principles of the Commonwealth of autonomous nations were recognized. Though the Balfour Declaration of 1926 formulated the metaphysical principles which best describe the meaning of the Commonwealth association, these principles were actually implicit in the outcome of the 1923 conference. For Dafoe, the conference was certainly one of the most important experiences in his life. From the outset he was taken into the confidence of the official delegation and was soon acting in the capacity of an "unofficial member of a board of strategy." Fortunately he kept a careful record of his observations.[22]

Once aboard the ship which carried the Canadian delegation overseas, Dafoe began to sound out the Prime Minister and his advisers. To his satisfaction he found that the material that had been prepared for the conference by the Canadians was "soundly Canadian in every respect

[21]Dafoe Papers, Dafoe to Sifton, Sept. 12, 1923.
[22]Ramsay Cook, "J. W. Dafoe at the Imperial Conference, 1923," *C.H.R.*, XLI, no. 1 (March 1960), 19–40. All subsequent references in this chapter, except where otherwise noted, are to this diary of Dafoe's.

and advanced. Practically identical F.P. position." Moreover, King showed some interest in the possibility of presenting the conference with a definition of status—one which had been prepared by Sifton—but he was cautious because of the political ramifications of such a move. Throughout the conference, as each critical stage was reached, Dafoe continued to press the Prime Minister to demand a clearly defined statement, but King continued to shy away from the proposal.

Despite the refusal of King to go as far as Dafoe wished, Dafoe was nevertheless very pleased with the Canadian leader's performance. King's opening speech emphasized the view that Canada had to be responsible for its own foreign affairs, and could not accept a commitment to a common imperial policy. Canada, King told the delegates, was not interested in the affairs of Europe and did not want the responsibility of advising the British Government on matters that were beyond the Canadian sphere of interest. King, Skelton and Dafoe watched every move by the British which might undermine the Canadian position. One such incident arose when the Colonial Office suggested that a means of formulating imperial policy might be provided by dividing possible questions into two lists. One would carry questions which the dominions would deal with alone; the other would contain matters of common interest. Dafoe immediately saw a joker in the pack; all the really important questions would be included in the common list, so that the dominions would still be committed to a common foreign policy despite the theoretical concession of a right to formulate their own policy. He was furious, but King proved an alert player in the game and refused to accept the arrangement.

Dafoe's suspicions of the intentions of the British Government never flagged for a moment. How could they when Lord Curzon kept referring to the "Empire's foreign policy" and even acting as if the conference were a cabinet of the Empire? At one point Curzon sent off a cable to the United States, concerning German reparations, in the name of the conference. The message sent, he then reported his action to the assembled delegates. Was any further proof needed of the utter barrenness of the concept of a common foreign policy? Dafoe thought not, recording in his diary that "if Curzon can thus ignore Dominions when their premiers are in conference in London, what is their chance for controlling foreign policy in any measure under normal conditions?"

Since Dafoe had been doubtful about the procedure followed by Canada in the Halibut Treaty negotiations, he was keen to see the matter of signing authority perfectly clarified. Here there was no difficulty since the British Foreign Office was ready to accept the Canadian suggestions. But while this subject was easily settled, the conference had still to deal with the extremely sensitive matter of resolutions. King did not want any resolutions since they might suggest that commitments had been made. If there had to be resolutions, Dafoe thought, why not have one that defined the autonomy of the Dominions?

At the end of October, as the matter of resolutions was just coming up, Dafoe was absent from the English capital visiting Paris, which had so attracted him in 1919. When he arrived back on November 6, he found the Canadian delegation in an uproar. Skelton wanted to see him immediately; the "imperialist" drive was on. During his absence the British Government had presented the Prime Minister's Conference ("an ingenious device to keep India and Ireland out of the confidential confabs," Dafoe suspected) with a report of the proceedings of the conference. On seeing the document, Dafoe's worst suspicions were immediately confirmed:

> It was a remarkable document. Not only did it represent the Conference as giving its general approval to the conduct of the joint common affairs since the last Conference, but it announced that the Conference had laid down policies for the future which the Foreign Office would be authorized to carry out. It meant the acceptance in its most unqualified form of the doctrine of the joint foreign policy with joint responsibility.

A further section committed the Dominions to the Lausanne settlement, and another promised the support of the dominions for any measures necessary to ensure British control of the Suez Canal. Dafoe was relieved to hear that King had exploded and given Curzon a "piece of his mind," taking the line that the conference was a meeting of governments, not an imperial cabinet. The result of this bombshell was an amendment which, Dafoe felt, still left the report open to serious objection. "I suggested that the right place for this report was the wastepaper basket or the fire because it did not seem to me that it could be amended, and that another attempt at a report [ought to] be made." King, still cautious, demurred at this violent suggestion, fearing the political consequences of appearing to oppose the rest of the conference. He suggested that a "caveat" be entered, stating Canada's view that no policy commitments were possible at such a gathering as the Imperial Conference. Dafoe was disturbed at King's trepidation, especially when he saw the proposed "caveat"—two good, clear clauses by Skelton, and two more by King that were "a jumble of words."

Curzon was naturally unhappy about the Canadian suggestion and at first refused to consider any "caveat." Sir Maurice Hankey, of the British secretariat, told Skelton that the problem was that the British Government was puzzled at the shifts in Canadian policy. Borden had asked for a share in formulating imperial policy; Meighen had agreed to the idea of a common imperial foreign policy; now King wanted something quite different. But the Canadians had little sympathy for these complaints. Skelton insisted that the King Government wanted a return to the traditional Canadian policy of no prior commitments. This explanation did nothing to reduce Curzon's adamance.

Dafoe now returned to his original suggestion; have a clear definition of Canada's position included in the report. King was not convinced, for he "feared the effect on Ontario public opinion, wondered what the Globe would say, etc., etc." Dafoe, who had no worries about a political future, was blunt: "I said that if the choice was between disagreement and the surrender of his position, King had really no alternative; moreover, in my judgment, a reservation along the lines of the drafted memorandum would be so strongly supported in Canada that it would be attacked only by the Imperialists who were against King anyway." If King showed his hand to be a strong one, Dafoe predicted that the other dominion prime ministers would scurry to his support. Skelton and George Graham agreed to urge this view, and finally King was convinced.

After what was likely a restless night, Dafoe learned that King had been forthright in his attitude at the November 7 session of the conference. And he had carried the day, especially with Smuts, "who no doubt foresaw in a glance what use could be made by his enemies in South Africa of his failure to agree to the Canadian point of view." Smuts carried out the final negotiations, convincing Curzon that the Canadians should be allowed to include a statement of their position in the report. The "caveat," which made no specific reference to Canada, simply noted that the conference was a meeting of governments and that its decisions were subject to ratification by the various Dominion parliaments. Dafoe was not entirely satisfied with the statement; "rather thin," he complained, "much less pronounced than the drafts I have seen."

Still, imperial affairs seemed to be back on the right track. Though a final definition of Dominion status had not been achieved, there had been no compromise of the Liberal nationalist position that an independent foreign policy was an aspect of full status. And while there may have been some bruised feelings, there had certainly been no rupture of relations among the various dominions. Dafoe went home feeling that the Canadian delegation was returning with a welcome gift for the Christmas of 1923.

The fact that the Imperial Conference had reached no binding policy decisions was its strongest recommendation, in Dafoe's view. The meeting could be "accounted a success by virtue of the things it declined to do." But it also had positive achievements to its credit, for "the conception of the Conference as a body governing the Empire—the idea plainly indicated by Mr. Hughes in his statement to the Australian parliament—has been either destroyed by the proceedings of the late Conference or put in abeyance until conditions are favorable to its revival." This achievement had only been attained by defeating a well-planned and politically inspired attempt by a group of British politicians, who had hoped to use the conference as a springboard for an election, Dafoe thought. "I made up my mind very shortly after I got to England," he wrote to a friend, "that Amery, the Morning Post crowd, etc., were keen to have an early election and were trying to steer the Conference into a course which would help them. They tried to play a big game, only part of which I could see; and they certainly have come a cropper." Did such a plot really exist? Dafoe was naturally suspicious of the people he tagged imperialists. But his view was given a little support when the Baldwin Government did call a general election in December of the same year. Whatever basis there was for Dafoe's suspicion, the *Free Press* was quick to draw a moral from the coincidence of the Imperial Conference and the British election. It remarked (December 17):

> Some fairly obvious morals can be drawn from these developments. One is that it is not wise for the Imperial Conference to raise issues which have to be settled by elections. This can only result in a political party undertaking to identify the Empire's interest and existence with its own fortunes; and the effect cannot but be unfortunate whatever the result of the elections—victory would be only a shade less ruinous than defeat.

The result of the 1923 Conference was, in Dafoe's view, a triumph for the ideal of a voluntary association of autonomous nations.[23] In this triumph, Dafoe had played a significant role. This was only possible, of course, because the Canadian Prime Minister agreed essentially with Dafoe's views. But King was notoriously cautious; Dafoe's role was to urge him persistently to go the second mile. King, always conscious of his political situation, must have realized that if he hoped to win Dafoe and the *Free Press* back to the Liberal party, he would have to listen to the Winnipeg editor. Still, the Liberal leader could not accept everything he heard, and he went only an extra half-mile. But the implication

[23]Dafoe, "Did the Imperial Conference Fail?" *Maclean's Magazine*, Jan. 15, 1924, 15; Dafoe Papers, Dafoe to John Stevenson, Jan. 28, 1924.

of the stand which he took was enough to convince Dafoe that King really was a stalwart nationalist.

Gradually Dafoe came to the conclusion that the Imperial Conference of 1923 was an important milepost in the development of the Commonwealth, and he gave credit for its establishment to Mackenzie King. "I am pretty clear in my own mind," he remarked in 1935, "that 1923 was the decisive moment and that in 1926 it was simply a case of mopping up the situation." But in 1923 Dafoe was not quite so certain that the battle had been won; the imperialists and centralizers, both in Canada and abroad, would still bear close watching. The man who was especially suspect was Arthur Meighen, who might become Prime Minister of Canada again. Nor was Dafoe's regard for King a full-blown admiration. The Liberal leader had proved himself capable of handling the issues in London, but there was still much room for improvement in his management of affairs at Ottawa.[24]

[24]Dafoe Papers, Dafoe to R. MacG. Dawson, May 23, 1935; Dafoe, "At the Imperial Conference," *M.F.P.*, Oct. 19, 1923.

IX. Lord Byng Intervenes
1924 - 6

✦✦

THE IMPERIAL CONFERENCE only brought Dafoe and King together on the imperial question, and did nothing to bridge the gulf that continued to separate them on domestic issues. Dafoe expressed his ambivalent attitude regarding King to one of the Prime Minister's sharpest critics, John Stevenson, when he wrote, "you see I don't think much of King as a party leader in Canada. But I am bound to say he handled himself pretty well in London." The narrowing of the area of difference was nevertheless extremely important, for, if an issue arose which combined the imperial question with domestic politics, the way would be open for Dafoe to fall completely into step with King.[1]

The reason that Dafoe lacked confidence in King as a party leader was that after two years King had failed to fashion a new Liberal party out of Progressives and low tariff Liberals. In short, Dafoe was sceptical of the Prime Minister's willingness to take the steps necessary to break the hold of Eastern protectionism on the existing Liberal party. Until this development took place, he believed that the Progressives should continue to represent the views of the true Liberals in Canadian politics.

In particular, the Progressives had to remain in existence until it was possible to revive the Liberal party in the West. That revival would not be possible as long as the Eastern Liberals, "without doubt the most 'Conservative' political influence which there is at present in Canada," remained wholly opposed to the policies which the West believed necessary for its economic growth. "As things stand at present," Dafoe told a Western Liberal in November 1923, "it is the Montreal element that will control the Liberal party, and if the West sends Liberal members to Ottawa they will find themselves subject to this control

[1] Dafoe Papers, Dafoe to John Stevenson, Jan. 28, 1924.

with only the right to make protests in the party caucus, which will be listened to tolerantly and ignored." Obviously, then, the Progressive party could not be abandoned. If the Liberals and the Progressives could be induced to co-operate in the West they could become the vanguard of a low tariff party. Moreover, the Progressives served another purpose; they helped to keep the Prairie electors "from casting their votes against the Government in favor of Conservative candidates."[2]

Dafoe had little hope that the existing Liberal Government could be refashioned to increase its appeal in the West. While in office, governments naturally grew more conservative, and it was only by moving to the left that the Liberals could hope to win support on the Prairies. "The decision which King made in December 1921," Dafoe told W. A. Buchanan, "when he accepted the dictation of Sir Lomer and the interests which he represents, is not, I think, reversible at least during the life of the present session of parliament." Since he believed that the Government faced an inevitable reduction of its forces at the next election, the best thing that could happen would be for the West to return a strong Progressive bloc, which would be able to co-operate with the liberals in the Liberal party, and force the conservative Liberals into alliance with Meighen. "I don't know which coalition would be the stronger and would therefore take office," he wrote, "but in any case there would emerge a real Liberal party which would be of service to the country whether it were in office or in opposition." Would King lead the new coalition of Liberals and Progressives? A year earlier Dafoe had expressed fairly conclusive doubts, but, having seen King in action in London, he was now less uncertain. Yet he had not made up his mind completely.[3]

There seemed little hope that the Canadian political situation would clarify itself before a new election. And in the West clarity could easily come at the expense of the Liberals. "All this talk about the revival of Dominion Liberalism in the West is just moonshine," Dafoe warned. King had implemented few policies which had satisfied the farmers. Nor was policy the only difficulty; there was also prejudice. King had stimulated an important Western prejudice, shared by Dafoe, when he lavished his favours on the Laurier Liberals, believing that the Unionist Liberals, hungry for patronage, would thus be forced to return home. But the prodigals had not returned and showed no intention of doing so. Dafoe felt sure that the only way to bring the West back to the Liberal party was a Liberal-Progressive fusion. The man that Dafoe thought

[2]*Ibid.*, Dafoe to W. A. Buchanan, Nov. 30, 1923.   [3]*Ibid.*, Dec. 6, 1923.

might engineer this union was Charles Dunning, Premier of Saskatchewan. Dafoe had been watching Dunning's activities for some time and rated him highly. Under such a leader, the Western forces could easily be united, for "the average Liberal and the average Western Progressive are twins, and they are bound to come together, given time."[4]

Dafoe knew that at the end of 1923 King was again exploring the possibility of attracting some of the Western leaders into the Government. Crerar was disposed to go in and Dafoe thought that A. B. Hudson and Dunning might also be ready to accept office. But since King still refused to offer policy guarantees, nothing came of the negotiations. Dafoe concluded that this failure proved finally that King's method of approach to the Progressives was at fault. "Things will now go on swiftly or slowly," he told John Stevenson, "but certainly to a smash, giving way to new combinations and adjustments the precise character of which I cannot foresee." Neither Crerar nor Dunning would be disposed to make any more pilgrimages to Ottawa, and King would be forced to continue along the unsure course he had followed since becoming Prime Minister. As for the Progressives, they were attempting to "turn themselves into a National political party" and since they needed time to accomplish this purpose, they would not be in a hurry to upset the Government.[5]

ii

For the next eighteen months Dafoe surveyed the Canadian political scene with growing concern. All the evidence suggested that the Liberal party's fortunes were on the decline. He was not entirely regretful but he feared that the result might be a triumph for the Tories in the West. The best hope for the West, he thought, was to keep its money on the Progressives. Speaking of the Western electorate in a future contest Dafoe told Sifton early in 1924, "It may be partly Liberal in its complexion, but it will probably be quite solid on two or three issues, among them the tariff and the construction of the Hudson Bay road." But such predictions depended very much upon the performance of the Government in the parliamentary sessions of 1924 and 1925.[6]

The Speech from the Throne at the opening of the 1924 session was encouraging. The *Free Press* (March 1) gave it cautious commendation. "For the first time in many years," it claimed, "the Speech from the

[4] *Ibid.*, Dafoe to Sifton, Dec. 27, Jan. 13, Dec. 27, 1923.
[5] Sifton Papers, Dafoe to Sifton, Jan. 2, 1924; Dafoe to John Stevenson, Jan. 28, 1924.
[6] Dafoe Papers, Dafoe to Sifton, Feb. 13, 1924.

Throne is not a piece of pretentious humbug, but a document of interest and value to the country. Of course, the menu does not always give a just idea of the viands that are to follow." To the Progressives, the *Free Press* a week later offered the advice that as long as the Government partially met Western demands there was no justification for opposition. A co-operative attitude would help to advance the "readjustment which promises to put our politics on the basis of reality." Dafoe was confident that the session would not produce anything startling. Unless the Government acted with "extraordinary stupidity" the Progressives would not threaten its existence.[7]

The viands that followed the appetizer were not without their savour. The *Free Press* interpreted the budget as an important sign that the Liberals were beginning to realize the strength of Western sentiment on the tariff, a sentiment which was becoming a "kind of obsession." With journalistic hyperbole the 1924 budget was described as a "Turning Point in History," not because of the trifling changes which it made in the tariff, but because it indicated a trend that was bound to frighten the Eastern protectionists. This editorial praise was more than the expression of a pious hope; it was also an apology. Would not the Western electorate be more susceptible to the blandishments of the Conservatives if some indication of sympathy for Western needs was not found in the Liberals' policies? Moreover the Progressives had been placed in a particularly difficult position during the budget debate when J. S. Woodsworth moved an amendment almost identical with the one put forward by Robert Forke at the previous session. Forke, however, no doubt believing that King's promises of a lower tariff were better than Meighen's threats of a higher one, chose to stand by the Government, and was deserted by fifteen of his followers in the division on the amendment. Perhaps the *Free Press*'s comments on the budget were designed to create a smoke-screen for the embarrassed Progressive leader.[8]

Whatever the 1924 budget may have meant in terms of political or economic relief for the West, there were other questions in the same session that suggested the Prairies had little hope of complete appeasement. Transportation costs were again in the forefront in 1924 and 1925. Western politicians had no lack of suggestions for providing cheaper means of transporting bulky agricultural produce to the markets of the world. But every effort to obtain lower freight and ocean rates, increased competition among grain carriers, or added transportation facilities

[7]*Ibid.*, Dafoe to John Stevenson, March 6, 1924.
[8]*Ibid.*, Dafoe to Sifton, Feb. 13, 1924; *M.F.P.*, May 17, 1924.

seemed to be opposed by Eastern interests. The projected railway to Hudson Bay, long believed to be the answer to the need for shorter and thus cheaper rail haulage, went forward only at a snail's pace. All the parties were committed to its construction, but Dafoe was sure that its completion was delayed by the pressure of Easterners. "If Montreal could block the route, tear up the rail and close the Bay, it would be the worst day's work for national solidarity that has ever been done," he told an Eastern business man. And not only was there opposition to the Hudson Bay project, but also there were equally serious rumours that the Canadian Pacific was carrying on an insidious campaign to destroy its competitor, the Canadian National. Dafoe was vigorously opposed to any suggestion of railway merger under either public or private auspices.[9]

The most immediate problem, however, was the revival of the controversy over the Crow's Nest Pass Agreement. In 1924 the King Government allowed the agreement to become fully effective for the first time since 1918. Three months later, the Board of Railway Commissioners ruled that the rates covering westbound goods could be raised. This action was followed by a Supreme Court judgment, on an appeal from the Prairie provinces, which held the Railway Commissioners' decision was invalid. Once more the problem was thrown into the Government's lap. To the *Free Press*, the Crow's Nest Pass Agreement was a "fundamental and inalienable right." A clarion call was sounded, summoning all Western members of Parliament to stand solidly for the agreement.[10]

The whole matter was very disturbing. Once more the Government's paralysis seemed certain to lose it the friendship of the Progressives. Equally distressing was the fact that every Government blunder played into the hands of the Western radicals or "Ginger Group" as they were now called. This group contended that nothing could be expected from either of the old parties and, in Dafoe's judgment, it hoped to exterminate the "moderate Progressives and take possession of Western Canada, a development which it is impossible to regard with complacency." But perhaps the Ginger Group was right about the old parties. When King presented the House with a bill which in effect terminated those sections of the Crow's Nest Pass Agreement which governed westbound goods, even the *Free Press* had to admit "A Complete Defeat for the West."[11]

[9]Dafoe Papers, Dafoe to J. M. Macdonnell, May 3, 1924; Dafoe to D. C. Coleman, June 10, 1924; Dafoe to Sifton, April 29, 1925.
[10]*M.F.P.*, Sept. 20, 1924, Jan. 27, 1925.
[11]Dafoe Papers, Dafoe to Sifton, Dec. 10, 1924; *M.F.P.*, June 8, 1925.

Of no less importance was the problem of ocean freight rates. According to a report drawn up by W. T. R. Preston, who had been appointed by the King administration to examine the ocean shipping trade, there existed a North Atlantic shipping combine which controlled freight rates. The *Free Press* strongly urged the Government to take some action which would protect Canadians against this monopoly. The Liberals decided to act upon the information supplied by Preston and drew up an agreement with an English shipping magnate, Sir William Peterson. The agreement was intended to provide the Government with a fleet of ships to compete with the North Atlantic combine. The plan received Dafoe's full approval, and he saw in every criticism of it the surreptitious activities of the C.P.R. interests. Whatever the merits of the Peterson contract, and it came under sharp criticism from the Conservatives, it was prevented from becoming effective by the death of the English shipowner. But so far as the West was concerned, the ocean freight rates fiasco was just another example of the inability of the Liberals to find solutions for the farmers' problems.[12]

There was no doubt that by early 1925 discontent was growing more shrill in the West. In January Dafoe confessed to Sifton that "there is more secession sentiment throughout the West than I would care to admit." He came down on the secessionists with a heavy hand, warning that although there was no limit to the discussion of panaceas for Western problems within the Canadian polity, the permanence of Confederation was beyond question.[13] But there was no use denying that there were very severe strains on the Canadian political system. The cause of this tension, the *Free Press* argued on Dominion Day, was the fact that the federal government since 1867 had imposed upon the whole nation the policies desired by only one section. A pessimistic note ran through the editorial's concluding plea for sectional tolerance:

Dominion Day is a good day for Canadians to think about matters of national concern. This country is not a unitary state in subjection to a highly organized centre; it is a political federation which implies the right of all units going to make up the federation to consideration in excess, perhaps, of what it is within their power to enforce by their political strength. This principle has been rather ignored in the past, and there has been a disregard for the legitimate desires of outlying sections which lack the political power to force consideration. The geographical disabilities under which the country labors are thus paralleled by resulting political disabilities; and the result is a problem of growing complexity which calls loudly for the attention of our statesmen—if we have any.

[12] *M.F.P.*, Feb. 18, March 13, 1925.
[13] Dafoe Papers, Dafoe to Sifton, Jan. 22, 1925; *M.F.P.*, Feb. 3, 1925.

Dafoe himself placed more confidence in power than in pleas for toleration from the stronger sections of the country; or at least he recognized that strength is more easily tolerated than weakness. Throughout the spring and summer of 1925 he watched the political scene closely, trying to see how the West could most advantageously use its political strength. After the blunders and failures of the parliamentary session, there seemed less hope than ever for the Liberal party in the West. The only salvation for the Government that Dafoe could foresee was the same he had advocated before—to join forces with the Progressives, a feat which might still be accomplished by deft handling. The weakness, as always, was King, who seemed to accept the worst available advice about the Prairies. "I know that Dunning talks to him pretty plainly at times," Dafoe reported, "but King is perhaps developing the weakness of all Prime Ministers—that of only wanting to hear what fits in with his preconceptions."[14]

The one thing that was clear to Dafoe was that the Conservatives had to be prevented from obtaining office. "If by any chance Mr. Meighen were to get into office with a substantial majority behind him he would probably smash the country trying to make it conform with his theories," Dafoe told Sifton. In view of the fact that Meighen's strength appeared to be growing, a coalition of Liberal and Progressive forces was more necessary than ever. Dafoe thought that because the Progressives, apart from the Ginger Group, were essentially Liberals, "they would be content to serve as a sort of Western wing of the Liberal party" if the correct formula for fusion could be found. So far, the fusion had been prevented by elements in both groups who refused to make any sacrifice of their views. The only way that the strife between the groups could be overcome, and the West united, was through the adoption of the alternative vote. This reform would make co-operation between Liberals and Progressives possible and ensure the defeat of the Conservatives in the West. The next step would be a union of Liberals and Progressives. "If under these conditions," Dafoe predicted, "there were forty Progressives in the next House, and their support was necessary to keep the Tories out, it would be comparatively easy, I think, to bring about a fusion or merger which might establish Liberalism on a fairly substantial foundation."[15]

Dafoe thought that he could see the way events were moving, but it was impossible for him, or anyone else, to control them. His paper

[14]Dafoe Papers, Dafoe to Sifton, March 26, 1925.
[15]*Ibid.*, April 3, 1925.

advocated the adoption of the alternative vote, but the Liberal Government showed no sign of interest. The public advocacy of this reform was conducted on the high ground of principle, though Dafoe privately saw it as a means of weakening the Conservatives in the West. "The case for the transferable vote," the *Free Press* argued on April 22, 1925, "is not that it will help this or that political party, but that it is in the public interest as ensuring a parliament that will represent pretty accurately the views of the people." But neither principle nor expediency seemed to arouse any sympathy in official circles in Ottawa. As the day of the election drew nearer, it was increasingly clear that the three-way struggle of 1921 was to be repeated.

Dafoe was not in Winnipeg when the election writs were issued in 1925. Late in the summer he accepted an invitation to attend, for the third time, the Imperial Press Conference, meeting in Australia. He had never been away during an election before, but he had no regrets about his absence this time. He doubted if anything would be settled by the contest, though the ground would likely be laid for a post-election realignment of forces. He was rarely more accurate in his predictions than when he wrote in a mood of gaiety, "I think the fun will be *after* the election. Mr. King in his handling of the West & its representatives has bn. either a Napoleon or a damnphool, and the voting will show which." Whatever fun Dafoe may have had in mind, he could not have foreseen the exciting events of the next twelve months or the part that he and his paper were to play in them.[16]

While Dafoe was in Australia, the *Free Press* carried on the battle for "progressive" government. As in the 1921 election the paper avoided direct identification with any party, though its sympathies were most obviously with the Progressives and against the Conservatives. The old parties had failed the West and although the Liberals had been given an opportunity to mend their ways in 1921, they had refused it. As for the Conservatives, they were incorrigible. By the process of elimination, if for no better reason, the paper's choice was the Progressives.

Since 1921, Conservative strength had grown appreciably; even with a high tariff programme its appeal had increased in both East and West. Dafoe had feared this would happen. But what he did not anticipate was the disastrous cooling of the Progressive fervour among the Western electors. The election results showed that, although the people had not completely decided which of the parties should have control of the government, they had at least narrowed the choice by virtually eliminat-

[16]Sifton Papers, Dafoe to Harry Sifton, Sept. 6, 1925.

ing the Progressives. Only twenty-four Progressives were returned in 1925 and, ominously, the radicals now practically equalled the moderates. Both Liberals and Conservatives had gained something from the Progressive decline. In Ontario, where the farmers' party was nearly wiped out, the Conservatives gained most, but even in Manitoba seven of seventeen seats went to Arthur Meighen. The Progressive decline was also evident in the other two Prairie provinces; Dunning's Saskatchewan was the scene of a notable Liberal revival despite the national trend towards the Conservatives. The final tally showed Arthur Meighen's party with a plurality on the basis of 117 seats, while the Government's supporters had been reduced to 101. The 24 Progressives and 3 independents were thus of crucial importance.

The immediate question was what action the Liberals would take in the face of this serious loss of the country's confidence. The *Free Press*, in its election post mortem on October 30, assumed that the result was clear enough to justify the conclusion that Meighen had "earned the right to be called upon to form the next Government of Canada." The newspaper's owner thought differently. Dividing the members on the basis of their attitude to the tariff, Sifton found a majority favoured a low tariff, and he advised King "to stand to your guns & fight it out." King readily agreed with this advice. Despite personal and party defeat he might still be able to perform some miracle that would save himself and his party from oblivion, and the country from the evils of Tory rule.[17]

King was fighting for his political life. His position as party leader had always been precarious; his failure after four years of office to produce a winning combination suggested that all his critics had been correct in pronouncing him politically naive and inept. Shortly after the 1925 election a move was set afoot to replace him, probably with Charles Dunning. The latter had proved his effectiveness by keeping the Liberals in power in Saskatchewan during the Progressive onslaught and saving the province for the Liberals in 1925. Two of Dafoe's political confidants, A. B. Hudson and H. J. Symington, a former Winnipeg lawyer who had moved to Montreal, were close to the movement to dethrone King. Dafoe, just back from Australia in November 1925, was probably aware of the plan. Dunning was reluctant to take any action that might appear conspiratorial; he wanted King deposed by the Eastern Liberals before he stepped into the picture. But these calculations failed to include two important factors—King's political finesse and ambition. With grim determination King chose to remain in office and meet Parliament in the

[17]*Ibid.*, Sifton to W. L. M. King, n.d.

hope that the Progressives and independents would give their support to him.[18]

Constitutionally King had a complete right to meet Parliament. The *Free Press* noted this fact, but indicated that the only satisfactory resolution to the deadlock would be a new election. This reality was accepted at Ottawa, the paper claimed on November 3, and the party leaders were already manœuvring for post position. The editorial concluded with this realistic appraisal: "There will be a lot of talk about the moral aspect of the thing and of what is required in the national interest. Most of it can be taken with a grain of salt. The public can make up its mind that it will be political strategy and not the moral aspect that will govern the moves at Ottawa during the next few weeks." This was hardly a reassuring observation in view of the serious constitutional issues that were to arise in the near future. Nevertheless it provides an important insight into the activities of Dafoe and the *Free Press* during these hectic events.

Dafoe was no sooner home from Australia than he was swept into the negotiations started by the parties interested in resolving the political deadlock. The talks took place in Toronto between Liberal and Progressive leaders. Dafoe, no doubt in the East to consult with Sifton on the situation, took the responsibility of outlining the programme that would make co-operation between the two groups possible both in the coming session and a future election. In the talks Dafoe did not find Mackenzie King in quite the frame of mind that he had hoped. In fact the Prime Minister still seemed to think he could win the West by taking a couple of Westerners into his cabinet. But there were also more reassuring signs, especially the other Liberal leaders' willingness to show "a good deal more readiness to listen to the West than formerly—Quebec has come off the high horse under the whip of necessity; and I have no doubt a united West could get terms worthwhile in the event of a showdown."[19]

Back in Winnipeg Dafoe realized that King's stock had fallen to a new low level in the West. But there were growing signs that Dunning might be just the catalyst needed to bring together the disparate elements of Eastern and Western Liberalism. Even Henri Bourassa had suggested Dunning's name and offered to support a combination that would keep Meighen at bay. Then, too, there was the problem of the so-called Maritime Rights group. Though they had been elected as Conservatives, these members might prove sympathetic to a Liberal Government which

[18]Hudson Papers, H. J. Symington to A. B. Hudson, n.d., 1925.
[19]Dafoe Papers, Dafoe to Charles Dunning, Nov. 16, 1925; Dafoe to Robert Forke, Nov. 16, 1925.

offered some alleviation to the difficulties of the Atlantic provinces. "The more the situation is studied, the more its strategic possibilities are revealed—given the master tactician," Dafoe ruminated. "But where is he? Not I fear in the P.M.'s chair."[20]

Early in December Dafoe talked with some of the leaders of the Western splinter groups, and reported his observations to Sifton. Robert Forke believed that King intended to follow the tactics adopted in the last Parliament of depending upon the Progressives to keep him in power without making any open commitments to them. This course could only end in disaster. The Progressive leader saw some hope if Dunning went into the Government "with a view to the early accession to the leadership," but Forke had little confidence in King either as a man or a politician. On policy Forke, as usual, was lacking in clear ideas, though he said he would be satisfied if the tariff was kept at the existing level. Next, Dafoe consulted J. S. Woodsworth, Labour M.P., and his associate, William Irvine. Irvine was prepared to have King defeated immediately and replaced by someone more capable as Liberal leader. Woodsworth agreed that matters would be more satisfactory if King were replaced, but feared that a defeat of the Government would result in a long spell of Conservative rule. "I should say," Dafoe commented, "judging from the conversations, that in the event of a Liberal-Progressive combination Woodsworth could be relied upon for one session at least." Summing up, he concluded that if disaster was to be avoided, King would have to agree to definite terms with the Progressives about both the personnel and policies of his administration. Dunning should be taken into the cabinet and allowed wide powers to negotiate with the farmer members, whose suspicions of the Eastern Liberals might thus be overcome. "They may have a doubt about going tiger-hunting with King and his inner advisers whoever they may be. But the only option for the Progressives is taking a chance and pulling the building down upon themselves. Therefore I think they will take a chance on Dunning if he will take the risk of going in."[21]

There was no longer any question in Dafoe's mind about the continuance of the Progressives as a third party. Though he had always viewed the movement as a detached wing of the Liberals, he had never been in a rush to see a reunion take place. Now the situation had changed. The Conservatives were waiting anxiously for office, and once in they would not readily relinquish power. There was no time for any

[20]*Ibid.*, Dafoe to Sifton, Nov. 20, 1925; Sifton Papers, Dafoe to Sifton, Nov. 21, 1925.
[21]Dafoe Papers, Dafoe to Sifton, Dec. 5, Dec. 18, 1925.

further coquettish courting between Liberals and Progressives; the marriage had to be celebrated now or not at all.[22]

By January 1926 Dafoe was straining every means at his command to force the Liberals and Progressives together. Repeatedly the *Free Press* warned of the dangers that lay ahead if the two groups remained at odds. The essential problem was for the Government to accommodate its policies to the needs of the "unofficial Liberals." In the previous Parliament the Government's "desire was not to conciliate but to excommunicate." But that attitude could no longer be safely maintained, for, "no matter how much the anti-Meighen elements may snarl and rail at one another they are in the same boat. They have either got to co-operate to sail the ship or they will go on the rocks and the sharks will get them." Over and over again Westerners were warned that everything they stood for would be destroyed if Meighen were allowed to take office. After all, Meighen was a man of "courage and character," who would never reject his well-known principles to obtain office. And Meighen's principles were all anti-Western. The Progressives had to be brought to realize that the time had passed when they could reasonably expect to receive any further sympathy from the public if they refused to accept responsibility for their own actions. In effect accepting responsibility meant giving their support to the King Government.[23]

From the general warnings of the dire consequences that awaited both Liberals and Progressives if they failed to co-operate, Dafoe moved to the particular pressures that he could bring to bear on the Progressive leader. He advised Robert Forke to impress upon the members of his caucus that the Progressive influence would be greatly strengthened if some of the group entered the cabinet. Forke found that, apart from the recalcitrant Alberta members, his followers were in sympathy with this view. But this pointed up the next difficulty. Dafoe warned that unless Forke could be sure that all, or nearly all, his members would follow him into the Liberal camp, the move would be fruitless.[24]

Almost daily Dafoe discovered new factors that had to be weighed on the delicate political scales. This was the kind of crisis that made or destroyed political careers and every participant's move required careful assessment. The central figure under scrutiny was Arthur Meighen. Dafoe heartily disagreed with everything Meighen stood for; but he never made the mistake of under-estimating his political and intellectual

[22]*Ibid.*, Dafoe to Robert Borden, Jan. 29, 1926.
[23]*M.F.P.*, Dec. 9, 18, 1925.
[24]Dafoe Papers, Robert Forke to Dafoe, Jan. 28, 1926; Dafoe to Robert Forke, Feb. 1, 1926.

ability. Dafoe had heard reports that the Eastern Tories were unhappy with their leader and were awaiting an opportune occasion to put R. B. Bennett in his place. He believed that Meighen was aware of this threat and was therefore fighting desperately to gain office. In February 1926, Dafoe wrote of Meighen's tactics:

> If Meighen can get in and demand a dissolution, he is safe; otherwise he may have serious trouble on his hands. One of my reasons for wanting to see a coalition was that if a new deal of this kind were made, the Government, in the event of defeat, might reasonably ask the Governor General for a dissolution; whereas a purely party government, already in a minority, would probably be obliged without question to turn over the reigns of office to Meighen.

Though Dafoe had probably not considered the constitutional aspects of the political deadlock at this stage, he was here committing himself fairly definitely to the view that King's minority Government had no right to a dissolution. In this appraisal of the constitutional position of the King Government, Dafoe was repeating an opinion which he had formed four years earlier when a somewhat similar problem arose in Manitoba. In the 1920 provincial election, the Norris Liberal Government was reduced from the position of a majority party to one which held only a plurality in the Manitoba legislature. When the possibility of an immediate appeal to the country was mooted, Sifton warned Dafoe not to commit the *Free Press* to the view that Norris had a right to a dissolution. Dafoe had replied that he expected Norris would ask for dissolution if defeated in the legislature, but without any expectation of obtaining it. He continued: "I have said to Ministers of the Crown with whom I have spoken that they could not expect a dissolution under the circumstances, but that, of course, it was within the power of the Lieutenant-Governor to grant them one if he chose to take the responsibility." When the defeat came, Premier Norris took the position that he had no right to ask for a dissolution. Thus, both in 1921 and again in February 1926 Dafoe admitted that a Lieutenant-Governor or a Governor General could refuse a dissolution to a minority government that was defeated in its first session. More correctly, he took the view that such a government had not the right to expect a dissolution.[25]

If the change which took place in Dafoe's view on the royal power of dissolution by the summer of 1926 is to be understood, his attitude to politics in general and to Arthur Meighen in particular must be made clear. Dafoe was associated with politics and politicians most of his life

[25]*Ibid.*, Dafoe to Robert Forke, Feb. 15, 1926; Sifton to Dafoe, Feb. 23, 1921; Dafoe to Sifton, Feb. 26, 1921.

and he was not disposed to take an idealistic view of the latter's motives. Political crises always brought out men's true colours, and from the first Dafoe had expected that the indecisive election of 1925 would result in a scramble for power, motivated by self-interest. No matter what dedication to high principle was claimed, Liberals, Conservatives and Progressives were all seeking gratification for their appetites for power. More particularly both Meighen and King were fighting for their positions as party leaders. Since politics was largely a matter of competing interests, one simply had to choose between the lesser and the greater evils, or rather choose the party which came nearest to representing one's own interest. Some such belief was the unstated major premise of Dafoe's acitivities during the hectic events of the spring and summer of 1926. He harboured no illusions about the Liberal party, and on many counts was highly critical of it. He worked to promote a Liberal-Progressive alliance simply because he thought a government formed of these groups was much more to be desired than a Conservative administration. But he was anything but enthusiastic about the Liberals. He confessed his private view to Sifton, a man who never suffered much from political idealism:

> I may say that I have been able to understand and to some extent sympathize with the insurgent Progressives. Like them I have only been able to bring myself to give the Government a hand by contemplating the probabilities of the Conservatives coming to power. I don't want to see them in Ottawa with a majority of fifty or sixty behind them because I am pretty sure that the result would be that the country would be handed over to the corporations. I doubt, in this event, whether Mr. Meighen would make any resistance; and if he did he would be dealt with. It is the contemplation of the possibilities of Conservative ascendency that has bestirred me to activity on behalf of the Government.... I quite realize that the time may come, perhaps may not be very distant, when we may regret that we intervened and helped to save the Government from its fate.

Dafoe had chosen to throw in his lot with King because the alternative was thought to be far worse.[26]

In May 1926 he discovered further evidence of the unreliability of the Liberals. The evidence took the form of an unexpected revival of the separate school question, this time in Alberta. The Ottawa Government had reached an agreement with Alberta for the transfer of natural resources to the province. These resources included certain lands set aside for educational purposes. When the agreement came before Parliament in the spring of 1926, Henri Bourassa took the initiative in demanding that guarantees be written into the agreement to ensure that

[26]*Ibid.*, Dafoe to Sifton, Feb. 19, 1926.

the Roman Catholic minority in Alberta would continue to receive its share of the proceeds from the school lands. Despite assurances that the guarantees were already contained in the Alberta Act of 1905, the French Canadians apparently forced King to give further security. Immediately Premier Brownlee refused to accept the agreement and the volatile school question once more threatened to become an issue. Dafoe was angry at King for allowing the issue to arise, and complained that the Quebec Liberals "cannot help trying to put something over the Western Canadian provinces whenever opportunity occurs." He was even more infuriated when complaints were made to Harry Sifton about the *Free Press*'s criticism of the Alberta legislation. "I have long observed," he wrote sharply, "that public men in the matter of newspapers act like idiots." They failed to realize that a newspaper that constantly apologized for a government could never hope to influence the public. As for the Alberta school question it could easily cost the Liberals office, and if so "they will get what is coming to them." When the Government finally lost control of the House in June, Dafoe had no doubt that the basic reason for some of the Progressive antagonism to King was due to the clumsy handling of the Alberta natural resources question. King had blundered again, and for no apparent reason. "Upon the whole I think this is the stupidest performance that any political party was ever guilty of," Dafoe wrote.[27]

Still, Dafoe believed that King's blunders and shortcomings were far outweighed by the evils that would accompany the prime minstership of Arthur Meighen. The Conservatives advocated two policies in particular which were utterly abhorrent to Dafoe: a high tariff and a common imperial foreign policy. "There are two things that are not desirable for Canada," Dafoe told an English friend, "extreme economic nationalism and abject political colonialism. The Tories exploited both sentiments last election and it would have been a tragedy if they had succeeded thereby in attaining power." For these same reasons Dafoe was convinced that the Tories should at all costs be prevented from obtaining office. This was the prime consideration in determining Dafoe's attitude in the election of 1926.[28]

iii

The Customs Scandal, the issue which finally brought the breach between King and his Progressive allies, was of little interest to Dafoe.

[27]*Ibid.*, Dafoe to Robert Forke, May 25, 1926; Dafoe to Harry Sifton, May 26, June 30, 1926.
[28]*Ibid.*, Dafoe to W. L. Griffiths, May 4, 1926.

The *Free Press* gave it but scant attention on its editorial pages. The one thing that became clear as soon as the problem arose was that King had held on as long as he could. But was it long enough? As the crisis developed, the *Free Press* blandly informed its readers on June 17 that, had a Conservative motion of non-confidence been accepted, an immediate election would have been in order. "The Government's claim to a dissolution under the circumstances could not have been denied by the Governor General having regard to the precedents set in Great Britain in 1924." Privately, Dafoe approached the subject with more circumspection. Since events were moving to a rapid climax, everything depended upon the circumstances in which an election took place. He thought that if the Government was defeated there would be an immediate appeal to the country either on the initiative of the Government, "if it can get a dissolution," or by the incoming Conservative administration. "A dissolution under the latter auspices, would, I think, result in a Conservative victory," he predicted, "although not by any such wide margin as would have been obtained under similar conditions in January." On the whole it was political strategy rather than consitutional practice that interested Dafoe, though he thought he had found firm constitutional ground in the British instance in 1924.[29]

The validity of this constitutional argument, which Dafoe called forth repeatedly during the election campaign of 1926, deserves examination. The facts of the "precedent" suggest that Ramsay MacDonald was in a rather different position in 1924 than was King in 1926. MacDonald had formed his Government in January 1924 after Stanley Baldwin, who had been returned to office in December 1923 with a minority government, had been defeated in the House. Ten months later MacDonald was also defeated in the House and was granted an immediate dissolution by the King. George V granted the dissolution reluctantly, because there had already been two elections in two years and also because he was dubious about the right of a minority government to request a dissolution. He granted it, apparently, because he did not wish to appear to discriminate against a Labour government. This situation differed from the one in Canada in two important respects. First, MacDonald had not had a previous dissolution; King had. Secondly, MacDonald resigned after a vote of non-confidence had been passed in the House of Commons; King resigned when a vote of non-confidence was still being debated in the House of Commons, in order to avoid defeat. Finally, the fact that George V granted a dissolution to MacDonald in 1924 can hardly be generalized into the contention that

[29]*Ibid.*, Dafoe to Harry Sifton, June 23, 1926.

the Crown can never refuse a dissolution. Thus the MacDonald precedent seems irrelevant to the Canadian case.[30]

Dafoe believed that politicians acted first and sought their constitutional justification later. On June 26 the King administration was breathing with death-like gasps. Dafoe surmised that King was simply feigning in order to manœuvre himself into a strong position to request a dissolution. "I have no doubt the dying tactics of the Government are intended to make it plain to the Governor General that the parliamentary deadlock is so unbreakable that there is nothing for it but a reference to the people." He conceded that Byng might refuse the request for an appeal to the country, but the constitutional authorities indicated that "it would be a highly arbitrary act on his part."[31]

When the climax came and Lord Byng refused Prime Minister King's request for a dissolution, the *Free Press* relied on the British precedent of 1924 for its claim that "at every point the Governor General has departed from the precedent set by the King." But no mention was made of the peculiar circumstances which surrounded the request of the Liberal leader; a motion of non-confidence in the Government was being debated in the House of Commons. As E. A. Forsey has written, "No Government in this position had ever been refused a dissolution. No Government in this position had ever asked for a dissolution. The refusal was unprecedented; so was the request."[32]

A Conservative Government, the very thing which Dafoe had exerted every effort to prevent, was at last a reality. King had bungled, and now Arthur Meighen, with an assist from Lord Byng, was to have his opportunity. As on many previous occasions, Dafoe was prepared to see King's career brought to an abrupt end. It was obvious that "as an opposition party the Liberals need a new leader, who of necessity must be Dunning." Once more Dafoe under-estimated the Liberal leader.[33]

The Conservative administration was a short affair. Meighen, anxious for office and wishing to finish the session before adjourning to allow his cabinet colleagues an opportunity to seek re-election, formed a ministry by the curious, though not illegal device of appointing temporary ministers without portfolio. He presented only himself for re-election, claiming that his colleagues had not assumed the full responsibilities of ministers, received no salaries from the Crown, and therefore

[30]H. Nicolson, *King George V* (London, 1952), 400.
[31]Dafoe Papers, Dafoe to Harry Sifton, June 26, 1926.
[32]*M.F.P.*, June 29, 1926; E. A. Forsey, *The Royal Power of Dissolution in the British Commonwealth* (Toronto, 1943), 144.
[33]Dafoe Papers, Dafoe to Harry Sifton, June 30, 1926.

were under no necessity to resign their seats. For three days this "shadow cabinet" tried to carry on while their frustrated leader watched from the sidelines. Finally on Dominion Day, as if to give one last exhibition of the Progressives' confusion, T. W. Bird inadvertently broke his Parliamentary pair and stood up to be counted in a division that, by a single vote, ended Meighen's term of office. Now there was no alternative but an appeal to the electorate. In commenting on this midsummer madness on July 3, the *Free Press* accurately forecast that all the important political and economic issues would now be set aside while the country debated the "constitutional crisis" that had resulted from Lord Byng's refusal to grant the Liberals the dissolution that had now been given to the Conservatives.

Since the war, even during elections, the *Free Press* had attempted to maintain an attitude of independence. Of course, its anti-Conservative bias had always been evident, but it had not returned to the Liberal partisanship which had characterized its pages before 1914. Facing the prospect of a long term of Tory rule, the paper dropped all pretence of independence in 1926. It offered its full support to the Liberals, and made the "constitutional crisis" the central issue of the campaign. As in other elections, the *Free Press* attempted to express the views of the West. It presented a five-point programme, including maintenance of the Crow's Nest Pass Agreement, statutory grain haulage rates, freer trade, completion of the Hudson Bay Railway, and definition of Dominion status. But, in relation to the constitutional question, these demands paled into insignificance.

In the *Free Press*'s campaign the distinction between the Liberals and the Progressives was erased. The Prairie electors were warned that the advantage would be handed to Meighen if the opposition was divided in Western constituencies. Liberals and Progressives were exhorted to unite to avoid the "idiocies of last year." Certainly there were still problems that divided the Eastern Liberals and the Western "unofficial Liberals," but the most critical issue united them. Meighen had to be defeated not only because his party stood for policies destructive to Prairie progress, but also because it subscribed to a constitutional doctrine that flew in the face of the entire history of Canadian development. This was the way that Dafoe chose to interpret Meighen's acceptance of the responsibility for Byng's refusal to allow King a dissolution. There had been no suggestion of these tactics in Dafoe's earlier reflections on the political and constitutional confusion at Ottawa. But in the fury of an election campaign all the important problems of maladministration, economic recovery and even constitutional subtlety were reduced to the simple dialectic of nationalism *versus* imperialism.[34]

Dafoe assumed that the Crown's grant of a dissolution to MacDonald's minority Government in 1924 represented a final proof that the King could no longer exercise the right to refuse a request for an election. Was the Canadian parliamentary system to be governed by a contrary set of rules? Surely equality of status was meaningless if the imperial Government's representative in Canada was allowed to exercise powers obsolete in Great Britain. But Arthur Meighen had defended Lord Byng's decision to reject the advice of his chief minister. Therefore it was crystal clear that the Conservatives accepted the view that Canada's elected representatives did not exercise the same authority as was allowed to the elected representatives of the British people. In sum, the faulty logic of this contention led to the conclusion that the Conservatives believed Canada was a colony and Britain a nation. On July 5 the *Free Press* declared:

> Clearly Mr. Meighen thinks we fall under the Colonial and not under the British procedure. We are, again in Mr. Meighen's judgment, not competent to deal with these questions ourselves as the people of Great Britain are, but must submit ourselves to be "governed" by an official responsible not to us but to the head of a department of state who sits in Downing Street.

On this theme Dafoe played a multiplicity of variations, but the underlying harmony was the same: was Canada to be a colony or a nation? The electors were advised to cast their ballots for King to ensure that "the well-defined procedure which has been observed for a century in Great Britain should be followed at Ottawa." Inadvertently the *Free Press* singled out the real cause of the constitutional confusion when it remarked that "the present constitutional crisis in Canada is another direct result of the failure to define our status." Here was the root of the matter, though not in the sense that Dafoe's paper maintained. The fact that Canada's status remained undefined allowed room for exactly the kind of misinterpretation that the *Free Press* and the Liberals indulged in during the summer of 1926. In the days before the Balfour Report, the Governor General was the appointee of the British government alone; there was no clearly defined relation between Britain and the dominions. These considerations in no way affect the constitutional question of 1926, but they do help to explain why it was possible to dress the constitutional question in the myth of Downing Street domination.[35]

[34] *M.F.P.*, July 22, 1926.   [35] *Ibid.*, July 6, 31, 1926.

The argument that in the election of 1926 the Canadian people were presented with a choice between national autonomy and colonial subordination is specious. In fact Byng's refusal to grant King a dissolution had little if any bearing on imperial relations. Dafoe argued that if Canada was equal to Britain, then the constitutional procedure of the two countries should be identical. But why should it be so? Difference in constitutional procedure might be even more indicative of equality of status, since it would illustrate the Dominion's intention of striking out in an independent direction. But the central piece of evidence in destroying the nationalism *versus* imperialism interpretation of the 1926 affair is Mackenzie King's letter of resignation of June 28, 1926, in which he advised Lord Byng to refer the dissolution question to the Secretary of State for the Dominions for an opinion. King's suggestion represents a request for British interference in Canadian affairs; Byng's rejection of the suggestion illustrates his rectitude in the matter of Dominion autonomy. Dafoe refused to consider this incident in the story of 1926. Seventeen years later, when asked directly about his interpretation of this suggestion, he replied that King "had acted with much common sense."[36]

Dafoe never moved an inch from his 1926 position. In 1943 when E. A. Forsey's book, *The Royal Power of Dissolution*, appeared, Dafoe chose to view it as part of a campaign to discredit King during the critical days of the war. He pronounced the book

> a campaign document, apparently planned to appear at the moment when Mr. Meighen, re-emerging from the shades into which the electors of Canada at the instance of Mr. King cast him in 1926, would take belated vengeance upon the victor.
> If in the presentation of his case Mr. Forsey's skill had matched his venom, this would have been one of the greatest political pamphlets in the English language. As it is, it is a pretentious "dud".

Despite Forsey's reasoned, but increasingly angry protests, Dafoe refused to meet his contentions with facts. The final answer he gave was: "There was an authority whose judgment was decisive but to which Mr. Forsey gives no heed. The authority was the Canadian electorate. . . . When the text-books clash with this decision they are obsolete so far as Canada is concerned." In short when pressed into a corner, Dafoe took refuge in plebiscitarian rather than parliamentary democracy.[37]

---

[36]R. MacG. Dawson, *Constitutional Issues in Canada, 1900-1931* (London, 1933), 73; W.F.P., "Excitable Letter Writer," June 12, 1943.

[37]Dafoe Papers, Dafoe to Grant Dexter, April 19, 1943; W.F.P., "The King-Byng Episode," May 10, 1943. One example of Forsey's later replies indicates that it was not only Dafoe who could command invective. "To you, on this

No fair-minded reader of this exchange could fail to sympathize with Forsey's exasperation, nor doubt that Dafoe had met his master But rather than concede, the Winnipeg editor used his powerful newspaper in a manner that can command little admiration. There can be no doubt, either, that Dafoe remained convinced that he was right. Quite apart from the natural human disinclination to admit error, Dafoe believed that Forsey's book was a part of a plot to overthrow King. In 1943 Dafoe was even more convinced than he had been in 1926 that Arthur Meighen should be prevented from replacing King as Prime Minister. Therefore he struck out in all directions in an effort to kill the Meighen revival. Eugene Forsey absorbed a great many of the blows.

Both in 1926 when the "constitutional crisis" was first fought out, and again in 1943 when it was re-enacted in a lesser way, political tactics played a far more important role in determining Dafoe's views than any theoretical consideration of the constitutional issues involved. In both cases the desire to prevent Meighen from obtaining office was primary. To this was added the nationalist cry. Dafoe sincerely believed that a Governor General appointed by the British was a symbol of Canadian subordination to Britain—at least if the Governor General exercised any important powers. His attitude to Lord Byng in 1926 was very similar to his attitude to Lord Minto in 1901. Dafoe failed to distinguish between the Governor General as an official of the British Government and the Governor General as a necessary part of Canadian parliamentary democracy. In 1926 he believed he had struck a blow against imperialism, when in fact he had more likely struck a blow against parliamentary government.

In its comments on the 1926 election results, the *Free Press* illustrated Dafoe's dual motivation in the campaign—opposition to Meighen, and belief that the nationalist cause was at stake. It declared on September 15:

The people of Canada have indicated their disagreement with the view that our Governor General comes to Canada in the capacity of an umpire to put Canadian parties in their place if, in his wisdom and discretion, he

---

subject," Forsey wrote (*W.F.P.*, June 9, 1943), "precedent is nothing, authority is nothing, common sense is nothing; you cheerfully consign to the dust-bin Australia, New Zealand, South Africa and all the provinces of Canada, and Peel, Russell, Gladstone, Dicey, Jennings, Evatt and a host of others, Conservative, Liberal, Labour. Who are these, what is history itself, to weigh in the balance against such giants as Mr. John S. Ewart and the editor of the Winnipeg Free Press? But would it not have saved time and ink if you had simply announced at the outset that the Winnipeg Free Press, speaking ex cathedra on a constitutional question, is infallible?"

thinks it necessary to discipline them. All future Governors General will understand that they are constitutional monarchs who will have to content themselves with powers and privileges which are sufficient to the King himself.

History will say that the election of 1926 was one of the most crucial in the life of Canada. A wrong decision would have been a serious thing for Canada. It would have saddled us with policies which would have bred sectional feuds threatening Confederation, and it would have gone far to put us back to a status from which we long ago emerged.

The election result was the triumph of Canadian nationalism over colonialism and sectionalism.

Thus the constitutional issue of 1926 was settled by an appeal to the people. Yet Dafoe did not think that the rejection of the Byng doctrine of dissolution by the electorate made the Governor General a complete rubber stamp. On the contrary he argued both in 1926 and again in 1943 that there still existed a prerogative right that could be used to protect the people from a government that refused to relinquish its authority, that is, a royal power to force a dissolution. "It is in the last resort a right of dismissal, that is, of appeal to the people," the paper explained on September 29, 1926. In his view of the forced dissolution, as in his opinion that the electorate settled the question of the right of the Governor General to reject a request for dissolution, Dafoe based his conclusions on a doctrine of popular sovereignty. The logical implication of this view is plebiscitary government in which constitutional practice is reduced to the decision of the people in the latest general election. Its result is to increase enormously the power of the Prime Minister and his cabinet at the expense of the Governor General on the one hand, and more important, the houses of Parliament on the other.

Dafoe was particularly gratified by the tune which the voice of the people sang in 1926, for it was the song of nationalism. If the crucial issue of the 1926 campaign was the constitutional one, then Dafoe was correct in interpreting the election as a triumph of his version of nationalism. Quite apart from the validity of the Liberal view of the constitutional question, the fact that it was presented as an aspect of the conflict of nationalism and imperialism gave Canadian electors the opportunity to express their preference for the nationalist, autonomist viewpoint. But the nationalism expressed in the election meant more than an assertion of Canadian autonomy. It also meant at least a temporary triumph of national unity over sectional disharmony. In 1926, so far as Dafoe was concerned, nationalism replaced progressivism. The constitutional issue had forced all the stock questions which agitated Western Canada during the early post-war years to take a weak secondary place. More important, it provided the guise by which Western Progressives of the Dafoe variety could fold their tents and silently steal into the Liberal camp.[38]

Dafoe had been the supporter and mentor of the Progressive movement because he believed that the old parties had lost touch with Western needs. The purpose of the Progressive movement, in his view, was to drive the Liberals back to their original Garden of Eden innocence before the serpent of protectionism had left its venomous mark on the party. Originally he hoped to see the "Tory" element driven out of the party, and the remaining fragments unite with the farmers. As the possibility of this development dimmed he looked towards a coalition or alliance which would at least ensure the fulfilment of minimum Western demands. But by the beginning of 1926 he had come to realize that the luxury of continued Progressive independence could only be purchased at the heavy price of allowing the Conservatives to obtain office. Like many Canadian voters Dafoe turned to King less because of the Liberal leader's virtues than from fear of the supposed vices of his opponents. In 1926 when the constitutional issue arose, Dafoe grasped the issue with both hands since it was one on which the Liberals and Progressives could agree. In Western Canada co-operation between the Progressives and the Liberals, and the campaign of the *Free Press* (circumstances that were by no means unrelated) contributed largely to the Liberal victory. Association between Liberals and Progressives in 1926 was possible where it had been absent in earlier elections, because of the nature of the issues as they were presented by the Liberals and the *Free Press*. The West was aggressively nationalist in its attitude to imperial relations. So was the Quebec-dominated Liberal party. Here was a wide area where agreement rather than dispute was possible between Liberals and Progressives. Furthermore, there was a common antagonism to Arthur Meighen. In 1926 this antagonism was easily brought into focus because of the peculiar circumstances of the election; the "constitutional crisis" made it possible to represent Meighen as the willing handmaiden of an imperial scheme to prevent Canada from exercising complete powers of nationhood. To both Liberals and Progressives, Meighen represented everything that was reactionary in both domestic and imperial affairs. The constitutional issue dressed in nationalistic garb provided the opportunity for Meighen's enemies to bury their differences in the face of the Conservative threat.[39]

Thus by the autumn of 1926 Mackenzie King had taken the majority

[38]Dafoe Papers, Dafoe to G. M. Wrong, Sept. 17, 1926.
[39]Hudson Papers, A. B. Hudson to W. L. M. King, Sept. 18, 1926.

of the Progressive voters into camp without having made any definite policy commitments to them. He was able to win this easy, though late, victory because he, like the Progressives, was an autonomist who turned the constitutional issue into a problem of imperial relations. Dafoe had first been attracted to King at the Imperial Conference of 1923. He returned home convinced that King shared his views on imperial policy, but sceptical of his ability to cope with domestic problems. In 1926 Dafoe and King were brought together on an issue of both domestic and imperial significance. Whatever opportunism there may have been in Dafoe's discussion of the "constitutional crisis," he nevertheless believed that the success of the autonomist view of the Empire depended upon the outcome of this election. A victory for Meighen would set the movement in reverse. Though King had his weaknesses, he was infinitely more attractive to Dafoe than the Conservative leader. This was what he meant when he told Sifton after the election that "our fight in the West was more *against* Meighen and his policies than *for* King." This sentence may well be the only necessary explanation of the success of King's career.[40]

Dafoe was much closer to King in 1926 than he had ever been before. There was now no talk of a new Liberal leader. King had fought the good fight and won; perhaps now his grasp on the problems facing the country would be firmer. Despite the heat of the campaign, the election of 1926 had a settling effect on Canadian politics. King was in office with his first majority; Arthur Meighen's career was destroyed; the Progressives had virtually disappeared from the scene. And what of Dafoe? After a decade of wandering he was back in the Liberal party, and somewhat uneasy about it. The immediate task before him was to re-establish the independence of the *Free Press* which, he admitted, had been undermined by his vigorous campaign on behalf of the Liberals in the preceding months.[41]

[40]Dafoe Papers, Dafoe to Sifton, Sept. 27, 1926.
[41]Willison Papers, Dafoe to Sir John Willison, Sept. 17, 1926; Dafoe Papers, Dafoe to Grant Dexter, Sept. 17, 1926; Dafoe to Sifton, Sept. 27, 1926.

x. Canada,
the Commonwealth and the World
1923-30

ALTHOUGH MUCH OF DAFOE'S ATTENTION in the twenties was devoted to domestic politics, he never lost interest in imperial and international affairs. Of course, as the election of 1926 graphically illustrated, there was no real division between domestic and external affairs. As imperial and international events developed, Dafoe's views broadened. His widening interests, in turn, were accompanied by an enhanced reputation. Rapidly he was becoming known as the leading Canadian journalist not only in his own country, but through the English-speaking world. Each time the Imperial Press Conference met—in Canada in 1920, in Australia in 1925 and in Britain in 1930—the Winnipeg editor was in attendance. In addition to having an increasing number of speaking engagements in Canada, he was heard by audiences in Great Britain and the United States. In short, Dafoe was becoming one of the best-known spokesmen of Canadian Liberal nationalism. Sometimes his views were not appreciated. Geoffrey Dawson, editor of *The Times*, decided in November 1924 that Dafoe's influence on imperial matters was reaching undesirable proportions. He hoped that an editorial in *The Times* might do something to undermine the autonomists. "It is addressed (though not by name) partly to Mackenzie King, and partly to Dafoe, who is really quite obsessed with getting a formal 'declaration' about Dominion status," Dawson explained to Sir John Willison.[1]

Not all Dafoe's speeches and writings in the twenties were devoted to the well-worn theme of developing Canadian nationalism. In addition, and as a logical extension of this theme, he gave increasing attention to

---

[1] Willison Papers, Geoffrey Dawson to Sir John Willison, Nov. 12, 1924; *The Times*, Nov. 11, 1924.

Canada's role in international affairs and the problems of Canadian-American relations. Canada, the Commonwealth, the United States and the League all formed part of a single pattern evolving in Dafoe's mind.

During the early years after the war the question that most often claimed Dafoe's attention when he turned from Canada's domestic concerns was that of Dominion autonomy. He was afflicted with a severe case of the "status complex," and never missed an opportunity to assert his conviction that a clear definition should be given to the standing of the dominions. Logically nationhood was a prerequisite of full, independent involvement in international affairs, though Dafoe also realized that international activities could raise Canada's national importance. Yet for all his preoccupation with status, he still found time to consider the problems of the League and world peace. Certainly in the twenties he was not the single-minded supporter of the League that he became in later years, but he did realize that Canadian nationhood was of little value if the world was to be repeatedly engaged in destructive warfare. He saw the League as an instrument through which nations, large and small, could co-operate in the preservation of peace. And since the Geneva organization was precisely what its name suggested, a league of nations, Canada's membership was an open recognition of nationhood. Here it could act, not as the subordinate of an Empire, but as the equal of other nations in an organization which included all the emancipated dominions. Gradually Dafoe came to regard the League as the machinery that made it possible for the British nations to co-operate among themselves and with other nations, without bearing the stigma of imperialism.

Though Dafoe had not personally fought in the Great War he was acutely conscious of its horror. To him it represented a collapse of civilization that would take a long time to get over. The convalescence would be neither automatic nor rapid, but would be painfully slow, requiring every available assistance. The disease of war had ravaged the world and if the germs were not extirpated, the illness would recur. Dafoe believed that his generation was the one that had to pay the price in harsh penance for the sins of 1914–18. He told a Winnipeg audience in 1919:

> You and I, alive by the sacrifices of better men, are in a position to help in this work. Today we are in troubled waters, but we hope that somewhere downstream these waters will be smoother and there will be peace and happiness. That will, however, be in the day of a future generation. For this one there can be no abiding peace. The whole world is in travail, and must jointly bear its burden.

It was not simply the ruinous nature of war that impressed Dafoe, but more important the fact that, once started, war produced more problems than it settled. The fighting of the war was child's play in comparison with the making of peace. "One of the reasons why the world cannot enjoy the doubtful excitement of war," he wrote in 1923, "is that under modern conditions you can make war, but you cannot make peace."[2]

In writing of the League, its promises and projects, Dafoe had always to be mindful of the inhibiting isolationism of his employer. Sifton was very much opposed to Canadian entanglement in European affairs, and was especially perturbed about the possibility that Canadian membership in the League would cause friction with the United States.[3] Dafoe had some reservations about the League, but he had no doubt about the necessity of the organization. Canada shared to some degree the objections of the United States to the League—it should not be allowed to limit Canadian sovereignty nor draw Canada into European imperial ambitions. "But the distrust does not justify an isolation which is not possible in the growing interdependence of people, but suggests rather co-operation upon a basis which does not detract from our national integrity," the *Free Press* explained on April 21, 1921.

Dafoe believed that the United States had made a grievous error in rejecting membership in the League, and that she would eventually recognize this mistake. A world organization without the United States was not only practically useless, but also it might be dangerous. The European powers might make it the instrument of their "imperialistic" ends, thus destroying its "democratic and anti-imperialist" character. Until the United States engaged in League activities, Canada would have to tread softly to avoid undesirable complications. But it would certainly remain a member of the organization. After all, League membership was "a simply invaluable argument at the disposal of those who urge the opinion that the dominions have attained sovereign power." The real danger to Canada was imperial centralization and Geneva helped to offset this threat. These arguments had little effect on Sifton, with the result that *Free Press* comments on the League during the twenties were usually circumspect and non-committal.[4]

When speaking publicly on collective security, Dafoe's views were far more clearly defined than the editorial policy of his paper would suggest. His central theme was usually the necessity of recognizing the

[2]Dafoe, "Canada and the Peace Conference" in *Speeches of the Year* (Winnipeg: Canadian Club, 1919), 103; Dafoe, "Impressions Overseas," *Bulletin of the League of Nations Society* (Dec. 1923), 2.
[3]Sifton Papers, Sifton to Dafoe, April 25, 1921.
[4]Dafoe Papers, Dafoe to Sifton, May 18, 1921.

revolution in diplomatic methods that the League had produced, or at least, could produce if member nations fulfilled their obligations. The bad old days of imperialism, militarism, secret diplomacy and autocracy had been forsaken in favour of the new world of democracy, open diplomacy, self-determination and international co-operation. The League provided the machinery for this transformation, but it did not make the change inevitable. The old categories of thought remained strong and could even capture the League. Dafoe told an audience in 1924 that "to minds steeped in pre-war wisdom and philosophy the League and all that it embodies is nothing but foolishness; and if they continue to direct the affairs of men the League will either die outright or, sadder still, it will be taken captive and set to grinding corn in the mills of the Philistines." Only a thoroughly enlightened public opinion could save the League from this fate.

Dafoe admitted that the League was not perfect, but he pointed out that the weaknesses frequently stemmed from public misunderstanding of the organization's real nature. The fundamental fact about the League was that it was made up of nations; it had no power apart from that given it by the member nations. "It is not a stream full of potential energy," he noted. "It is a flume which is dry and useless until water is turned into it." The weaknesses of the League were therefore the weaknesses of its members who failed to fulfil their obligations under the Covenant.

The success of the League demanded that individuals and nations have faith in its objectives and its ability to achieve them. Surely the nations of the world had seen enough of war to be ready to seek peaceful solutions to their problems. Surely mankind had reached a point in its moral development where the barbarism of war was totally repugnant. This was the faith, with its overtones of nineteenth-century optimism, that was embodied in the League of Nations. In 1924 Dafoe was not sure it was a faith that would convert the whole world. The Messianic signs had appeared, but whether the new revelation would overcome the old tribal gods remained uncertain. "The issue is not settled," he admitted prophetically; "a nation insane with nationalist ambition; a national leader, vain, reckless, glory-seeking, might bring the whole fabric to the ground."[5]

When Dafoe moved from generalities about the League to specific questions of Canada's role in international affairs, his vision was often obstructed by his preoccupation with status. Until a clear definition of Dominion powers was obtained, the practical objectives of Canadian

[5]*Ibid.*, notes for a speech, April 22, 1924.

foreign policy received scanty attention. The *Free Press* sometimes recognized that a policy of negation, which was what the quest for status amounted to, was not a foreign policy. "Is it not time for Canada to consider this question of foreign policy in all its relations and with all its implications?" Dafoe's paper queried on February 5, 1923. But the question usually went begging for an answer as long as Canada's status remained undefined. No doubt it was easier for Dafoe to write about the question of status, a subject on which there was complete accord between editor and publisher, than to write on questions of policy relating to the League, where there was discord.

Several incidents in the twenties illustrate the way in which the quest for status affected Dafoe's thinking on the subject of Canadian foreign policy. The Chanak crisis in 1922 was an obvious case. Then in 1924 came the debate over the Lausanne Treaty, which finally ended the war with Turkey. Since Canada had not been involved in the peace negotiations, the Liberal Government took the position that Canada was free of obligations connected with the treaty. Dafoe believed that this stand was in complete agreement with the principles laid down at the 1923 Imperial Conference. Only a "freemasonary of Imperial diehards" refused to recognize this fact. But was Canada left at war with the Turks? The whole confused question, a confusion further compounded by Mackenzie King's fine distinction between "legal" and "moral" obligations created by the treaty, only presented a further example of the anomalous position of the dominions. "We pretend among ourselves that the Dominions are nations," Dafoe reflected, "but no foreign country is under any obligation to accept us at that valuation."[6]

Canada's relations with the League were also confused by the status question. During 1924 and 1925 several attempts were made at Geneva to meet France's desire to strengthen the collective security provisions of the Covenant. The Geneva Protocol, sponsored by the MacDonald Labour Government, contained some features which Dafoe thought were wholly unacceptable. He feared that any attempt to strengthen League obligations would further harden the isolationism of the United States. But if it was made clear that the Protocol intended nothing more than a restatement of the principles already embodied in the Covenant, Dafoe thought Canada should support it. Then the suggestion that the Dominion prime ministers should go to London to consider the Protocol roused Dafoe's opposition. Such matters could only be decided by the individual Dominion governments, the *Free Press* maintained on Decem-

[6]Sifton Papers, Dafoe to Sifton, April 10, 1924; Dafoe Papers, Dafoe to Grant Dexter, April 11, 1924.

revolution in diplomatic methods that the League had produced, or at least, could produce if member nations fulfilled their obligations. The bad old days of imperialism, militarism, secret diplomacy and autocracy had been forsaken in favour of the new world of democracy, open diplomacy, self-determination and international co-operation. The League provided the machinery for this transformation, but it did not make the change inevitable. The old categories of thought remained strong and could even capture the League. Dafoe told an audience in 1924 that "to minds steeped in pre-war wisdom and philosophy the League and all that it embodies is nothing but foolishness; and if they continue to direct the affairs of men the League will either die outright or, sadder still, it will be taken captive and set to grinding corn in the mills of the Philistines." Only a thoroughly enlightened public opinion could save the League from this fate.

Dafoe admitted that the League was not perfect, but he pointed out that the weaknesses frequently stemmed from public misunderstanding of the organization's real nature. The fundamental fact about the League was that it was made up of nations; it had no power apart from that given it by the member nations. "It is not a stream full of potential energy," he noted. "It is a flume which is dry and useless until water is turned into it." The weaknesses of the League were therefore the weaknesses of its members who failed to fulfil their obligations under the Covenant.

The success of the League demanded that individuals and nations have faith in its objectives and its ability to achieve them. Surely the nations of the world had seen enough of war to be ready to seek peaceful solutions to their problems. Surely mankind had reached a point in its moral development where the barbarism of war was totally repugnant. This was the faith, with its overtones of nineteenth-century optimism, that was embodied in the League of Nations. In 1924 Dafoe was not sure it was a faith that would convert the whole world. The Messianic signs had appeared, but whether the new revelation would overcome the old tribal gods remained uncertain. "The issue is not settled," he admitted prophetically; "a nation insane with nationalist ambition; a national leader, vain, reckless, glory-seeking, might bring the whole fabric to the ground."[5]

When Dafoe moved from generalities about the League to specific questions of Canada's role in international affairs, his vision was often obstructed by his preoccupation with status. Until a clear definition of Dominion powers was obtained, the practical objectives of Canadian

[5] *Ibid.*, notes for a speech, April 22, 1924.

foreign policy received scanty attention. The *Free Press* sometimes recognized that a policy of negation, which was what the quest for status amounted to, was not a foreign policy. "Is it not time for Canada to consider this question of foreign policy in all its relations and with all its implications?" Dafoe's paper queried on February 5, 1923. But the question usually went begging for an answer as long as Canada's status remained undefined. No doubt it was easier for Dafoe to write about the question of status, a subject on which there was complete accord between editor and publisher, than to write on questions of policy relating to the League, where there was discord.

Several incidents in the twenties illustrate the way in which the quest for status affected Dafoe's thinking on the subject of Canadian foreign policy. The Chanak crisis in 1922 was an obvious case. Then in 1924 came the debate over the Lausanne Treaty, which finally ended the war with Turkey. Since Canada had not been involved in the peace negotiations, the Liberal Government took the position that Canada was free of obligations connected with the treaty. Dafoe believed that this stand was in complete agreement with the principles laid down at the 1923 Imperial Conference. Only a "freemasonary of Imperial diehards" refused to recognize this fact. But was Canada left at war with the Turks? The whole confused question, a confusion further compounded by Mackenzie King's fine distinction between "legal" and "moral" obligations created by the treaty, only presented a further example of the anomalous position of the dominions. "We pretend among ourselves that the Dominions are nations," Dafoe reflected, "but no foreign country is under any obligation to accept us at that valuation."[6]

Canada's relations with the League were also confused by the status question. During 1924 and 1925 several attempts were made at Geneva to meet France's desire to strengthen the collective security provisions of the Covenant. The Geneva Protocol, sponsored by the MacDonald Labour Government, contained some features which Dafoe thought were wholly unacceptable. He feared that any attempt to strengthen League obligations would further harden the isolationism of the United States. But if it was made clear that the Protocol intended nothing more than a restatement of the principles already embodied in the Covenant, Dafoe thought Canada should support it. Then the suggestion that the Dominion prime ministers should go to London to consider the Protocol roused Dafoe's opposition. Such matters could only be decided by the individual Dominion governments, the *Free Press* maintained on Decem-

[6]Sifton Papers, Dafoe to Sifton, April 10, 1924; Dafoe Papers, Dafoe to Grant Dexter, April 11, 1924.

ber 30, 1924. Further reflection and some straightforward urging from Sifton caused Dafoe to move into complete opposition to the proposed League reform. Sifton's unvarnished isolationism manifested itself in vigorous hostility to the Protocol, which he suspected would draw Canada further into European affairs. Support for the League might do some good, he thought, but he was deeply "suspicious of the bunch of second-rate professors that are congregating around Geneva; busybodies who think in small dimensions but long-winded sentences." Since he was already worried about the Protocol, especially the effect it might have on Canadian-American relations, Dafoe accepted Sifton's candid advice and attacked the MacDonald proposal. "Make the League into a superstate in the present stage of evolving international morality and it will inevitably become an agency of Imperialism decked out in the attractive garments of peace," the *Free Press* warned.[7]

The failure of the Protocol led to the Locarno pacts, which, by guaranteeing Germany's western boundaries, made an attempt to calm the fears of its neighbours. At the same time Germany was admitted to the League of Nations. The *Free Press* gave warm approval to this arrangement, which it interpreted as a realistic admission of Germany's place in world affairs. More important, the Locarno agreements made no attempt to commit the dominions to any obligations, unless they specifically approved the terms. In this, the *Free Press* quite rightly saw a definite international recognition of the independent status of the dominions.[8]

Dafoe's comments on Locarno again illustrated that the quest for status was of greater concern to him than the actual consideration of specific questions of foreign policy. He was not an isolationist, but he believed that until the constitutional relation of the members of the Commonwealth was clearly defined, Canada should avoid entanglements in European affairs. Such involvement might be mistaken for a commitment to a common imperial obligation, which, in Dafoe's view, would constitute a limitation on Canadian autonomy.

ii

Even after the outcome of the 1923 Imperial Conference Dafoe was not satisfied with the state of Canada's relations with the other members of the British family of nations. In January 1925 he began publishing

[7]Dafoe Papers, Dafoe to Sifton, Nov. 24, 1924; Sifton to Dafoe, March 10, 1925. *M.F.P.*, Jan. 24, 1925.
[8]*M.F.P.*, Dec. 2, 1925; Feb. 18, 1926.

in the *Free Press* monthly literary section a series of articles on the constitutional development of the Empire. This series, which ran for eight months, represents one of the best statements of Dafoe's Liberal nationalist viewpoint. The central theme was the story of the struggle for full self-government within the Empire carried on by the British colonies after the American Revolution. Self-government, Dafoe held, was the supreme achievement of Englishmen. The lesson of the American Revolution was that to refuse to grant self-government to Englishmen wherever they settled was to court disaster. After the revolt of the Thirteen Colonies, British colonial policy-makers were chiefly concerned with the attempt to find a solution to the problems which had resulted in the destruction of the First Empire. The point at issue was the question whether the colonies were subject to the authority of the British Parliament, or merely to the authority of the Crown. The history of the Empire since the American colonists had rejected subordination to the British Parliament was the story of the gradual emergence of the idea of colonial self-government under the Crown. But the idea of colonial subordination had not been completely discredited by the revolt of the colonies; it had been unsuccessfully revived late in the nineteenth century. Thus imperial history was the account of the conflict between the idea of centralization and the idea of local autonomy.[9]

The American Revolution, Dafoe wrote, was an unfortunate mistake which had resulted from failure to apply the distinctive British doctrine of self-government to the colonies. There was no need in 1775, or later, for insoluble conflicts between colonies and imperial authorities; self-government prevented friction and at the same time preserved unity. The well-worn tale of imperial development led to the single irrefutable, Whig conclusion:

> This study of Imperial constitutional development is the story of a continuing tendency in which the working of the political instinct of the British people is revealed. Sooner or later the instinct has prevailed against artificial barriers intended to control it, however deeply rooted they may have seemed to be in political necessity, whatever the buttresses of sentiment which appeared to uphold them. This is the instinct of self-government. It has the vitality, the unconquerability of natural force; and its pressure towards full expression is steady and, in the end, irresistible.

Dafoe was a journalist, not a historian, but he read widely and wrote with confidence of his nation's past. Whig history it certainly was in its searching of the past to justify the present, but it had the virtue of all

[9]Dafoe, "The Rise of the Commonwealth," Part I, "The Destruction of the First Empire," *M.F.P.*, Jan. 5, 1925.

Whig history in its emphasis on liberty and self-government. In true Whig fashion Dafoe had a moral to draw from his survey of imperial development in 1925. The moral was that the lesson of self-government taught by the past should be enshrined in a final constitutional declaration that would stand as a recognition of the equality and independence of the dominions under the Crown.[10]

Dafoe feared that without a definition of equality the programme of a common imperial foreign policy would again rear its ugly head. He objected to the idea of a joint foreign policy not only because it placed a limit on Canadian powers of self-government—"the old centralization donkey dressed up in a new disguise"—but also because he thought it would produce an isolationist reaction in Canada. Canadians were simply not interested in commitments to Britain's far-flung imperial interests and attempts to force them to become interested would cause them to turn away from the outside world completely. Certainly Canada would act as Britain's ally in any major crisis, but that was a different matter from persistent involvement in every picayune quarrel. If the dominions were allowed to pursue quietly their own diplomatic course, they would learn to think in international terms and the end result would find the Commonwealth united on everything of consequence. Only faith could make such a system work, faith in the moral unity of the British nations. At bottom the proponents of a common foreign policy were without faith. "The trouble with the Round Tablers," Dafoe told H. H. Wrong,

> Mr. Amery, Mr. Curtis, and the rest of them, is that at heart they have no faith in the Dominions. They do not believe in a nationalism for Canada which leaves this country free to make its own decisions. They say they favor Canadian nationalism if before it comes [sic] effective, we commit ourselves to a scheme of Imperial relationship which in fact and in operation would be a denial of national status.[11]

In 1926, on invitation, Dafoe invaded the Round Tablers' own territory and told them in an anonymous article "Why Canadian Nationalists Are Dissatisfied with the Status of Canada." This forthright and uncompromising statement contained little that Dafoe had not stated elsewhere. He argued that the most unsatisfactory aspect of Canadian status was its lack of definition. What was needed, he wrote predictably, was a final declaration that the Commonwealth was a mansion with many separate rooms—rooms large enough for each adult member of the family to

[10] Dafoe, "The Rise of the Commonwealth," Part X, "From Empire to Community of Nations," *M.F.P.*, Sept. 7, 1925.
[11] Dafoe Papers, Dafoe to H. H. Wrong, April 5, 1926.

go about its private concerns without parental interference. If the dominions were not allowed to live their separate existence, they would never become adult nations. But why should they become adults? Canada was a country composed of a multiplicity of peoples, Dafoe pointed out, and could only become a homogeneous and united nation if a common denominator of Canadian nationalism was established. Non-British immigrants would never lose their European characteristics unless they could exchange them for truly Canadian traits. "They cannot be turned into British imperialists; they must either become Canadians or remain undigested elements in the country." Furthermore, unless Canadians were allowed to achieve full nationhood and a national spirit, the danger of annexation to the United States would be increased. "This prospective danger is very real to the Canadian nationalist, who can see no permanent defence against the ever increasing pull to the southward except the establishment of a Canadian nation which will give its citizens opportunities and satisfactions which they will prefer when the temptation comes, to material advantages involving their loss," Dafoe concluded.[12]

The comments of the *Round Table* editor on the Canadian nationalist's views were moderate, conceding everything except what Dafoe considered to be the fundamental point of his argument. Certainly Canada should be allowed the status of full nationhood. But did not nationhood demand responsibility in world affairs? To this question, Dafoe would have replied in the affirmative. He would not, however, have agreed that the responsibility should be shouldered through participation in a common Commonwealth foreign policy, as the editor of the journal suggested. Here again was an example of the lack of faith that the "centralizer" persistently exhibited. The real unity of the Commonwealth was a moral unity which held the members together when their interests were threatened. If these interests diverged, no commitment to a common policy could hold the nations together, and might lead to serious unresolvable differences. Dafoe held that "if our interests differ to a point beyond the possibility of statesmen co-operating with one another, the Empire is bound to blow up anyway no matter what the machinery is." The difficulty with the proponents of a joint foreign policy was that they lived in fear of a war that would find the Commonwealth divided. Dafoe had two assurances against this fear. First, if Britain did find herself at war, Canada would be technically committed

[12]*Round Table*, XVI (March 1926), 369–76. Editorial comment is found in the same issue, 229–33. Dafoe's authorship is established by a letter in the Wrong Papers, Dafoe to G. M. Wrong, July 19, 1926.

because of its allegiance to the Crown. Moreover, he believed that if the Commonwealth was a true association of equals, the converse would also be true—if a Dominion engaged in war, Great Britain and the other dominions would also be committed. There was no need to fear the prospect of a divided Commonwealth in wartime, provided the war was just. Closely connected with this view was Dafoe's belief that writers on imperial relations were too preoccupied with the fear of war. Surely the League of Nations provided the resolution of this problem. "I do not foresee any major war in which England will be concerned which will not be a League of Nations war as well, in which case we shall be doubly called upon to take part," Dafoe told Sir Frederick Whyte. There was an association of nations, Commonwealth and League, for the preservation of world peace. If the peace were threatened the aggressor would be met by the members of the Commonwealth, united in their dedication to the moral principles of the League of Nations Covenant.[13]

In Dafoe's mind this scheme of collective security was always accompanied by the belief that before it could be worked out the autonomous status of the dominions would have to be declared. In 1926 he believed that the time was at hand when this definition would be possible. There were signs in Canada that the last bastions of the defenders of the joint policy were falling. At Hamilton in November 1925, Arthur Meighen declared his opinion that in time of war an election should precede the dispatch of Canadian troops overseas. The *Free Press* interpreted this statement as an acceptance of the autonomists' theory of the Empire. Meighen was acclaimed for his new-found enlightenment, and his Conservative critics subjected to a fierce attack. But Dafoe did not really believe in the sincerity of Meighen's conversion. Only King could be trusted to represent Canada at the forthcoming Imperial Conference. The century-old struggle for the recognition of full Canadian autonomy was approaching its culmination and the surrender of the "last outpost" would be accelerated if King remained general of the Canadian forces. Meighen himself was probably not a reactionary, but in the face of the critics in his own party, he would likely be content to allow the imperial question to remain unsettled. King, on the other hand, could probably be expected to go the full distance and would receive the support of the Irish and the South Africans.[14]

Dafoe's faith in King's complete acceptance of autonomist principles was an important factor in determining the role that the *Free Press* played

[13] Dafoe Papers, Dafoe to Sir Frederick Whyte, May 13, 1926.
[14] *M.F.P.*, Nov. 23, 26, 1925; Wrong Papers, Dafoe to G. M. Wrong, July 19, 1926.

in the 1926 election. Yet, after it was over Dafoe had a renewed sense of uneasiness about King. It was not that he doubted the sincerity of King's attachment to the autonomist cause, but rather exasperation at the Liberal leader's well-known caution. The South Africans and the Irish would set the stage for a declaration on the status question and the British Government would agree if the pressure was persistent enough. "But I am a little fearful that King will 'stall' and content himself with some platitudinous generalities," Dafoe fretted. He probably would have liked to repeat his 1923 experience by travelling to London with King in 1926, but he decided not to do so. The recently fought election campaign had brought him dangerously close to the position of a Liberal party propagandist and he wished to dispel this notion as rapidly as possible. Nevertheless he was kept well informed about the proceedings of the Conference through D. B. MacRea, assistant editor of the *Free Press*, who attended the London gathering.[15]

In Dafoe's view the chief business of the 1926 conference was to draft a statement that would clearly explain the nature of the autonomy of the dominions. This declaration would serve notice upon the world that the dominions were full-fledged nations, co-operating under a common Crown. This last point, the common Crown, was one that Dafoe insisted upon. He was a staunch, though unsentimental monarchist, and looked upon the common Crown as the symbol of Commonwealth unity rather than the symbol of Canada's subordination to Great Britain. The evidence was soon forthcoming that the conference in London was considering a declaration along the lines desired by Dafoe. MacRea reported that Hertzog of South Africa was pressing for a straightforward declaration of equality. The Canadians were more cautious, contending that an empirical approach which dealt with specific issues would be more useful than a statement of abstract principle. As Dafoe had expected, King and Lapointe were temporizing on the declaration. "In this they may be politically discreet," he conceded, "though my judgment is that if they were to clear up the situation once for all the consequences to them in a political sense would be wholly beneficial."[16]

MacRea produced some colourful comments on the activities of the Canadian delegation which must have amused Dafoe as well as increasing his uneasiness about King. In one letter he wrote of the foibles of the Canadian delegates:

[15]Dafoe Papers, Dafoe to W. D. Gregory, Sept. 17, 1926; Wrong Papers, Dafoe to G. M. Wrong, Oct. 29, 1926; Dafoe Papers, Dafoe to Sifton, Sept. 27, 1926.
[16]Dafoe Papers, Dafoe to Sir Robert Borden, Oct. 16, 1926; D. B. MacRea to Dafoe, Oct. 29, 1926; Dafoe to Sifton, Nov. 1, 1926.

Skelton says Hertzog has ability and sincerity but is inclined to be diffuse and to split hairs. He [Skelton] was of the opinion that [Hertzog] had said too much in public before the conference and has to take home something definite to his party. He also says that Lapointe is making a better stand than King. The latter is the despair of his secretaries. He hasn't time to see anybody. [Speaks of King missing a Press Conference]. . . . The result was that they [the reporters] all went away feeling piqued. Moyer put it up to him today and he said he was too damn busy to have time for the newspapers. He goes out to lunch every day, to dinner at night, gets in late and sleeps until after 9. Then he dashes off to the Conference. He is also having his picture painted by Orpen and thinks, apparently, that this is of the utmost importance. Lapointe is much better but is cautious. Massey is fair but appears to be falling for the social stuff. . . . Maybe I'm all wrong but it would be like a breath of fresh air to hear somebody get plain Canadian and call something a son of a bitch. . . . Skelton is alright on the main issues but cannot get too far ahead of the procession. . . . The boys are to attend the Buckingham Palace reception. Lines are already out for suits and high hats. God Save the Queen!

In an effort to put some starch into the Canadian delegation, both Dafoe and Sifton let the Prime Minister know that they thought the conference should promulgate a clear statement of Dominion autonomy. At least according to MacRea, this bracer seemed to shake the Canadians out of their lethargy. Despite the opposition of New Zealand, Newfoundland and some Britons, King took up Hertzog's line and got the idea of a declaration of autonomy accepted.[17]

Throughout the conference Dafoe kept up a steady flow of commentary on the proceedings, urging that the problem of definition be taken by the horns and finally settled. When the Balfour Declaration was made public, the *Free Press* (November 23) pronounced it the "Charter of Dominion Independence." Dafoe was naturally extremely pleased with this outcome, particularly by the fact that King's dilatory tactics had been defeated by the Irish and the South Africans. The representatives of the British Government, too, deserved great credit for their realistic acceptance of the full autonomy of the dominions. With good humour Dafoe remarked, "Of course in my comments, I shall not try to pluck any laurels from W.L.M.K.'s brow. I have just seen a cable from British United Press in which it is explained that K. by his masterly statesmanship did the whole thing. Perhaps this will go down in history wh. as Henry Ford once observed is mostly 'bunk'." In fact, the *Free Press* did not try to excuse King's timidity at the conference. Leadership in the evolution of imperial relations had always fallen to Canada, the paper pointed out on November 26, but in 1926 General

[17]*Ibid.*, D. B. MacRea to Dafoe, Nov. 4, 21, 1926.

Hertzog had taken over this position "and Canada's record, highly creditable though it is, falls a little short of what it might have been."[18]

Despite his chagrin at King, Dafoe was satisfied with the Balfour Declaration. Reviewing the events of the recent conference he observed that King's qualities "become less and less admirable as they are more closely observed." But other, more courageous leaders had emerged elsewhere in the Commonwealth to carry through the last steps to full partnership in the British association of nations. Certainly anomalies remained but these, Dafoe thought, were negligible compared with the impressive declaration of equality. Some missionary work was still necessary, especially to remove the "colonial complex" from the minds of the French Canadians, but the path to full sovereignty now seemed unobstructed.[19]

What was left of the traditional imperial allegiance, now that the Balfour Declaration had made the autonomy of the dominions clear beyond dispute? Dafoe had no doubt that the most valuable feature of that association remained unimpaired. In fact, he believed that with the last vestiges of imperialism swept away, the real strength of the Commonwealth would emerge in power and glory. Speaking to an American audience at the University of Chicago in the summer of 1927, Dafoe set out his conception of the post-Balfour Commonwealth: "What remains is an association of free nations who have a pecular relationship to one another—a moral, more than a legal, obligation to one another which ensures common action in matters of high policy because failure to act together would reveal a moral disunity which would mean the dissolution of the community."[20] The sceptics, those of little faith, of course asked what a moral unity meant in the face of the realities of power in the modern world. But Dafoe believed that a faith such as his would bring forth the good works when the time demanded. On the one hand there were those who held that the salvation of the Commonwealth depended on good works guaranteed by a common foreign policy. On the other were those who claimed that the phrase "moral unity" was a meaningless euphemism. Dafoe rejected both views. While the Balfour Declaration had undermined the diplomatic unity of the Empire as certainly as Luther's theses had destroyed the unity of Catholic Christendom, there remained a moral unity which could only exist among nations with the common heritage of the British Commonwealth. There was no longer any

[18]*Ibid.*, Dafoe to Sifton, Nov. 20, 1926.
[19]*Ibid.*, Dafoe to Sifton, Nov. 23, 1926; Dafoe to O. D. Skelton, Dec. 28, 1926; Dafoe to J. S. Ewart, Dec. 28, 1926.
[20]Dafoe, "The Problems of Canada" in Sir Cecil J. B. Hurst *et al.*, *Great Britain and the Dominions* (Chicago, 1928), 208–9.

vestige of British authority over Canada, but that did not make the relations between Britain and Canada the same as those between other nations, Dafoe explained to his sceptical friend, J. S. Ewart. "The relationship is a moral one, and the obligations arising from it are moral." Of course that moral unity might be destroyed if one of the partners set out on a course of action that was morally unjustifiable, but Dafoe thought this hypothetical situation very unlikely. Barring this possibility, which would only arise if Britain pursued a blatantly imperialistic policy, the Commonwealth would always be united in war. This unity would be further strengthened by association with the League of Nations, for a British war would undoubtedly be a League war.

Essentially this moral unity was to be found in the English-speaking nations. Thus the Indian Empire was by its very nature precluded from membership. "India," Dafoe remarked, "is a great historic accident and remains the insoluble anomaly of the British Empire." But apart from what he called the "brown empire," there would be close co-operation between the English-speaking members of the Commonwealth in the conduct of international affairs, especially at Geneva. Since one of the uniting factors was language, Dafoe believed that the United States "could be brought into sympathetic contact with this 'moral unit'." American imperialism would have to be watched as carefully as its British counterpart, but the danger seemed slight in 1928. In the final analysis, Dafoe told Ewart, the unity of the Commonwealth was not capable of definition; it had to be accepted on faith. But it was no less real for that. If moral unity did not preserve the Commonwealth, then nothing could, and the association would come to an end. "This may be its fate, but I doubt it," Dafoe concluded. "At any rate it will not arrive in your time or mine."[21]

National autonomy was not an end in itself for Dafoe, though it often seemed to be for the persistent Liberal nationalist status-seekers. Status had to be accompanied by stature, freedom of activity by the assumption of the responsibilities that accompany self-determination. The Canadian national spirit, Dafoe felt, should never be allowed to grow petulant and isolationist. This was the danger of the nationalism of the French Canadians. Canada should co-operate with all the nations of the world and especially with Britain. "Where co-operation is difficult owing to desire by Great Britain to pursue Imperialistic policies," Dafoe remarked, "it will be Great Britain, I think, and not Canada that will make the sacrifice which will permit co-operation." Once the old fears that Canadian autonomy was insecure were allayed, Dafoe's chief concern was

[21]Dafoe Papers, Dafoe to J. S. Ewart, Jan. 9, 1928.

that the negative policy of status-seeking should be replaced by a positive foreign policy that would justify Canada's claim to nationhood.[22]

iii

Dafoe, like all Canadians, was aware that in foreign policy Canada's first considerations involved Britain and the United States. Historic relations and geographic proximity made these two countries Canada's natural allies. Differences between them were usually detrimental to Canada. In short, Canada's position in the world was conditioned by its membership in the North Atlantic Triangle. The triangle was not an equilateral, and Canada was the smallest side of the figure, but none the less essential. Geographically Canada was a North American nation like the United States, but unlike the Republic it had maintained its political and sentimental ties with Great Britain. Thus Canada played its part in the triangle "as a sort of *liaison* between the English-speaking nations." The idea of the unity of the English-speaking world was a primary postulate in Dafoe's thinking. He emphasized it even to the point of virtually forgetting the French Canadians. When criticized for this blind spot by Henri Bourassa, he admitted that the French Canadians were an important bulwark against American assimilation. "If we should ever have a non-adjustable feud between French and English it would be the end of all things Canadian," he admitted. "The pieces of a disrupted Canada would be sucked into the American maelstrom against any resistance which they might offer." But quite beyond this consideration, the same faith in the unity of the English-speaking people which caused him to conclude that India was an insoluble anomaly in the Commonwealth brought him to view the United States as a silent partner in the British association of nations. He told his audience in Chicago in 1927 that beyond the moral unity of the Commonwealth there was a wider association that included the United States; a unit bound together by a common language and common habits of mind. He looked upon every step which brought these relations closer, such as the establishment of Dominion diplomatic delegations at Washington, as steps towards an association that "might easily prove the greatest stabilizing influence in the world."[23]

Dafoe's attachment to the British Commonwealth was not weakened

[22]*Ibid.*, Dafoe to Arthur Hawkes, Jan. 6, 1928.
[23]Dafoe, "The Problems of Canada," 256. Dafoe Papers, Henri Bourassa to Dafoe, April 26, 1928; Dafoe to Henri Bourassa, May 12, 1928. Dafoe, "The Problems of Canada," 259. *M.F.P.*, May 5, 1928. Beginning in April 1928 it is possible to establish the authorship of *Free Press* editorials through the *Free Press* Library's filing system.

by his belief that close co-operation with the United States was necessary for Canada and the other English-speaking nations. Indeed, he more frequently looked to Britain than anywhere else for lessons in politics and economics that might be helpful to Canada. Writing to the Canadian High Commissioner in London in the summer of 1929, he remarked that he wanted to take a trip to Britain very soon "to look at closer range at British conditions in view of all the changes that are going on over there. After all Great Britain is the home of change: the Dominions are, in comparison, staid, conservative communities." He did not believe, however, that Canadian society should be a pale replica of the mother country. In a brilliant exposition before the Royal Institute of International Affairs in June 1930, he summed up his views on Canadian society and Canada's place in the world.[24]

In this address he emphasized, as he had frequently done before, the underlying unity of the English-speaking world. He told his audience of his firm belief that the "English race was tragically divided" by the unnecessary American Revolution. But even this political division had been unable to destroy the deeper affinities of the English-speaking people. The peculiar position of Canada emphasized that continuing unity. Canadians and Americans were the "joint fashioners and practitioners of what may be called American civilization, which, although in part derived from the Western civilization of Europe, is indigenous to the American continent." British people who shook their heads in dismay at what they called "American" characteristics in Canada misinterpreted the true nature of the North American Dominion. These characteristics were, in fact, Canadian, part of the conglomeration of traits that made Canada a separate nation with a national consciousness, a sense of destiny, and a permanent membership in the British Commonwealth. Rather than decrying Canada's close relation with her neighbour and prophesying doom, Englishmen should be filled with hope for the future built upon the co-operation of all the nations of the English-speaking world. Dafoe summed up his theme:

> One of the consequences of the intimate relationship between Canada and the United States, which so many people deplore, is that it enables us to fill the role of interpreter. In the moral consolidation of the English-speaking peoples the whole of the future rests. I have noticed that all over the world English-speaking people naturally tend to take the same point of view; and if we can create relations based primarily on those between Canada and the United States, we shall create a power which may make some of our dreams, or what look like dreams, actual realities. You cannot have too many relationships between Canada and the United States; the political consequences

[24]Dafoe Papers, Dafoe to P. C. Larkin, July 2, 1929.

of such relationships, so far from resulting in the absorption of Canada into the United States, will operate to make the United States part of the larger English-speaking world.

In emphasizing Canada's close relation with the United States in the North American environment, Dafoe was expressing a view that was fairly common in the inter-war years. But it was not simply a dual relation that Dafoe looked forward to; it was a multiple relation among all the nations of the English-speaking world. Nor did he mean that Canadians should become "duplicate Americans." On the contrary he thought there were deep differences in social, educational and political values which were very much to the advantage of Canadians. They had evolved from the British system of government, a political structure "infinitely more adaptable than the stereotyped pre-revolutionary system of the United States."[25]

But Dafoe's increasing emphasis on the unity of the English-speaking world stemmed from his realization that efforts to promote world peace were seriously weakened by the absence of the United States from her proper place in world affairs. Only through co-operation could the world avoid a return to war. If the English-speaking nations failed to set an example, what could be expected of other nations which did not have a common heritage? These considerations were frequently on Dafoe's mind as the world moved from the illusory prosperity and peace of the late twenties into the economic depression and threatening international tensions of the thirties.

[25]Dafoe, "Canada and the United States," *Journal of the Royal Institute of International Affairs*, IX, no. 6 (Nov. 1930), 721–39.

XI. Bennett, King and Chaos
1927-37

ONCE THE FURIOUS 1926 election campaign was over, a temporary lull descended upon Canadian politics. The election had one interesting personal sidelight for Dafoe. The Liberal Association in Portage la Prairie offered to nominate him. Had he accepted, his Conservative opponent would have been none other than the Prime Minister, Arthur Meighen. He, of course, refused the offer. His ambitions were not those which motivate the active politician. Dafoe had been with the *Free Press* for twenty-five years and he had no second thoughts when he wrote: "When, if ever, I am a candidate for Parliament I shall first give up the editorship of the Free Press; and, as upon the whole I think I would sooner be editor of the Free Press than Prime Minister of Canada, I don't think I am likely to be a candidate in any constituency for some time to come." Dafoe was too happy with the independence that editing a powerful newspaper gave him to exchange it for the insecurity of active politics. With the election over and the Liberals firmly established in office for the next four or five years, he wanted to sit back and watch events develop.[1]

Dafoe's main theme when commenting on domestic politics after 1926 was that, if the West expected to have its problems given sympathetic attention, it should remain united within the Liberal party. This represents a reversal of the position he had held since 1920 and indicates his complete disillusionment with the Progressive movement. Meighen's near triumph in June 1926 had convinced Dafoe that a continued division of anti-Conservative forces was extremely dangerous. The Progressives would simply have to work for their objectives from inside the Liberal party. The handful of farmer politicians who remained independent of the King Government were severely criticized by the *Free Press* for dividing the West.

[1] Dafoe Papers, Dafoe to J. H. Metcalfe, July 27, 1926.

But Dafoe was not really worried about the few radical Progressives who insisted on carping at the Liberals, or the Conservatives who were attempting to rebuild their party. In 1927, R. B. Bennett took over the Tory leadership at a convention held in Winnipeg. Dafoe did not think that he was a first-class contender because of his explosive temperament and his close identification with big business. *Free Press* readers were advised not to pay much attention to the new Conservative platform with its low tariff plank, for the important fact was that Bennett was a protectionist. There was even a note of unusual complacency in the editorial of June 12, which branded Bennett as a true-blue Tory. "He will have difficulties in a country like Canada, essentially Liberal, in contrast to Mr. King who appears to be that phenomenon—a Liberal statesman who grows more Liberal as his tenure of office lengthens." The future certainly looked bright for the Liberals.[2]

The country was experiencing its most prosperous period since the war. Accompanying this prosperity were business developments—growing monopolies and an increasing number of bank mergers—which occasionally worried Dafoe. Moreover these consolidations of the financial power were being permitted by a Liberal Government. The public interest had to be defended against the predatory activities of the financial power, if for no other reason than that "the excesses and greed of capitalism sow the seeds of socialism." This was a prospect no more welcome than a government controlled by Eastern business. But these danger signs were only ripples on the generally calm surface of Canada's political and economic scene during the last few years before the depression. Like most people in 1928 Dafoe expected the calm to last indefinitely, and with it the Liberal Government. Late in that year Dafoe told his friend, John Stevenson, "I don't think Bennett can turn King out unless he has some luck on his side through the emergence of difficult questions beyond King's capacity to handle." The latter contingency seemed most unlikely. If conditions remained normal, as Dafoe thought they would, Bennett's "anti-American crusade" would not likely receive any widespread approval.[3]

The spring of 1929 brought one unmistakable sign that an old era was passing and a new one about to begin in Dafoe's career. In April Sir Clifford Sifton died in a New York hospital. For almost twenty-eight years Dafoe and Sifton had worked in close collaboration, dividing seriously only once—in 1911. There is no doubt that Sifton's influence

[2]*Ibid.*, Dafoe to Sifton, Oct. 15, 1927.
[3]*Ibid.*, Dafoe to Sifton, April 13, 1927, July 17, 1928, July 28, 1927; Dafoe to John Stevenson, Nov. 15, 1928; Dafoe to P. C. Larkin, July 2, 1929.

on the policies of the *Free Press* was very great; Dafoe never denied it. Commenting on this matter, Dafoe once told a friend, "He does not concern himself very directly with the paper, but I have always found it expedient and valuable to get his views when any large question of policy has to be decided."[4]

Sifton and Dafoe thought very much alike on social, political and economic issues, though there was a measure of crusading spirit in the editor that was largely lacking in his employer. After his retirement from active politics, Sifton never lost contact with public affairs, and frequently urged Dafoe to follow suggested courses. Yet he trusted Dafoe completely and allowed him and his associates to formulate the paper's policies as they thought best for the interests of the newspaper and Western Canada. Dafoe firmly believed that the task of a newspaper was educational and propagandist; its editorial page was the most important section. Sifton had less faith in the value of the editorial page, but he allowed his editor to shape the paper as he preferred. Thus the editorial page was always the most important part of the paper, and the reason for the *Free Press*'s widespread prestige. "The vital element of a newspaper's life is prestige," Dafoe told his employer in 1927, "and it can only be got from legitimate news columns and from the editorial page."[5] Probably few editors since the day when newspapers were transformed from organs of an editor's opinions into valuable business enterprises have had the freedom to develop a paper's character that Dafoe had at the *Free Press*.

Dafoe sometimes modified his views or held back his fervour for a cause in the face of Sifton's opposition. On the subjects of freer trade and the League of Nations, Dafoe was never able to say all he wanted in the *Free Press* while Sir Clifford was alive. But the relation was not simply one which limited Dafoe; he also benefited greatly from it. Sifton, in addition to being a shrewd politician, was an extremely capable business man. Dafoe frequently appealed to him for assistance in unravelling the complexities of railroad problems, finance and legal questions. In the large campaigns, such as the drive for definition of national status, Dafoe was able to persist in his course, even though it may have lost the *Free Press* some business, because he knew that he had Sifton's backing. "I do not know any other man in Canada," Dafoe confessed, "who, if he had been chief proprietor of the *Free Press*, would have let me pursue my apparently reckless course unchecked."[6]

[4]*Ibid*. Dafoe to A. Bridle, June 14, 1921.
[5]*Ibid*., Dafoe to Sifton, July 25, 1927.
[6]*Ibid*.

Sifton's death in 1929 therefore left a vacancy at the *Free Press* that could not be filled. Dafoe felt the loss very heavily. But Sir Clifford's death also meant that Dafoe was able to increase his independence. Sifton's sons, John, Clifford, Harry and Victor assumed their father's position. They were capable young men, but Dafoe was already the much respected grand old man whose name was synonymous with the *Free Press*. Perhaps, also, these younger men were more in agreement with the liberal side of Dafoe's nature than their father had been. It is no mere accident that some of the *Free Press*'s best known crusades for freer trade, constitutional amendment and the League of Nations were carried on after the death of Sir Clifford. In the critical decade before the Second World War when economic depression, constitutional deadlock and growing international tension threatened to destroy the world that Dafoe knew so well, he used his independence and prestige to give unfettered expression to views he had long held.

ii

The portents of disaster in the coming of the economic depression that enveloped the world in the autumn of 1929 were largely unforeseen. Trade depressions had been experienced many times before; recovery had usually been achieved after hardship but without radical alterations in society. Western Canadians might have been expected to realize that the times were out of joint, for the post-war period had been one of only partial and fluctuating prosperity for agriculture. But the last years of the twenties were good ones and hopes were high that all the necessary economic readjustments had been made to guarantee years of glowing prosperity. When the explosion came in 1929, few believed that it was anything more than one of the brief crises which had punctuated the past decade and had soon been followed by recovery. The *Free Press* shared this optimism. The unseen god of free enterprise was a just and kindly deity and would rapidly, indeed almost automatically intercede to save its worldly creation.[7]

Dafoe himself subscribed to this faith, though he thought that man's work could contribute to regeneration. The sins of protectionism could be expiated by tariff revision which would lighten the load borne by the primary producers, increase world trade and cut living costs. With a Liberal Government in office, these alterations should not be long in coming. Trade stagnation only further indicated the error of R. B.

[7] *M.F.P.*, Oct. 30, 1929.

Bennett's protectionist doctrines. Mackenzie King, solidly in office, must now produce the long-awaited tariff reductions, Dafoe thought.[8]

But what if the Liberals decided to go to the country for a renewed mandate before the end of their legal term of office was reached? In the spring of 1930 rumours were abroad that this was exactly what Mackenzie King was planning. The Government should get on with the business of fighting the depression rather than worry about an election, the *Free Press* advised on March 5. Dafoe wrote the Prime Minister pleading with him not to take any precipitate action. He appealed to King's pride, pointing out that he had already won himself a safe place in history by his imperial policy, but that the Imperial Conference expected in 1930 would set the crown on these achievements. If Bennett represented Canada the whole structure of Dominion status might be demolished. "The plow is in the furrow; the end is but a few months away," Dafoe wrote. King was unmoved; in fact he thought that his record on imperial relations might well serve as part of the election programme.[9]

The Dunning budget in May 1930 further convinced Dafoe that an election should be postponed until the effects of tariff revision were felt. It was a good budget, especially those features that were designed to divert some of Canada's trade from the United States to the United Kingdom and Europe. If only King would stand up to the truculent opposition of the Conservatives and avoid the appearance of panic that an unexpected dissolution would give. "I find my old-time distrust of King's political judgment reviving," Dafoe complained. But his warnings found no response; King decided to use the Dunning budget for an appeal to the country. Dafoe was probably glad of the opportunity to attend the Imperial Press Conference during June, for it meant that he was absent from Canada during a large part of the campaign. Despite the urgings of the *Free Press* that the country and especially the West should stand behind the Liberals, the protectionists were triumphant and R. B. Bennett was called upon to form an administration.[10]

Dafoe had been correct in fearing the results of an election in 1930. He was not sure why King had blundered but he suspected that the Quebec ministers had forced him to act prematurely because of their fear that the Quebec Liberal machine was falling apart. Then the general social discontent in the country had played into the hands of the Opposition. The result of the election was the expression of a desire

[8]*Ibid.*, Dec. 16, 1929; Jan. 24, 1930.
[9]Dafoe Papers, Dafoe to W. L. M. King, April 22, 1930; W. L. M. King to Dafoe, April 25, 1930.
[10]*Ibid.*, Dafoe to T. A. Crerar, May 8, 1930; Dafoe to Harry Sifton, May 8, 1930.

for change rather than any widespread agreement with the Conservative protectionist programme, Dafoe thought. "Man is never less entitled to be called Homo Sapiens than when he is engaged in performing his first duty of citizenship," he remarked bitterly.[11]

Though the Conservatives had campaigned on a "Canada First" programme, Dafoe refused to believe that the result indicated an upsurge of Canadian nationalism. Rather it was the acceptance of a "Sinn Fein policy of 'Ourselves Alone'." This result was a great disappointment to Dafoe, who five years earlier had thought that a majority of Canadians had at last seen the truth of his freer trade doctrines. Writing to W. D. Gregory, an old free trade Liberal in Ontario, he explained:

> I have always kept my political nationalism free from economic entanglements. I have a loathing for narrow nationalistic selfishness which is, I think, stronger than my objection to political imperialism; and my regret over the election arises chiefly from the revelation that it afforded that the Canadian people are equipped with minds capable of being influenced by the absurdities and crudities of the Bennett campaign. For the first time in my life I am a little ashamed of my country.

Perhaps, he thought, the election marked the opening of a period of Canadian history when the "American theory of government" would be applied to Canada; the theory that "it is the people who have a million dollars and over who are entitled to run the country." The Conservatives had apparently succumbed to this view; would the Liberals be able to resist it?[12]

Prime Minister Bennett was the leading example of this "American theory." Dafoe thought that Bennett was a very dangerous man, misled in his views and strong-willed in his determination to carry them out.

> He is chock-full of self-confidence and conceit. If he were an ordinary politician prepared to do anything or say anything to reach office he would forget the extravagance of the campaign. I do not think, however, that Mr. Bennett is a politician in this sense at all. I think he regards himself as a man of destiny. I should be very much surprised if he does not try to impose his views, whatever they may be, and his projects, however they may shape up, upon parliament and the country.

No doubt serious domestic and international tensions would result from placing such a man in office. His policies would place a sharp strain on Confederation, rupture Canada's relations with Great Britain and leave the country without a friend in Europe, Dafoe predicted gloomily. One

[11] *Ibid.*, Dafoe to Harry Sifton, Aug. 11, 1930; Dafoe to R. J. Deachman, Aug. 6, 1930.

[12] *Ibid.*, Dafoe to W. D. Gregory, Aug. 13, 1930; Dafoe to D. A. McArthur, Oct. 7, 1930.

feature of Bennett's ultranationalism which was particularly distressing was its anti-American tone. The puzzling part about this attitude, Dafoe remarked, was that the people who gave the fullest support to it were the "Canadians who admire your fiscal system and play sedulous ape to it."[13]

Not all Dafoe's comments about the Conservative victory in 1930 were pessimistic. There was some consolation in the fact that the Bennett régime would be handicapped by the necessity of implementing its policies in a period of economic depression. In such circumstances it could hardly be expected to succeed. Bennett "will be the Conservative 'Mackenzie' and his party will be lucky if it does not fix in the public mind for a generation the idea that the Conservative party is a hoodoo and a bringer of hard times." Once this stigma was attached to them, the Tories would be banished to the political wilderness for an extended term, Dafoe thought rather gleefully.[14]

A second consolation was the fact that a Conservative Government presented a "shining mark" for a Liberal journalist's sharpest arrows. Political alternatives, as Dafoe frequently repeated, were usually confined to "something not very good and something worse." The Dunning budget would hardly have warmed the heart of a free trader, but at least it was greatly preferable to the Conservative offerings. Therefore the *Free Press* set about assisting the Liberals in their efforts to regain office. Its attacks on the Tories would not have to be limited to anything the Liberal Opposition would have to say. In the end, Dafoe expected, the *Free Press* would be more effective than the politicians.[15]

Before turning all his energies to assail the sins of the new Government, Dafoe said a final farewell to the Progressive movement. Writing in the *Free Press* on August 6, 1930, he totalled up the successes and failures of this movement of protest. It had won some victories for the West in its defence of the Crow's Nest Pass Agreement and in its advocation of the Hudson Bay Railway. Moreover it had forced the old parties to give fresh consideration to the country's problems. But as an unorganized expression of Western opinion the movement could not last indefinitely. The realists had joined the Liberals, while a handful continued the course of futile independence which only aided the Conservatives. This was Dafoe's obituary on the Progressive movement. In death it was crowned with the wreaths of success that he had hoped it would win. He stood with those Progressives who had envisaged a future within

[13]*Ibid.*, Dafoe to C. P. Craig, Aug. 14, 1930; Dafoe to Brooke Claxton, Dec. 29, 1930; Dafoe to Hon. Wm. Phillipps, Oct. 25, 1930.
[14]*Ibid.* Dafoe to John Stevenson, Dec. 29, 1930.
[15]*Ibid.*, Dafoe to D. A. McArthur, Oct. 7, 1930; Dafoe to R. J. Deachman, Sept. 16, 1930; Dafoe to Grant Dexter, Aug. 8, 1930.

a reformed Liberal party, fighting for lower tariffs and freight rates. His reformist views stopped far short of the agrarian radicalism that burned in the breasts of the Ginger Group and was soon to manifest itself in new political heresies. In 1930, Dafoe's words of valediction on the passing Liberal Government—"this Government served Canada with distinction, with ability and with foresight"—indicated that he now stood sure-footed within the ranks of Mackenzie King's army. For Dafoe, the Progressive movement as a separate organization of Western reform sentiment was ended; it had coalesced with the Liberal party. While pointing up the deficiencies of the new Conservative administration, Dafoe knew that he would have to keep an eye on the Opposition to ensure that the progressive flame continued to burn on the Liberal hearth. If it was allowed to go out, a new, more radical, progressivism might be kindled on the Western plains.[16]

iii

For almost five years Dafoe concentrated his editorial thunderbolts on a single aspect of the Conservative Government's programme. There were, of course, minor shafts directed at a wide variety of issues, but the principal target was the tariff. Dafoe had always been a low tariff man, but now, with Sir Clifford's restraining hand removed and the Liberals in Opposition, his emphasis on freer trade as a panacea for Canada's economic problems grew markedly. He saw in the rejected Dunning budget a fiscal ideal. "The more I study the Dunning budget," Dafoe told J. M. Macdonnell, "the more I see that it sought, and in a measure found, the middle way. It was rejected both by the protectionists and the ultra-low tariff men."[17]

As the depression settled in, Dafoe realized that the Prairie farmers were falling into a pitiful state. The world demand for wheat had shrunk to a point which made the 1929 crop virtually unmarketable. The farmers' financial prostration was partly a result of their own failure to make the best of the prosperous years. Now, without reserves to fall back on, they were in desperation. None of the various solutions which were being offered—soft money, compulsory grain marketing or least of all, an increase in the tariff— appealed to Dafoe. "Unless the international commercial situation improves—of which there is no sign whatever—the West will get a lesson in economics that perhaps it will learn so thoroughly that never again will it be forgotten," Dafoe told a Queen's professor.[18]

[16]*M.F.P.*, Aug. 8, 1930.
[17]Dafoe Papers, Dafoe to J. M. Macdonnell, Dec. 31, 1930.
[18]*Ibid.*, Dafoe to D. A. McArthur, Oct. 7, 1930.

Bennett had promised the people during the 1930 campaign that Canadian trade and industry would be given new stimulus and direction by the application of Conservative tariff policy. The first step would be a higher tariff to protect Canadian manufacturers against unfair foreign competition. This tariff would then be used as a bargaining weapon; in this way Canada would, as Bennett put it, "blast her way into the world's markets." The second phase of Tory fiscal policy envisaged a scheme of reciprocal imperial preferences. This arrangement would provide for a preference for Canadian raw materials in the British market in return for Canadian preference for British goods. Both propositions involved the erection of trade barriers against the free flow of world trade. The idea was anathema to Dafoe.[19]

In December 1930 Bennett began his campaign for imperial preference at the Imperial Conference. Dafoe was happy to find that Bennett made no effort to undo the work of the autonomists in imperial relations, but he offered no support for Bennett's trade proposals. The idea of asking Great Britain to reject her century-old free trade system to meet the demands of the Canadian Prime Minister for a preference on Canadian goods was scandalous. Dafoe was not unaware of the growing protectionist sentiment in Britain. While attending the Imperial Press Conference in the summer of 1930 he had carefully observed the movement. At its centre was the crusade being carried on by Lord Beaverbrook for Empire free trade. Dafoe thought that the programme was doomed to failure, for quite apart from the apparent reluctance of the British Conservatives to adopt an unpopular tax on food, there was the obstacle presented by Canadian manufacturers, who would never agree to serious competition from British imports. "If you put a tax on food for Canada, Mr. Bennett will expect a full preference," Dafoe warned Beaverbrook; "he will bellow, roar, snort, quote scripture and prophesy death and damnation if this is not given. But in return you will get nothing half as valuable as that which Canada has voluntarily given Great Britain under the Liberal government."[20]

The most important event in the evolution of Bennett's tariff policy was the Imperial Economic Conference that met in Ottawa in the summer of 1932. The unexpected had happened: the British Government had committed what Dafoe consider to be the worst folly, in adopting a protective tariff. If the world's one paragon of free trade virtue fell from grace, there

[19] *M.F.P.*, Dec. 18, 1930; Dafoe Papers, Dafoe to John Stevenson, Dec. 29, 1930; *M.F.P.*, Oct. 28, 1930.
[20] Dafoe, "Politics in Great Britain," *M.F.P.*, July 15, 1930; Dafoe Papers, Dafoe to Lord Beaverbrook, Sept. 16, 1930.

would be little hope left for the rest of the unregenerate nations. Now when in 1931 the National Government committed itself to a protectionist or what was euphemistically called a retaliatory tariff policy, Dafoe's traditional argument against a system of reciprocal imperial preferences was undermined. As long as Britain had clung to free trade, Canadian Liberals could argue that there should be no attempt to bargain with Britain for preferences, as to do so would involve Canada in the internal politics of Great Britain. But once Britain had equipped herself with a tariff, Dafoe had to admit that bargains could now be struck among the members of the Commonwealth for a freer exchange of goods. He refused to believe, however, that Bennett's policy could increase trade; he suspected that the Conservative leader wanted to gain entrance for Canadian foodstuffs and raw material into the British market without conceding much to British manufacturers in return. But Dafoe's basic opposition to Bennett's policy was his belief that, no matter how valuable the British market was to Canada, it alone was insufficient to meet Canadian export needs. If the system of imperial preferences limited Canada's access to markets outside the Commonwealth, the results would be crippling to Canadian primary producers. Dafoe did believe that, if the Imperial Economic Conference resulted in a lowering of trade barriers throughout the Commonwealth without raising them against the rest of the world, its results would be very beneficial. This was exactly the advice he gave to Prime Minister Bennett, on the latter's request, in the summer of 1932. Bennett was at least impressed with the power of Dafoe's arguments, for he was reported to have remarked to Geoffrey Dawson of *The Times* that, "I am bound to say that Dafoe, although one of my most *malignant* opponents, is one of the ablest men in this country." But no matter how much Bennett might have been impressed, he certainly was not convinced. Nor did Dafoe expect he would be.[21]

Apart from his objections to Bennett's fiscal theories, Dafoe was suspicious that the Economic Conference might be a smoke-screen for a plan to centralize the Empire. He had always suspected that L. S. Amery, who attended the conference, was a centralizer, and now he feared that Amery had won Bennett's confidence. Perhaps it was on Amery's urging that Bennett had put forward his scheme for imperial preference at the 1930 conference in order to embarrass the British Labour Government. Now

[21] Dafoe Papers, Dafoe to Evelyn Wrench, Nov. 16, 1931; Dafoe to Lady Astor, Dec. 24, 1931. *M.F.P.*, Feb. 21, 1930. Dafoe Papers, Dafoe to John Stevenson, April 28, 1932. *M.F.P.*, Oct. 30, 1931. Dafoe Papers, Dafoe to R. B. Bennett, July 2, 1932; Geoffrey Dawson to Dafoe, July 7, 1932; Grant Dexter to Dafoe, July 12, 1932.

the scene was to be repeated at Ottawa with the objective of driving the Liberal and Labour members out of the National Government in order to get an administration in Britain that would be committed to imperial centralization. Dafoe was not certain enough of this suspicion to pursue the theme openly in his editorials. Instead he took a line that was much closer to that of the British delegation than the Canadian: Ottawa should be the first step towards wider world trade rather than an attempt to ring the Empire with prohibitive tariffs. But as the conference progressed, he became more convinced than ever that Bennett, with the approval of some British Conservatives, was attempting to force the British Government to accept a policy which would result in the establishment of an imperial *Zollverein*. According to Dafoe, the Canadian Prime Minister persistently pressed the view that the British should raise their tariffs to levels that would prohibit the entry of non-Commonwealth goods; when faced with refusal he threatened to force the conference to adjourn without an agreement. Ultimately the British were forced to accept a large measure of Bennett's proposal. By a series of bilateral agreements the Commonwealth countries arranged tariffs between each other without reducing existing tariff rates. The largest sacrifices were made by Britain in the hope of exchanging her foreign markets for increased Commonwealth trade.[22]

After the Commonwealth Economic Conference had ended, Dafoe received some information to substantiate his suspicions about Bennett. The Prime Minister approached Grant Dexter, the Ottawa correspondent of the *Free Press*, and delivered a blistering attack on the newspaper for the support it had given the British position during the trade discussions. He claimed that he had cornered the British delegation, and with the assistance of the Australians and South Africans, had forced them to make great concessions to the Canadian export trade. His position had been made very difficult, however, by the traitorous course that the *Free Press* had followed. Whether L. S. Amery was actually working in collusion with the Canadian Prime Minister, as Dafoe suspected, is at least doubtful. Amery denied the charge, though it is clear that some of the British delegates were as suspicious of his activities as was Dafoe.[23]

The imperial economic agreements, as Dafoe predicted, tended to restrict not only world trade, but also exchanges between the Common-

[22]Dafoe Papers, Dafoe to T. B. Roberton, July 23, 1932. *M.F.P.*, July 21, 1932. Dafoe Papers, Dafoe to Geoffrey Dawson, Aug. 29, 1932; Dafoe to C. L. Burton, Oct. 22, 1932.
[23]Dafoe Papers, Grant Dexter to Dafoe, Oct. 16, 1932; L. S. Amery, *My Political Life* (3 vols., London, 1955), III, 86.

wealth countries. The preferences offered to Britain were negligible in comparison with the general tariff increases effected by the Bennett Government. The whole system, Dafoe concluded, "reveals in too many instances a roundabout way of increasing protection to Canadian manufacturers." The single benefit that he could see arising from the agreements was that they forced the Liberal Opposition to take a firm stand in favour of a low tariff and of increased British preference. Canada, whose trade depended upon markets wider than those of the Empire, could only suffer from the agreements. Particularly important in the Canadian trade picture was the United States; if an opportunity arose for a trade agreement with that country, Canada would have to forgo the Ottawa agreements. Perhaps the only good words that the *Free Press* had for the Tory economic policy during Bennett's term of office came when it was learned late in 1934 that a trade agreement was being sought with the United States. Even then Dafoe doubted if Bennett's protectionist convictions would allow him to offer terms that would be acceptable to the United States.[24]

In fact, of course, the Bennett Government could do nothing to win the approval of the *Free Press*. Dafoe deeply distrusted the Prime Minister, whom he once described as "Alger boy hero plus Mussolini." He was by no means "a chore boy of the big interests," for his self-confidence was too great to allow him to bow to anyone. But his policies were all directed towards allowing the business barons of Canada to exert a large measure of control over Canada's economic life. Particularly distressing was the perennial railway question. The depression had placed both the national systems in financial jeopardy and Dafoe's old suspicion of the C.P.R.'s designs on the Canadian National revived. "A complete merger of the two systems is not practicable unless it takes the form of the absorption of the Canadian Pacific Railway by the Canadian National," he contended. Dafoe appeared in person before the Duff Commission, which was established in 1931 to examine the railway situation, and came away with the uneasy feeling that the commission's recommendations might undermine the independence of the nationally owned railway. He hoped to see the two companies operate separately with some accommodation between them to increase financial viability. The one security that the Canadian National had, he believed, was the fact that the Liberals could make a political issue out

[24]Dafoe Papers, Dafoe to Sir Robert Donald, Oct. 26, 1932; Dafoe to Geoffrey Dawson, Jan. 10, 1933. *W.F.P.*, Nov. 15, 1934. Dafoe Papers, Dafoe to Grant Dexter, Jan. 26, 1935.

of an attempted amalgamation and thus save the railway from annihilation.[25]

Dafoe never expected the Conservative Government to last for long. The depression was its greatest enemy, and from the tariff reformer's viewpoint there was no possibility that Bennett's policies would do anything to ease the situation. But the Tory leader had to be watched closely for fear that through some sleight-of-hand he would find a means of extending his reign. There was always the chance that he might persuade some of the more conservative Liberals to join him in a coalition. There were rumours of this possibility in Ottawa as early as December 1931. The proposition, Dafoe believed, was merely a ruse to perpetuate Conservative rule under the cloak of non-partisanship. The more control big business exercised over government, Dafoe thought, the greater was the danger of the growth of a socialist movement in Canada. "I do not myself believe that the socialist movement is going to be formidable unless the Liberals give them a chance either by falling for some national government humbug, or by refusing to commit themselves to a definite policy of reform," Dafoe remarked at the end of 1932. The only reasonable alternative to the Bennett Government that Dafoe could envisage was a "union of the Liberal and Progressive forces of all parties." Such a government was necessary not only to undo the unacceptable policies of the Conservatives, but also to nip in infancy the left-wing and socialist sentiments that were beginning to attract the attention of some Canadians. Throughout the years of Conservative ascendancy, Dafoe was re-examining his position as a Liberal in an effort to work out a programme of moderate reform for King's party.[26]

iv

Both in his criticisms of the Conservatives and his advocacy of Liberal reforms, Dafoe's ideals were based on assumptions about the cause and nature of the depression. He did not believe that the country's economic malaise was the result of faulty economic institutions. The depression was not a domestic phenomenon at all, but rather was a world-wide crisis with international causes. The free flow of international trade upon which the prosperity of the world depended had been blocked by a

[25]Dafoe Papers, J.W.D. to T.B.R., Feb. 2, 1935; Dafoe to Sir Henry Thornton, Oct. 3, 1932; Dafoe to Grant Dexter, Sept. 16, 1931; Dafoe to Sir Henry Thornton, Aug. 10, 1932; Dafoe to J. L. McDougall, March 13, 1935.
[26]*Ibid.*, Grant Dexter to G. V. Ferguson, Dec. 31, 1931; Dafoe to Grant Dexter, Dec. 30, 1932; Dafoe to Harry Sifton, Jan. 2, 1932.

proliferation of protective tariffs. "Each nation, determined to beggar its neighbor, has succeeded in beggaring itself," he commented. The stagnation of world trade resulted in an especially critical situation in the Canadian West, which was heavily dependent upon international markets. Since Dafoe believed that the "real source of Canadian wealth came from the farm, the forest and the mine," the whole economy floundered when the markets for natural products dried up.[27]

There was no doubt about the seriousness of the economic upheaval of the thirties; Dafoe realized that it was not merely a slight tremor in the economic framework. After eighteen months of steadily declining prosperity he admitted that the situation was critical enough to produce revolutionary social consequences. But despite the evidence of social dislocation and individual suffering, Dafoe held firmly to the opinion that the situation was international in origin and therefore incapable of cure by domestic remedies. Only measures that would lead to a revival of world trade could assist in economic recovery. In short, tariffs would need a general levelling down. "I find myself sceptical of local or national expedients designed to counteract the fact of these world-wide causes of the trouble," he explained. "I doubt whether anything could be accomplished beyond a purely temporary improvement which, in the continued absence of wider remedial measures, would result, with no great loss of time, in a further let-down."[28]

Dafoe's faith in classical answers to problems of depression remained unshaken by the growing popularity of the economic ideas usually connected with the name of J. M. Keynes. He read Keynes. He also observed "Keynesian experiments" in the United States with government controls, currency management and "pump priming," but he remained convinced that the only real solution to economic stagnation rested on a reliance on the gold standard and the revival of international trade. He told Professor C. R. Fay in 1932:

> I read with interest everything that your old comrade Keynes writes; but I find myself stubbornly refusing to believe that he can work any such miracle as he has in mind by a managed inflation of the currency. The world which has been defying all the economic laws for twenty years—indulging in war and all that derives from it, economic war and all the follies that go with it—cannot escape punishment by monkeying with the currency. We are getting what we jolly well deserve; and the nations will have to repent and do penance before the conditions will be righted.

---

[27]*Ibid.*, Dafoe to R. J. Cromie, Sept. 16, 1930; Dafoe to Grant Dexter, July 29, 1931.

[28]*Ibid.*, Dafoe to Harry Sifton, Feb. 28, 1931; Dafoe to Robert Cromie, Jan. 6, 1933.

Currency inflation was no cure; the world simply had to face the first of the Cobdenite commandments—all prosperity derives from international trade.[29]

Just as he had little faith in Keynes's "experiments in magic," so he had slight trust in the other unorthodox expedients he heard advocated. He paid a good deal of attention to socialist writing—John Strachey and R. H. Tawney, especially. But in Dafoe's opinion all the economic planners were open to the same criticism—they attempted to turn nations into self-sufficient economic units. Less sophisticated economic reformers, afflicted with the "Douglas craze," were simply fanatics: William Aberhart was a "blend of Father Coughlin and Dr. Townsend." He found the furious activities of the American New Dealers very unimpressive. He had heard Raymond Moley speak and decided he had "very obvious limitations"; Rexford Tugwell's New Deal writings were "very cheap and unsatisfactory." "The events of the past six months," he told J. T. Shotwell in October 1933, "have shown how dangerous it is to have the Prime Minister and the Chief of the nation the same man. The immense experiment [the New Deal] has been entered upon and is being carried out with about one percent of the examination that a similar programme would get in any British country." Though Dafoe admitted that Roosevelt was a superb political tactician, he found him lacking in a sound knowledge of economics, one opinion that Dafoe shared with J. M. Keynes. Resting at his summer cottage in the autumn of 1934, Dafoe offered his pessimistic, though revealing, reflections on the sad state of democratic leadership to G. M. Wrong:

> This is the age for political freaks to rise to power.... Ferguson was nothing but a village cut-up & smart aleck; I cannot but think Hepburn the better man. Bennett is a rowdy and a braggart—but fortunately his day is passing. Roosevelt, though personally charming, is the playboy of the western world. He is like a little boy in the powerhouse of a great city, playfully pulling switches and wondering what will happen.
> The kind of leaders that you and I were used to in our youth—Mackenzie, Blake, Mowat, Laurier, etc.—are no longer acceptable to Demos. Let us be thankful that King in some considerable degree measures up to their standard & that he will shortly be in a position where he may keep Mr. Hepburn & others like him in check.

Just as Dafoe admired T. A. Crerar as the leader of the Progressives because he stood in the tradition of nineteenth-century Canadian Liberalism, so he measured the politicians of the great depression against the standard of Mackenzie, Blake and Laurier. He found all of them

[29]*Ibid.*, Dafoe to C. R. Fay, May 30, 1932; Dafoe to Victor Sifton, June 17, 1932.

wanting, except Mackenzie King, whose views on economic depression had more in common with Blake's than with Roosevelt's.[30]

When charged with being a Cobdenite, yearning for the lost and largely mythical world of nineteenth-century laissez-faire, Dafoe pleaded guilty. But, he argued, Cobden had never been properly understood by the world, and his system never fully tried. Dafoe was extremely sensitive to the criticism that his political and economic philosophy was stale in an age of radical experimentation. He even feared that, now he had reached his sixties, he was not adaptable enough to remain in the editor's chair at the *Free Press*. His own firm conviction was that the new radicalism was nothing more than a return to the closed society which preceded the triumph of nineteenth-century liberal economics. The hard road of liberalism was being deserted for short-cuts that would eventually lead through bogs and fens. Ultimately, Dafoe was certain, the world would get back on the liberal road, but in the meantime the *Free Press* might be smothered in the multiplicity of voices clamouring for radical reform. Even its old Western stronghold might fall to armies bearing the standard of "social credit, that is, fiat money; producers' guilds embracing every variety of agricultural production; import and export boards, and the rest of the socialist and fascist bag of tricks." Perhaps, Dafoe thought, the best interests of the *Free Press* would be served if he stepped down from the editorship, for his own views were immutable. "I am all for staying with the colors & going straight ahead in faith, resolutely believing that we shall be part of a goodly company," he told Harry Sifton.[31]

Naturally Dafoe's colours continued to fly at the *Free Press*. In December 1931 the *Manitoba Free Press* became the *Winnipeg Free Press* but the change was only nominal. Dafoe's trumpet sounded even louder than before, for the editor believed that Mackenzie King was the

---

[30]*Ibid.*, Dafoe to Vincent Massey, April 8, 1933; Dafoe to Harry Sifton, Aug. 19, 1933; Dafoe to Harry Sifton, June 4, 1932; Dafoe to Dr. J. T. Shotwell, April 8, 1935; Dafoe to George Iles, Oct. 2, 1933. Wrong Papers, Dafoe to G. M. Wrong, Sept. 18, 1934. Dafoe was usually well informed on most subjects, though curiously he seems often to have been badly informed about American domestic politics. For example, his opinion of Roosevelt, expressed in the letter to Wrong, was based on a reading of three articles on Roosevelt, written by H. F. Pringle for the *New Yorker* for June 16, 22 and 29, 1934. These magazines had been left by Dafoe's son at the summer cottage. The articles were superficial, impressionistic and largely concerned with personal details. For Dafoe's later view of Roosevelt see Dafoe's review of *The Public Papers and Addresses of Franklin D. Roosevelt* in *A.H.R.*, XLVII, no. 4 (July 1942), 907–9.

[31]F. H. Underhill, "J. W. Dafoe," *Canadian Forum*, XIII, no. 145 (Oct. 1932), 23–4. Dafoe Papers, Dafoe to F. H. Underhill, Oct. 17, 1932; Dafoe to Harry Sifton, Jan. 1, 1934.

Liberal Moses who could lead the Canadian people out of the economic wilderness and back to the Promised Land. But Dafoe wanted to be certain that the Liberal party would not stumble along blindly without a map. After the defeat of 1930 he worked diligently with other Liberal intellectuals to draw up a programme that would strengthen the progressivism of the party. In 1921 he had worked to support a Progressive party that would reform the Liberal party from outside; after 1930 his main aim was the same, only this time he hoped to see the transformation work within the existing framework of Mackenzie King's party.

V

As always Dafoe's main interest was in the Liberal party's appeal in Western Canada; his concern was that it should adopt policies that would be radical enough to prevent Prairie voters from espousing the doctrines of the new parties of agrarian protest. Dafoe believed that anti-Conservative sentiment in the West would not automatically accrue to the benefit of the Liberals; only by moving to the left could King hope to strengthen his party among the farmers. "The spirit of 1921 may revive wilder than ever," Dafoe warned. Above all he wanted to prevent the party from rejecting the low tariff views that had been expressed in the Dunning budget.[32]

The first step in the Liberal revival could be taken without an immediate declaration of policy. All that was necessary was to concentrate on the weakness of the Tories' fiscal policies. Gradually a new platform could be evolved. Offering his advice to a Liberal politician, Dafoe set out the core of his reformist views: "I should like to see the Liberal party turn its back on all the specious fiscal doctrines that have flourished in Canada in recent years and get back on the firm ground that we cannot thrive unless we can export our primary products, which means permitting imports under tariff rates which will be competitive but not prohibitive." In his attitude to the tariff Dafoe was essentially a Westerner of the old school. Without world markets for their grain, the people of the Prairies faced tragedy, and that tragedy would rapidly spread to the rest of Canada because of the dependence of the whole economy upon the products of the West. The country's chief economic problems resulted from "our noble Canadian determination to industrialize Canada beyond the limits of economic justification." When criticized for failing to consider the requirements of the country's industrial and transportation interests, Dafoe replied that "the farmers as the

[32]Dafoe Papers, Dafoe to Grant Dexter, Nov. 3, 1930.

primary producers subject to the conditions of world competition cannot be penalized in the slightest degree in order to help out any other Canadian industry." The same conservatism which inspired Dafoe to support the Progressive movement, a conservatism based on a desire to preserve agriculture as the prime factor in the Canadian economy, was the underlying premise of the policies which he hoped to see the Liberal party adopt in the thirties. These policies were rarely more radical than freer trade and sound currency. The depression did not alter his views on government-sponsored grain boards, quota systems and monetary reform.[33] Clearly, Dafoe was losing touch with his Western constituents, who were becoming increasingly interested in the new, collectivist radicalism of the thirties.

One feature of the Liberal party which had frequently been criticized by Dafoe in the past was now fully accepted by him: King's leadership. Even the Beauharnois scandal, which momentarily weakened Dafoe's faith in King, did not seriously shake it. If King was tainted with Beauharnois money he would have to resign, but Dafoe felt that the Liberal leader was in the clear. The hope was strengthened by the belief that King "certainly has a truer idea of the policies necessary for Canada than his adversary." When King came out of the investigation with little or no mud stuck to him, Dafoe was relieved. He could now turn from personalities to programmes.[34]

By the end of 1931, Vincent Massey, one-time Liberal cabinet minister and diplomatist, was leading a movement to modernize the Liberal platform. Dafoe was quick to offer a variety of suggestions. He told Massey that the Liberals' main problem in the West was that Mackenzie King had no real appeal; he was dull, drab and suspected of mistrusting farmer politicians. Yet he would simply have to find a way to appeal to the progressive Western voters if he hoped to regain office. The way was a programme that showed an understanding of Western problems. This did not mean that the Liberals should adopt all the "fads" of the socialists, Douglasites and other cranks, for Dafoe believed that the "lunatic fringe" would go its own way no matter what the Liberals offered. The group that the Liberals had to appeal to was that of the moderate progressives who formed the majority of the voters. Dafoe outlined the platform that he thought would appeal to these people. First, it should contain a straightforward declaration in favour

[33]*Ibid.*, Dafoe to J. L. Ralston, May 26, 1931; Dafoe to Vincent Massey, April 8, 1935; Dafoe to Harry Sifton, June 4, 1932; Dafoe to Grant Dexter, June 12 and July 7, 1931.
[34]*Ibid.*, Dafoe to N. W. Rowell, July 28, 1931.

of a low tariff. Such a declaration would place the Liberals definitely on the side of the low tariff forces, and "end, once for all, the long-established custom of trying by compromising its principles, to retain within the party men enamoured of Tory performances which should excite the ire of every Liberal." The long-delayed occasion for a purge of the conservative Liberals had come, and Dafoe admitted that he would "shed no tears if the exit should be somewhat imposing." Confirmation of the tariff proposals of the 1930 budget, though they were not radical enough, would be a good starting point for the Liberal tacticians. Secondly, to meet the threat of the numerous monetary and banking reformers in the West, the Liberal party should pledge itself to a "policy of banking reform which will include the establishment of a central bank of discount and some measure of control over credit through the re-discount rate." Thirdly, the party should firmly uphold the "independence and integrity" of the Canadian National Railways. In doing so they should express their opposition to any programme of amalgamation of the two national roads, and also pledge themselves to the establishment of a board of directors for the C.N.R. which would be free from political interference. Finally, the Liberals should live up to their often expressed devotion to electoral reform, including the alternative vote, proportional representation and legislation limiting the use of privately solicited campaign funds. These policies, sincerely adhered to, could win the West for the Liberals: "If the party has not the 'intestinal fortitude' to avow these policies and stay with them through good and evil report it has no particular future, and I do not know that on these terms it deserves any. If the country has to submit to Tory government it might as well patronize the holders of the patent rights in place of preferring an imitation."[35]

Two points about Dafoe's proposed reform programme seem most obvious. First, it was composed of policies which he thought had a particular appeal to the voter in the agricultural West. The programme's central plank was tariff reform—a plank which had been in the platform of every farmers' pressure group since the opening of the West. Secondly, the programme contained not a single social reform. But even in the West in the 1930's the old tariff reform programme was wearing a bit thin, as witnessed by the development of radical movements of such differing character as the C.C.F. and Social Credit. In the atmosphere of the 1930's Dafoe reform programme was, therefore, an extremely cautious one. Perhaps it was well that the programme was cautious, for so was the leader, Mackenzie King, whom he expected to put it into practice.

[35]*Ibid.*, Dafoe to Vincent Massey, Dec. 7, 1931.

Dafoe took an exceptionally active part in the efforts made by the Liberal party to hammer out a new programme. The *Free Press* blasted away at the Tory Government, and after 1933 at the C.C.F. But these were the usual chores. Dafoe was also involved in the more interesting task of joining with the party leaders in discussions of policy. In September 1932 he attended a high-level conference at Massey's Batterwood House, where the whole range of party strategy and policy was discussed with King, Lapointe, Massey, Ralston and Lambert. In 1933 he was one of the theme speakers at the Liberal summer school held at Port Hope. On each of these occasions he stressed his view that the Liberal party had to adopt the cause of reform, especially tariff reform and international co-operation.[36]

In 1932 Vincent Massey was planning a book on Canadian Liberalism, and approached Dafoe for advice. Dafoe had studied this and allied subjects with care for years, and so he readily offered Massey both his own opinions and some suggested readings. He recommended a wide list of Conservative, Liberal and Socialist writings—M. J. Bonn, R. H. Tawney, Ramsay Muir and R. M. MacIver whose *Modern State* he called the "handbook of modern liberalism." Some of the writings of Walter Lippmann and Woodrow Wilson were included, though Dafoe observed that "it is astonishing how the fact that the United States is under a rigid constitution of checks and balances makes American political writing inapplicable to our more fluid situation." Turning to the content of the proposed book, Dafoe suggested that twentieth-century liberalism in Canada should be based on the belief that

in a state fully conscious of its social obligations and equipped with the machinery necessary to discharge them, there is still room for individual initiative and freedom. Implicit in the political philosophies of the Tories and Socialists is the conception of the state as a power which can obliterate at will all individual rights. Implicit in them also is the idea of dictatorship—Fascist in one instance, and by a minority of zealots in the other. As I have put it on occasion, the state is the unit in one case and the individual is the unit in the other.

The liberal philosophy should manifest itself in policies which would attract all moderate reformers and drive the reactionary parasites from the party. If the Liberals lacked such a programme, the conservatives would remain in the party and the moderate reformers would move over to the C.C.F.[37]

[36]*Ibid.*, Dafoe to Harry Sifton, Aug. 9, 1932; Dafoe to N. W. Rowell, Sept. 30, 1932. Dafoe, *The Challenge to Democracy*, reprinted from *The Liberal Way* (Toronto and Vancouver, 1933).

[37]Dafoe Papers, Dafoe to Vincent Massey, Oct. 1, 1932.

Dafoe kept a watchful eye on the activities of the growing Canadian Socialist movement, though he was not very worried about its chances of attracting a wide support. Personally he had no sympathy for its objectives, believing that a slightly reformed capitalist system operating within a world economy governed by moderate tariff policies was the most satisfactory economic system that man could devise. He was quick to point out in the *Free Press* that the C.C.F. was not a continuation of the Progressive movement. The latter was an "outbreak of insurgent Liberalism" which hoped to reform the Liberal party; the C.C.F. was a definite third party with Socialist aims, the paper noted on March 1, 1933. Nor was there any room for compromise between Liberals and Socialists, for the latter denied the very individualism upon which the former was based. Both the Liberals and Socialists might claim to be reform parties, but the C.C.F. was just as serious a threat to freedom as the reactionary forces of the far right. The essential difference between Liberal and Socialist reform, the *Free Press* explained on August 9, 1933, was that "one aims at the freeing and equipping of the individual for the better living of his own life; the purpose of the other is to submerge the individual in a collectivism which recognizes and serves nothing but the state."

Dafoe believed that the theory of Socialism was unacceptable; in practice its prospects in Canada were thin. The Western farmers would never relinquish their inherent individualism, as a Socialist policy would necessitate. Furthermore, collectivist policies ran counter to the free trade principles that an agricultural society had to accept if it wished to prosper. The Socialists' objective of winning a balance of power in Parliament was quite unrealistic. The lesson of 1925 had been that the expectation of controlling Parliament by a balance of power was an illusion. In the end, Dafoe predicted, the Liberals would be the beneficiaries of the C.C.F. agitation for reform.

The farmers would shatter the C.C.F. hopes in the West, Dafoe expected. When King was planning a Western tour in the summer of 1933, Dafoe advised him to concentrate on the rural districts. In these areas he would get a sympathetic hearing because the radical reformers were all economic nationalists who refused to accept the fact that the West was a low tariff heaven. Dafoe urged King to get down to fundamental points, for he distrusted the Liberal leader's "constitutional reluctance to elucidate principles." He wanted him openly to repudiate any possibility of co-operating with the C.C.F., but at the same time to make it clear that the Liberal policy was one of definite reform. This would prevent the movement of Liberals into the C.C.F. column. The Liberal party had to be cleared of the stigma, placed on it by both Tories and the C.C.F., that "Canadian Liberalism is an arid political faith without works, subscribing to some kind of nineteenth-century policy of laissez-faire."[38]

As the Conservative term of office neared its end, Dafoe increased the tempo of his campaign for a return of the Liberals. At the head of his list of Liberal principles remained the demand for the enlargement of Canadian trade through tariff reduction. He admitted he was "far to the Right of the hosts that are rushing Utopia-wards," but he never doubted the justice of his denunciations of collectivism and economic nationalism. At times his voice rose almost to a hysterical pitch in his denunciations of the C.C.F.:

> Liberalism can never come to terms with Socialism, but it is the advocate, and when it is in power, the practitioner of social reform. The objective of Socialism is the destruction in all its forms of the profit motive and the standardization of life under the control of bureaucrats in conformity with a "planned economy" socialistic in purpose. As a practical policy Socialism and Communism are the same thing; the divergence is with respect to the tactics by which this obliteration of individualism and the transformation of men into ants can best be brought about.

These denunciations of the Socialists along with his endless attacks upon the Conservative Government left Dafoe in the centre position which he wished to see the Liberal party occupy. At the party's summer school in 1933 he told the audience that the "challenge to democracy" came from both the right and the left, the parties on either extreme advocating national self-sufficiency and collectivism. Democracy could only be saved from these dangerous doctrines by Liberals united together to promote the principles of "international goodwill and co-operation." His editorials in the *Free Press* came to represent the gospel of Liberalism so well that the party organization suggested that a selection of them be made for campaign purposes. Dafoe declined the offer in the belief that he was of more use to the party as an independent editor. Of course, he was only independent in a very technical sense. He was completely committed to the Liberal cause and had no illusions about the position his paper would take when the active campaigning began for the 1935 election.[39]

[38]*Ibid.*, Dafoe to Vincent Massey, Dec. 29, 1932; Dafoe to F. H. Underhill, Oct. 17, 1932; Dafoe to W. L. M. King, June 15, 1933; Dafoe to Harry Sifton, July 24, 1933; Dafoe to W. L. M. King, Aug. 8, 1933.
[39]*Ibid.*, Dafoe to Dr. J. T. Shotwell, Dec. 28, 1933. *W.F.P.*, June 12, 1932. Dafoe, *The Challenge to Democracy*. Dafoe Papers, Dafoe to Norman Lambert, Feb. 13, 1935.

vi

Even a casual reader of the *Free Press* could have predicted what the paper's attitude would be towards the Bennett "New Deal" which was presented to the Canadian public early in 1935. On two counts—their Tory origin and their collectivist nature—these proposed social and economic reforms were anathema to the *Free Press*. These "experiments in the impossible," as the paper had branded the Roosevelt New Deal, were interpreted as a completely opportunistic stratagem by a millionaire Prime Minister anxious to preserve his slipping hold on office. "This is one of the most cynical and dishonest performances recorded in Canadian politics, and will have a long train of disastrous consequences," Dafoe warned an Eastern Conservative. Bennett's new pose was a deathbed conversion, the *Free Press* announced in the extreme tones of denunciation which it sometimes adopted:

If Capitalism is corrupt, avaricious, predacious, heartless, regardless of human suffering, greedy and whatnot, how does it come that Mr. Bennett did not find out until December 1934, when the millions having been safely amassed and salted down, Mr. Bennett turned his ambitions not to further triumphs of capitalism, but to the capture of a political position which will make him just as much the dictator of Canada as Mussolini is the dictator of Italy?

Admittedly the Royal Commission on Price Spreads had collected some impressive information on poverty, hardship and unethical business practices in Canada, but the collectivist policies of the Tories were no answer to the problem. Similar policies had failed in the United States and were doomed to an ignominious fate in Canada.[40] It was perhaps a sign of the times that in his condemnation of Bennett's "New Deal" proposals, Dafoe was joining hands with such spokesmen of Eastern big business as the Montreal *Gazette*. Even the *Financial Post* was a good deal more moderate in its comments than the *Free Press*. Indeed Dafoe's attitude to social reform during the thirties suggests several variations on Arch Dale's well-known cartoon which depicted R. B. Bennett trying to get into bed with J. S. Woodsworth. One variation could certainly have included J. W. Dafoe with bedfellows from Bay and St. James streets.

Dafoe felt confident that Bennett's new policies would fail as an election device. In fact, he thought that they would be "disintegrating and disastrous to the Conservative party." The whole Canadian New Deal

[40]*W.F.P.*, Aug. 15, 1934. Dafoe Papers, Dafoe to J. M. Macdonnell, Aug. 27, 1935. *W.F.P.*, Jan. 23, 1935; April 15, 1935.

scheme was concocted in the United States, under the guidance of Bennett's brother-in-law, William Herridge, Dafoe had reason to believe. The Prime Minister aspired to the title of a Canadian Roosevelt, but he would fail. "Canada is not the United States. Bennett is certainly not Roosevelt, and 1935 is not the year 1933," Dafoe asserted confidently. Two years earlier Bennett might have succeeded, but now the rot in his party had gone too far to be stopped. Writing to Lord Lothian from Ottawa in March, Dafoe described "the most astonishing political situation that we have had since the convulsions of 1895–96 wh. marked the dissolution for the time being of the Conservative party. History is abt. to repeat itself, I think."[41]

As the election campaign of 1935 got under way, Dafoe could see little but Liberal complacency to prevent the defeat of Bennett. Once the Liberals were back in power, there would be no attempt to enforce the New Deal until an appeal was made to the Supreme Court, which would no doubt deal with it as the American Supreme Court had dealt with its counterpart. The *Free Press*'s advice to the electorate was to keep its attention on the primary issue of the campaign: "that of liberating and reviving trade with the outside world." Western voters could ensure the achievement of this objective by voting solid for the Liberal party.[42]

The election of 1935 was a victory, though not a landslide, for the Liberal party. Only in Quebec did King's followers carry everything before them, while they actually suffered a net loss in votes in the rest of Canada. The Conservatives were soundly trounced, but much of the anti-Conservative vote went to the minor parties, especially the C.C.F. and Social Credit—a fact which indicated the declining attraction for Western voters of Dafoe's "liberal reforms." Once more the province of Quebec was the predominant influence in the Liberal party. This fact was highly significant in view of Dafoe's hope that the Liberals would actively support the League of Nations.

Dafoe was delighted with the Liberal victory. Bennett had been a particular obsession of the Winnipeg editor. Writing to Mackenzie King after the election Dafoe explained that he had given his best efforts to prevent Bennett from carrying the Prairies into the Conservative camp.

---

[41] Dafoe Papers, Dafoe to Grant Dexter, Jan. 10, 1935; Chester Bloom to Dafoe, Jan. 11, 1935; Dafoe to Tom King, Feb. 19, 1935. Lothian Papers, Dafoe to Lord Lothian, March 7, 1935. On Herridge's part in Bennett's New Deal, someone quipped: "Mr. Bennett has drawn a red Herridge across the trail." "Backstage at Ottawa," *Maclean's*, March 1, 1935, 54.

[42] Dafoe Papers, Dafoe to Tom King, May 30, 1935. *W.F.P.*, Sept. 9, Oct. 12, 1935.

"I made it my particular business to block him & it certainly kept me busy," he wrote. Dafoe's hope was to see the past years of high tariff reversed, but he realistically noted that the prospects were not entirely promising. An examination of the election returns showed that many manufacturing districts had changed their 1930 verdicts and returned to the Liberal fold. The result would be "a tremendous rally of the protectionist elements in the country to induce Mr. King to follow an ultra-cautious policy." As usual King would need watching.[43]

Dafoe might have assumed a position of direct influence in the new Government: in recognition of his services he was offered a cabinet position or the Washington diplomatic post. He thought that the suggested cabinet post was a "courtesy offer" and refused it immediately. The diplomatic post, however, was a more serious offer on the Prime Minister's part. Dafoe was not really tempted to accept, but he spent some time considering. After a decent interval he wrote to King declining the position. "The only job I feel competent to fill or wh. I wd. be happy in filling," he explained, "is the one I have, & when it comes to an end, I shall pass into retirement, absolute or otherwise." Explaining the decision to his brother Wallace, Dafoe said he did not doubt that he could have handled the Washington assignment, for the Embassy staff did most of the work anyway. But, he wrote disarmingly, "I have no particular ambitions left except to be left alone as much as possible in order that I may carry out some plans which I have in mind, the chief among them are the writing of a couple of books."[44]

Whatever books he had in mind, they were, unfortunately, never written. Though a contemplative man for a journalist, Dafoe was far too interested in the affairs of the world around him to isolate himself often enough to write anything as long as a book. Early in 1931 he had found time to retire to Bermuda for a few months to compose his biography of Sir Clifford Sifton, but by 1935 events were moving too quickly to allow another extended retreat. There were the critical problems of international affairs that demanded an increasing amount of his attention. There were also many important domestic questions to be attended to. After all, a mere change of government was no guarantee

[43] Dafoe Papers, Dafoe to W. L. M. King, Oct. 19, 1935; Dafoe to R. J. Deachman, Oct. 16, 1935.
[44] *Ibid.*, Dafoe to W. L. M. King, Oct. 19, 1935; Dafoe to Wallace Dafoe, Nov. 25, 1935. Some years later Dafoe suggested that the reason for his refusal to accept the Washington post was his reluctance to become associated with King's foreign policy (*ibid.*, Dafoe to J. M. Macdonnell, Sept. 16, 1940, and Dafoe to Henry Luce, Aug. 5, 1941). This may have played a part in his decision, but I suspect it was an afterthought, for in 1935 Dafoe had hopes that King would adopt an internationalist foreign policy.

that the frightful conditions of the depression would be immediately improved.

The tariff question was still of first importance. The overtures to the United States that had first been made by the Conservatives could now be brought to a successful culmination. The *Free Press*, veteran of many battles for liberalized trade with the United States, commented on December 6, 1935:

> A highly important difference between the circumstances in 1911 and in 1935 is that the Canadian people have learned by hard experience the value of markets and the importance of closer trade relations with our big neighbor to the south. And they know that that market can be cultivated without seriously disturbing our relations with Great Britain and the other British Dominions.

King was able to get the much-desired trade agreement which Dafoe hoped would mark the beginning of a general levelling down of the tariff. He soon realized, however, that his old dream of a solidly united low tariff West was no nearer realization than ever. Indeed the coolness of the C.C.F. and Social Credit members to low tariff proposals had "reduced almost to nullity" the West's power. Dafoe's old friend, T. A. Crerar, now a member of the Liberal cabinet, reported that the pressure on the Government to maintain the tariff at a protective level was very strong, and what was worse some of the pressure came from Western members as well as Ontario Liberals. Dafoe was distressed at the failure of Canadians to admit the truth of his views on trade and tariff. None of the inceasingly popular schemes for government marketing, quota systems and compulsory pools fitted into his liberal ideals.[45]

He admitted that his principles were old-fashioned, but he never lost faith in their ultimate triumph. Writing on his seventieth birthday, he expressed his faith with a strength of conviction that had characterized nineteenth-century liberals:

> I am myself profoundly convinced that in a free society the principles of liberalism will steadily justify themselves until in the procession of the decades—perhaps of the centuries—they will become universal. But this is an expression of faith—I have no expectation that in the span of life that remains to me there will be any clarification of the immense confusion in which the world now wallows; in fact the chances are that it will be increased.

Were the lights of liberalism dying everywhere in the world? Perhaps they had been growing dim for a longer time than Dafoe would admit to himself. He had thought he saw a new flicker of life in the autumn

[45] *W.F.P.*, Feb. 13, 1936. Dafoe Papers, T. A. Crerar to Dafoe, March 4, 1936.

of 1935, but only a few years later he realized that the battle for his brand of liberalism was no nearer to victory. The world's chaos seemed everywhere compounded. The one bright light was the announcement that the King Government intended to do something about Canada's constitutional confusion.[46]

[46]*W.F.P.*, March 21, 1936. Dafoe Papers, Dafoe to Graham Spry, April 16, 1936.

XII. Remodelling the Canadian Constitution

THE GREAT DEPRESSION OF THE THIRTIES, the "dirty thirties," brought out many of the weaknesses of the Canadian social and political structure. It provoked serious questions about the country's free enterprise economy, the traditional political parties and even democracy and parliamentary government. Few doubted that the times were out of joint. One point on which nearly all critics were agreed was that Canada's nineteenth-century constitution was no longer capable of meeting the demands of a twentieth-century society. Indeed it was not even the original constitution prescribed by the British North America Act in 1867 that governed Canadian political life in the depression decade; it was a constitution so stretched and pulled as to modify many of the primary ideas of the Fathers of Confederation. The constitution, which in 1867 had envisaged a strong central power functioning for the "peace, order and good government" of Canada and surrounded by provincial satellites, had become by 1930 a constitution in which the federal power was straitened while the provinces were encouraged to grow in power. The chief villain of the piece was the Judicial Committee of the Privy Council whose judgments had seriously crippled the federal government's authority to deal with national catastrophes on the scale of the depression. The provincial governments' increased authority offered no real solution, for the difficulties of the depression were national in scope. Furthermore, while the Privy Council had given the provinces increased responsibilities, it had failed to offer any suggestions about methods of acquiring the funds necessary to carry them out. The social crisis of the thirties necessitated a full-scale re-examination of the Canadian constitution in all its aspects—the division of powers, methods of public finance, and not least of all the question of amendment.[1]

[1]D. G. Creighton, "Federal Relations in Canada since 1914" in Chester Martin, ed., *Canada in Peace and War* (Toronto, 1941), 29–58.

Canadian nationalists had long been humiliated by the fact that the country's final court of appeal was in London rather than Ottawa. What could a court of English judges know about Canadian constitutional needs, they asked. The nearer Canada approached full national status, the more galling this anomaly became. What a curious nation it was that had to rely on English law lords to settle its constitutional controversies. And worse still, it had to depend upon the imperial Parliament to enact desired constitutional changes. The fact was, of course, that this unusual situation existed because Canadians simply could not agree on how to alter it. Some thought that the abolition of appeals to the Privy Council would sunder the last of the silken bonds of Empire. Others felt that entrenched minority privileges were safer in the hands of the British Parliament than they would be if the amending machinery were transferred to Canada. The discussion of these points had a history as old as Confederation itself. The depression made it plain that it was time for the discussion to end and action to begin.

Premier Bennett, perhaps hoping that the decisions in the *Air Navigation Case* and the *Radio Case*, both in 1932, signalled a revival of the federal authority, chose largely to ignore the constitutional problem in enacting his New Deal social legislation in 1935. Mackenzie King, more cautious, chose a different and probably more sensible course. Bennett's legislation was referred to the court, and for the most part found unconstitutional.[2] With its powers thus seriously delimited, the federal Government had to discover a new approach to the problems of social and economic plight evident throughout the country.

ii

On August 14, 1937, the Royal Commission on Dominion-Provincial Relations, popularly known as the Rowell-Sirois Commission, was established by the King Government to examine the constitutional stalemate that had been reached in Canada. Its breadth of purpose was well summed up in a clause of its terms of reference, which called for "a re-examination of the economic and financial basis of Confederation and the distribution of legislative powers in the light of the economic and social developments of the last seventy years." The composition of the commission, which produced the most famous state paper in Canadian history after the Durham Report, included representatives of every section of the country. Chief Justice N. W. Rowell of Ontario was appointed chairman. Chief Justice Thibaudeau Rinfret of Quebec was forced to retire after three months, but was replaced by another eminent

[2]Maurice Ollivier, *Problems of Canadian Sovereignty* (Toronto, 1945), 185–209.

French-Canadian jurist, Dr. Joseph Sirois. From the Maritimes the Government chose Dr. R. A. MacKay of Dalhousie University, and another professor, H. F. Angus, to represent the Pacific Coast province. As the representative of the Prairies, John W. Dafoe was selected.[3]

Dafoe, it will be remembered, had rejected King's offer of a cabinet post and then refused the suggestion that he become Canadian Minister to Washington. But the Royal Commission post offered an opportunity to participate in a fascinating and extremely important task. And it had the added advantage of requiring only a temporary retirement from the *Free Press*. Prior to a telephone conversation with the Prime Minister on July 23, 1937, Dafoe apparently had not thought of himself as a serious candidate for membership on the commission. His own view was that perhaps a commission of five—"three Canadians and two outsiders, one Englishman, one American or Australian"—would be the most satisfactory arrangement. He also thought that his friend, Dr. J. T. Shotwell, would be a useful member. So, when the position was offered to him, Dafoe was modestly self-deprecating about his qualifications. Nevertheless his interest was obvious when he wrote to King that

nothing would deter me from giving my services if I could convince myself that I could make a contribution of real value to a task of immense importance, nothing less than the re-modelling of our whole national structure, which is beginning to have a jerry-built appearance. On this point I must say, I am more than a bit sceptical. The journalistic method of rapid and confident generalization from a few related facts has its uses: but I do not know that—particularly in view of my years—I am fitted for the prolonged intellectual assault upon a most complex problem that is called for here.

Dafoe was vastly underrating his ability to make a contribution to the commission's work. Perhaps he was also anticipating the criticisms that would be directed at a commission on which he was a member. After all, he had made a good many enemies in his years of controversy. And his anticipations were fulfilled. Some attacks came from French Canadians who recalled Dafoe's attitude to conscription and separate schools. Others came from politicians such as Premier Aberhart of Alberta, and R. B. Bennett who described the Winnipeg editor as "one of the most violent partisan journalists the country had produced." Still, Dafoe accepted the appointment, for here was an opportunity to put to use, in a new way, the extensive knowledge of his country and its constitution that he had acquired over the years. He told Dr. Shotwell that he could think of a dozen reasons why the appointment should not be given to

[3]*Royal Commission on Dominion-Provincial Relations*, Book I, *Canada, 1867–1939* (Ottawa, 1954), 9 (hereafter cited as *Report*).

him, and another dozen why he should refuse, but he admitted that he did not "lack views as to what shd. be done if our constitution, in the Carlylean phrase, is to 'march'."[4]

These views had evolved over a period of years, and especially since the Great War. As a journalist Dafoe's interest in this question had never been that of a detached scholar, but rather of a well-informed advocate. His nationalist views were just as important in shaping his ideas on the Canadian constitution as they were in forming his attitude to the constitution of the British Commonwealth.

It had not required a depression to make Dafoe conscious that the Canadian constitution was not an entirely satisfactory instrument of government. As part of the post-war campaign for full national status, he had often turned his attention to the British North America Act, its construction and interpretation and possible methods of altering it. As a nationalist he believed that Canada should acquire full control of its constitution. On March 22, 1924, for example, the *Free Press* criticized both Liberals and Conservatives for refusing to face this issue when it was presented to Parliament by J. S. Woodsworth. As long as the power to change and interpret the constitution remained outside the country, the Canadian governmental structure was subject to the whims of the Judicial Committee of the Privy Council, whose judgments repeatedly threatened the authority of the national power. Dafoe believed that a strong federal government was a prerequisite of Canadian nationhood and he suspected that perhaps the motives of the British judges were not altogether unadulterated by imperial considerations when judgments weakening the federal government were handed down. The whole problem was brought sharply to his attention in 1925 when the Judicial Committee in the case of the *Toronto Electric Commissioners* v. *Snider* invalidated the Industrial Disputes Investigation Act on the ground that it infringed upon the powers ascribed to the provinces. Dafoe's suspicions were reflected in his comments to Sifton:

> It seems to me that this judgment pushes to an extreme the view that Canada is a federation of sovereignties tied together by tenuous bonds, the central power having very nominal powers, or none at all, over many matters of national concern.
>
> If this constitutional development goes on under repeated judgments limiting or destroying federal activities, will it ever be possible to give national cohesion to this country?
>
> Is there some such idea as this behind these Privy Council judgments?

---

[4]Dafoe Papers, Dafoe to W. L. M. King, July 24, 1937; Dafoe to A. R. Carman, Nov. 5, 1937. *Winnipeg Tribune*, Oct. 23, 1937. Dafoe Papers, Dafoe to Dr. James T. Shotwell, Dec. 21, 1937.

Sifton, who was much less nationalist in constitutional matters than Dafoe, thought the Judicial Committee's judgment quite correct. Anyway, he added, it was best that labour legislation should be left in the hands of provincial legislatures, which were dominated by farmers and therefore unlikely to be influenced by the pressure of organized labour. Dafoe was certainly on the right track when he suggested that the Snider judgment was a further limitation on the federal power. Lord Haldane made this fact quite clear when he asserted in his judgment that "the real contest was between Sir John Macdonald and Lord Watson." In the *Free Press*, Dafoe took the opportunity to point out that the judgment again indicated that the time had come for Canada to assume full control over its constitution. To leave the authority with Britain was to provide one more possible source of friction between Canada and the mother country.[5]

Dafoe knew that it was one thing to terminate British authority over the Canadian constitution, and quite another to find suitable substitute machinery. The Canadian Supreme Court could fulfil the judicial functions, but the question of constitutional amendment was much more complex and explosive. The French Canadians, Dafoe was convinced, were the greatest obstacle to progress in finding a solution; they believed that their minority rights were safer in the hands of the imperial Parliament than they would be if a Canadian authority were substituted. Dafoe had some frank comments to make about this situation to Henri Bourassa:

> How can we ever be a nation until we get over the beliefs that only an external parliament can be trusted to change our constitution, and only a court not of our appointing is competent finally to interpret our laws? On these points the French Canadians seem to be pretty nearly unanimous; and while they hold these views no real progress can be made towards establishing Canada in the world's eyes as a nation.

Not only were the French Canadians an obstacle to full Canadian control of the constitution, but also their position on the amending process was completely at odds with Dafoe's. The French Canadians looked upon the British North America Act as a compact which could only be altered after the unanimous agreement of the contracting parties. Dafoe believed that the worst disaster that could befall the constitution would be the acceptance of this view. To accept it would be to give the country an

---

[5]Dafoe Papers, Dafoe to Sifton, Feb. 11, 1925; Sifton to Dafoe, Feb. 16, 1925. F. R. Scott, "French Canada and Canadian Federalism" in A. R. M. Lower, F. R. Scott, *et al., Evolving Canadian Federalism* (Durham, N.C., 1948), 72. *M.F.P.*, Feb. 20, 1925.

unchangeable constitution "like that of the Medes and the Persians." In truth, Canada had never recognized this paralysing doctrine; if a joint address of the Canadian Parliament requesting a constitutional amendment was presented to the British Parliament, the amendment would be allowed as a matter of course. There was no guarantee of consultation with the provinces, and certainly none that amendment would only follow upon unanimous consent, the *Free Press* maintained.[6]

National peace would not, of course, be found by having the federal government assume all responsibility for constitutional amendment. Dafoe admitted that where minority rights or provincial powers were in question, no government with any sense of justice or political acumen would dare act without consulting the provinces. His own proposal was simple, but it gave full recognition to all the interests involved: certain minority rights would be guaranteed absolutely, but changes in other sections of the constitution would require "the support of some reasonable percentage of the provinces." If the provinces refused to agree to this suggestion, Dafoe thought that the issue might be forced if the Dominion would renounce its right to apply to the imperial Parliament for constitutional changes.[7]

The Balfour Declaration in 1926 brought a new sense of urgency into Dafoe's thoughts on the constitution. The Declaration made it evident that the Canadian government could take over the amending and judicial powers at will. What worried Dafoe was the possibility that the Liberal Government under the influence of "Mr. Lapointe and his friends [would] try to tie this country up to procedure which would make it impossible for anything whatever to be done in amending our constitution." The first necessity was to prove beyond doubt that there was no constitutional convention which required the federal government to obtain the agreement of all the provinces before approaching the imperial government for an amendment. In the *Free Press*, January 5, 1927, Dafoe argued that "this whole elaborate theory ... is a hallucination. It finds no support in law, in practise, or in the intentions of the Fathers of Confederation, as revealed by the documents of the Confederation period." He found the claims of Premier Taschereau of Quebec and Premier Ferguson of Ontario at the Dominion-Provincial Conference of 1927 irritating in the extreme. To accept their view that each province had a veto on suggested constitutional changes would cramp the country into a strait-jacket from which it would eventually break out with such violence that Confederation would be endangered.

[6]Dafoe Papers, Dafoe to Henri Bourassa, April 24, 1926; *M.F.P.*, March 4, July 18, 1925.   [7]Dafoe Papers, Dafoe to Sifton, March 11, 1925.

He never doubted that certain minority rights would have to be given absolute guarantees, but in other matters "such as the distribution of powers between the Federal and Provincial Governments" the constitution had to be made alterable by a simple formula. He told Grant Dexter:

> This is the one question upon which Lapointe may prove himself a reactionary. If he and King try to tie this country up in a constitutional straitjacket, the last fate of this country with respect to the amendment of the constitution will be worse than the first. Unfortunately there is a possibility that the provinces might fall in with this preposterous scheme as it flatters their sense of being important.[8]

Dafoe would not have described himself as either a centralizer or a champion of provincial rights. As a nationalist he believed that the country should control its own constitutional procedures, and that the national government should be entrusted with sufficient powers to deal with all problems of national concern. At the same time he fully recognized the fact that the diverse nature of the country made a federal system inevitable; some matters had to be placed beyond the reach of the federal government. Like many English Canadians Dafoe preferred a unitary system of government with some federal modifications rather than a federal system with some unitary modifications. His case against the Judicial Committee of the Privy Council, apart from its location, was that its judgments had weakened the authority of the federal government as conceived by the nation's founders. As always, he appealed to history to support his views. Careful research satisfied him that there was no historical basis for the compact theory of Confederation. In 1930 he set out his conclusions with supporting evidence in an admirable article entitled, "Revising the Constitution." Here he carefully analysed the views of the founders of the constitution on the nature of the system of government established in 1867, and the methods that had been used in subsequent amendments. Two years later, reviewing Norman McLeod Rogers' celebrated article on the compact theory, Dafoe wrote confidently, "The compact theory breaks down under any one of a dozen tests."[9]

But it was one thing to prove in a convincing manner that there was no basis for the compact theory and quite another to get a government to act in the matter of setting up machinery for constitutional amendment.

---

[8]*Ibid.*, Dafoe to Sifton, Dec. 16, 18, 1926; Dafoe to Grant Dexter, Oct. 6, 1927.

[9]K. C. Wheare, *Federal Government* (3rd ed., London, 1956), 20; Dafoe Papers, Dafoe to Brooke Claxton, Dec. 2, 1931; Dafoe, "Revising the Constitution," *Queen's Quarterly*, XXXVII, no. 1 (Winter 1930), 1–17; Dafoe, "The Compact Theory of Confederation," *C.H.R.*, XIII, no. 1 (March 1932), 32.

King's Government had failed to find a solution to the problem at the Dominion-Provincial Conference in 1927. When Bennett was first elected, Dafoe thought that he might be the man who would act resolutely on the matter. But very soon the proponents of the compact theory were on Bennett's doorstep. The occasion for a new and extreme expression of this old view was the Report of the Committee on Dominion Legislation which was to form the basis of the Statute of Westminster. Before Bennett departed for the Imperial Conference that was to draft the statute, Premier Ferguson of Ontario let him know in no uncertain terms that since the constitution of Canada was a compact among the provinces, "the province of Ontario holds strongly to the view that this agreement should not be altered without the consent of the parties to it." The suggestion made Dafoe livid. Its acceptance, he wrote in the *Free Press* on October 1, would be "humiliating in the extreme to most Canadians." When Premier Taschereau added his voice to that of the Ontario leader, Dafoe called up his sharpest fighting words. "The claims of the provinces to be consulted," he wrote on December 29, "voiced by Mr. Ferguson and Mr. Taschereau, have no foundation beyond the egregious, overweening conceit of these gentlemen.... The impudence of the proposition is amazing, colossal!" When Bennett accepted the draft Statute of Westminster subject to prior consideration by the provinces, Dafoe was not especially perturbed. He announced gleefully, "We are all 'extreme autonomists' now." The agreement to discuss the matter with the provinces was simply a means "for the saving of Ferguson's face," though Dafoe felt that in providing for this arrangement Bennett had "made a rod for his own back."[10]

During Bennett's term of office no solution to the problem of amending the constitution was provided, though his decision to consult the provinces on the Statute of Westminster may have been a "precedent" or at least an "instance" to support the opinion of those who held that the British North America Act could only be amended on the unanimous consent of the provinces. What disturbed Dafoe was a belief that the high-handed actions of the Conservatives, especially in their last months in office, had stimulated anti-federal sentiment. In this atmosphere the normal difficulty in the way of settling the constitutional problem was vastly increased.[11]

[10]Dafoe Papers, Dafoe to Graham Spry, Sept. 30, 1930; G. H. Ferguson to R. B. Bennett, Sept. 20, 1930, in R. MacG. Dawson, *Constitutional Issues in Canada*, (London, 1933), 79; *M.F.P.*, Dec. 18, 1930; Dafoe Papers, Dafoe to John Stevenson, Dec. 29, 1930.
[11]K. C. Wheare, *The Statute of Westminster and Dominion Status* (London, 1947), 190; Dafoe Papers, Dafoe to Brooke Claxton, Aug. 26, 1935.

The depression made it patently obvious that the question of constitutional readjustment had to be faced. Everywhere, and especially in the West, provincial governments were floundering in their efforts to meet social problems that could only be dealt with satisfactorily by the federal government. Somehow the Ottawa administration had to be given the means of coming to grips with these difficulties. Dafoe thought that the discussion of specific constitutional amendments should be postponed until after the amending machinery had been devised. Naturally he felt that there was a definite need to consider the reallocation of the powers of taxation and responsibility for social services, but he feared that these questions might become red herrings if the principle of amendment was not settled first. At the conference of Liberal leaders held at Batterwood House in 1932, he strongly urged the party's policy-makers to give serious attention to this problem. Two years later he outlined his views with some precision in the *Free Press*:

All questions of particular amendments and how they are to be obtained should be suspended and attention centred on the procedure to be followed. In a Conference called for this purpose, the Dominion would not be in such a helpless position in the face of unaccommodating provinces as it is when it asks for approval for desired amendments because there is a public opinion that could, upon an issue of this kind, be invoked against intransigent provincialism.

This was purely a question of tactics. Dafoe thought that the majority of Canadians favoured the principle of constitutional amendment through Canadian machinery; on specific amendments that majority might be divided.[12]

Dafoe hoped that the return of the Liberals to office in 1935 would open the way to a quick solution to the constricting difficulties of the country's constitution. Despite the fact that the Liberals were traditionally the party of provincial rights, he thought that both King and Lapointe were at last convinced of "the necessity of a whole series of adjustments prominent among which must be some provision for amending the constitution and some actual re-adjustment of powers." But it was soon evident that the new Liberal Government was to be no more successful in finding a means of carrying out amendments than it had been in 1927. Even though Premier Ferguson had been replaced by that redoubtable Liberal, Mitchell Hepburn, the Dominion-Provincial Conference of 1935 was a practical re-enactment of the futilities of 1927.[13]

[12]Dafoe Papers, Dafoe to N. W. Rowell, Sept. 30, 1932; *W.F.P.*, Nov. 10, 1934.
[13]Dafoe Papers, Dafoe to Brooke Claxton, Aug. 26, 1935.

King's Government had failed to find a solution to the problem at the Dominion-Provincial Conference in 1927. When Bennett was first elected, Dafoe thought that he might be the man who would act resolutely on the matter. But very soon the proponents of the compact theory were on Bennett's doorstep. The occasion for a new and extreme expression of this old view was the Report of the Committee on Dominion Legislation which was to form the basis of the Statute of Westminster. Before Bennett departed for the Imperial Conference that was to draft the statute, Premier Ferguson of Ontario let him know in no uncertain terms that since the constitution of Canada was a compact among the provinces, "the province of Ontario holds strongly to the view that this agreement should not be altered without the consent of the parties to it." The suggestion made Dafoe livid. Its acceptance, he wrote in the *Free Press* on October 1, would be "humiliating in the extreme to most Canadians." When Premier Taschereau added his voice to that of the Ontario leader, Dafoe called up his sharpest fighting words. "The claims of the provinces to be consulted," he wrote on December 29, "voiced by Mr. Ferguson and Mr. Taschereau, have no foundation beyond the egregious, overweening conceit of these gentlemen.... The impudence of the proposition is amazing, colossal!" When Bennett accepted the draft Statute of Westminster subject to prior consideration by the provinces, Dafoe was not especially perturbed. He announced gleefully, "We are all 'extreme autonomists' now." The agreement to discuss the matter with the provinces was simply a means "for the saving of Ferguson's face," though Dafoe felt that in providing for this arrangement Bennett had "made a rod for his own back."[10]

During Bennett's term of office no solution to the problem of amending the constitution was provided, though his decision to consult the provinces on the Statute of Westminster may have been a "precedent" or at least an "instance" to support the opinion of those who held that the British North America Act could only be amended on the unanimous consent of the provinces. What disturbed Dafoe was a belief that the high-handed actions of the Conservatives, especially in their last months in office, had stimulated anti-federal sentiment. In this atmosphere the normal difficulty in the way of settling the constitutional problem was vastly increased.[11]

[10]Dafoe Papers, Dafoe to Graham Spry, Sept. 30, 1930; G. H. Ferguson to R. B. Bennett, Sept. 20, 1930, in R. MacG. Dawson, *Constitutional Issues in Canada*, (London, 1933), 79; *M.F.P.*, Dec. 18, 1930; Dafoe Papers, Dafoe to John Stevenson, Dec. 29, 1930.
[11]K. C. Wheare, *The Statute of Westminster and Dominion Status* (London, 1947), 190; Dafoe Papers, Dafoe to Brooke Claxton, Aug. 26, 1935.

The depression made it patently obvious that the question of constitutional readjustment had to be faced. Everywhere, and especially in the West, provincial governments were floundering in their efforts to meet social problems that could only be dealt with satisfactorily by the federal government. Somehow the Ottawa administration had to be given the means of coming to grips with these difficulties. Dafoe thought that the discussion of specific constitutional amendments should be postponed until after the amending machinery had been devised. Naturally he felt that there was a definite need to consider the reallocation of the powers of taxation and responsibility for social services, but he feared that these questions might become red herrings if the principle of amendment was not settled first. At the conference of Liberal leaders held at Batterwood House in 1932, he strongly urged the party's policy-makers to give serious attention to this problem. Two years later he outlined his views with some precision in the *Free Press*:

> All questions of particular amendments and how they are to be obtained should be suspended and attention centred on the procedure to be followed. In a Conference called for this purpose, the Dominion would not be in such a helpless position in the face of unaccommodating provinces as it is when it asks for approval for desired amendments because there is a public opinion that could, upon an issue of this kind, be invoked against intransigent provincialism.

This was purely a question of tactics. Dafoe thought that the majority of Canadians favoured the principle of constitutional amendment through Canadian machinery; on specific amendments that majority might be divided.[12]

Dafoe hoped that the return of the Liberals to office in 1935 would open the way to a quick solution to the constricting difficulties of the country's constitution. Despite the fact that the Liberals were traditionally the party of provincial rights, he thought that both King and Lapointe were at last convinced of "the necessity of a whole series of adjustments prominent among which must be some provision for amending the constitution and some actual re-adjustment of powers." But it was soon evident that the new Liberal Government was to be no more successful in finding a means of carrying out amendments than it had been in 1927. Even though Premier Ferguson had been replaced by that redoubtable Liberal, Mitchell Hepburn, the Dominion-Provincial Conference of 1935 was a practical re-enactment of the futilities of 1927.[13]

[12]Dafoe Papers, Dafoe to N. W. Rowell, Sept. 30, 1932; *W.F.P.*, Nov. 10, 1934.
[13]Dafoe Papers, Dafoe to Brooke Claxton, Aug. 26, 1935.

In 1935, after the failure of its negotiations with the provincial premiers, the King Government simply could not sit back and nurse its wounded pride. Nor could it rest on its tattered laurels by claiming that it had tried without success to find a solution to the constitutional deadlock. The depression had produced social and economic conditions in the country that cried aloud for attention, and the new administration had promised to take action. If it did not, the 1935 campaign cry "King or Chaos" might become "King and Chaos" in a later election. But what action could a government take when its powers were severely limited on the one hand by provincial politicians jealously hoarding their authority, and on the other by the courts, which had swept aside the main provisions of the Bennett New Deal? The Liberal Government chose to follow the time-honoured practice of appointing a royal commission to examine the division of powers between the Dominion and the provinces. In appointing Dafoe to the commission Prime Minister King served notice on the extreme proponents of provincial rights that their submissions would be met by a convinced nationalist.

iii

Dafoe was in his seventy-second year in the autumn of 1937 when he took up his duties as royal commissioner. It was no small task for a man of his age to follow the perambulating commission around the vast country for almost a year. Yet he endured it all very well. "I am alright, and not too tired," he told a solicitous inquirer, "thanks to the 'philosophic mind' that seven decades of battling life have imposed on me." Indeed, he thought that perhaps his age was an advantage; with no more ambitions to fulfil he could assume an attitude of indifference to the criticisms that were constantly directed at the commission. "I did not take this work in any expectation that it would be easy or that I shd. thereby make a popular hero of myself," he told James Shotwell, and added whimsically, "Well, as Morley, the old rationalist, used to say to his friends when he was in a jam, 'Pray for me'."[14]

Naturally Dafoe was keenly interested in the work of the investigation. He did not look upon his particular task as that of a representative of any limited section or group, and believed that his fellow commissioners should adopt a similar attitude. Writing in the *Free Press* on August 17, 1937, just before the commission began its work, he stated:

While the five members of the Commission are chosen from the five main sections of Canada, that does not mean at all that they are expected to look

---

[14]*Ibid.*, Dafoe to Clifford Sifton, June 3, 1938; Dafoe to Dr. J. T. Shotwell, Dec. 21, 1937.

at matters from sectional viewpoints. That would destroy the usefulness of the enquiry, which is intended to be of a national character, taking cognizance of the conditions and claims of different parts of the country, but keeping always in view the welfare of Canada as a whole.

Dafoe attempted to fulfil his duties as a Canadian rather than a Westerner. And he was certainly anxious that all viewpoints, especially the French Canadian, were well represented. When Mr. Justice Rinfret found it necessary to retire from the commission, Dafoe was insistent that a suitable substitute should be found, for it was "highly desirable that the French member of the Commission should be thoroughly representative and should be prepared to insist that the French point of view receives full consideration." Dafoe's own contributions to the public hearings were, with one exception, limited. But this was true of all the commissioners who were faced with the necessity of hearing a mass of representations in a short period of time. When Dafoe spoke he always showed a consciousness of the tremendous responsibility that had been placed on the commission. His strong sense of history caused him to hark back seventy years to the conferences which had led to the founding of the Dominion. These events were certainly in his mind when he replied to the address of welcome extended by the Quebec legislature in Quebec City in May 1938. "I think we have a very special sense both of our obligations and our responsibilities here in Quebec," he reflected, "because it was in this city over seventy years ago that the miracle—I use the word deliberately—the miracle of Confederation was achieved in intention, in the face of difficulties and obstacles far outranking any of the difficulties of today." As the old man sat and heard the disputes over national development, trade, tariffs, railways and the whole multiplicity of questions that came before the commission, his thoughts went back to the days when he first sat in the Parliamentary Press Gallery only two decades after Confederation and heard Macdonald, Blake, Thompson, Laurier and others disputing the same questions. "I have sometimes felt," he told the Canadian Political Science Association in 1939, "as though I were witnessing a later if not final act in a drama, the opening acts of which I saw long ago, with a twist in the theme which had changed it from melodrama to tragedy."[15]

Yet no matter how much the affairs of the commission intrigued him, his thoughts were never far from the editorial offices of the *Free Press*.

[15]*Ibid*., Dafoe to A. R. Carman, Nov. 5, 1937; *Royal Commission on Dominion-Provincial Relations, 1937, Report of Hearings, Quebec*, I, 8127 (hereafter cited as *Hearings*); Dafoe, "Canadian Problems of Government," *C.J.E.P.S.*, V, no. 3 (Aug. 1939), 287.

Shortly after he had begun his new employment, G. V. Ferguson, who had been left in charge in Winnipeg, informed him that some local Liberals had suggested that since its editor was on a royal commission, the *Free Press* should hold its fire on subjects embarrassing to the King Government. Dafoe exploded. It had only been after much serious consideration that he had accepted the appointment. "But," he told Ferguson, "if my service on the Commission is to be regarded as justifying any constraint on the Free Press of the kind hinted at then I'll cease forthwith to be a member of the Commission, and the public will be informed as to the reasons." Nothing more was heard of this suggestion.[16]

Not unnaturally Dafoe found it difficult to still the hand that had written editorials almost without pause for thirty-five years. The years that were consumed by the commission's work were terrible ones that shouted for comment. Crisis piled upon crisis on the international scene and the frustrated Dafoe was rarely able to find time to scribble out a column on the League and the aggressiveness of the dictators. Struggling in bureaucratic Ottawa with the commission's Report, Dafoe wrote to his substitute in Winnipeg, "Not a day goes by that I do not have a desire to write something for the paper or to bat up suggestions to you; & it is just as well for you perhaps, that I am tied down here with unending work ever renewing itself."[17]

But he stuck to his task, hearing submission after submission, reading endless documents, mulling over countless ideas about possible roads out of the constitutional and financial swamp that the country had landed in. From the outset Dafoe had fairly well formulated the general lines that he thought the Report should follow. In constitutional matters the paramount position of the Dominion government would have to be affirmed. In fact, he decided that if necessary he would write a separate report expressing the view that "while the provinces' rights must be strictly guarded they have to stop horning in on Dominion matters." With regard to fiscal relations he held from the beginning that the commission would have to devise a means of establishing "throughout the Dominion certain minimum standards both with regard to the individual and the provinces."[18]

During the public hearings Dafoe's greatest interest was in upholding the power of the federal authority against the champions of provincial

---

[16]Dafoe Papers, Dafoe to G. V. Ferguson, Jan. 4, 1938.
[17]*Ibid.*, Dafoe to G. V. Ferguson, Nov. 19, 1938.
[18]*Ibid.*, Dafoe to G. V. Ferguson, March 12, 1938; Dafoe to Alex Skelton, Aug. 27, 1937.

rights who came forward as exponents of the compact theory. Of course the most determined defenders of provincial rights, Premier Duplessis of Quebec, Premier Hepburn of Ontario and Premier Aberhart of Alberta, either refused to meet the commission or repudiated its findings, so that Dafoe was left to exercise his forensic powers on lesser lights. His chief victim was W. P. Jones, M.L.A., counsel for the province of New Brunswick. Though Commissioner Dafoe repeatedly denied that he was advocating a viewpoint in his exchanges with the Maritimer, his statements were unmistakable criticisms of the compact theory. Jones argued that, since the compact of Confederation was based on the Quebec Resolutions, the federal government was pledged to honour all the promises made in the seventy-two resolutions, even those which had not been specifically included in the British North America Act. Dafoe replied that since the Quebec Resolutions had never been accepted by the legislatures of Nova Scotia and New Brunswick, they could hardly be called the treaty or compact of Confederation. Displaying a remarkable knowledge of the documents of the period, Dafoe argued that even though Sir John Macdonald had spoken of the resolutions as a "treaty" it was clear that the British North America Act was nothing of the sort. Having made his point, he remarked with obvious satisfaction, "I think that if that has been accomplished something has been attained." Since he was satisfied that the Canadian constitution was not a compact, Dafoe showed little sympathy for the New Brunswick argument that the federal government had failed to live up to its contracted obligations because the expected, indeed promised, trade had not developed between the Maritimes and central Canada. Nevertheless he was fully prepared to admit his sympathy for the plight of the Eastern provinces without partaking of the provincialist argument upon which their claims were based.[19]

The cross-country sessions of the commission were only a small part of the work that had to be done by Dafoe and his colleagues. Probably the biggest, and certainly the most important task was the writing of the Report. Dafoe believed that the success of the commission depended very much upon the commissioners' achieving unanimity in their conclusions. The views of Dr. Sirois, the Quebec representative, were thus of crucial importance. The French Canadian might have found the recommendations on debt-refunding, subsidies and reallocation of revenues "a stiff hurdle to hop over," Dafoe thought, but in fact he took it all in his stride. Dr. Sirois' attitude to the commission's work and recommendations was no small matter in the gradual growth of

[19]*Hearings, New Brunswick*, II, 9010, 9053.

sympathy on Dafoe's part for the French Canadians. Sirois was the kind of liberal-minded, broadly national, French Canadian with whom Dafoe could find much in common. Having won Sirois' support for the Report, Dafoe felt that the next important step was to place the commission's findings in the hands of the Government without any unnecessary delay. Delay would leave the commission open to the charge that it was holding back its conclusions until the Government had an opportunity to appeal to the country. Dafoe did what he could to hurry the Report on, but it was not a job which could be completed overnight.[20]

As the document moved into its final stages, an increasing amount of time was required to read drafts of the Report and the special studies that the commission had delegated to a host of Canadian scholars. These special studies were of particular interest to Dafoe; he had urged the commission to have them prepared and found the ones dealing with historical and constitutional subjects especially engrossing. The one thing that bothered him was that the commission was committed to a degree of objectivity that prohibited opinions on important subjects. Even the problem of the nature of Confederation, which had interested him so long, had to be slurred over with the observation that there were two viewpoints on the subject. Yet this was the key to the "riddle of federation" and without some definite conclusions the problem of the federal power of disallowance had also to be left without a satisfactory discussion. Dafoe's own views on this subject were quite definite:

> The power is there; it cannot be whittled down or explained away. It is without limit and the conditions under which it can be exercised are entirely political (that is, Federally political) ever since the Mackenzie government established the principle that for the advice tendered the Governor General, the Government was responsible to Parliament.

As a journalist Dafoe was anxious to set down hard and fast conclusions on these controversial constitutional questions, but as a commissioner he realized the importance of keeping the public document as free as possible from unnecessary tendentiousness.[21] Moreover, the Rowell-Sirois commissioners had not been asked to settle questions of the power of disallowance, techniques of constitutional amendment and repatriation of the British North America Act that Dafoe had considered so thoroughly in earlier years.

Before the commission completed its labours, the country was at war.

[20]Dafoe Papers, Dafoe to G. V. Ferguson, May 8, 1939; Dafoe to R. A. MacKay, July 7, 1939.
[21]*Ibid.*, Dafoe to Alex Skelton, July 24, 1939; Dafoe to R. A. MacKay, Aug. 15, 1939.

During the hearings Dafoe had never lost sight of the possibility that the world might slip into armed conflict at any moment. Indeed he had felt that this fearful prospect made the successful completion of the commission's work even more urgent, for in wartime the federal government would need to be absolutely certain of its sources of power and revenue in order to ensure the nation's safety. With war an actuality, the commission saw no reason to alter its findings for, as the chairman remarked, "it believes its recommendations to be appropriate to meet the new strains and emergencies of war conditions."[22]

The voluminous Report, presented to the Government in May 1940, was a superb survey of every aspect of Dominion-provincial relations, except the strictly political, from Confederation to the outbreak of the Second World War. Rarely, if ever, had a government sponsored such a thorough examination of a nation's history and problems. The commission's leading recommendations were far-reaching in their scope and momentous in their implications. The hoped-for unanimity among the commissioners had been achieved. The Report pointed out with permissible pride that this agreement was "not the result of compromise or of give and take, but reflects a sincere unanimity of judgment on the great issues which confront the nation." Apparently Dafoe played an important role in bringing this unanimity into being. One of the commission's secretaries, R. M. Fowler, looked on Dafoe as the chief architect of agreement, while Adjutor Savard, a French-speaking secretary, described the Winnipeg journalist as

the man who sat with his younger colleagues in order to try and find a way of compromise, of good will and harmony. With his prodigious recollection of dates and facts, and having met and known almost every politician whose name has been in the limelight during the last fifty years, he used all he knew and remembered as one more argument for national unity. Quite naturally his colleagues turned to him as their mentor. And thanks to him every national problem was quickly approached in its historical background. If the report is inspired by the highest and most noble patriotic conception, if it so carefully considers respectable traditions, acquired rights, ethnical, cultural and religious differences and even certain sensitive feelings, a great share of the credit goes to John W. Dafoe, a great Canadian.[23]

Although the commissioners disclaimed any intention of adopting either a centralizing or decentralizing viewpoint, they maintained that the country, national unity and indeed the existence of the provinces

---

[22]*Hearings, Ontario*, V, 7629–30; *Report*, Book I, Jos. Sirois to W. L. M. King, May 3, 1940.
[23]*Report*, Book II, 269; Dafoe Papers, R. M. Fowler to Dafoe, May 25, 1940; A. Savard to Dafoe, May 22, 1940 (transcript of speech).

themselves, depended upon the presence of a federal power armed with sufficient resources to fulfil its functions efficiently. The Report argued that the fiscal structure upon which such a system could be based would require that each province be allowed National Adjustment Grants commensurate with its need to provide "normal Canadian services with no more than normal Canadian taxation." The funds for these grants were to be acquired by the federal government through a reallocation of taxation, subsidies and provincial debts. The provincial governments were asked to relinquish their powers over corporate, income and succession taxes. Furthermore the complex web of federal subsidies to the provinces was to be untangled. In addition to providing National Adjustment Grants, the federal government was advised to assume the provinces' debts and, in the case of Quebec, part of the municipal debt. In effect, the Report recommended a rough equalization of minimum economic conditions for all Canadians regardless of their geographic location. These proposals, it was urged, were, "in terms of 1939, very similar to what the provisions of the British North America Act were in terms of the economic life of 1867." A host of less sweeping recommendations were included in the Report, such as those dealing with unemployment relief and old age pensions. No summary of the commission's findings and recommendations can possibly do justice to the Report's magnitude or impressiveness. Its two-and-a-half years' labour was time well spent. Dafoe and his fellow commissioners could be justly proud of the finished product.[24]

Shortly after the commission laid its Report in the hands of the Government, Dafoe returned to his editorial desk in Winnipeg. Naturally he was anxious about the fate of the results of these years of work. At first he was inclined to think that the war would help to ensure the adoption of the commission's recommendations. Writing to the Canadian High Commissioner in Australia, C. J. Burchell, he explained:

> The reception by the people of the Report has been all that we could have hoped. There has been no direct attack upon it from any quarter; but I doubt whether Hepburn, Aberhart or Pattullo are favorable to it. However, provincialism is very much subdued these days. There is an acute sense of danger which makes the Federal Government all-important; and I think this will continue all through the war and after it.

Dafoe was apparently much more sanguine than the Liberal Government, which was feeling its way very cautiously. Its most pressing con-

[24]*Report*, Book II, 269; 272, 273, 270. For a useful summary and critique of the *Report* see R. M. Burns, "The Royal Commission on Dominion-Provincial Relations" in R. M. Clark, ed., *Canadian Issues* (Toronto, 1961), 143–57.

cern was the war effort and it was not anxious to irritate any sources of possible national disunity. The experience of the commission in several provinces, notably Quebec and Ontario, was enough to moderate any action which might have been planned even under normal circumstances. And the war argued for additional caution—or at least Mackenzie King thought so. Dafoe knew that the cabinet was not at one on the course that should be followed with respect to the recommendations of the commission. T. A. Crerar and other Liberal ministers favoured a bold front in the face of the storm that Premier Hepburn was raising, but Prime Minister King and his coadjutor Ernest Lapointe were more circumspect.[25]

In November 1940, King announced the convening of a Dominion-provincial conference in January 1941 to consider the recommendations of the Rowell-Sirois Commission. Writing in the *Free Press* on November 9, Dafoe urged that at least the broad principles of the Report should be accepted. Any premier who opposed the recommendations should only do so if he had alternative proposals to suggest. He warned that "the Report of the Commission and the attendant studies have made it clear to all that our existing Federal system is no longer adequate to the requirements of Canada; and that to persist in retaining it intact will be to invite disaster and perhaps to make disaster inevitable." In private, Dafoe was not optimistic about the prospects of the Report being accepted by the premiers. He had no doubt that changes such as those recommended would have to be made, but for the moment too many provincial leaders were playing politics. Even the demands of war, which might have been expected to induce the provinces to agree to a rearrangement of powers and finances, seemed to have had little effect. "There is too much in evidence a feeling of complacency that somehow the war will take the course desired by Canada, and that there is no need for us to abstain from playing politics and pursuing personal interests in the good old way," he wrote gloomily. Still, he felt that the fact that the Government had chosen to present the Report to a Dominion-provincial conference was a laudable move. At least the commission's recommendations were to be placed out in the open for political discussion rather than being simply commended and then relegated to the shelves of forgotten royal commission reports.[26]

As the day of the conference approached, Dafoe's pessimism increased.

[25]Dafoe Papers, Dafoe to C. J. Burchell, Aug. 16, 1940; Grant Dexter to Dafoe, Oct. 25, 1940.
[26]*Ibid.*, Dafoe to J. T. Thorson, Nov. 19, 1940; Dafoe to R. M. Fowler, Dec. 18, 1940.

He knew that King was adamant in his refusal to make the Report an election battle-cry. He was also aware that Mitchell Hepburn was determined to centre his quarrel with Mackenzie King on the commission's recommendations. Deadlock seemed assured. "While personally I am not saying anything about the battle (and I observe the other Commissioners are equally discreet)," Dafoe remarked to his fellow commissioner, H. F. Angus, "I fortunately have a dual capacity, and as editor of the Free Press I am saying quite a bit and shall continue to do so."[27]

Dafoe's pessimism about the prospects of the conference proved fully justified. When the meeting convened in Ottawa on January 14, three of the premiers from English Canada refused even to enter discussions based on the Report. In the face of the opposition led by Ontario's Premier Hepburn, who was eloquently supported by two Western gallants, T. D. Pattullo of British Columbia and William Aberhart of Alberta, Prime Minister King decided to adjourn the meeting after two days filled with largely unedifying speeches. Hepburn termed the supporters of the Report "wreckers of Confederation" and called upon his fellow premiers to "set aside this Sirois Report, the product of the minds of a few college professors and a Winnipeg newspaperman who has had his knife into Ontario ever since he was able to write editorials." Though the language of Pattullo and Aberhart was more temperate, their views, if not their logic, were no less clear. Facing this blind alley, King admitted defeat. Despite firm speeches by some of his ministers and appeals from some provincial leaders, notably John Bracken of Manitoba, the Prime Minister lost heart. He had never expected the conference to succeed, a fact which likely explains the unusually uninspiring character of his closing speech.[28]

The three shrewd premiers had caught the federal Government completely off balance. T. A. Crerar admitted to Dafoe that there had not been the slightest suspicion that the opponents of the Report would refuse even to go into committee to discuss the suggested alterations in the governmental structure. Thus more than two years of demanding work was washed down the drain by a flood of petty provincialism and political partisanship. Dafoe was enraged. He vented his anger in an editorial pointedly entitled, "The True Wreckers." He warned that the failure of the conference meant that the federal government would be forced to invade the revenue fields of the provinces, not because it

[27]*Ibid.*, Grant Dexter to Dafoe, Dec. 30, 1940; Dafoe to H. F. Angus, Jan. 9, 1941.
[28]*Dominion-Provincial Conference, 1941* (Ottawa, 1941), 80, 103–8; J. W. Pickersgill, *The Mackenzie King Record*, I, *1939–1944* (Toronto, 1960), 159.

wanted to, but because, "confronted with the unreasoned and bitter prejudice of the three wreckers, it must." Three weeks later his anger had not yet subsided. In a lengthy article on February 3, he fulminated against the "wreckers" again: "Canada is at war; her existence is at stake; national unity is the dire necessity of the hour. But 'British Columbia is in a category by itself,' says T. D. Pattullo; and Hepburn and Aberhart echo his words on their own behalf and match his actions." Dafoe's thrusts drew blood; Premier Pattullo wrote angrily to the *Free Press* charging that most Canadian newspapers had been unfair to him. "In varying degrees the comments include error, misconstruction, misinterpretation, misrepresentation, falsification, lying and libel, and I am sorry to say that your paper seems to qualify in all these categories."[29]

For the three years that were left to him, Dafoe continued to fight for the acceptance of the main provisions of the Report that had commanded so much of his last precious time. He was unhappy that the defence of the commission's work seemed to fall largely on the *Free Press*, for he realized that his voice would not be accepted as that of a detached observer. But after all, what was one more battle added to the myriad that he had fought? And Dafoe never lost hope that he was fighting on the winning side. Perhaps the Rowell-Sirois scheme would not triumph immediately, but the exigencies of war and post-war reconstruction would surely force acceptance of the commission's plan. "I am pretty philosophical about the probable future of Dominion-Provincial relations," he told Alex Skelton, the commission's secretary. "I just cannot see how, in the post-war world, Canada can be other than a highly integrated country, with the provinces relegated to a relatively unimportant role." This was not the first of Dafoe's predictions to have been proved at least partly inaccurate by events. The principles of the Rowell-Sirois Report actually suffered the fate he had earlier feared they might; having received honourable mention they were retired to that crowded closet on Parliament Hill which is reserved for the recommendations of royal commissions. In place of the carefully worked out, but apparently impractical, schemes suggested by this great inquiry there has been substituted a maze of *ad hoc* arrangements between the provinces and the federal government. Dafoe feared that this would happen, and condemned the development in strong terms. But the country that had refused to listen to his plea for political parties based on principles was no more ready to listen to his advocacy of a rational,

---

[29]Dafoe Papers, T. A. Crerar to Dafoe, Jan. 16, 1941. See also Pickersgill, *Mackenzie King Record*, I, 161–2; *W.F.P.*, Jan. 16, 1941; T. D. Pattullo to *W.F.P.*, Feb. 12, 1941.

equitable, Dominion-provincial fiscal arrangement. His condemnation of the wartime tax agreements might be applied to any period of Canadian history. On March 19, 1941 he wrote that the system of separate settlements drawn up "under political pressure, with resultant charges, often well based, of unfairness, discrimination and political corruption, has poisoned the relations between the provinces themselves and the relations between the provinces and the Dominion for much too long a period; it is time, in the language of Mr. Pattullo, to make a 'clean up'."

Gradually the battle for the acceptance of the commission's recommendations was eclipsed by the more pressing demands of the war effort. Not that Dafoe ever let the matter slip entirely into the background, for he foresaw a post-war world in which the country would need the power to amend its own constitution to provide for the growing demand for social legislation. But the grim events of the world conflict limited the amount of useful consideration that could be given to the question of Dominion-provincial relations.[30]

In many ways the Rowell-Sirois Commission was the climax of Dafoe's career. His whole life was devoted to the consideration of public events and policies, not as a politician, but as an observer, critic and publicist. As a Westerner, his views were always coloured by the peculiar position of inequality which the Prairies occupied in the Canadian federal system by virtue of their economy, population and income. Whether as an advocate of low tariff, special freight rates or full provincial control of natural resources, Dafoe's objective was always to raise the West from that position of inequality. Perhaps his claims were sometimes extreme, and his strictures on the Eastern "interests" unfair, but his aim was nevertheless entirely justified. He knew that the nation could not endure half rich and half poor. Dafoe believed that only if all sections of his diverse country were allowed equal opportunities to develop and prosper would Canadianism destroy sectionalism and the basis of nationhood be laid. This, of course, had been the aim of the makers of Canada in 1867 and the fact that it had not been achieved seventy years later was due more to unpredictable circumstances than any serious failings on their part. The depression of the thirties made it distressingly clear to any who were not already aware of the fact, that all the provinces had not shared equally in the promised good things of Confederation. It was Dafoe's desire, and the desire of his fellow commissioners in 1937, to provide a plan that would lead to the fulfilment of the vision of 1867. The Rowell-Sirois Commission's aim was to equalize the burdens and rewards of Confederation. Though its well-

[30]Dafoe Papers, Dafoe to Grant Dexter, Jan. 31, 1941; Dafoe to Alex Skelton, May 20, 1941. *W.F.P.*, March 30, 1943.

devised scheme has never been fully accepted by the parties that make up the national whole, in so far as the process of equalization has been carried out in the years since 1940 some of the credit must be given to the authors of the Rowell-Sirois Report.[31]

Like many of the other enterprises to which Dafoe lent his support, from the Progressive movement to the League of Nations, the Rowell-Sirois equalization plan was only a partial success. But Dafoe was enough of a sceptic to realize that in the affairs of men, especially in a country as heterogeneous as Canada, partial successes are often the best that can be achieved. In his presidential address to the Canadian Political Science Association in 1939, he offered some reflections that might well have been applied to the best-laid plans of the commission on which he was serving. "I doubt even more than I did formerly," he confessed, "the engineering idea of statecraft, that you can build safely on the estimated carrying strength of the electorate or upon mankind's carefully determined stability. . . . I have seen too many fine ascending projections dip into the cellar these past few years."[32] But this scepticism did not prevent Dafoe from striving energetically to advance the causes that he believed were just and necessary. It seems very fitting that the last editorial written by John Dafoe, and published in the *Free Press* two days after his death, was a suggestion that the country pick up the principles of the Rowell-Sirois Report that had been dropped in 1941 and put them into practice as the first step in post-war reconstruction. His truly national spirit infused the conclusion:

> We failed as a nation at the last interprovincial Conference, but largely because of the parochial selfishness of three gentlemen who have since left the scene. Since then the nation has learned much about its physical strength and constitutional weakness. It is better prepared to face the fundamental issues. Another Conference must be called eventually, an agreement must be reached by at least a majority of the provinces and finally enforced. As the war in Europe is now entering upon what seems to be its last phase, there should be no undue delay in calling a new Conference so that Canada may be equipped to take its full part in the peace settlement.[33]

The editorial was characteristic of Dafoe, for the nationalism that inspired it was a nationalism that stressed not only his country's needs, but also its responsibilities to the wider world. This largeness of mind is the measure of Dafoe's stature and sets him in contrast with many of the smaller figures of his generation of public men.

[31]Dafoe, "The Canadian Federal System under Review," *Foreign Affairs*, XVIII, no. 4 (July 1940), 646–59.
[32]Dafoe, "Canadian Problems of Government," 287.
[33]*W.F.P.*, Jan. 11, 1944.

XIII. The Whole World in Travail
1929-39

THOUGH DAFOE'S MIND WAS CONCERNED with as wide a variety of public issues in the thirties as ever before, or perhaps wider, one major problem occupied more of his thoughts than any other—the peace of the world. And as the years of the depression decade wore on, his tempered optimism about the prospects of universal peace was replaced with a deep pessimism based on a certainty that the world was once more reeling headlong into armed conflict.

Throughout the twenties, despite many indications to the contrary, Dafoe had refused to be daunted in his belief that a new phoenix had risen out of the ashes of the Great War. Governments failed to live according to the new dispensation of the League of Nations, but Dafoe's faith was in the people, whose hearts, he thought, burned with Wilsonian idealism. Even as the depression with its awful potentialities was enveloping the world, Dafoe was able to write with undiminished optimism of the triumph of the spirit of peace during the first decade of the League's life. He did not, however, see the League in itself as a panacea that would cure the nations of the world of their sick penchant for worshipping the gods of war. He realized that its efficacy depended completely upon "the mighty moving power of appeal which its purpose makes to the hearts and consciences of man." Without the moral force of world opinion to compel peace, the nations of the world would inevitably lapse into their old ways of national animosities, and would resort to armaments and war as an instrument of policy. This was a liberal's faith in moral rather than physical force. In the world of the thirties, the saving power of this faith was gravely weakened as Mars, outlaw or hero, won numerous powerful adherents.[1]

[1]*M.F.P.*, Sept. 14, 1928; Jan 1, 1930; Jan. 10, 1930.

ii

The new powers in the field of foreign relations that the dominions had been granted carried responsibilities with them. The right to conduct an independent foreign policy implied the desire to formulate one. The Balfour Declaration had pointed out that "equality of status" did not automatically carry with it equality of "function." Dafoe's view was that Canada should acquire that second equality through the practice of a responsible foreign policy. Though he took second place to no one in his preoccupation with status, he was not satisfied that the end of the road was reached when full autonomy was recognized. It was an empty phrase unless the powers that it implied were used constructively for the promotion of a peaceful world. Here he differed from such Liberal nationalists as Mackenzie King, whose perpetual refusal to accept imperial commitments was equalled only by his persistent rejection of international responsibilities. Dafoe clearly perceived that the twentieth-century world was not composed of disparate national atoms living unto themselves, but was rather a molecular world of interdependent entities knit together by modern methods of communication and warfare. Maxim Litvinov expressed the view exactly in a phrase which was constantly on Dafoe's tongue in the thirties—"the indivisible peace."

In this world of interdependent nations, the relations between states were complex, being based on interests and traditions. Though Canada had been too long in the shelter of the imperial throne for a strong foreign policy tradition to have become rooted in the minds of the people, Dafoe thought that there were nevertheless certain facts which Canadian foreign policy planners could not afford to neglect. First, there was Canada's historic membership in the British family of nations. Secondly there was the geographic position of the country, which not only divided it from Europe, but set it alongside the United States. Finally Canada was a member of the League of Nations. In considering each of these relations, the overriding consideration in Dafoe's mind was the fact that "the comfortable theory that Canada is remote from the centre of world affairs and is therefore protected by distance and the sea no longer holds." Thus Canada's interests could best be served by formulating policies which would assist in the promotion of international co-operation.[2]

The three determinants of Canadian foreign policy—the Commonwealth, the United States and the League—had somehow to be kept from conflicting. In Dafoe's judgment, the nature of the Commonwealth

[2]Dafoe, "A Foreign Policy for Canada," *Q.Q.*, XLII (Summer 1935), 162, 164.

as an independent association of nations was crucial in preventing friction. Though he forcefully disclaimed the idea that the Commonwealth should act as a unit with a joint foreign policy, he also refused to take the position of the extreme autonomists that Canada could exercise the right of neutrality in a war involving the Commonwealth. "I may say," he wrote in 1932, "that I have always held the view that if one British nation declares war, all the other British nations are involved, though the extent of their participation must be a matter entirely within their own judgment." By this he meant that not only the United Kingdom, but also any member of the Commonwealth, could commit the other members to legal belligerency. "I cannot see how nations belonging to the same family and having the same sovereign can be divided into combatants and non-combatants in the event of war," he emphasized. Any other view would result in the complete disruption of the British association of nations. He did not, however, doubt that circumstances could arise that would encourage the growth of opinion in Canada favourable to the view that the country should remain neutral in a British war. The ranks of the neutralists, or isolationists, would be swelled, Dafoe feared, if an effort was made to weld the Commonwealth into a unit for purposes of foreign military policy. "The Dominions have feelings of loathing and fear for Europe and her hopeless insanities," Dafoe told Lord Lothian, "and when Great Britain gets pulled into a European massacre of the nations the desire of large elements of the population of those Dominions will be to keep away from the explosions and the falling walls." Of course this was not the only opinion; in Canada there were also the imperialists who would demand that the Canadian government come to the aid of Britain in any and every outbreak of hostilities. A conflict between the isolationist and imperialist sentiments would be of a most serious nature for both Canada and the Commonwealth. It might result in civil disorders, perhaps even civil war in Canada, and the end of the Commonwealth tie.[3]

Dafoe believed that it was possible to avoid an open break on this question. The League of Nations provided the means of preserving the peace of the world, and thus of preventing the destruction of Canadian unity. Therefore the Commonwealth was fitted into the matrix of the League, so that any armed conflict would be one for the protection of the principles of the Covenant. In other words there would be no more British wars or Commonwealth wars, but only League wars. Dafoe knew that isolationist sentiment was strong and growing stronger in Canada,

[3]Dafoe Papers, Dafoe to W. D. Gregory, Feb. 2, 1932; Dafoe to Hon. Wm. Martin, Aug. 2, 1932; Dafoe to Lord Lothian, Oct. 10, 1934; Dafoe to H. F. Armstrong, July 25, 1935.

especially after the Manchurian débâcle in 1931 had illustrated the weaknesses of the League. The only way to combat it was to educate opinion in the need for an effective system of collective security. Canadians had to be brought to realize that they could not "contract themselves out of the universe." Only a system with the moral appeal of the League could win widespread confidence and support. The best foreign policy for Canada would be one which would place the country, along with the other British nations, in the forefront of a movement to secure the establishment of a collectively guaranteed peace.[4]

Canadian foreign policy, then, should be directed towards making the League work as its founders had believed it could work. In order to transform the League from an ideal into an operating instrument of peace, it was necessary for nations to sacrifice their right of going to war for their own aggrandizement. Furthermore sacrifices were required of them in order to constrain or punish the powers that refused to take the necessary self-denying ordinance. Dafoe had no illusions about the obligations of the League system even though he was never wholly satisfied with Article X of the Covenant, seeing it as an unnecessary blunder which had kept the United States out of the League. In 1927 he argued in a speech to the Winnipeg Women's Canadian Club that the League had to be more than a mere debating society. Its first purpose was to prevent aggressive war, if possible by conciliation, but if necessary by the application of sanctions. "In part the obligation is specific and legal in the application of economic sanctions," he argued; "in the application of force the obligation is moral. But where there is a clear case, the moral obligation outranks in sanctity one which is merely legal." But the moral obligation to use force against aggressors was, like the League itself, dependent upon that nebulous force which Dafoe called world public opinion. He assumed that the people of the world, in their desire for peace, would support the League and force their governments to fulfil contracted obligations. In fact, in 1933 he characterized the years since the Great War as years in which a furious race had taken place between the consolidation of world opinion in favour of collective security and the re-emergence of power politics. In short, Dafoe's liberal optimism concerning the moral righteousness of the people's will led him to the conclusion that the League would work if the people's will were allowed to emerge. Like many liberals, he assumed that, once educated, the public would reach the same conclusions as he had about international problems. But what if the public reached the conclusions

[4]*Ibid.*, Dafoe to W. D. Gregory, Feb. 2, 1932; Dafoe to H. F. Armstrong, July 25, 1935. Dafoe, "A Foreign Policy for Canada," 170. Dafoe Papers, Dafoe to Loring Christie, July 6, 1935.

of Adolf Hitler or even Mackenzie King? Dafoe did not ask himself this question, for to have done so could have undermined the faith by which he lived. At least he did not ask any questions about democratic public opinion, for he knew that the facts did not support the view that the democracies were punctilious in their support of the League.[5]

For Dafoe, the central problem of the League was that many of the nations that belonged to it remained undemocratic, while the League was predicated on the assumption that its members would subscribe to the democratic creed. "The League," he wrote in 1934, "cannot be what its founders hoped until the nations comprising it accept the tests and practises of democracy." But was not such an admission a clear recognition of the hopelessness of the League conception? The organization was even further weakened by the absence from its ranks of the world's most powerful democracy, the United States. Dafoe knew that the League would not work properly until the United States overcame its sullen, self-righteous isolationism and assumed a position of leadership in preserving the peace. Year after year he expressed the futile hope that the Americans would recognize their international obligations. "Nothing can be done while they stay aloof," he wrote despondently. "Meanwhile the world proceeds hellward at an accelerated pace." Over and over he repeated that the world, for lack of the co-operation of the United States, was putting its feet "on the slippery slopes that will lead [it] to ruin." But despite fond hopes for a change of the American heart, he was resigned to the fact by 1934 that "Uncle Sam is wedded to his idols and will not, I fear, come out of his trance until the guns begin going off."[6]

Despite his realistic recognition that the League was a tragically weak instrument of collective security, Dafoe clung to it as the only hope for a peaceful world. Perhaps some miracle would convince the nations of the world, especially the democracies, that their security depended upon the effective carrying out of the Covenant. It was all there was to hope for, and Dafoe persisted with dogged determination in his faith that this alone could save civilization from renewed catastrophe. When he spoke to the Empire Club in Toronto in 1936, he was asked if the failures of the League had not convinced him the institution was useless,

---

[5]Dafoe Papers, Dafoe to W. T. Stone, July 2, 1938; Dafoe, "The League To-Day and Tomorrow," address to the Winnipeg Women's Canadian Club, April 27, 1927 (MS); Dafoe, radio address under the auspices of the Young Men's Canadian Club, Montreal, Dec. 10, 1933 (MS).
[6]Dafoe, "The World Outlook," *Interdependence*, XI, no. 3 (Oct. 1934), 111-12. Dafoe Papers, Dafoe to Mary C. McGeachy, Nov. 7, 1932; Dafoe to George Iles, Dec.11, 1933; Dafoe to Loring Christie, July 6, 1935; Dafoe to Lord Lothian, Oct. 10, 1934.

and he replied, "Well, I saw the brat born, and I am going to stay with it as long as it has a bit of life in its body." That was exactly what he did.[7]

The obstinancy of Dafoe's faith in the League was based upon the conviction that the Covenant provided the only system through which Canada could work out a coherent foreign policy. He firmly believed that Canada should remain in the British Commonwealth, but the peculiar nature of the country's population and its proximity to the United States created special problems for Canadian policy-makers. He feared that a war waged by the Commonwealth alone would find Canada divided and weak, and would place her in a dangerous position in her relations with the United States. But a League war, free from any trace of the stigma of "imperialism," might not only call forth the united efforts of Canadians, but also win the support of the American Republic. Like his friend Sir Alfred Zimmern, Dafoe believed that "the League of Nations is the *Deus ex machina* of the British Commonwealth." If the League failed, the whole basis of the British Commonwealth would have to be shifted. The alternatives would be either a centralized Commonwealth bloc, which Dafoe himself would not accept and believed would never gain the support of Canadians, or a Commonwealth in which each member would follow completely independent policies "in the light of their own problems and of such important considerations as geographical location and particular sectional interests or affiliations." Thus, in Dafoe's mind, not only the peace of the world but also the existence of the Commonwealth and the unity of Canada depended upon the success of the League of Nations. "The United States could survive a general war," he explained in 1937, "but Canada may need, and I think does need, a world under collective peace if she is to remain a nation, just as the Commonwealth does if it is to continue." These were the underlying principles of all Dafoe's writings on international affairs in the last years of peace.[8]

iii

As a newspaperman Dafoe saw his task as one of assisting in the formation of a world climate of opinion that would favour the full development of the peaceful potentialities of the League. One of the first necessities, Dafoe felt certain, was a world disarmament agreement.

[7]Dafoe, "Roads to the Future," speech to the Empire Club, Toronto, Jan. 30, 1936 (MS).
[8]Sir Alfred Zimmern, *The Third British Empire* (London, 1926), 63; Dafoe, "Canada, the Empire and the League," *Foreign Affairs*, XIV, no. 2 (Jan. 1936), 308; Dafoe Papers, Dafoe to R. A. MacKay, July 16, 1937.

Though he was revisionist with respect to the Treaty of Versailles, and highly critical of what he considered to be the French obsession with security, he was not blind to the possibility of a revival of German militarism if disarmament failed. The onus for the failure of the disarmament negotiations to make any progress was laid at the feet of the French and the Americans; the French refused to accept American assurances that real security was contained in the Paris Pact, while the Americans refused to recognize that the French fears had some foundation. The deadlock which resulted was a distinct threat to world peace, for if France could not be convinced of the need to decrease her armaments, Germany would demand the right to rearm. "And then there may be fireworks," Dafoe remarked.[9]

Another imperative, Dafoe believed, was to remove the causes of war. First, there was the friction that began with economic nationalism in the form of protective tariffs. This erosion of goodwill was aggravated by the complex problem of war debts and reparations which not only caused latent national jealousies to become inflamed, but also upset the world economic balance. Dafoe's remedy went beyond universal disarmament to include tariff reductions and the cancellation of war debts and reparations. These themes were frequently reiterated by him during the years of the depression. But despite his preachments, success never seemed to draw much nearer. And why not? Dafoe's answer was always that the world was the scene of a gigantic intellectual struggle in which the demonic forces of old world power politics were locked in a mortal contest with the new world ideals of collective security and the peaceful settlement of disputes. Eventually the people, with pure hearts and unselfish motives, would win the battle against the vested interests which fed upon national animosities. This idealistic faith did not make Dafoe completely blind to the hard realities of international life; much of what he said was more an effort to convince people that this was the way things should be, rather than the way they actually were. When the Conservatives were in power at Ottawa, it was easy for him to believe that the true wishes of the people were being thwarted, and he tended to think that this was so in the rest of the world. Once Mackenzie King was returned to office, Canada would assume its share of the responsibility for promoting world peace. This belief was one of the reasons why Dafoe personally worked so hard to discredit the Bennett régime. It also explains his efforts to permeate the Liberal party with his views in order to ensure the election of a government that would

[9] *M.F.P.*, Jan. 14, March 30, 1930; Dafoe Papers, Dafoe to Sir Robert Borden, Nov. 1, 1930.

not "make hanging on to office its first objective, but [would] show courage & vision in its policies."[10]

The crucial question was whether there was time to save the world from the destruction that would inevitably result from outdated policies. In 1933 Dafoe was beginning to doubt whether his liberal lessons were having any effect. In the summer of that year, the World Economic Conference failed to find a means of breaking down the trade and financial barriers that had been built up throughout the world. The cause of world disarmament seemed completely lost. In Germany Hitler was on the rampage and Dafoe had only the direst predictions about the Führer's future course. "He may give effect to plans of re-armament in default of authority from a Conference of powers, which would constitute a deliberate rejection of the Treaty of Versailles," Dafoe told his readers. "Any such course could only end in catastrophe for Germany and for the world." Clearly the worst was happening, for now two powers, Japan in Manchuria and Germany in Europe, were flaunting their power before the nations of the League. Their success gave substance to Dafoe's greatest fear—that the nations of the world had never really intended to live up to their covenanted obligations.[11]

As gangsterism revived in world affairs so isolationist sentiment grew in Canada. This growth was spontaneous, Dafoe insisted, resulting from Canadian fears of becoming involved in the armed anarchy that was spreading over the world. At the informal Commonwealth Conference held in Toronto in 1933, Dafoe predicted that, if the League failed, Canada would attempt to hide behind the boundaries of North America, and the Commonwealth would disintegrate. By the end of the year his predictions seemed about to be verified. Since an ostrich policy of isolationism was impossible for Dafoe himself to accept, he continued to place his faith in the League. What was necessary was to make "the obligations of its members more clearly defined and its powers of collectively enforcing peace more widely recognized." But his increasing pessimism and his jeremiads about the future suggested that he doubted if this could be done. "Everything suggests that things are working up to a grand smash," he told Chester Martin early in 1934. How could the Canadian people be so obtuse when the patent fact was that the world without the League would be a world in which inevitable war would again overshadow Canada? In the *Free Press* Dafoe attempted to break

---

[10]Dafoe Papers, Dafoe to John R. Dutton, Sept. 29, 1931; *W.F.P.*, Jan. 29, 1932; Dafoe Papers, Dafoe to Mary C. McGeachy, Nov. 7, 1932.

[11]*W.F.P.*, Nov. 9, July 4, 10, 1933; Dafoe Papers, Dafoe to Mary C. McGeachy, July 12, 1933.

through the thickening crust of isolationism. In an editorial of August 17, 1934, he wrote:

> They do not seem to be able to understand that if the League disappears and the vision of collective action to impose peace fades, Canada will find herself an integral part of a world which will be busily engaged with no great loss of time in the business of destroying civilization by means of war. Canada can either lend a hand to strengthen the cause of peace or she can, with other countries, look forward to participation in the "big show" that is inevitable once the idea which the League embodies is definitely rejected.

But combined with these declarations of despair was the faith that "there are reserves of common sense that will prevent war on a large scale." If the cataclysm could be prevented for a decade, a union of liberals of all shades could perhaps impress upon the world the fact that "the heady stimulants of nationalism" had to give place to the pure, sweet wine of international co-operation.[12]

Despite the apparent futility of the Geneva experiment, Dafoe continued to give it his support because he saw no other possible alternative to a new, more horrible bloodbath. "There are no alternatives but death, ruin and damnation," he warned Escott Reid. Not even an isolated country like Canada could look with hope upon the possibility of non-commitment. If the League vanished Canada would have to begin arming. Alone in North America alongside the gigantic United States, Canada's future was indeed dim. "For us it is the League or an armed North America with the virtual submergence of our nation," Dafoe argued. "The Commonwealth in such a world cannot protect us, nor can we make any worthwhile contribution to its defence." Nor did he think that a short-term policy of preventing war was of any real value; its permanent abolition was necessary. The slogan "peace for our time" would only lay up a store of disaster and sorrow for the future, and the fibres of civilization would be permanently rent. Appeasement had not yet become part of the popular vocabulary, but it was appeasement that Dafoe was condemning when he wrote with deep emotion that "Peace for our time—enforced if necessary—and for all time, this is my slogan; and I shall keep sounding it however fruitlessly for the now brief period of time in which these matters will affect me."[13]

---

[12]A. J. Toynbee, ed., *The British Commonwealth Relations Conference* (London, 1934). P. Noel-Baker, "The Drift towards War," *Yale Review*, XXXIII, no. 4 (June 1934), 662–82. Dafoe Papers, Dafoe to Wickham Steed, Nov. 2, 1933. W.F.P., Dec. 7, 1933. Dafoe Papers, Dafoe to Chester Martin, Feb. 20, 1934; Dafoe to Escott Reid, July 21, 1934.

[13]Dafoe Papers, Dafoe to Escott Reid, May 17, 1935.

Dafoe felt moved to give his readers a message of hope at the end of 1934 in which he suggested there were growing, though inconclusive, signs that the regenerating policies of economic and political liberalism were finding new adherents. But more often his voice was the trumpet warning of oncoming doom. In mid-1935 he foresaw that Mussolini's covetous glances at Ethiopia could easily destroy the League. "If there is any international opinion in the world," he wrote gloomily, "it has a very narrow margin in which to save the situation." He had seen Hitler repudiate the Treaty of Versailles with complete impunity and, though he had momentarily hoped that the nations of the League would take steps to prevent German expansionism, the blows began to fall on the tottering institution's head too quickly to be warded off.[14]

Dafoe had believed, or perhaps only hoped, that the new Liberal Government would at least attempt to live up to Canada's League obligations. Even the famous Riddell incident did not shake his faith. Riddell had been incautious in committing the Canadian Government to the extension of the sanctions against Italy, and the Government had been forced to repudiate this unwanted leadership. But this did not mean that Canada would attempt to cut the tie that bound her to Geneva. Privately Dafoe expressed the view that Canada was too much blamed for the Ethiopian fiasco, though Lapointe's statement on the Canadian attitude had been unfortunate. After all, the Hoare-Laval agreement, which offered Mussolini everything he asked for in the little North African country, showed the true intentions of the European powers, and they were the powers that really carried weight in the collective security system. Indeed, Dafoe was even able to find something that was heartening in the betrayal of Ethiopia; the outburst of public opinion which forced Sir Samuel Hoare's retirement suggested that perhaps the people really were fully behind the League of Nations. "Public instinct," he told Arnold Toynbee, "is that this is the time to save the League and that there can be no compensation for its loss. The officials and politicians whom they prime are prepared to abandon the League and take a chance." But the hour was late for public demonstrations to be effective. On all sides Dafoe saw the events which were gradually leading to renewed warfare on a global scale: the butchery of the Ethiopians, Hitler's cynical repudiation of Locarno, and the Spanish Civil War. Everywhere the power-hungry dictators were having a field day. "It foreshadows a resumption, with no great delay in time, of the age-long civil war in Europe in which the white races will proceed to exterminate

[14]*W.F.P.*, Dec. 31, 1934; Dafoe Papers, Dafoe to Harold Butler, July 12, 1935; *W.F.P.*, March 18, 1935; April 19, 1935.

one another with the lethal weapons of the twentieth century," Dafoe wrote in the *Free Press*.[15]

What was the explanation for the failure of the League? In Dafoe's view the prime responsibility rested with the English-speaking peoples. The United States had failed in 1919 to recognize that it could not escape its responsibilities in the world without leaving the system of collective security woefully weak. The British nations had paid lip service to the principles of the Covenant, but had failed to give practical effect to their promises. Here were the "chief wreckers of the League." But why had the English-speaking peoples, and especially the British countries, failed to fulfil their duties? For Dafoe, there gradually emerged one answer, whose premises had long governed his thought. The imperial centralizers, the villains of imperial history, were the true saboteurs of the League. British governments had never fulfilled their League obligations. Rather, each government, and especially the Conservative ones, had yearned with unrequited love for a united Empire acting as a bloc apart from the League. As war came ever nearer, the imperial demon crept more frequently into Dafoe's explanation of the League's weaknesses. Repeatedly he predicted the ultimate failure of the new plot to centralize the Empire but he feared that the plot would nevertheless produce results of the most awful kind. "The consequences," Dafoe told H. Wilson Harris, editor of the London *Spectator*,

which may not be very long postponed will be very surprising to my friend Mr. Amery and those of his way of thinking who have conspired for years to destroy the League owing to their belief that it prevents the establishment and development of a united, armed British Empire. When the League disappears, in my opinion, a time fuse will be lit which will ultimately blow the British Empire to pieces and a catastrophe may come much sooner than anyone at the moment would care to predict.

Not until the outbreak of the war was the ogre of imperial centralization far from Dafoe's mind as he viewed the pathetic efforts of the democracies to preserve the illusion of world peace.[16]

iv

Even before the Ethiopian débâcle Dafoe had warned that, if Britain failed to remain faithful to her League obligations, the alternative as

[15] *W.F.P.*, Oct. 22, 1935; Dafoe Papers, Dafoe to Justice MacDonald, Dec. 13, 1935; *W.F.P.*, Dec. 31, 1935; Dafoe Papers, Dafoe to A. J. Toynbee, Jan. 10, 1936; *W.F.P.*, March 17, 1936.
[16] *W.F.P.*, June 8, 1936. Dafoe Papers, Dafoe to James T. Shotwell, Dec. 21, 1937; Dafoe to H. Wilson Harris, June 12, 1936.

far as Canada was concerned would not be a common imperial foreign policy but a retreat into isolationism. "In the shaping of any such policy our geographical position and such protection as this affords will determine the policy to the exclusion of traditional or emotional considerations," he claimed. The Hoare-Laval agreement simply reaffirmed his conviction that isolationism was the direction that Canadian policy would now take. "I have just spent three weeks in Ottawa," he told an English journalist in June 1936, "where I found isolationist sentiment universal in all the political parties and in the official Civil Service." Coupled with the belief that Canadians were increasingly isolationist in their point of view, Dafoe had the gnawing suspicion that by refusing to fulfil its League obligations the Canadian Government might be aiding, perhaps even co-operating with, the British government in its efforts to emasculate the League. Perhaps the Canadian Government had been "jockeyed from London into giving the first lead to surrender" on the question of placing sanctions on Italy.[17]

Though Dafoe attempted to fight the growth of isolationism, he found that it was a discouraging battle. In the absence of any convincing sign that the League would be revived, he began to urge that the obvious course for Canada to follow would be to develop her defences in North America. He suffered no illusion that this policy of self-interest would succeed either in preventing war or keeping Canada safe in time of war, but at least it was what he considered a realistic recognition of Canada's place in the world and the resources available to defend it. In one sense this was admitting defeat to the isolationists, but the tide now seemed to be running so strongly that perhaps something could be salvaged if the country at least prepared itself for war. Nor was Dafoe any kinder to the expressions of the isolationists. At the end of September 1936, Prime Minister King, the man who Dafoe had hoped would give Canada a foreign policy centred on collective security, delivered a speech at Geneva which, as far as Canada was concerned, reduced the League to the status of a highly expensive debating union. In the speech, Dafoe said sarcastically, "the League of Nations, with assurances of the most distinguished consideration, was ushered into the darkness by Mr. Mackenzie King." In the *Free Press* on October 1, he summed up Canada's contribution to the League in the bitterest terms. King's declaration was "the last of a long series of acts by successive Canadian governments intended to circumscribe the League's power; and it is the most discreditable of them because it amounts to the rejection by Canada of the

[17]Dafoe, "A Foreign Policy for Canada," 167. Dafoe Papers, Dafoe to H. H. Wilson, June 12, 1936; Dafoe to N. W. Rowell, July 21, 1936.

League." He realistically pointed out that Canada, as a small power, could hardly be held chiefly responsible for the League's collapse, but that it was nevertheless near the head of the list of powers which had retracted their obligations under the Covenant with few signs of regret.[18]

Once he was convinced that the League was paralysed, Dafoe found himself in difficulty as to the line he should take in his writing. Of course he could, and did, suggest that the Commonwealth should take the responsibility for reviving the League. More specific policies were harder to suggest. As he saw the situation, there were three possibilities: complete isolation and refusal to consider the possibility of Canadian involvement in a European war; secondly, isolation accompanied by rearmament without commitments; and thirdly, a united Empire defence policy. For Dafoe the first was foolhardy, and the third undesirable and impossible. The policy of armed non-commitment seemed the safest position, though he admitted that "if war should break out the whole situation would blow up." On the whole he felt that a policy of caution was best, making it plain that "there is trouble ahead and that we are bound to some extent to be involved in it." As for the Liberal Government, Dafoe felt certain that King's course would be one of complete isolationism, though he would never make the policy completely unambiguous. "I am satisfied in my own mind," he observed, "that Mr. King's private hope is that it will be possible for Canada to keep out of external wars, whether League or Imperial, without thereby setting up reactions in Canada which would lead to internal strife. I myself am far less hopeful that this could be accomplished."[19]

Nor did Dafoe have any lingering doubts that King represented the feelings of the majority of Canadians. What he called "Great Britain's treachery to the League" in the Ethiopian crisis had provided the opportunity for the isolationists in Canada to grasp command of public opinion. Until this point, he had been confident that Canada would have followed League leadership in opposition to Mussolini. But now the sources of isolationism had become manifold. Isolationism was by no means limited to the French Canadians, but was shared by English Canadians afflicted with the same disease as the people of the United States. In addition there were the Canadian Socialists whose opposition to the League was based on a belief that it was merely the tool of capitalist imperialism. Finally, there were the timid politicians who refused

[18] *W.F.P.*, Sept. 18, 1936; Dafoe, "Canadian Foreign Policy" in *Proceedings of the Conference on Canadian-American Affairs* (Montreal, 1937), 225; *W.F.P.*, Oct. 1, 28, 1936.
[19] *W.F.P.*, Nov. 14, 1936; Dafoe Papers, Dafoe to Grant Dexter, Oct. 20, 1936.

to assume any international responsibilities on behalf of Canada, claiming that national unity would be rent asunder if the Government took any positive action. This latter excuse carried little weight with Dafoe because he "could imagine issues arising which would make such an appeal to some Canadian sensibilities that not to go to war would provoke internal dissension." In fact, Dafoe had no sympathy either for King's isolationist policy or the reasons that were offered to justify it. In 1937 at the Conference on Canadian-American Relations held at Kingston, he pointed out that national unity was being preserved, not because of King's policy, but because of the existence of a precarious peace. When the day came when peace was shattered, the unsoundness of King's policy would be painfully evident. These were strong words coming from a man who for three successive elections had placed the full weight of his powerful newspaper behind Mackenzie King. But by 1937 Dafoe's disillusionment with King was almost complete. It had reached this point because Dafoe believed that Canada's national status should be used to promote a constructive policy of international cooperation. King, like Laurier before him, emphasized status, but attempted to avoid the responsibilities that Dafoe believed were part of a mature nationalism.[20]

The chief danger which Dafoe saw in King's refusal to attempt seriously to make the collective security system work was the possibility that he would be used by the imperial centralizers in their efforts to deliver the final blow to the Covenant, the blow that was necessary before a programme of imperial unity could be made effective. For this reason all his old suspicions of imperialist influence were revived as the Imperial Conference of 1937 approached. He told T A. Crerar, one of the ministers who attended the conference, that King was likely to find that he would have been better off if he had not repudiated all League obligations, for in repudiating them he had weakened his defences against the partisans of a common imperial foreign policy. Dafoe's fear was that while King would likely be able to avoid making commitments to a common imperial policy, he might be prepared to give his approval to a plan that would nullify the Covenant.[21]

In Dafoe's review of the 1937 Imperial Conference, the paradox of his position was perhaps more evident than at any other time. As a Canadian Liberal nationalist, he was pleased that the policy of no com-

[20]Dafoe Papers, Dafoe to Escott Reid, Nov. 10, 1936; Dafoe to Rt. Hon. Lord Davies, Jan. 7, 1937. Dafoe, "Canadian Foreign Policy," 230-1.
[21]Dafoe Papers, Dafoe to T. A. Crerar, April 20, 1937; Dafoe to Philip Noel-Baker, May 29, July 31, 1937.

mitments to a common imperial front had again triumphed. But as a supporter of collective security, he was frustrated by the conference's failure to pay any open respects to the League system. With some bitterness he wrote:

> What the statesmen of the nations, with incredible blindness, would not see was that the conception of the Commonwealth as a brotherhood of kindred nations co-operating in peaceful measures for their mutual advantage was only possible in a world obedient to principles embodied in the Covenant of the League and the Pact of Paris; and that it was incumbent upon them, not as an organized *bloc*, but in co-operation with other nations of like intent, to make it certain that the League was duly established.

The only alternative now was the one which Dafoe had never sought, indeed had dreaded—the policy of every country for itself. He had not been opposed to a common imperial foreign policy provided it threw the support of the Commonwealth behind the League of Nations. What he now feared was that the anti-League forces had triumphed and that Mackenzie King had agreed with, indeed supported them. Lord Lothian, whom Dafoe looked upon as one of the chief architects of the anti-League policy, suggested that in fact the conference had subscribed to the view that the League should be stripped of those aspects which prevented it from becoming universal, and had agreed to find peaceful solutions to the demands of the revisionist nations of Europe. In other words the conference had accepted appeasement—a claim which is verified by its report. Dafoe was right in fearing that King had acccepted this policy. Thus the policy which Dafoe most deplored, that of retreating from League principles in the face of the threats of Germany, Italy and Japan, won acceptance at the Imperial Conference of 1937 because it was a negative, do-little-or-nothing policy that the excessively prudent Canadian Prime Minister could accept. King had always rejected imperial commitments because they demanded action; in 1937 he accepted, at least tacitly, an imperial commitment because it required no action.[22]

After the conference of 1937, Dafoe had few optimistic moments about the possibility of world peace. Since he had always believed that the continuance of peace depended upon the successful operation of the Geneva system, the only conclusion that was left for him after the practical destruction of the League was that war would come very soon. "The world," he wrote in despair in 1937, "is at the mercy of fools,

---

[22]Dafoe, "The Imperial Conference of 1937," *U.T.Q.*, VII, no. 1 (Oct. 1937), 8, 4, 12; Maurice Ollivier, Comp. and ed., *The Colonial and Imperial Conferences from 1887 to 1937* (3 vols., Ottawa, 1954), III, 437.

madmen and incidents." Even his old optimism that somehow Woodrow Wilson's dream would become a reality became "academic because the League is prostrate and is likely to be more so when the chariots of war pass over its body, as will inevitably happen if the nations persist in the courses which now seem wise to them." When the Japanese troops landed at Shanghai in August 1937, Dafoe wrote a sentence which summed up his resignation of spirit: "Shanghai is just a burning signpost on the highway along which the nations press," he prophesied.[23]

V

During the last two years of uneasy peace before the outbreak of the Second World War, Dafoe was engaged in the work of the Rowell-Sirois Commission. Nevertheless his interest in world events never flagged, and perhaps his greatest moments were spent in the futile denunciation of appeasement. His mood was one of depressed acceptance of the inevitable. "It is no satisfaction to have one's pessimistic views verified to an extent which completely outruns his direst fears," he told Professor Shotwell, "but this has been my experience now for about two years." Nor did he expect that the immediate future held anything but a repetition of the experience. The statesmen of the world seemed paralysed in the face of totalitarian threat. The high point of this paralysis was Munich.[24]

Dafoe believed that the British surrender of League principles, which took place at Munich in September 1938, was largely due to the nefarious influence of a coterie of important Britons who were anxious to appease Nazi Germany in order to provide a counterweight against Communist Russia. This was the famous "Cliveden Set"; Lord and Lady Astor, Lord Lothian, Geoffrey Dawson of *The Times*, and A. L. Garvin of the *Observer* were among its leading members. In addition to their belief in the need to appease Hitler, these people had another common characteristic which made them suspect in Dafoe's estimation—they were "Imperialists." Dafoe believed that the Cliveden Set convinced Prime Minister Neville Chamberlain and his colleagues that Hitler's demands were just, that the League was dangerous because it divided the world into ideological blocs and that Russia was the real threat to European peace. These were the people who were prepared to sacrifice Czechoslovakia on the Nazi altar.

As the Czechoslovakian crisis approached, Dafoe feared that the end

[23]Dafoe Papers, Dafoe to J. A. Aikens, July 15, 1937; Dafoe to R. A. MacKay, July 16, 1937. *W.F.P.*, Aug. 31, 1937.
[24]Dafoe Papers, Dafoe to J. T. Shotwell, April 13, 1938.

of the uneasy peace was in sight. "The chances are," he wrote from Ottawa, "that between the fools and cowards in London and the madman in Berlin, the guns will go off." Of course the result was even worse— the Czechs were forced to give in to Hitler's insatiable demands without a single blow being struck. Momentarily Dafoe believed that the British intended to save the little Eastern European democracy, and that perhaps out of a bold front would develop a system of collective security capable of holding the Nazis in check. But these hopes were ill founded. When the Munich agreement was announced, and the world resumed its complacency, the *Free Press*, in Dafoe's unmistakable tones, cried "What's the Cheering For?" Munich left the most important question unanswered. "Austria yesterday, Czechoslovakia today; what of tomorrow and the day after?" Never was Dafoe more cutting than in his castigation of the Municheers. He suspected that Mackenzie King had been working in cooperation with Chamberlain throughout the humiliating affair. Dafoe had talked with the Prime Minister in November and concluded that "he is one of the Makers of the World To-Day & perhaps his responsibility is greater than we have thought." Dafoe must have shuddered when he read King's letter of congratulation and gratitude on behalf of the Canadian people to Chamberlain for "the service that you have rendered to mankind."[25]

The Munich agreement threw Dafoe into the depths of despair. For weeks he had poured out his thoughts to George Ferguson in Winnipeg. He seemed unable to write of anything but the betrayal of Czechoslovakia. Munich clearly meant another triumph for the Cliveden Set in their eagerness to destroy the League once and for all. This was not the group's ultimate objective, however; as always the ubiquitous imperial centralizer was lurking behind the scenes—now that the League was buried the pallbearers would soon begin to drive for a centralized Empire. Dafoe had set his hopes on the probability that the National Government in Britain would go too far in the appeasement of the dictators and be chased from office by a public inspired by the views of Winston Churchill. Munich, with its widespread popular approval, showed the barrenness of this hope. "The League is at last in ruins," he wrote in November. "The countries in Europe that would have joined an Anglo-French front are now suitors in the courts of the dictators. France has shown herself craven and irresolute, Russia has withdrawn. The wreckage is complete."[26]

[25]*Ibid.*, Dafoe to G. V. Ferguson, Sept. 1, 1938; *W.F.P.*, Sept. 3, 29, 30, 1938; Dafoe Papers, Dafoe to G. V. Ferguson, Oct. 11, Nov. 29, 1938.
[26]Dafoe Papers, Dafoe to G. V. Ferguson, Oct. 28, Nov. 5, 1938.

It was Neville Chamberlain whom Dafoe reserved for his cruelest lashes. Dafoe had been briefly misled by this man, but the Munich agreement made it evident that only the worst possible interpretation could explain the British Prime Minister's actions. He had never intended to stand out against Hitler's demands; his only concern had been to gain for himself a reputation of peacemaker. Dafoe wrote with a mixture of anger and dismay:

> Chamberlain was concerned not at all about Cz., but he did not want Hitler to march into that country and dismember it by force which would show that he, Chamberlain, counted for nothing in the plans of the Gt. Conqueror. He wanted to be around, helping to hold down the victim, while the raping was proceeding, in order to share the credit.

The old man was never more bitter, nor more justified in being so. For years he had fought for his conception of the best means of securing world peace, always warning that "appeasement" of aggressors would end in bloody disappointment. In 1938 he knew that once more, as in 1914, the world was about to be launched on a career of bloodshed and destruction. The leadership of second-rate men had failed to build a firm foundation for peace. Dafoe was convinced that even after Munich there was no sign that the lesson had been learned.[27]

Dafoe's reaction to Munich caused him to make a searching reappraisal of the country's relation to the world in this dangerous situation. He had long ago predicted that, if the League was destroyed, Canada would have to resort to armed isolationism. The events of September 1938 re-emphasized this "Fortress North America" viewpoint. Dafoe now began to think that perhaps the time had arrived for Parliament to enact legislation defining Canada's right to neutral status in the event of war; but perhaps to take this step would only intensify the divisions in the country. One thing he was certain had to be impressed upon Canadians and their Government: the country must arm. In November 1938 he told George Ferguson that

> I do think we might say as a matter of record, & perhaps repeat it upon occasion, that the govt. cannot affirm, as it does by its avowed policy, our right to be neutral & yet decline to provide the measures by wh. that neutrality can be made effective, thus taking long chances of precipitating the most dangerous of all divisions in Canadian public opinion when war breaks out. (You will notice I say "when" not "if".)

Further consideration of the question of neutrality legislation led Dafoe to the conclusion that such a measure might even contribute to the

[27]*Ibid.*, Dafoe to G. V. Ferguson, Nov. 19, 1938; Dafoe to Sir James Barrett, Jan. 9, 1939; Dafoe to L. S. Amery, Jan. 14, 1939.

country's unity when the inevitable war came. After all, if there was a minority opposed to Canadian participation in the war, this group might be more easily convinced of the justice of the cause if the decision to intervene was a purely Canadian one, rather than one which might have the appearance of being imposed from outside. Dafoe had no doubt that Canada would be involved in the war when it broke out; his chief wish was to ensure that the country was united when the day came.[28]

What irritated him most was his certainty that Canada would have entered the war as a united country if the League had not been destroyed. A League war would have had the support of nearly all Canadians, he believed. Furthermore the cause would have been strengthened by the adherence of numerous nations to the anti-totalitarian front if only the punitive provisions of the League had been effectively set in motion against Mussolini in Ethiopia and later against Hitler. Dafoe thought that the argument that the Munich settlement was allowing the opponents of Hitler an opportunity to mass their forces and unite their countries was specious. In March 1939 he wrote:

> If Britain and France can stop Hitler now they cd. have done it more effectively in September when they cd. have invoked the Covenant & in any case cd. have relied upon Russia & Cz. One variant of the argument wh. I run into is that the British people wd. now be more united than they wd. have been in September & that this has had a deterrent effect in Germany. This is quite worthless to my way of thinking. Certainly this is not the case here in Canada. If Gt. Britain had got into the war in defence of a great principle a great mass of support wd. hv. bn. assured; if she fights now for her own hide Canadian participation will be on a lower—though probably equally effective—plane: that of calculation as to the best means of saving *our* hide.[29]

After Munich, Dafoe watched the Prime Minister with a suspicious eye. The Liberal leader seemed to have little interest in, and less understanding of, the darkening international scene. The conviction that King and Chamberlain were working hand-in-glove rankled, and when Dafoe heard that King had denounced Churchill and Duff Cooper in the Liberal caucus he was completely disgusted. All that seemed to interest the Prime Minister was the forthcoming tour of Canada by the King and Queen. Sarcasm and uneasiness exuded from Dafoe's comment that

> I havn't been able to find out what kind of despatches are coming in to the govt. It is a fair bet that W. L. M. King hasn't read them, his mind running on really important things such as—well let us say the kind of

[28]*Ibid.*, Dafoe to G. V. Ferguson, Nov. 29, 1938, Feb. 19, 1939.
[29]*Ibid.*, Dafoe to H. V. Hodson, March 20, 1939; Dafoe to G. V. Ferguson, March 4, 1939.

pillow the Queen will rest her head on as she travels through Canada. First things must come first.

Nevertheless, Dafoe still could not find an answer to the persistent question—what alternative was there as a national leader? He might be convinced that King would make a very poor war minister, but when his newspaper had to take a stand on an actual issue—the apparent confusion in the Department of National Defence—he could only advise that criticism be directed at the Minister, Ian Mackenzie, without damaging the Government.[30]

For the most part the spring and summer of 1939, which Dafoe spent in Ottawa working on the report of the Rowell-Sirois Commission, were months of depression for him. The world was crumbling, yet no one seemed to be trying to shore it up. Franklin Roosevelt made a speech in April which cheered Dafoe somewhat as evidence of the President's awareness of the folly of isolationism. Moreover there were signs in Great Britain that the long malaise of appeasement was over. Even the Conservatives were beginning to see the error of letting the League die, Dafoe thought. His own view of the League was unchanged. Sometimes, in the moments of optimism that occasionally punctuated his gloom he thought that a great awakening was taking place. But there was no time for a revival of the League; only time for makeshift preparations for war. The one thing which had to be avoided in Canada, Dafoe was convinced, was an election that would unnecessarily divide the country in the atmosphere of deepening international crisis. There was a rumour in Ottawa in May that King was planning a dissolution. The suggestion enraged Dafoe. He had no personal objection if King wanted to "jump off the wharf," but the idea of putting the Government's political future ahead of the country's safety was scandalous. However, the war could not wait on King's rumoured electoral plans.[31]

The relatively quiet summer of 1939, brightened for Canadians by the royal tour which even evoked expressions of pleasure from Dafoe, ended in August with the Polish crisis. Would Munich be repeated? Dafoe thought it might, though he did not doubt that it would only mean a short respite. "Any bona fide readiness of Hitler to fall in with some kind of general adjustment may be, I think, dismissed because if Germany wants to live at peace with the rest of the world she will get rid of Hitler," he wrote. At last, in Poland, the British decided to stand firm. "This is the Britain that we looked for & wh. failed us 4, 3, 2,

[30]*Ibid.*, Dafoe to G. V. Ferguson, March 23, 19, 23, and June 8, 1939.
[31]*Ibid.*, Dafoe to G. V. Ferguson, April 19, 23, and May 11, 1939.

years ago, or is it? But certainly if the sequel is war we shall have to go all out in approval of her stand," Dafoe told George Ferguson.[32]

By September, war was obviously only a matter of days away. The country seemed steeled for the worst, though Dafoe had lingering doubts about the ability of King and Lapointe to lead a war administration. Perhaps the transfer of Colonel Ralston to the Ministry of Defence would give the Government the needed starch. On September 3, Dafoe spent most of the day beside his radio in Ottawa. The announcement that Hitler was at last to be put to the test of military opposition gave him the first sense of full relief that he had experienced in months: "I thought the actual announcement of war wd. knock me out, but it hasn't as yet anyway. I have been so ashamed of my race as it has been represented by Chamberlain & co. that I think a burden that rested somewhere lifted when the sword came out of the scabbard in a good cause—nearly 4 years too late." Without waiting for Parliament to decide, the *Free Press* leader on September 4 began with the declaration that "whatever the technical constitutional situation may be until Parliament meets on Thursday, the fact is that Canada is at war."[33]

A momentary fear that the appeasers in or near the Canadian Government might swing King towards a policy of neutrality passed through Dafoe's mind just before the country entered the war, but mercifully the fear was unfounded. At long last the country's will to stop wanton aggression had been stirred, and Dafoe sensed a mood of resignation and calm resolve in the people. The unity of the country seemed assured, though Quebec could still cause trouble. The Government's problem was to handle the Quebec isolationists on the one extreme, and the fire-eating conscriptionists on the other. Probably the general feeling of the country was a safe one—"a grim determination which excludes careless optimism and hysterical enthusiasm." As for the people both inside and beyond Government circles, who had thought that Canada could avoid participation in a world war by a policy of non-commitment, Dafoe thought, perhaps hoped, that they were suffering a rude awakening from their self-induced somnolence. But for such morally blind people, the British nations might have been at war as part of a large coalition rather than standing alone against the Axis powers. "If I were one of this crowd," he wrote grimly, "I'd jump in the river."[34]

Dafoe was prepared to forget the past, admitting that "nothing counts

[32]*Ibid.*, Dafoe to G. V. Ferguson, May 20, 31, and Aug. 29, 1939.
[33]*Ibid.*, Dafoe to G. V. Ferguson, Sept. 2 and Sept. (n.d.) 1939.
[34]*Ibid.*, Dafoe to G. V. Ferguson, Sept 7, 1939; Dafoe to E. C. Carter, Sept. 10, 15, 1939.

now but tenacity, power to endure and a determination to endure." But after so many years as a supporter of collective security he could not prevent moments of regret that the war was not an unambiguous fight on behalf of League principles. And then there was the continued and astonishing blindness of the United States. Why the childish refusal to admit the responsibility that bore so heavily on the betrayers of Wilson? he asked an American friend. If the war was to be brought to a successful conclusion, the United States would somehow have to be brought to bear its responsibilities.[35]

But Dafoe was not a man to brood on the failings of the past. Now that the issue was joined, every muscle had to be turned to forwarding the cause at hand.

vi

The strongest trait in Dafoe's liberalism was evident in his thoughts on international relations. He believed, like liberals before him, in the necessity and possibility of peaceful, voluntary association among nations and the settlement of international disputes by arbitration. He knew that, if these means failed, the peace had to be enforced by military and economic sanctions. The League of Nations was a monument to this way of thinking and he spent much energy in defending it against its detractors. What he saw in the League was a means by which the nations of the world, especially the democratic nations, could co-operate to preserve peace. If co-operation failed, the League also provided the means for the collective punishment of aggressors. The Commonwealth, as a free association of British nations, fitted nicely into the pattern of the League, for its objective, like that of the Geneva organization, was the preservation of peace.

The League was magnificent on paper, but in the end it had failed to fulfil its promise. Why? Dafoe found the answer in the kind of leadership that had risen to the top in the democracies. Speaking in 1940, he offered a liberal's critique of democracy:

One of the primary weaknesses of democracy has been its faith that if the majority will not see a fact, the fact does not exist; and that if it declines to adopt policies indicated as necessary by the facts it prefers not to see, it does not thereby prejudice its future freedom of action by putting itself at the mercy of conditions created by external developments. What may well become the classic example of this weakness was the admission of a British Prime Minister some years ago that he had declined to advocate policies

---

[35]*Ibid.*, Dafoe to Prof. H. M. Cassidy, Sept. 30, 1939; Dafoe to E. C. Carter, Sept. 15, 1939.

which it is now clear were essential for the defence of the country out of a fear of political results if he were frank with the electorate. Of course, the explanation is that he believed that there was plenty of time for the leisurely processes of trial and error to find a solution for this and for all other difficult problems; and that meanwhile there was no impending danger. That attitude was typical of the leadership of all the democracies during the fatal twenty years of procrastination, of hesitation, of retreat and repudiation.

Of course this criticism was based on hindsight, but Dafoe had seen as early as 1931 that the drift in international affairs which characterized the policies of the democracies could only lead to a fool's paradise. He persistently maintained that the drift could be halted by a firm adherence to League principles.[36]

But Dafoe's dilemma was that as a liberal and a nationalist he had to place his faith in voluntary co-operation and unfettered association. Indeed it was in the nebulous promises of the Paris Peace Pact rather than the binding commitments of the Geneva Protocol that Dafoe placed his hopes. His world was made up of independent nations, and he had no wish to see the great quest for Dominion status concluded by national subordination to some other external body, even the League of Nations. His view was that independent nations had to recognize the necessity of voluntary co-operation to preserve peace because it was in their interest, not because there was a supranational organization to call them to their duty. Dafoe never became reconciled to the view that the League should be provided with armed forces with which to enforce peace, for this implied an authority higher than national authority. Nor would he agree to suggestions that the League should become an agency for international economic planning. Dafoe's faith was in a world which subscribed to doctrines of liberal economics and voluntary national co-operation. It was a world in which inequalities of power were abolished, or rather forgotten. It had to be such a world if the League was to operate successfully. What Dafoe did not anticipate, apparently, was that power rivalries and ideological competition could frustrate the purposes of a League that did include all the great powers. Because League membership was never accepted by all the powers, Dafoe was able to contend that support of the Geneva scheme for collective security was, by itself, a desirable policy.[37]

The success of the League presupposed the equality of nations, and the eradication of the evils of "power politics." This was a view that

[36]Dafoe, *Let's Face the Facts* (Ottawa: Director of Public Information, Nov. 1940), 31.
[37]Dafoe Papers, Dafoe to Rt. Hon. Lord Davies, Jan. 7, 1937; Dafoe to Mary C. McGeachy, Dec. 31, 1934.

appealed to small nations like Canada and to liberal democrats like Dafoe. This is curious in a way, for Dafoe had no such naive belief about the abolition of power in domestic politics; he knew too well that the prizes of domestic political warfare went to the big battalions. But in international affairs, power politics and power blocs were anathema to him. There was a new-world innocence about his attitude to Europe and its military dissipations. The new world had offered Europe a means of curing its chronic bouts through the Covenant. If it failed to accept the medicine, the alternative for Canada was to withdraw from the scene of the prospective plague. This North American self-righteousness placed Dafoe on a vantage point with respect to the growth of European anarchy in the thirties. He was never blind to the motivating forces of the Nazis, and condemned them from the day they arrived in power, despite the protests of the German consulate in Winnipeg. Dafoe knew, as few others in Canada realized, that Hitler could not be appeased; his force had to be met with force. But force for Dafoe meant the force of the League of Nations. He never seriously considered any other alternatives. The same North American viewpoint which gave him an insight into the real meaning of Naziism caused him to reject any means but the League as a counterforce to Hitler. If the League disapppeared, "power politics" would be resumed, and a part of that prospect was the idea of a centralized British Empire. In 1937 Dafoe knew that the world was moving rapidly down the road to destruction, but his obsession with the idea that the situation might be used as an excuse to centralize the Empire caused him to reject the possibility, and it was a pretty remote possibility, that if the League failed, the Commonwealth might provide a united front against the Axis Powers.[38]

What Dafoe did not see was that the insistence upon Dominion status, which was at the basis of his objection to a common imperial foreign policy, was a partial explanation for the unheroic course of Britain and the dominions in the inter-war years. Perhaps this was inevitable, but to say so does not destroy the criticism that the status campaign was a double-edged sword. While it cut away the surviving vestiges of Dominion subordination to Britain, it also weakened the voice of the Commonwealth in foreign affairs when the testing time came in the late thirties. It is only fair to add, however, that in the long run it may have ensured the almost united front of the Commonwealth in September 1939, as Dafoe always said it would. But in 1937, Dafoe's unchangeable suspicion of the "imperial centralizers" meant that, instead of considering the best available means of meeting Hitler's threat, he introduced

[38]*Ibid.*, Dafoe to Dr. H. Seeheim, July 13, 1933.

the imperial bogey, which only confused the primary issue. The result of this confusion was that Dafoe almost slipped into the very isolationism he had so long deplored.[39]

But isolationism was never really a practical alternative for Dafoe, though he feared that it might be for the country. His own view was that Canadian participation in the war, and he never really doubted that the country would be involved, would result from a calculation of interest. Dafoe's own belief that Hitler would have to be met by force, and that Canada could not exist as an island unto itself, provided him with the score for his clarion calls for collective security. Since few people were prepared to pay heed, and as he could see no alternative means of preventing war, he concluded that another global catastrophe was inevitable. He was never in doubt as to his own sympathies. When Britain awoke from her dangerous sleep and determined to fight Nazi Germany, he did not question whether Canada should join the battle. When "the sword finally came out of the scabbard," as he put it, he knew it was for a good cause. But he also knew the personal sacrifices that it would demand. In December 1939, as he prepared to leave Ottawa and the Rowell-Sirois Commission for the more familiar surroundings of his office in the *Free Press* Building, he wrote a paragraph to his former employer's son that summed up all his inter-war thoughts on the affairs of the world:

> I have postponed my departure for a day in order to see my son Van off to the wars. I met the troop train at Smiths Falls on Tuesday morning and accompanied it to Montreal. They were a fine lot of young men, and I felt pretty sad seeing them going overseas to finish the job that we thought was finished twenty years ago, and would have been finished if the achievements of the army had been properly seconded by the statesmen.[40]

---

[39]Nicholas Mansergh, *Survey of Commonwealth Affairs: Problems of External Policy, 1931-1939* (London, 1952), chap. XI; Dafoe, "Canadian Foreign Policy," 220-1, 247. For the whole period see the essay by James Eayrs, "A Low Dishonest Decade: Aspects of Canadian External Policy, 1931-1939" in H. Keenleyside *et al.*, *The Growth of Canadian Policies in External Affairs* (Durham, N.C., 1960), 59-80.

[40]Dafoe Papers, Dafoe to Clifford Sifton, Dec. 29, 1939.

xiv. Canada Fights
1939-44

✦✦✦

"THE HIGHEST OBLIGATION OF CANADA is to fight side-by-side with Britain against Germany," Dafoe told an audience in St. Paul, Minnesota, in November 1940. Canada was tied to the Commonwealth culturally and historically, he maintained, and this fact outweighed the importance of being located on the North American Continent. In fighting on the side of Britain, Canada was fighting for the cause of the free world against the Axis Powers. The dreary prospect of armed isolationism that Dafoe had envisaged as Canada's last resort in the days when the destruction of the League carried him into the depths of disillusionment was swept away by the outbreak of war. Despite the increasing weight of his years—he was seventy-three when war was declared—Dafoe set his mind and pen to the purpose of winning. During four and a half years he anxiously watched the war situation change from the depressing defeats of 1939-40 to the hints of victory that appeared by the end of 1943.[1]

Like all the men of his generation, Dafoe witnessed the outbreak of two global wars within the space of a quarter of a century. In 1939 the very foundations of civilized life were again being threatened. For men who, like him, had spent much of the twenty-year period between the wars in the advocacy of international co-operation, the renewed conflict posed some basic questions. Had it all been to no avail? Was mankind incapable of learning the lessons taught by liberal tutors? Dafoe pondered these questions, wondering about "how many friends of mine had been busy for 20 years in saving the world," the money that had been spent, the books and articles that had poured off the presses. Then along came "a couple of crazy men who fifty years ago would have been locked up as bums or worse! and half the people of the world follow them as the

[1]*W.F.P.,* Nov. 29, 1940.

children did the Pied Piper into darkness, insanity and savagery." These were sobering thoughts. But for Dafoe, the liberal, the evidence was not conclusive. If Hitler and his friends could be stopped, then perhaps the investments of the inter-war years would "pay dividends to humanity as the forces of a sensible reconstruction of a ruined world."[2]

Dafoe never lost sight of the prerequisite of a world rebuilt on sensible principles—the defeat of Germany. As early as October 18, 1939, he wrote in the *Free Press*: "Subject to the condition that there can be no kind of peace short of the overthrow of Hitlerism, the discussion as to the uses to which victory will be put is desirable and necessary." He knew that the first task of the British nations and their Allies was to find the means by which the perpetrators of this new savagery could be brought to their knees. There were two things in particular that Dafoe thought were necessary for Canada and the Allied nations. First was the necessity of maintaining Canada's unity so that all its energies would be devoted to the war effort and none dissipated in domestic feuding. Secondly, the United States, with its massive industrial might and military potential, must be brought into the war. Though Dafoe never believed that the Axis Powers would emerge victorious, he did fear a stalemate that would leave Europe prostrate at Hitler's feet. Active American assistance would ensure the complete defeat of the Nazi armies. These two causes consumed a large part of Dafoe's time during the early years of the war.

ii

From the outset of the war Dafoe sought means to still the domestic political strife. Though the legal termination of the Parliament elected in 1935 was still a year away when war was declared, the *Free Press* suggested that an extension might be considered as a means of avoiding the inevitable pre-election partisanship. Premier Duplessis' attempt to make political capital out of anti-war sentiment in Quebec was condemned as a "sinister venture in national sabotage." Naturally Dafoe was greatly elated by the Liberal victory in the Quebec provincial election in October 1939.[3]

Again in early January 1940, when election rumours were abroad, the *Free Press* urged that an extension of the parliamentary term was preferable to an election. But when King sent Parliament packing, after an unprecedented one-day session, Dafoe was with the Liberal forces. He

[2]Dafoe Papers, Dafoe to E. C. Carter, Oct. 15, 1940.
[3]*W.F.P.*, Sept. 25, Oct. 16, Oct. 26, 1939.

could not resist one parting shot at the Liberal leader when King claimed that his pre-war foreign policy had ensured the unity of the country. "Commitments to proper ends set forth in express terms would not have divided the Canadian people any more than the decision to go to war divided them," Dafoe wrote solemnly on February 10. But with this one caveat, he was prepared to throw the influence of the *Free Press* wholeheartedly behind the Government. He was displeased with King's blanket rejection of the proposal made by the Conservative leader, Manion, for a National Government; but he agreed that there was nothing to be gained by the formation of a coalition at that time, although he thought popular demand might make it desirable at some later date. All his earlier doubts about King's ability as a war leader were banished as his pen poured out condemnations of the "Hepburn-Drew-Manion myth of Canadian laxity and unpreparedness." The revelation of the country's united support of the Government, which the sweeping Liberal victory displayed, was highly gratifying to Dafoe. He felt sure that this would be the last election contest that would command his energies.[4]

It was certainly not the last political quarrel. Indeed the battle had just begun. The conclusion of the spring election in Canada coincided with the end of the "phoney war" in Europe. As Hitler's land, sea and air forces moved into high gear, Dafoe decided that every sign of complacency about the Canadian war effort had to be stamped out. On June 8, he set out a programme of action which he thought every Canadian, not least of all the members of the Government, should strive to attain:

> The nation, listening to Mr. King's broadcast, will accept only with reserve his claim to foresight and preparedness. The story of our war effort up to now is a familar one. What the people want at this moment is the assurance that our Government has the ability and the vigor to snatch the initiative from our enemies forever, that it will not only accept burdens proposed to it, but will have the courage and strength of vision to create new opportunities of contribution to the common cause. We must mobilize our strength not only in men but in industry and production generally on a scale hitherto unknown, and forge here the vital links in the chain that will at last drag our foes down to defeat.

But the experience of the Great War must have reminded Dafoe that setting such an objective was a simple matter compared to solving the political difficulties that could arise in Canada in attempting to attain it. The First World War had created so many problems that Dafoe had become convinced that a party government was incapable of carrying

---

[4] *W.F.P.*, Feb. 26, March 7, 1940. Dafoe Papers, Dafoe to Brooke Claxton, March 31, 1940.

out the necessary, yet politically dangerous, policy of conscription. If the Second War fulfilled its promised longevity, surely this issue with all its disruptive complications would arise again. But during the Second World War Dafoe never seriously considered supporting a re-enactment of the 1917 campaign for union government. Gradually he came to believe that King was the indispensable man in Canadian politics and defended him with a vigour which he had given to no other politician except Borden during the years of the Union Government. For a time he thought that the Liberal administration might be strengthened, and made more national, if vacant cabinet posts were filled by nationally respected, non-partisan figures. This was a case which he repeatedly put forward, but he just as persistently asserted that the "case for strengthening the Government cannot be made to rest upon abuse of the Government, malignancy toward King, indiscriminate, wholesale and unbalanced attacks upon the war performance of the Government to date—all that sort of thing." Dafoe's admiration, indeed affection, for King was never stronger than during the first years of the war when the Prime Minister was subjected to increasingly severe criticism. One of the most personal letters the aging editor ever wrote was sent off to Prime Minister King at Christmas in 1940. He wrote:

> Just a line, my dear Prime Minister, to let you know that there are two old people in Winnipeg, Mrs. Dafoe and myself, who have you often in their thoughts and at this season want to convey to you their regards, their best wishes, and their gratitude for all that you are doing for the cause of human freedom. In your labors I hope that you are sustained by the knowledge that there are millions of Canadians—not to overlook Americans and Britishers all over the world—who are at one with us in this recognition of your courage, sanity and devotion to the greatest cause that free mankind has had to face.[5]

Dafoe knew, however, that personal eulogies were of little importance in the face of the swelling tide of criticism that was breaking over the Liberal Government. By the spring of 1941, conscription was already in the air and threatening to become a critical political issue. Perhaps partisan strife would be less bitter if King would broaden the basis of his Government. Dafoe was acutely aware of the rising feeling throughout the country that conscription was the only equitable enlistment policy. Perhaps, he thought, a plebiscite might be held to release the Government from its pledge to fight the war without compulsory enlistment. Though fully aware of the explosiveness of the conscription

[5]Dafoe Papers, Dafoe to Victor Sifton, Feb. 13, 1941; Dafoe to W. L. M. King, Christmas 1940.

question, Dafoe was not gravely concerned about the unity of the country in the late summer of 1941. In the Canadian people he sensed a "deep unbreakable unity, prepared to stay with the war until it is won." Perhaps it would have been better if Canada had been able to find a Churchill at the beginning of the war, but the contrast between the existing unity and the divisions of the First War suggested that "perhaps Mr. King's somewhat drab leadership has been more effective than appears on the surface."[6]

A month later, however, the enlistment controversy pushed every other political consideration aside. The *Free Press* straddled the fence on the issue, admitting that if it became clear that conscription was the best means of making the maximum contribution to the war effort, then it should be adopted. But the case had not yet been proved beyond doubt. Dafoe himself felt sure that the crisis had arisen not from any sincere desire to assist the war effort, but rather from the Tories' desire to forward their political fortunes. But once the issue had been raised it gained the support of many disinterested people. "To these people 'conscription' has become the symbol of their attitude toward the war," Dafoe explained to T. A. Crerar. "We had the same phenomenon in 1917 when there was a justification for it."[7]

Why was the situation different in 1941-2 than it had been in 1917? Dafoe examined this question very carefully, recalling the events of the earlier war, and considering the arguments that had brought about his break with Laurier. On December 29, 1941, an editorial appeared in the *Free Press* entitled "Comparisons: 1917 and 1941," in which Dafoe set out his conclusions. Central to the disruption of 1917 had been the dispute over Canada's position in the war; was it a principal or merely a supporting actor? The supporters of the first view had favoured conscription and union government; the proponents of the second view had followed Laurier into opposition. Dafoe's disguised self-analysis continued: "That Canada is in the war as a principal, with her fate as surely at stake as that of any other nation which is at war, is all but universally accepted. Upon this point, which was the real cause of the disruption of 1917, there can be no clash in principle." Nor did he find any of the other circumstances of 1917 present in 1941—the Government was widely supported; there had been no slackening in the war effort, and no falling off in recruiting. He had reached his conclusion:

[6]*Ibid.*, T. A. Crerar to Dafoe, April 30, 1941; Dafoe to T. A. Crerar, May 5, 1941; Dafoe to T. A. Crerar, May 23, 1941; Dafoe to Henry R. Luce, Aug. 5, 1941.

[7]*W.F.P.*, Oct. 15, Nov. 5, 1941. Dafoe Papers, Dafoe to Grant Dexter, Dec. 29, 1941; Dafoe to T. A. Crerar, Jan. 12, 1942.

Compared with 1917, the points upon which there can be differences between honest and patriotic Canadians (leaving out of account the would-be trouble makers, whose power to make mischief is in inverse ratio to their desires) are so limited and relatively unimportant that they ought to be readily adjustable with no serious present disturbance and no aftermath of bitterness or dissatisfaction. If this is not the result, the fault will be, not in the circumstances, but in the statesmanship of Canada's political leaders.

These were his stated reasons; but there was also something else. Dafoe's conception of the nature of Canadian unity had been modified. He had no doubt whatsoever that in theory conscription was the only just and efficient recruiting policy. But there was the political problem presented by the refusal of the French Canadians to accept the policy. The French Canadians, especially their leaders, had to be shown that to resist on a matter of such national importance would result in their own defeat, isolation and humiliation to a degree far more serious than in 1917. Dafoe had learned to sympathize with the French-Canadian viewpoint; bludgeoning tactics were impossible. Dr. Sirois had seen problems from a national viewpoint when he served on the Rowell-Sirois Commission. Was it too much to expect that other French-Canadian leaders might have a similar breadth of view about the conscription crisis? In the years since 1917 Canada had grown to a new maturity; John Dafoe had grown with it.

The conscription issue in 1941-2 was complicated by two completely unrelated events. The first was the entry of the United States into the war. Since the Americans had adopted a policy of selective service, Canadian conscriptionists insisted that the King Government should follow suit. Secondly, and more immediately important, was the decision of Arthur Meighen to leave the Senate and resume the leadership of the Conservative party.

At first the *Free Press* welcomed Meighen's decision to return to active politics. Before that, Dafoe had privately expressed the hope that steps would be taken to hasten the recovery of the Conservative party, since some alternative to the C.C.F. had to be offered to the Canadian electorate after the war. But Meighen's return in the midst of the growing manpower controversy was eyed with distrust—surely he was the tool of the nefarious interests which wanted to "unhorse" King. Dafoe's suspicion seemed to be confirmed by a letter he received about a week before the South York by-election that was being contested by Meighen and an unknown C.C.F. school teacher, J. W. Noseworthy. The letter came from Dafoe's old friend, John Stevenson, who was connected with the Toronto *Globe and Mail*. Dafoe had hoped that Stevenson's influence might moderate the views of the paper's new owner, George

McCullagh. But this hope was not to be fulfilled. In February 1942, Stevenson appealed to Dafoe for support in a move to replace King's administration with a union government which would exclude all the people who were opposed to conscription. The intransigence of the French Canadians, he argued, offered an opportunity for all loyal people to unite and form a new government.[8]

Dafoe waited a few days before answering the letter. Probably he wanted to see the results of three important by-elections that were to be held on February 9 before deciding how to word his rejection of the proposal. The by-elections were in Quebec East where Louis St. Laurent was fighting a nationalist candidate for the right to replace the late Ernest Lapointe at Ottawa; in Welland where Humphrey Mitchell, the new Minister of Labour, was opposed by a Hepburn-sponsored "Union" candidate; and in South York where Meighen, unopposed by the Liberals, was fighting what most people believed to be a winning battle against the C.C.F. Then the unexpected happened: both Liberal ministers were returned and Arthur Meighen sustained his final defeat at the hands of the Canadian electorate. In the *Free Press* of February 10 Dafoe interpreted these results as a complete vote of confidence in the Liberals and a serious rebuke to the "Warwicks" who had hoped to use Meighen's talents to gain control of the Government.[9]

He now turned with confidence to answer Stevenson's letter. Step by step he demolished the plan that his friend had offered, and in doing so illustrated the new breadth of his nationalism. His first objection to the suggested "National Government" was his belief that its chief purpose was to "eject King and the French members and replace [them] with a Government limited, in effect, to English-speaking Protestant Canadians." In short, it was a revival of the old doctrine of forcible assimilation through British domination of Canada. Such a movement could only prove "denationalizing and destructive." "If there must be division," Dafoe wrote, "let it be between parties and not between races." The only government that could truly claim to be national was one which contained the representatives of both cultures, and this condition was fulfilled by the King Government to a far greater extent than by any suggested alternative. And even the King Government was threatened with disunity by the conscription question. But Dafoe thought that a plebiscite was the way out of this dangerous situation, for the "more

[8] *W.F.P.*, Nov. 13, 1941. Dafoe Papers, Dafoe to J. M. Macdonnell, Oct. 18, 1940. *W.F.P.*, Nov. 18, 1941. Dafoe Papers, Dafoe to Geoffrey Dawson, May 27, 1941; John Stevenson to Dafoe, Feb. 2, 1942.
[9] *W.F.P.*, Feb. 10, 1942.

enlightened French" were desirous of finding a means of avoiding racial disruption. The French, Dafoe affirmed, were here to stay, "and as a condition of our nationhood they must be given their place in the sun." Of course, they could be flooded out, drowned in an English-speaking sea, but the precondition of this achievement would be for the rest of Canada to allow itself to be submerged in the United States. Here was a prospect that no Canadian could anticipate with pleasure.

Turning to Stevenson's complaints about the unfortunate effects of the French-Canadian bloc in Canadian politics, Dafoe said he agreed that it was undesirable for the French Canadians to vote solidly for one party. But, he said, the Conservatives made this inevitable by their anti-Quebec attitude. With some anger, he continued:

> Our present business is to keep internal friction down to a minimum and to make our own maximum contribution to the war. We cannot do this if we have a racial split in this country; it is our business, as a majority race, to see that if there should come a split, it will be due not to the arrogance of the majority but an intransigent minority.

If this view was accepted by all Canadians, there would never be a racial crisis, he claimed, but "upon the basis of the McCullagh-Hepburn-Drew-Bassett plan this country would this very day be in pieces." Nor would Dafoe give any weight to Stevenson's fear that the country could not trust a King-led, French-dominated Government to ensure Canada's place in a rationally ordered post-war world. In the post-war settlement, he held, nations would have to surrender some of their sovereignty, but national identities would be maintained. If such a plan was not put into effect, the world would be divided into "warring Empires" and Canada would take her place in the English-speaking Empire whose capital would be at Washington. "I no more want to see the Canada of the future bossed from Washington, than I favored having it bossed from London as was the case not so long ago," he declared. Mackenzie King and Louis St. Laurent could be trusted to protect Canada's national identity.

Finally, Dafoe turned to an estimation of King's record and ability. Both sides of the ledger had to be totalled up, he told Stevenson. Down to 1935, King had a fair balance to his credit; many of his domestic policies left something to be desired, but he had a good imperial and international record. Chanak, the Halibut Treaty, the 1923 Imperial Conference and the dispute with Byng were all marked in heavy black in King's account book. After 1935 the entries were more frequently in red. But even here it had to be admitted that King was no more blameworthy than the other leaders of the League countries. Since 1939 the record was again in his favour. Dafoe, while conceding that the systematic disparagement of King since the outset of the war had made him "somewhat of a partisan on his behalf—something I never was previously," felt that King's accounts showed a surplus. In summing up he pleaded for a fair estimate:

> No doubt he has made many mistakes; his methods of doing business may exasperate people; he may at times have confused national and party interest. In short, he is a miserable sinner. But aren't we all? But also are we not all according to our lights trying to help the cause to which our lives and the lives of our children are pledged? I am as sure of King's integrity in this matter of the war and his devotion to duty as he sees it, as I am of my own.

Here was a transformation in Dafoe that was truly remarkable, and might simply be written off as inconsistency. He had cast the national unity argument to the winds in 1917, accusing the French in their opposition to conscription of being "the only known white race to quit." Faced with a similar situation in 1942 his viewpoint was entirely changed. Was it simply that in 1917 the Government had been Conservative, and the public demand for conscription irresistible? Whatever part these considerations played in Dafoe's thinking in 1942, it was not a major one. For him the 1942 situation was not parallel to that of 1917, and this was because of the changes which had taken place in himself and in the country. Dafoe's transformation had been gradual, but in the interwar period he had grown a great deal in stature; grown from a party journalist in the strictest sense to a man with breadth of view. He had come better to understand his country, to see that its uniqueness rested in the fact that it was an experiment in cultural relations and that its very existence depended upon the success of that experiment. Moreover Dafoe had grown to appreciate the role that the French Canadians had played in the successful campaign for Dominion status. "There are several instances in Canadian history," he told Stevenson, "where the [French-Canadian] bloc came in very handy in offsetting abject Tory colonialism." At the centre of this change in Dafoe was Mackenzie King, who, for all his failings, had convinced Dafoe of his ability to keep the elements of the country working together. Dafoe never accepted King as the infallible leader, but only as the least fallible of the alternatives. In short, in 1942, Dafoe's intellectual convictions led him into full communion with the Liberal party.[10]

[10]Dafoe Papers, Dafoe to John Stevenson, Feb. 12, 1942. Dafoe described this whole incident to King, and according to King's Diary, said of his letter to Stevenson "that he had written a letter which he thought would be of historic value and would make real reading some day when it was published." J. W. Pickersgill, *The Mackenzie King Record, I, 1939-1944* (Toronto, 1960), 389.

In one respect, at least, Dafoe's views in 1942 were very similar to those of 1917. He believed as firmly as ever that every step necessary for the successful prosecution of the war must be taken. Among these steps was the application of conscription for overseas service when circumstances demanded. But at the same time he realized that the means by which this measure was effected could be as important as the measure itself. The means was the 1942 plebiscite to release the Liberals from their pledge to oppose conscription. The only justification for the plebiscite, Dafoe argued, was that it could help to prevent national disruption. In the *Free Press* he wrote (February 2, 1942):

> The plebiscite is an unheroic expedient to protect this country against the dangers and consequences of ill-considered courses urged by reckless men. It is not necessary for anybody to be enthusiastic about it; it will be sufficient if it is accepted as the only available road out of an impasse and loyally supported on those grounds.

He was prepared to admit that the Government had failed fully to accept its responsibility for educating Quebec in the facts of modern war. Lapointe had been largely responsible for this failing. But the only way out of the crisis was to avoid the conflagration risked by the extremists in English Canada who had fired the sparks of racial conflict, and the extreme nationalists in Quebec who had fanned them with delight. Only King's moderation could carry the country through a situation which threatened the very existence of the nation. "I think that in this moment in which we have arrived King is about as indispensable for Canada as Roosevelt is for the United States or Churchill for Great Britain," Dafoe told a Conservative friend.[11]

Dafoe realized that the plebiscite was a daring gamble; it might end in increasing the country's disunity. Especially dangerous was the possibility that the French Canadians might refuse to agree to release the Government from its pledge. Should this be followed by a refusal on the part of the French-Canadian members of Parliament to accept conscription, "the fat would be in the fire with a vengeance." Nevertheless Dafoe hoped that there would be no such crisis and felt that, if the intemperate discussion was adjourned and all efforts turned to obtaining an affirmative vote, "we shall lay once and for all the bogeyman of conscription in Quebec."[12]

The conscription plebiscite, if the ambiguous question can be so definitely described, revealed exactly the division that Dafoe had feared; Quebec was 72 per cent opposed, all the rest of Canada 80 per cent in

[11]Dafoe Papers, Dafoe to J. M. Macdonnell, Feb. 16, 1942.
[12]*Ibid.*, Dafoe to John Stevenson, March 21, 1942.

favour of releasing the Government from its pledge. The result made two conclusions clear to Dafoe. First, the country was disunited, and that unpleasant fact had to be accepted. Secondly, there was the overriding consideration that the majority of the country favoured conscription. Compulsory enlistment had therefore to be implemented by the Government. Dafoe thus interpreted the affirmative vote as one not merely releasing the Liberals from their promise, but as one which definitely favoured conscription. Nevertheless he was still prepared to allow the Government a margin of flexibility in fulfilling the people's wish. "Not until all the other expedients of delay and adjustment are exhausted should Canada face the stark division of this country into conscription and anti-conscription camps," the *Free Press* argued on May 22. Again Dafoe stressed the necessity of preserving national unity if the country was to make the ultimate effort in winning the war. But he was firm in his conviction that the Government could not avoid its obligation to provide the means of applying conscription if the necessity arose. He lauded King's decision to amend the National Resources Mobilization Act to provide for conscription while leaving the date of application indefinite. This seemed the only means of avoiding the rupture between French and English.[13]

On one point Dafoe was especially firm: the only way in which the disruption of the community could be avoided was for the French Canadians to accept the decision of the majority on conscription. He was cautiously confident that a majority of Liberals could be brought around to this viewpoint, provided the Quebec nationalists and the C.C.F. could be prevented from playing politics with the issue in the French province. Firmness by the Government in pressing through the legislation empowering it to enforce military service was the best way to meet the situation, Dafoe believed.

On the whole Dafoe was satisfied with the Government's handling of the conscription issue. Bill 80, authorizing the implementation of compulsory service when it was deemed necessary, was passed by Parliament in July 1942. One aspect of the measure caused Dafoe distress: King insisted that even with the powers of Bill 80, the Government would still ask for a vote of confidence before applying conscription, and Dafoe feared that the whole controversy would thus be thrown open again. Even so, he felt that a bad situation had been avoided by King's curious circumambulations. Perhaps the future was brightening at last.

[13]*W.F.P.*, April 29, May 28, 1942. For a sensitive account of the Quebec case see André Laurendeau, *La Crise de la conscription, 1942*, Montréal: Editions du Jour, 1962.

At the end of 1942 Dafoe was able to write, as the crisis was passing, "I think the stock of all three Governments—British, United States and Canadian—is up and going higher in spite of the yelpers."[14]

The conscription crisis of 1942 was the last large domestic issue that commanded Dafoe's attention; not because he lost interest in dispute, but because the war effort seemed to move along smoothly during the last year of his life. What interested him most in domestic affairs was the future of the various parties. King seemed to be firmly in power for the duration of the war, but Dafoe expected that the Liberals would likely suffer the same fate that had befallen the Unionists after the First World War. The worst he could foresee was the possibility that the C.C.F. would benefit from the inevitable disenchantment with the Liberals. In an effort to prevent this result, he persistently urged his Conservative friends to begin mending their party's fences. Though Dafoe had a high regard for Arthur Meighen's talents, he was certainly not sorry to see him lose the South York by-election. Apart from the fact that Dafoe disagreed with Meighen's principles, he did not believe that the former Prime Minister was the type of leader who could rebuild the Tory splinters into a national party. Nor did he think that the discontented Conservatives would be well advised to scrap the old party and found a new one; that would take too long. What the Tories needed was a new, effective leader who could appeal to the electorate on a programme of broad Canadianism. Otherwise the threat of a successful radical revolt would be increased, and the Conservatives overcome. Dafoe saw the C.C.F. as a real threat—a group that could succeed where the Progressives had failed. Speaking of the years after the First War he remarked that had the Progressive group not disintegrated, "it might have gone on to greater strength under leadership more radical than that supplied by Crerar." Here was the advantage that the C.C.F. would have when the Second War ended.[15]

When the Conservatives' efforts to revive their party resulted in the choice of Manitoba's John Bracken as leader, Dafoe wished the party every success. At the same time he warned that if this remarkable gamble failed, the results would be disastrous. Actually Dafoe was sceptical about Bracken's ability to provide the Tories with a tonic. He told his old friend Senator Buchanan not to worry about the turn of events that had placed a Progressive at the head of the Conservative

[14]Dafoe Papers, Dafoe to A. R. M. Lower, July 2, 1942; Dafoe to W. R. Givens, July 3, 1942; Dafoe to T. A. Crerar, July 14, 1942; Dafoe to Hon. Leighton McCarthy, Nov. 14, 1942.
[15]*Ibid.*, Dafoe to J. M. Macdonnell, Oct. 18, 1940; Dafoe to John Stevenson, Feb. 10, 1942; Dafoe to J. M. Macdonnell, July 20, 1942.

party. In the first place it would be a good thing if the Conservatives were revived. But secondly, there was the distinct possibility that Bracken would have exactly the reverse effect on the party to that which his supporters envisaged.[16]

The Canadian political scene remained in a rather confused state during the last year of Dafoe's life. Bracken was something of an enigma, but Dafoe continued to doubt whether he was winning many new votes for the Conservatives. Furthermore, though he believed that the Liberals had lost some support during the conscription crisis, he thought that King's personal stock had risen with the voters. The real danger, as the Ontario provincial election in 1943 illustrated, was the C.C.F. Accordingly Dafoe set his assistants to the task of exposing the Socialists as the precursors of totalitarianism and the exponents of economic nationalism.[17]

Dafoe's own commitment was to Mackenzie King as it had never been before. King had proved his ability as a war leader and Dafoe was prepared to give his last strength to ensuring that the post-war reconstruction would be carried on under the same man. Only a few weeks before his death he wrote the Prime Minister: "In 1935 I said to Lapointe that, as that would surely be my last campaign, I intended to put everything I had into the campaign against R.B.; but I am rather counting on taking a hand in the next electoral battle."[18] He was not allowed to fight that one last battle. But one thing was definite: after twenty-five years of uncertainty, he had come to rest finally in the Liberal fold. King had proved invincible against the years of Dafoe's criticism, as against the criticism of so many others.

iii

The coming of the war did not dim Dafoe's interest in affairs outside Canada. Indeed the conflict increased his concern about the neutralism of the United States. The war offered an opportunity for an expression of that unity of English-speaking people which Dafoe saw not only as an ideal, but as a necessity, if firmly founded international co-operation was ever to be achieved. Moreover, in the dark days of the war he looked enviously at the unused military potential of the United States. So he

[16]*Ibid.*, Dafoe to Hon. T. C. Davis, Dec. 15, 1942; Dafoe to Senator W. A. Buchanan, Dec. (n.d.) 1942.
[17]*Ibid.*, Dafoe to T. A. Crerar, Jan. 4, 1943; Dafoe to Sir Frederick Whyte, Feb. 17, 1943; Dafoe to Chester Bloom, Aug. 8, 1943; Dafoe to G. V. Ferguson, Sept. 12, 14, 1943.
[18]*Ibid.*, Dafoe to W. L. M. King, Dec. 20, 1943.

set himself the task of contributing whatever he could to educating Americans in the true meaning of the war.

At the beginning of the war two features of the American attitude caused him deep concern. First, there was the neutrality legislation which was an insuperable barrier to the British nations' war effort. Sometimes it seemed that the whole fate of Western civilization was being jeopardized by the exigencies of party politics in the United States. Even more infuriating was the neutralism of American intellectuals who refused to see any moral question at issue in the war against the Nazis. Dafoe was deeply distressed by the frequent suggestion that the United States might intervene in the war to force a negotiated peace. Such foolish talk arose out of a complete failure to understand the critical issues that hung in the balance, he believed.[19]

Dafoe made every effort to appeal to the American liberal conscience in order to enlighten the citizens of the Republic about the facts of international life. He was convinced that the battle to win the minds of the American people was as important as the actual physical battle in Europe. His main tactic was to explain that the responsibility for world chaos rested heavily upon the United States because of its refusal to take an active role in promoting international security. Admittedly the other English-speaking democracies had played only a hesitant, half-hearted part, but in the end they had redeemed themselves by taking up the cudgels against Nazi Germany. The American opportunity for a similar redemption was ever at hand, if only the people would realize that their security was tied up with that of the British nations.[20]

These sermons to the Americans in the *Free Press* naturally reached only a very limited audience. It was obvious that some more extensive means of promoting the Allied cause in the United States was necessary. Early in the war Dafoe made an effort to have the Canadian Government erect a powerful short-wave station for beaming Allied propaganda to the United States, but the Government had not been receptive to this "Voice of Canada" proposal. Dafoe then turned to a much more modest undertaking: the publication, in co-operation with several of his colleagues, of a book describing the Canadian attitude to the war and arguing for American assistance. This was the origin of the book, *Canada Fights*, published in the spring of 1941.[21]

[19]*Ibid.*, Dafoe to Thomas F. Holgate, Sept. 30, 1939; Dafoe to J. T. Shotwell, April 5, 1940. *W.F.P.*, Feb. 14, 1940.
[20]Dafoe Papers, Dafoe to Angus Fletcher, July 30, 1940; *W.F.P.*, May 27, 1940.
[21]Dafoe Papers, Dafoe to W. R. Givens, Feb. 12, 1941. The collaborators were Dr. Percy Corbett, then of McGill, Grant Dexter, Bruce Hutchison, G. V. Ferguson and B. T. Richardson.

Its central theme was the necessity of co-operation between Canada and the United States as North American democracies. "The belief behind this book is that the Ogdensburg agreement is the symbol and a turning point in the history of the world and a change for the better," the authors pointed out. The part that Canada had played in obtaining American co-operation in the defence of North America was seen as an expression of Canada's function as the linchpin in the union of that wider community of English-speaking people. Canada as a North American nation had been able to win the support of the United States without doing violence to its "commitments to the other British nations overseas." Thus, while Canada was a North American nation, this was not the same thing as saying that the United States was a North Americn nation. Canada had characteristics which expressed its individualism, characteristics which could be explained partly by its continuing relation with the Commonwealth. But it was not to be thought, the writers claimed, that Canada had rejected North American isolationism because of any purely sentimental attachment to the Commonwealth. Canada's entry into the war had been based on a recognition of the truth that the issues raised by the war were of fundamental importance to free nations everywhere. Here was the real significance of Canadian-American co-operation. It was a partial acceptance of the crucial truth that the interests of the United States were also at stake in the war wih the Axis. Furthermore this co-operation pointed to the inevitability of world leadership through the association of the English-speaking nations. That future leadership would embody "some type of co-operation by the free world, led by Britain and the United States who together must wield the sceptre which, in the years that lie before our generation, will be the most potent weapon of order and security in the world."[22]

Canada Fights was primarily a journalistic propaganda piece which overlaid these ideas with the facts and figures of Canada's war effort and post-war aspirations. Nevertheless it contained the intellectual assumptions of Dafoe's mature thought. For him the long-desired goal of English-speaking co-operation had been made even more pressing by the war. American co-operation in every field, including active military participation, was imperative if the war was to be won and a secure post-war world constructed. Dafoe knew that close co-operation with the United States might entail some disadvantages for Canada, but on balance he thought that the advantages would be far greater. He was so convinced of the necessity of American participation in world affairs that he worried very little about the immensely disadvantageous power

[22] Dafoe, ed., *Canada Fights* (Toronto, 1941), 3, 9, 34–5, 81, 210, 234–5.

ratio that existed between Canada and the United States; or at least he thought that this would be offset by Canada's membership in the Commonwealth and a new League of Nations. His chief concern was to lure the Americans out of their isolationist lair in order to prevent a repetition of the events which had followed the First World War. "During the long years of American withdrawal from participation in world affairs ...," he told Henry Luce, "I have felt a deepening apprehension, which in recent years became a certainty, that this abstention meant ultimate disaster for the world, including the United States." This correctly anticipated disaster had convinced him that if English-speaking people were to preserve their heritage, "a far greater unity of attitude and action in matters of international concern" was required.[23]

Thus Dafoe did not see Canadian-American relations in a void, but always in the wider context of the English-speaking community of interests. The joint defence of North America was simply part of the co-operation necessary to preserve that community. Commenting on the series of agreements between Canada and the United States in the early years of the war, Dafoe gave expression to a fundamental premise of his thought on international affairs when he praised them for bringing "the whole English-speaking world together in closer and more permanent relations than they have ever before seen." The growing interdependence was epitomized, in Dafoe's opinion, by the signing of the Atlantic Charter, which marked the re-entry of the United States into the world arena. Franklin Roosevelt was accepting America's responsibilities. Now every effort had to be made to ensure that there would be no repetition of the events of 1919-20. The United States could not be allowed to retreat again into isolationism or the result would be another ruinous war.[24]

The Japanese attack on Pearl Harbor brought the long, frustrating days of waiting to an end: the United States was in the war. Dafoe was now optimistic about the future; surely the United States had taken an irrevocable step into world affairs. It could only result in a commitment to "international policies which will give effect to the views and convictions of Roosevelt's old chief, Woodrow Wilson." Dafoe was at last

[23] Dafoe Papers, Dafoe to Prof. W. R. Livingstone, Aug. 26, 1941; Dafoe to Henry R. Luce, March 10, 1941.
[24] *W.F.P.*, May 9, 1941; Dafoe Papers, Dafoe to John Russell, Aug. 26, 1941. By 1942 Dafoe's view of F.D.R. had altered substantially from the days before the war. While he still had reservations about the President's domestic policies, on the basis of his foreign policy he was able to award F.D.R. the title of "Liberator and Defender of Mankind." See Dafoe's review of *The Public Papers and Addresses of Franklin D. Roosevelt* in *A.H.R.*, XLVII, no. 4 (July 1942), 909.

able to be confident that two of his most cherished hopes would be fulfilled. The first was the short-term, but primary, concern of winning the war. "I have discarded the use of the word 'if' with respect to victory and have substituted 'when' now that the United States is definitely in the war a united and determined nation," he told an American friend. But there was more involved than winning the war. American participation would bring about the positive co-operation of the English-speaking peoples, which heralded a new day in international relations. "There are going to be developments of the most interesting kind regarding the co-operation of the British nations with the United States both in war and in the following peace," he told Chester Bloom, the *Free Press* correspondent in Washington. Here was the basis upon which he could begin to organize his thoughts about the post-war world and Canada's place in it.[25]

iv

By 1939 Dafoe's views on the best means by which world security could be achieved had fully matured. His opinions on the subject of post-war reconstruction were essentially the same as the views which he had consistently put forward in the thirties. He was a nationalist who believed that any rational scheme of world organization must begin with the recognition that the world was composed of nation-states which had not reached a stage where they would accept the overruling authority of a supranational organization. He was a liberal democrat who believed that all nations should be given equal recognition in the councils of the world, and that the democratic nations should band together to prevent the aggression that was the life-blood of dictatorships. He was an economic liberal who argued that international co-operation could only be based on free competition and that friction was the inevitable result of policies that promoted economic exclusiveness. Basic to all these assumptions was the belief that, given favourable conditions, nations would co-operate and that the original sin which causes men and nations to strive for power could be overcome. Or at least he believed that through conscious effort a world could be created from which the evils of power politics could be excluded.

Dafoe looked upon the Second World War through the eyes of a Wilsonian internationalist; once again the free nations were doing battle to make the world safe for democracy. Here was the essential justifica-

[25]Dafoe Papers, Dafoe to Dr. Hu Shih, Dec. 17, 1941; Dafoe to E. C. Carter, Dec. 19, 1941; Dafoe to Chester Bloom, Feb. 14, 1942.

tion for Canadian participation in the war. He told an American correspondent in 1941:

> It is not a case of Canada being either American or European—the time is passed when the world can be thus compartmentalized. This is not a war between territories, but between states of mind; and the issue is just what your President has said it is: freedom or slavery, civilization or savagery, not for particular regions but for the whole world.

This was the kind of world that Dafoe believed in—a world of cooperating democracies. It was the kind of world he hoped to see emerge from the years of military upheaval.[26]

As far as Canada was concerned, the first line of defence, from Dafoe's point of view, was the protection of Canadian status against any efforts by the British to gain centralized control of the war effort. The war was only two months old when Dafoe began tracking imperialist moves, and his suspicious nose kept picking up the scent to the last days of his life. The Imperial War Cabinet which had attempted to correlate the efforts of the various parts of the Empire during the First War was not an institution which Dafoe believed could be profitably revived during the Second War. Here he was in agreement with Mackenzie King, who in February 1941 indicated that he felt the existing means of communication between the dominions were entirely satisfactory.[27]

Yet despite his suspicion that the British might use the war to centralize the Commonwealth, some of Dafoe's most complimentary words about the British association of nations and British leadership were written during the war years. He recognized that the British war effort was superb and he had been an admirer of Churchill since the thirties. In 1943 he described the British Prime Minister as "the greatest man the race has produced in a thousand years"—a rather large claim. It is easy enough to pass over this type of encomium, but Dafoe went much further. Perhaps surprisingly, he took it upon himself to defend the British record in India against cantankerous criticism in the United States. Great Britain had promised India self-government after the war, he pointed out, so that those who attacked the British in India—the Luce publications in the United States, or Gandhi and the Congress party in India—were doing nothing but harm to the Indian cause and to the war effort. He directed a couple of his most pointed editorials at *Life* in October 1942 for what he called the "journalism of cheek, cockiness and bounce in its extremest form." After all the British nations had been fighting the cause of all free nations, even of the

[26]*Ibid.*, Dafoe to Mrs. E. B. Shipman, June 9, 1941.
[27]*Ibid.*, Dafoe to G. V. Ferguson, Nov. 20, 1939; *W.F.P.*, Oct. 1, 1941.

United States, during the first years of the war, he noted testily. His own great pride in the achievements of the Commonwealth were obvious in the editorial's concluding paean of praise:

> History will amply confirm General Smuts' estimate of the contribution which the family of British Nations has already made to the defence of civilization. It was indispensable in the testing-time of 1940—failing it Hitler would have been at this time Lord of the Universe. Of all the political experiments of the last half century, none has been so vindicated by the testing of events as the transformation of the British Empire, as it was at the turn of the century, into today's league of British Nations.

The Empire had never been all profit for Britain and loss for the dependencies. Countries such as India had greatly benefited from British rule. This was never more evident than during the war when, had it not been for British military forces, they might easily have fallen prey to some predatory power.[28]

While Dafoe lectured the Americans on the virtues of British imperialism, he was none the less insistent that the term "British Empire" be permanently replaced by "British Commonwealth" in the public statements of British and Dominion politicians. He personally disliked the term "Empire," but his chief concern was that the use of it left a serious misunderstanding in the minds of some Americans who were frequently only too willing to misunderstand.[29]

Once the United States was in the war Dafoe began to fear that Canada's independence was threatened from two sides—the British and the American. He felt that, from the start, Canada had played a part in the war second only to Great Britain. Therefore the Canadian government had the right and the duty to ensure that the country's interests were constantly consulted before any decisions touching them were taken by the two senior partners. He recognized that Canada had to avoid being obstructive in insisting that its rights be given due attention, and admitted, "We are useful and indispensable, but it is only in certain respects that we are in the first line, and we should show a due sense of proportion." The difficulty of the dominions' position was that all the larger powers, including the United States, failed "to take our claims to sovereignty very seriously," and were satisfied to assume that Britain spoke for the Commonwealth. To some extent this was to be expected. The best plan for his country to follow, Dafoe thought, was to impress upon the British that Canada refused to be committed to any policy

---

[28]Dafoe, *Sixty Years in Journalism* (Winnipeg, 1943), 11. *W.F.P.*, Aug. 6, Oct. 16, Oct. 28, 1942.
[29]*W.F.P.*, Dec. 16, 28, 1942.

decisions without prior consent. Given a proper system of "continuous consultation," Dafoe thought Canada should be willing to accept the fact that in wartime there was no reason why the views of the British nations "should not be expressed by a single voice (not necessarily that of Britain at all times), provided that it is made clear that it is in reality a multiple voice." Perhaps in the post-war world distinctions of national sovereignty would be somewhat blurred, but in the interim Canada should make it clear that it made its own decisions. "We cannot act like a colony of either Britain or the United States," he asserted. Here was the same old battle that Canada had fought during the First World War, but now it had to be won over both Britain and the United States. Dafoe's one fear was that the King Government lacked the resolution that had characterized the Union Government's leading figures, Borden, Arthur Sifton and Doherty. "They were alert and on the job at all times," he reflected.[30]

Clearly Dafoe was not entirely satisfied with the methods that had been provided for consultation among the Allied nations. He was not alone in his uneasiness; by 1943 several Commonwealth leaders were publicly expressing their dissatisfaction with the want of co-ordination within the Commonwealth. Neither Prime Minister Curtin of Australia nor General Smuts of South Africa offered any specific institutional proposals, but both made it clear that they were unhappy about the lack of effective consultation within the Commonwealth, a lack which sometimes led Britain to assume more authority than was warranted by prior agreement. In addition Smuts was worried about the possibility of a post-war world divided between two super-powers and suggested that the Commonwealth, in co-operation with some European nations, might unite to form a third force. For Dafoe, as for Prime Minister King, these proposals could mean only one thing—the black sheep of imperial centralization had once more crept into the flock. After a lifetime of fighting real or imagined plans of this kind, Dafoe reacted like Pavlov's dog to the 1943 proposals. In the *Free Press* on November 24, Curtin's suggestion was interpreted as calling for the establishment of an Imperial Council which would undo all the work of Laurier, Borden and King. It was an attempt to "turn the clock back." Once again the Round Table movement was at work, Dafoe suspected. When the much-respected voice of General Smuts was added to the discussion, Dafoe told J. B. Brebner that "I think Smuts in his London performance is flying a kite for a combination wh. includes Curtin, Bennett and various Britishers—

[30] *Ibid.*, March 26, 1943; Dafoe Papers, Dafoe to Chester Bloom, March 22, 1943.

possibly Churchill too. . . . We have been flying storm signals in the Free Press."[31]

Two features of the Smuts proposal evoked bitter criticism from Dafoe. First there was the implied suggestion that the British nations should form a single power. In short, the whole story of the development of Dominion status was to be wiped off the board and replaced by the long-deprecated common policy in foreign affairs. The Commonwealth that had been established between the wars was thus to be junked. This suggestion would mean the destruction of what Dafoe considered the essence of Canadian sovereignty: the right to act independently in international affairs. Canada had entered and was fighting the war as an independent nation, and would insist on taking part in the peacemaking, and on living in the post-war world, as a nation. All the talk about a consolidated Empire would only play into the hands of American isolationists who would use it, as they had done in 1919, as an argument for American neutrality in the post-war world.[32]

But this was not the only, not even the chief, objection to Smuts's proposal. The idea of dividing the world into three power blocs was an acceptance of power politics, pure and simple. To Dafoe, this meant the acceptance of the necessity of a world eternally posed on the brink of war. With emotional intensity, Dafoe crisply condemned Smuts's suggestion as a desertion of the ideal of the League in favour of the madness of power politics:

> If the United States is going to demand military and naval bases all over the world; if Russia is going to make vassal states of all the adjoining European states; if Britain is to be the head of an armed Western European confederacy plus the Dominions, then there will always be enough powder available to blow up the universe if these powers, armed, jealous of their prestige, and inflamed with imperialistic ambitions go totalitarian in keeping with dreams of world domination. Impossible? Who seventy years ago would have foreseen that Germany in the supposedly civilized Twentieth Century would be ruled absolutely by a criminal lunatic, Italy by a posturing blatherskite, and Japan by a coldly calculating and murderous racial fanatic?

No, this was not the kind of world that Dafoe had spent twenty-five or more years of his life arguing for and writing about. It denied all the features of international life that he most cherished—Canadian independence, world-wide co-operation among nations and the close association of the members of the English-speaking world. The kind of post-war

---

[31]Dafoe Papers, Dafoe to Dr. J. T. Shotwell, Nov. 1, 1943; Dafoe to J. B. Brebner, Dec. 5, 1943.

[32]W.F.P., Dec. 6, Dec. 16, Nov. 1, 1943.

organization that Dafoe planned was very different from that suggested by the South African Prime Minister.[33]

The only road to world security, the only alternative to power politics, in Dafoe's view, was a return to the principles of collective security as they had been established in the Covenant of the League of Nations. He was willing to accept some modifications in the League structure, but he believed that the foundation was sound. In addition he was convinced that a lowering of the trade barriers established by the nations in the thirties was a prerequisite of international amity. Only if the "evils of nationalism and the follies of autarchy" were completely destroyed could collective security be made effective.[34]

None of the multiplicity of plans for world government, supranational authorities or regional federations caught Dafoe's imagination. These were all too idealistic, too impractical. "I have not in the least changed my mind," he wrote in June 1940, "that the founders of the League were on the right track." Though he was prepared to listen to the proponents of the more far-reaching schemes, such as the "Union Now" people, he personally refused to join in the advocacy of these ideas. Good liberal that he was, he took the moderate view that what was needed was "not as loose as the League nor as tight as Union Now."[35]

He was convinced that "the primary responsibility for the destruction of the League and for the present war rests upon the United States." If a repetition of disaster was to be avoided, a world organization that would command the support of the United States was imperative. Gradually Dafoe moved towards the view that the most satisfactory organ of collective security would be one composed almost exclusively of the democracies. Confident that democracy and the desire for peace were analogous, he believed that since totalitarian nations inevitably threatened world peace, the democratic nations would have to band together for self-preservation. "Nations outside the alliance would be kept out until they were fit company for the free nations; inevitably this means a League headed up, at least at the outset, by Great Britain and the United States," he argued. His idea for a new League, then, was not a universal association of nations. Just as in the thirties he had called upon the democracies to stand up against Hitler, now he demanded that they stand together to enforce the peace of the world. Only if this were achieved could he foresee the eventual abolition of war and the forma-

[33]*Ibid.*, Dec. 23, 1943.
[34]Dafoe Papers, Dafoe to Dr. Jacob Viner, March 20, 1940.
[35]*Ibid.*, Dafoe to E. C. Carter, June 5, 1940; Dafoe to Goldwin Gregory, Nov. 16, 1940; Dafoe to Clifford Sifton, Oct. 27, 1941.

tion of a more catholic world organizaton. "With fifty years of enforced peace," he predicted cautiously, "even the threat of war might be banished from the world."[36]

At the heart of Dafoe's conception of a new, democratic League was his belief in the need for close association among the English-speaking nations. He shared the deep concern of those internationalists who feared that there would be strong influences in the United States insisting on a return to isolationism. The crucial question was: "Can the Republican leopard change his spots?" Dafoe was cautiously hopeful. He took his shots at the incorrigible isolationists at every possible opportunity, arguing that a successor to the League was inconceivable without the "United States playing a leading role in creating and directing it."[37]

By 1943 Dafoe was quite certain that a new League would be founded upon the basis of the Allies' wartime coalition. It would have to be built on the recognition that nations in the traditional sense would continue to exist, though there would naturally be some pooling of sovereignty in the new organization. He thought that the need to give exact definition to aggression and strict formulation of the obligations of the member nations was of first importance. Finally he insisted that unless the world accepted some attenuation of sovereignty in economic affairs, its future after the war would be an anxious truce which in a short time would collapse into renewed war "beside which the present encounter will look like a Sunday School picnic." To the end he remained optimistic that a new and better world, the one that had not been achieved in 1919, would follow the conclusion of the war. World public opinion, so deathly sick of war and destruction, would force the nations to find a means to abolish war. "If I did not think this, the daily record of horrors would do me in," Dafoe wrote a month before he died.[38]

In October 1943 Dafoe was invited by Prime Minister King to accompany the Canadian delegation to the expected post-war peace conference. But on January 9, 1944, he died. No doubt he would have enjoyed a second opportunity to witness the activities of peacemakers, perhaps offering advice to the Canadian delegation as he had done in Paris in 1919, and at the Imperial Conference in 1923. There is no doubt what form that advice would have taken. Three days before his death, under the title "Blunders and Achievements," he summed up his views on the

[36]*Ibid.*, Dafoe to Dr. J. T. Shotwell, April 14, 1940; Dafoe to E. C. Carter, Jan. 27, 1941. *W.F.P.*, June 17, 1940.

[37]Dafoe Papers, Dafoe to Dr. J. T. Shotwell, Dec. 29, 1942. *W.F.P.*, June 3, 1943.

[38]Dafoe Papers, Dafoe to R. B. Inch, Feb. 8, 1943; Dafoe to Dr. W. C. Graham, Dec. 10, 1943.

League and the future in a defence of Woodrow Wilson. "Whatever mistakes Wilson may have made," he wrote, "they are dust in the balance in judging the greatness of his work and its enduring qualities. Whatever form the future structure of the world peace may take, it will rest on the foundations laid by Wilson and his co-workers in Paris in 1919."

Dafoe's vision of the post-war world was essentially the same in 1944 as it had been after the First World War. With an optimism that is no longer fashionable, he persisted in clinging to the belief that the world could be made a safe place through international co-operation. To the day he died, he believed that the League of Nations provided the essential pattern for international life. Only in such a world could nations like his Canada live free from subordination to the imperialism of the Great Powers.[39]

[39]*Ibid.*, W. L. M. King to Dafoe, Oct. 30, 1943. *W.F.P.*, Jan. 6, 1944.

xv. Western Liberal Nationalist

JOHN WESLEY DAFOE WAS A JOURNALIST, or more accurately a newspaper editor—"one of those who essay to hurl the bolts of Jove," as he once described his profession. He believed that journalism was a high calling which offered to its practitioners great opportunities, but also demanded heavy obligations from them. A newspaper editor, he contended, had to live in the faith that his readers were intelligent and critical. He gave no sanction to the claim that "people are vulgar, vicious and corrupt and that the art that appeals to them must have these qualities." No newspaper based on this assumption could ever hope to influence the public or expect its leadership to be followed. Furthermore a newspaper's independence from "outside control for ulterior purposes" had to be established if it hoped to win widespread consideration for its opinions. When a journal acquired an audience, it also acquired the duty of maintaining its integrity at the highest level, subjecting to the severest criticism "policies which it believes to be wrong and experiments which it regards as dangerous." But independence, integrity and respect for the intelligence of the reading public were not enough to secure that position of leadership which Dafoe thought it was the duty of every editor to seek. To win a position of leadership in a community a newspaper had to establish itself, through its editorial page, as the proponent of a recognizable set of views and values. As Dafoe told his journalistic colleagues in 1924, "a newspaper to attract and hold public support must have politics, convictions, loyalties, principles—in short it must have 'personality'." These were the qualities Dafoe gave to the *Free Press*.[1]

Dafoe believed that a newspaper editor's task was an important one in a democratic community, because the effectiveness of democratic

[1]Dafoe, *The Editorial Page* (n.p. 1924), 1, 4, 5; Dafoe, "Freedom and Public Opinion," *Canadian Forum*, XV, no. 77 (Aug. 1935), 342; Dafoe, *The Editorial Page*, 4.

government depended upon an informed public opinion. As a liberal he had faith in the basic rationality of men, and a belief that through education a society could be built on the just foundations of peace and human welfare. Public opinion he defined as "an expression of dominant conviction backed by an intention to give effect to it." The journalist's task was to give direction to that opinion.[2]

An editor's pronouncements, Dafoe knew, were fallible and limited because of the wide field of activities over which he had to spread his all too human capabilities. Speaking at the Convocation of the University of Manitoba in 1923, he summed up the strengths and weaknesses of his trade as he saw them:

> A journalist is hardly an authority upon anything—unless perhaps upon the appraisal of the drift of public opinion. His writings on economics are likely to be greeted by your professors of economics with a polite snort. Eminent lawyers disagree with his constitutional pronouncements. Preachers do not subscribe to his theological views. Transportation experts regard his comments on freight rates as wholly uninformed; and the financial magnates consider his ventures into the mazes of finance as the triumph of reckless ignorance over prudence. And yet in spite of all these limitations the journalist must go forward laying hands upon these and other mysteries with a sort of reckless courage; and unless he is to fail, he must, out of his half knowledge and his intuitions, and his sense of values and his knowledge of life, tell a story which may not be accurate but is still true and which does not altogether lack suggestive power.[3]

Dafoe himself made every possible effort to overcome these limitations. Though largely self-educated, he was exceptionally well read, and more important he had a strong intellect which could digest what he read. He gave much hard thought to the subjects upon which his readers expected him to make daily pronouncements. Only a man with a wide knowledge and powerful mind could have written those two solid contributions to Canadian history, *Clifford Sifton in Relation to His Times* and *Laurier: A Study in Canadian Politics*. In his more than forty years as editor of the *Free Press* Dafoe raised his newspaper from the level of a provincial party journal to one whose opinions were worthy of national consideration. Even if the views rarely had the unanimous support of the nation, they nevertheless acquired a widespread respect. It may be an exaggeration to say, as was said during Dafoe's lifetime, that "for the past generation now it has been generally true that what the *Free Press* thinks today, Western Canada will think tomorrow and

[2]Dafoe, "Public Opinion as a Factor in Government" in Q. Wright, ed., *Public Opinion in World Politics* (Chicago, 1933), 5–6, 7.
[3]Dafoe, *The University Graduate and the Community* (n.p. 1923), 4.

the intelligent part of Eastern Canada will think a few years hence," but it is true that much of what Dafoe wrote has become part of the national consciousness.[4]

The opinions which Dafoe continually advanced with clarity and forthrightness, for over four decades, were varied and sometimes inconsistent. As a publicist his ideas were largely arrived at empirically; his opinions developed in relation to the daily happenings in the world around him. Yet behind his massive outpourings was a set of presuppositions which shaped the character of the *Free Press*. These were the intellectual assumptions of a Western Liberal nationalist.

Though an Easterner by birth and early training, Dafoe became a Westerner not only by adoption, but by conviction. The Western atmosphere appealed to him. He had been born in an Ottawa Valley community which had hardly advanced beyond the pioneering stage of the West, and he understood the problems of pioneers. He was a self-made man who sympathized with people who were attempting to raise their status by self-exertion. His personal predilection was for the egalitarian ethos which characterized the pioneering agrarian community. Thus Dafoe readily found his place on the Prairies and his ideas developed in close relation to the needs and aspirations of the people of the grain-growing Western plains.

As a Westerner by conviction and sympathy, and a Liberal whose party affiliations had largely been formed before Liberalism was sanctified by the success of 1896, Dafoe was suspicious of those aspects of the National Policy which seemed to favour the ambitions of Eastern Canadian industrialists. Moreover he had that strong belief in the virtues of the tillers of the soil which is often typical of people born on the farm. His criticisms of the policies of the party in power at Ottawa, whether Liberal or Conservative, were based on the conviction that the viability of the Canadian economy was founded on the prosperity of the primary producers, especially the farmers. Successive governments were therefore exhorted to attune their policies to the needs of agriculture, rather than follow the false sirens of urban industrialism.

Dafoe's fiscal views were based on two beliefs that were both liberal and Western in their bias. First, he saw a low tariff as the only means of ensuring a prosperous West, which depended so heavily on the international market. This belief provides the key to Dafoe as a Progressive. Since the Progressive movement stood for the conservation of the Western agrarian way of life against the growing strength of Eastern

[4]F. H. Underhill, "J. W. Dafoe," *Canadian Forum*, XIII, no. 145 (Oct. 1932), 23.

industrialism, Dafoe gave his support to it; or rather he gave his support to the wing of the movement which followed T. A. Crerar and was largely interested in tariff reform. He had no sympathy with the group in the farmers' movement which followed Henry Wise Wood and espoused more radical, class-conscious views. Nor did he have anything but scorn for radical protest movements such as the C.C.F. and Social Credit, both of which, at least at the beginning, looked towards drastic changes in the country's economy.

Dafoe looked upon the independent farmers' movement as a means by which the Liberal party could be brought back to the temperate life it had led before it tasted the spoils and temptations of office. The first step towards regaining this healthy simplicity, in Dafoe's plan, was for the West to send to Ottawa a solid bloc of Western members pledged to a low tariff programme. The experience of Union Government, which had been backed by an almost solid West, further emphasized the possibilities of "bloc voting" to him. For Dafoe, as for many Westerners, Union Government was the purgatory through which they passed on their way from the hell of the old parties to the heaven of Progressivism. Dafoe hoped that a low tariff Progressive bloc would soon find allies in the Liberal party. Together these groups would deliver the Liberal party from the sin of protectionism into which it had fallen when in office. This new liberal Liberal party, in the resurgence of its faith in low tariffs, would then overcome the protectionists. But Dafoe failed to take into account the political acumen of W. L. M. King or the instability of the Progressives. Gradually the farmers' movement disintegrated, and its more moderate wing was absorbed into the Liberal party despite the continued presence of the protectionist elements. Dafoe helped to force this union in 1926 because of the peculiar circumstances of the election of that year. He never stopped advocating a low tariff but after 1926 his hope was to evangelize the Liberals by working from inside the party. By the thirties, Dafoe's simple faith in tariff reduction as a solution for nearly every economic problem became increasingly unacceptable even to Prairie farmers. In a decade when collectivism and government intervention in economic affairs won many advocates, Dafoe remained a spokesman for the past.

In addition to the Western sentiment which made Dafoe an exponent of freer trade there was his inherited nineteenth-century liberal faith which made him see protectionist policies as a cause of international friction. As an internationalist, Dafoe therefore advocated tariff reductions not only as a necessity for Western agriculture, but also as a prior condition of international co-operation. He kept on repeating his liberal trade doctrines to the world of the inter-war years, but they fell on deaf ears.

Dafoe's interests were never devoted solely to Western Canada. Indeed he always argued that his views were national rather than sectional, though he frequently took the position that what was good for the West was good for the nation. Still, he was a nationalist, even though he sometimes mistook sectional desires for the national interest. In so far as his nationalism was emotional, it was based on a profound love of his country. All his writings have an obvious undercurrent of patriotism, though none more than his now forgotten *Over the Canadian Battlefields*, published after the First World War. His complete commitment to the Canadian war effort in both wars was an expression of his nationalism. So too, of course, was his campaign for Dominion status. But Dafoe was a man whose emotions always required intellectual expression. Therefore much of his writing was devoted to explaining his views on the nature of his country and its place in the world.

Perhaps the most obvious characteristic of Dafoe's nationalism was its anti-imperialist tone. He was not an Anglophobe, for he always expressed a deep attachment to Great Britain and especially to what may loosely be called the English liberal tradition. He recognized that Canadian political institutions were of British parentage, and believed that this was as it should be. But what he did object to was every sign, real or imagined, of British interference in, or control over, Canadian affairs. His nationalism, exemplified by the belief that Canada should have complete sovereignty over all its affairs, thrived on the suspicion, even the myth, that if Canada was to preserve its autonomy it had always to be on guard against the blandishments and surreptitious scheming of British governments. Scratch an Englishman, especially a Conservative, and you will find an imperialist, often seemed to be Dafoe's view. Therefore, just as his liberalism was expressed in a defence of the virtuous, free-trade West, so it was manifested in his efforts to protect the young Canadian nation against the somewhat dissolute possessiveness of its imperial mother.

Dafoe assumed that all schemes for imperial organization implied the subordination of the dominions to Great Britain. For this reason he had no more sympathy for the proposals of Curtin and Smuts in 1943 than he had for Chamberlain's in 1902 or Lionel Curtis' in 1916. One reason for this outright rejection of all schemes to institutionalize the unity of the Empire was that Dafoe had a North American democrat's suspicion of European power politics. Every plan for imperial unity, whether expressed in terms of federation, a common foreign policy, or a third force, worked from the premises of power as the significant factor in international affairs. Dafoe was convinced that a world which approved of power politics was a world doomed to constant war or the threat of war. His alternative was a decentralized Commonwealth of equal partners, co-operating with the other nations of the world through an organization like the League of Nations.

Dafoe's view of the Commonwealth was the traditional Liberal view —an association of self-governing British nations bound together not by political ties but by common ideals. He never doubted that despite differences of opinion on various subjects, the members of the Commonwealth would be united on the important issues such as war. Here the experience of two wars in his lifetime proved him correct except about Ireland. This association of British nations, shorn of all the traits of imperialism, was an institution in which Dafoe took great pride. He took particular pride in it because it was an organization shaped in conformity with ideas evolved by Canadians. In this Commonwealth of self-governing equals, there was no conflict between nationalism and attachment to a historic association. Nor was this Commonwealth an obstacle to wider international co-operation.

Why had Canada played so large a role in the evolution of the British Commonwealth? Dafoe found the answer to this question in the nature of Canada itself, specifically in Canada's North Americanism. This theme is found in many of his writings, but it is best set forth in a series of lectures delivered at Columbia University in 1933 and published under the revealing title, *Canada an American Nation*. In this slim volume, Dafoe presented the essence of his nationalism.

It is a truism to state that Canadian history is the expression of a tension between geographic location and historic ties. The relative strength of these two forces has been the subject of eternal debate among Canadian politicians, perhaps unconsciously, and more consciously among Canadian historians. No one of any sophistication would deny that both geography and history have been of fundamental importance; the question has always been one of emphasis. In considering the nature of Canada, Dafoe struggled with this antithesis. In describing Canada as an American nation he seemed to come down on the side of the environmentalists. He did not intend to, though he knew the title of his book was provocative:

> As for a general title I have had, from such thought as I have been able to give to it, no luck. If I thought Mexico would not regard it as a casus belli, I might suggest "North America's Other Democracy." "America's Other Democracy" is a more accurate, but very flat. "Canada—A North

American Nation" might earn me a lambasting from my Imperialistic friends, but I am hardened to this usage.

In each of the suggested titles, except the one finally accepted, Dafoe's emphasis was on "democracy" as well as North America. This, too, was the emphasis of the book. In fact, Dafoe was not a complete environmentalist, though Canada's geographic position was for him the first fact to be considered in understanding the country.[5]

Dafoe was a continentalist who saw North America as a single geographic unit. It was not a political unit because of the quite different historical experiences of Canada and the United States. Both North American countries had been founded by members of the same family, in Dafoe's view; the view ignored the French. After the offspring of the family had left home to settle in North America, a basic difference had divided them. One group had found the continued parental guidance intolerable and had severed its connection entirely in 1776. The other group, while not entirely pleased with the maternalism of Britain, was much less radically inclined, and rather than cut the home tie completely had separated from the radicals and moved north. Thus while Canada and the United States were founded by people of the same stock, one group had become Revolutionaries, the other Loyalists. Those who moved to Canada, Dafoe held, were inspired by the same ideals of democracy and self-government as their revolutionary relatives, but they were not convinced that it was necessary to give up the British connection to attain their ideals. After 1776 the history of British North America was an exercise in achieving self-government and democracy without duplicating the tactics of the Thirteen Colonies. The Canadian achievement, then, was to have worked out a system of self-government within the British association of nations which, had it been possible at the time, would have prevented the tragedy of the American Revolution. Canada's struggle was the same as that of the revolutionary colonies—"the struggle between the democratic conception of Government that was carried there from the English colonies along the Atlantic, and the imported and imposed scheme of Government which the British statesmen of the day regarded as the embodiment of the lesson taught by the Revolution." But in winning the struggle Canada had refused to cast off its British heritage and had thus consciously rejected the American pattern.[6]

[5]J. M. S. Careless, "Frontierism, Metropolitanism and Canadian History," *C.H.R.*, XXXV, no. 1 (March 1954), 1–21; D. G. Creighton, "The Discovery of Canada," *U.T.Q.*, XXV, no. 3 (April 1956), 269–82; Dafoe Papers, Dafoe to Dr. H. L. McBain, Jan. 20, 1934.

[6]Dafoe, *Canada an American Nation* (New York, 1935), 11–12, 25–6, 39.

The second aspect of Canadian independence was that the country was always faced with the danger of absorption into the American union. To avoid this ever-present threat, a union of the British North American colonies had been agreed upon in 1867. Dafoe, since he was, like Goldwin Smith, a continentalist, looked upon Confederation as "a defiance of geographical and economic facts." But his continentalism increased his political nationalism, for it emphasized the necessity of resisting what he thought were the natural geographic pressures for union with the United States. In establishing the "artificial" structure of Confederation, Canadians again rejected the American example in favour of the heritage of Britain. "When Canadian statesmen were framing our constitution," Dafoe maintained, "they went to the United States not for a model but for warnings." The result was that Canadian institutions of government and Canadian political parties had a superficial similarity with those of the Republic, but "in the thing that really matters, the means by which Canadian democracy makes the policies of the country and determines its courses, we have adapted to our own ends the British methods of government which have developed down the centuries."[7]

Despite these efforts to cling to the British heritage, the fact remained that Canada was a North American nation. North American because democratic, a term which Dafoe equated freely with self-governing. This was the area in which Canada and the United States had a shared experience. Both countries had completely rejected the idea that colonies should be ruled in perpetuity by an imperial power. Canada had not adopted the American means, but its drive for self-government and democracy had been no less ardent. "The recorded facts are, I think, conclusive that it was the essential North Americanism of the Canadian people that led them into courses of thought and action with which the theory of government embodied in the Second Empire could not be permanently reconciled." The democratic impulse had caused Canadians, like Americans before them, to reject a centralized Empire.[8]

Thus for Dafoe the chief glory of Canadian history was the achievement of full self-government by means which allowed Canadians to remain true to both their North American environment and their British traditions. In this way Canada's existence as a separate nation in North America had been ensured. Dafoe believed that by the twentieth century

[7]Dafoe, "The Problems of Canada" in Sir Cecil J. B. Hurst *et al.*, *Great Britain and the Dominions* (Chicago, 1928), 137. (The well-known answer of Harold Innis to the continentalists was, "The present Dominion emerged not in spite of geography, but because of it." See *The Fur Trade in Canada* (rev. ed., Toronto, 1956), 393.) Dafoe, *Canada an American Nation*, 76, 74.
[8]Dafoe, *Canada an American Nation*, 73.

Canada had no further need to worry unduly about the preservation of its separate existence in North America. Twentieth-century Canada was strong enough to rely on its own resources for self-preservation; the British connection, though desirable, was not necessary for this reason. In fact, Canada would possibly suffer if the British connection made for imperial interference in its affairs. The moral that Dafoe drew in 1933 from the story of the Alaska Boundary dispute was not a warning of the persistence of Americans in gaining their full demands, but of British perfidy in allowing the Americans to take what they wanted. Thus Dafoe, believing that Canadian-American relations were not a serious source of worry, concentrated his attention on the winning of complete freedom from Britain.[9] Yet it is only partly true to say that in the fight for Dominion status Dafoe believed that "one of the best ways of doing this was to use the influence of the United States as a counterbalance against pressure from Westminster."[10] Certainly he emphasized the view that Canada's proximity to the United States necessitated consideration of American interests on matters which related to Canada's association with the Empire. But at the same time he repeatedly noted that Canada's rise to nationhood within the Empire was neither a parrot-like emulation of the United States nor the expression of a desire to draw away from the British association into closer relations with Canada's southern neighbour. Indeed, he pointed out in unmistakable terms that Canadian nationhood developed as a reaction to the United States, and claimed that the Republic made no direct contribution to the development of Canadian autonomy. Dafoe's agitation for national autonomy was not based primarily on a fear that continued colonial status would increase the danger of absorption into the United States, though he used this argument too, but rather on the belief that once the dominions were fully self-governing, the way would be open for close co-operation among all the English-speaking nations.[11]

One feature of Dafoe's nationalism which deserves special emphasis was his obvious neglect of the influence of the French Canadians in his assessment of Canada's national structure. Though he spent some of his early career in Montreal he never came to understand fully the people of Quebec or to sympathize with their aspirations. As a Liberal of the English-Canadian Protestant variety he was deeply suspicious of the Roman Catholic Church. One of his most persistent fears was that

[9]*Ibid.*, 69–72, 92.
[10]G. V. Ferguson, "Likely Trends in Canadian-American Political Relations," *C.J.E.P.S.*, XXII, no. 4 (Nov. 1956), 438.
[11]Dafoe, *Canada an American Nation*, 69; Dafoe, "The Unguarded Frontier," *U.T.Q.*, XII, no. 2 (Jan. 1943), 224–5.

Quebec politicians, either surreptitiously or openly, were carrying on a constant campaign for the extension of separate schools to every part of Canada. In his attitude to separate schools Dafoe was very much a Westerner and a democrat. He believed that the polyglot population of the Prairies had to be transformed into Canadians. One means of achieving this end was the common school. All minorities, French Canadians as well as others, had to be subjected to the nationalizing process, a process which in practice turned all minorities into English Canadians.

A second cause of Dafoe's lack of sympathy with the French Canadians was his belief that their essential conservatism prevented the Liberal party from adopting progressive policies. Though some French Canadians held progressive views, Dafoe was convinced that the proper home for the majority of them was in the Tory party. In his plans for a political realignment in the twenties, the splitting of the French-Canadian bloc in the Liberal party was an important step. Similarly, the conservative, "colonially-minded" French Canadians always presented an obstacle to the fulfilment of Dafoe's desire to see Canada assume full control of its constitution. In federal politics Dafoe was a moderate centralist, and this cast of mind naturally brought him into conflict with the provincial rights views of Quebec.

Finally Dafoe's nationalism with its strong internationalist flavour clashed with the isolationism that was an essential factor in the nationalism of the French Canadians. In both world wars Dafoe's nationalism was expressed in his conviction that Canada should exert itself to the limit. For him the most national and democratic means of reaching this goal was the adoption of compulsory military service. The French Canadians expressed their nationalism by opposing conscription, which they viewed as the symbol of their subjection to the English-Canadian majority. On conscription, as on the school question, Dafoe was a democrat and a supporter of majority rule, always an easy position for a member of the majority. It is true that by 1942-3 Dafoe's attitude had moderated and his sympathies for the French Canadians grown more generous. But he never wavered from the position that when conscription proved necessary it would have to be applied, as it had been in 1917, despite the opposition of Quebec. In this attitude Dafoe had a democrat's belief in equality of treatment for all groups rather than a liberal's respect for minority rights.[12]

But the principal explanation of Dafoe's attitude to the French Canadians, as well as to the United States and the Commonwealth, is found

[12]Lord Acton, "Nationality" in his *The History of Freedom and Other Essays* (London, 1922), 290.

in the one big idea that engendered all his thoughts about Canada. That idea was embodied in his frequent variations on the theme of English-speaking unity. Where did the French Canadians fit into this scheme? Dafoe did not try to answer this awkward question; indeed he ignored it. He simply assumed that Canada was primarily an English-speaking nation and, while recognizing the existence of the French-speaking minority, he apparently did not think that any special place need be found for this group in the moral unity of Anglo-Saxondom. Here he exhibited the English Canadian's tendency to assume the self-evident superiority of his own culture.

Dafoe's vision was of a reunion of the English-speaking people that would reconcile the estrangement caused by the American Revolution. Perhaps, too, it was designed to eradicate the guilt that lay on the conscience of a descendant of the United Empire Loyalists. He never thought in terms of political reunion. Both the Americans and the Canadians had rejected the institutional ties with Britain which involved subordination. Canada had likewise shown its determination to avoid absorption into the United States. But Dafoe believed that despite this permanent political separateness there was a moral unity among the English-speaking peoples which, once equality among them was accepted, would form a permanent bond of friendship. In Dafoe's view Canada formed the bridge between the United States and the rest of the English-speaking nations. Like the United States, Canada was North American, but it was also a member of the British Commonwealth "with a window on every continent." In this flexible and informal community of interests lay the basis for the kind of co-operation which Dafoe believed was "one of the world's great hopes."[13]

The real hope of the world, in Dafoe's view, was international co-operation through an organization like the League of Nations. For the successful functioning of such an organization, he saw the necessity of leadership from the morally united English-speaking world. But only an organization which accepted the existence of national sovereignty could win the support of the English-speaking nations, jealous of their individualism. He saw the world united for peace or divided for destruction by the technological advances of the modern age. Only collective security could save it from the horrors of war which would result from the rejection of co-operation and the revival of power politics. Dafoe, with the faith of a liberal democrat, believed that power

---

[13]Dafoe, "The Problems of Canada," 257, 259. The psychological interpretation of Dafoe's vision of the unity of the English-speaking world was suggested to me by Professor F. W. Gibson of Queen's University.

politics could be abolished from the affairs of the world. Because of his blindness to the nature of power in a world of nation-states, Dafoe did not foresee the difficulties that have beset the new world organization. Nor did he see the potential danger in his view of the unity of the English-speaking world. The decline of Britain and the rise of the United States to the status of a super-power have left Canada in a particularly vulnerable position in a relation which has its roots not only in moral strength but also in military and economic power. Perhaps to say this is only to admit that Dafoe's answers to Canada's problems were meant for his day only, and that new ideas must be applied to new problems.

Dafoe's Canadianism had a Western Liberal bias, but it was essentially broad and unusually generous. It was a sentiment derived mainly from a pride in his country without being blind to its shortcomings. More important, it was a nationalism which inspired him to see that no nation in the twentieth century can exist in isolation from the rest. In his view, Canadian nationalism carried responsibilities in a world of nation-states. The greatness of J. W. Dafoe of the *Free Press* lay in this conviction.

A Note on Sources

The Dafoe Papers provide the primary source of information for this study. The collection is housed at the Library of the University of Manitoba, and a complete microfilm copy is on deposit at the Public Archives of Canada in Ottawa. When the collection was organized, a largely successful attempt was made to recover either the originals or copies of all the letters which Dafoe had sent without retaining a carbon copy. Prior to 1910 Dafoe either burned on Sifton's direction, or lost, much of his correspondence with his employer. Sifton, however, seems to have kept most of his original letters, and his papers provide a valuable supplement.

In the period before 1920, the background of Canadian politics is well filled by the numerous collections of well-organized papers available in various public archives throughout Canada. After 1920 the story is different: the main collections—the King, Meighen and Bennett papers—remain closed to all but the official biographers for the time being. This has not been a serious problem since my emphasis has been mainly on Dafoe's ideas, but it would have been valuable to have been able to obtain a more complete picture of the events and personalities that Dafoe was commenting upon.

The richness of Dafoe's unpublished writing is infinitely multiplied in quantity, if not quality, by the published material. The *Free Press* is naturally the major source. Dafoe's full control of the paper allows one to use it confidently at all times. For the period after 1928 this confidence is increased by the fact that in April of that year the Free Press Library adopted a filing system which definitely identifies editorialists. I have also consulted the other newspapers that Dafoe wrote for in his younger days, but on the whole it has been nearly impossible to identify his contributions with any certainty. Indeed for the years before Dafoe became editor of the *Free Press* I have relied almost entirely on the slim amount of definitely identifiable material available. In addition to *Free Press* editorials and articles, Dafoe published scores of articles and left many manuscripts of unpublished addresses. A fairly complete list of his published writings, "Bibliography of J. W. Dafoe (1866–1944)," was compiled by Inga Thomson and Marcella Dafoe and published in the *Canadian Journal of Economics and Political Science*, vol. X, no. 2 (May 1944), pp. 213-15. I have been able to add a few items to this list and, if they are of importance, they appear in the notes.

As for secondary sources the notes indicate my indebtedness to a whole range of writing about Canada. No useful purpose would be served in compiling the list. Therefore I shall include only the manuscript collections.

1. PUBLIC ARCHIVES OF CANADA: Dafoe Papers, Sifton Papers, Laurier Papers, Borden Papers, Willison Papers, Rowell Papers, Hudson Papers, Flavelle Papers, Minto Papers

2. PUBLIC ARCHIVES OF MANITOBA: Ewart Papers, Crerar Papers (Dafoe's diary of the 1923 Imperial Conference)

3. UNIVERSITY OF TORONTO LIBRARY: Wrong Papers, Walker Papers, Mavor Papers

4. TORONTO PUBLIC REFERENCE LIBRARY: Dafoe Papers, Main Johnson Papers

5. PUBLIC ARCHIVES OF ONTARIO: Whitney Papers

6. SCOTTISH PUBLIC RECORD OFFICE: Lothian Papers

7. IN THE POSSESSION OF MR. HENRY BORDEN, Q.C.: Borden Diaries

The following abbreviations have been used in the footnotes.

A.H.R., American Historical Review
C.A.R., Canadian Annual Review
C.H.R., Canadian Historical Review
C.J.E.P.S., Canadian Journal of Economics and Political Science
M.F.P., Manitoba Free Press
Q.Q., Queen's Quarterly
U.T.Q., University of Toronto Quarterly
W.F.P., Winnipeg Free Press

Index

ABERHART, WILLIAM, 201, 216, 226, 229, 231, 232
Alaska boundary dispute, 26–7, 292
Alberta schools, 159–60
American Revolution, 4, 22, 176, 185, 290, 294
Amery, L. S., 144, 177, 196, 197, 245
Anglo-Japanese alliance, 134, 135
Angus, H. F., 216, 231
Article X, 89, 90, 238
Asquith, H. H., 36
Astor, Lord and Lady, 250
Atlantic Charter, 275
Autonomy bills, 32
Aylesworth, Sir Allen, 134

BALDWIN, STANLEY, 144, 161
Balfour Declaration, 140, 164, 181, 182, 219, 236
Bassett, J., 267
Batterwood House conference, 206, 222
Beauharnois scandal, 204
Beaverbrook, Lord, 195
Bennett, R. B., 158, 191, 192–3, 198, 201, 241, 279; leader of Conservatives, 188; attacks Dafoe, 196, 197; "New Deal," 209; on Canadian constitution, 215, 221; on Dafoe's appointment to Rowell-Sirois Commission, 216
Bilingual schools, 55, 69, 70. *See also*: Manitoba school question; Regulation 17
Bill 80, 270
Bird, T. W., 163
Blake, Edward, 201, 224; influence on Dafoe, 7–8
Bloom, C., 276
Boer War, 13–14, 19
Bonn, M. J., 206
Borden, Sir Robert, 39, 46, 47, 49, 50, 51, 53, 57, 66, 77, 81, 87, 88, 96, 115, 131, 132, 139, 143, 279; naval policy, 61; denounced as imperialist, 62; bilingual schools, 69; manpower problem, 73; view of Dafoe, 74, 77, 88, 90, 133; announces conscription, 75; proposes coalition, 75; at Peace Conference, 88; Resolution IX, 89; seeks to strengthen Union Government, 105; retirement, 107
Bourassa, Henri, 40, 46, 47, 56, 57, 62, 70, 72, 76, 79, 82, 84, 155, 159, 184, 218
Bowell, Mackenzie, 12
Bracken, John, 231, 271–2
Brebner, J. B., 279
British North America Act, 4, 214, 226
Brittain, H. E., 37
Brown, George, 74
Brownlee, J. E., 160
Buchanan, W. A., 147, 271
Budget (1924), 149
Burchell, C. J., 229
Byng, Lord, 162, 163, 164, 165, 267

Canada an American Nation, 289–92
Canada Fights, 273–5
Canadian Council of Agriculture, 97, 106
Canadian National Railways, 150, 198, 205
Canadian Pacific Railway, 8, 15, 115, 121, 150, 151
Calder, J. A., 78, 80
Cecil, Lord David, 88
Chamberlain, Sir Joseph, 9, 20, 25, 288
Chamberlain, Neville, 250, 251, 252, 253, 255
Chambers of Commerce of the Empire, 36
Chanak, 137, 174, 267
Churchill, Winston, 251, 253, 264, 269, 277, 280

Citizens' Committee of One Thousand, 99
Cliveden Set, 250, 251
Confederation, 219, 220, 224, 227
Cooper, Duff, 253
Co-operative Commonwealth Federation, 205, 206, 207–8, 212, 265, 270, 271, 287
Côté, Thomas, 71, 86
Crandall, C. F., 109
Crerar, T. A., 77, 80, 87, 107, 109, 113, 114, 119, 124, 125, 148, 201, 212, 230, 231, 248, 271, 287; resigns Union Government, 102; farmers in politics, 103, 109; on post-war politics (1919), 104; negotiates Liberal-Progressive coalition, 118; wheat board, 121; radical Progressives, 123; retires from Progressive leadership, 123
Crow's Nest Pass Agreement, 15, 121–2, 150, 163, 193
Curtin, John, 278, 288
Curtis, Lionel, 58, 93, 177, 288
Curzon, Lord, 21, 141, 142, 143
Customs Scandal, 160

DAFOE, CALVIN WESLEY (J. W. D.'s father), 4, 5
Dafoe, John Wesley: goes to Winnipeg (1901), 3; on United Empire Loyalists, 4, 294; ancestry and childhood, 4–5; education, 5; on education, 5; school teacher, 5–6; becomes journalist, 6; early journalism in Montreal, 6–7; on Edward Blake, 7; attitude to Laurier, 8, 42, 70, 72, 77; on Riel, 8–9; edits *Ottawa Evening Journal*, 9–10; reporter for *M. F. P.*, 10; Manitoba school question, 11–12, 13; edits *Family Herald and Weekly Star*, 12; role in 1896 election, 12–13; attitude to Roman Catholic Church, 13; marriage, 13; Boer War, 13–14; writer of fiction and poetry, 14; relations with Sifton, 16, 17, 45–6, 188–90; becomes editor of *M.F.P.*, 16–17; relations with E. H. Macklin, 17; view of West, 20, 41, 286; concept of Empire (1901), 21–4; attacks Lord Minto, 21–3; on Laurier's imperial policy, 24–5; attitude to United States, 26–7, 178, 243, 267, 292; attitude to Liberals and Conservatives, 28; tariff, 28–9, 43, 54, 110–11, 114, 122, 194, 287–8; West and Liberals, 29, 30, 70, 187; *Free Press* policy, 29–30, 114; big business, 30, 188; Hudson Bay Railway, 30, 150; electoral lists, 31; Northwest schools, 31; French Canadians, 31, 83–4, 86–7, 182, 184, 265, 266–7, 292–3; separate schools, 32, 293; Autonomy bills, 32–3; Sifton's resignation from Laurier Government, 33; visits England, 36; naval policy, 36–7, 39–41, 56, 57–8, 60–5; attends Imperial Press Conference (1909), 37–9; concept of Empire (1909), 38–9; Imperial Council, 40; Roblin Government, 41, 55–6; reciprocity (1911), 43–7; election of 1911, 46–8; Conservative party, 52, 62, 160; Liberals after 1911, 52; criticisms of Borden Government, 53–4; bilingual schools, 55, 69, 70; Bourassa nationalism, 57, 70–1, 77; Canadian nationalism, 57; Great War, 66–7, 68; critical of Borden's war effort, 68; Lapointe Resolution, 70–1; political situation (1916), 73; manpower problem (1916), 73; Union Government, 73–4, 76–7, 78–9, 80, 81, 87, 98, 106–7; view of Borden, 74, 88, 94, 106, 131; urges Laurier to join coalition, 75; conscription (1917), 75, 76; breaks with Laurier, 77; Western Liberal convention, 78–9, 80; on Quebec (1917), 78–9; election of 1917, 81, 82; racial division (1917), 82–3; breaks with Liberals (1917), 83–4; contrast with Laurier's nationalism, 84–5; attitude to W. L. M. King, 87, 106, 114, 123, 126, 142, 145, 146, 152, 156, 160, 169, 180–2, 204, 254, 263–4, 267–8, 272; at Peace Conference, 88–90; *Over the Canadian Battlefields*, 89–90; League of Nations, 90–1, 171, 172–3, 235, 238, 245, 246–7, 253; U.S. and League, 91–2, 172, 239; development of nationalism during Great War, 93; on Lionel Curtis, 94; development of Dominion status, 95–6, 129–30, 131–2, 138, 143, 171, 177–8; Winnipeg General Strike, 100–1; social views, 101–2; on post-war politics (1919), 103–4, 106–7; farmer-labour alliance, 104–5, 122; National Liberal

convention, 105–6; farmers in politics, 106, 108; H. W. Wood, 108; Liberal party, 108, 113, 147; political realignment, 109; division in farmers' movement, 109–10, 113; Progressive party, 110, 116–17, 124, 146–7, 193–4; on Crerar, 111–12, 119; Liberal-Progressive alliance, 111–14, 116, 118, 122, 126–7, 148, 152, 155, 156–7; Progressivism, 112, 286–7; on politics, 112–13, 158–9; Progressives and tariff, 114, 149; railway problems, 115, 150; Western natural resources, 115; Conservative party prospects (1921), 120; wheat board, 121; J. S. Woodsworth, 122–3; Robert Forke, 124, 157; farm debt, 125; ocean freight rates, 126–7; divisions in King Government, 126; Imperial War Cabinet, 129; J. S. Ewart, 129–30; "Kingdom of Canada," 131; independent foreign policy, 132–4, 139; common imperial foreign policy, 132, 141, 177; Commonwealth as counterweight, 133; "imperialists," 133–4; "colonialists," 134; on Meighen's imperial views, 135–6, 179; Anglo-Japanese alliance, 135; Washington Conference, 136; on King's imperial views, 137, 138, 140, 180; Lloyd George, 137; Chanak, 137–8; Halibut Treaty, 138; Imperial Conference (1923), 141–3; Smuts at Imperial Conference (1923), 143; importance of Imperial Conference (1923), 144–5; Charles Dunning, 148; 1924 budget, 149; "Ginger Group," 150; Western secessionism, 151; attitude to Meighen, 152, 157–8, 159, 265–6; alternative vote, 152, 153; plan to replace King, 154–5; political situation (1925), 156; royal power of dissolution, 158, 161–2, 163–4; 1926 election, 163–4, 166–7; dispute with Forsey, 165–6; royal power of dismissal, 167; Progressives in 1926, 168–9; Lausanne Treaty, 174; Geneva Protocol, 174–5; status and foreign policy, 175, 184–5, 236; "Rise of the Commonwealth," 176–7; American Revolution, 176, 185; Canadian isolationism, 177, 237, 242–3, 246, 247–8, 259; Commonwealth and war, 178–9; Imperial Conference (1926), 180–1; King's role at Imperial Conference (1926), 181–2; Balfour Declaration, 181, 182–3; India, 183; Commonwealth and U.S., 183; "The Problems of Canada," 184; English-speaking unity, 184, 185–6, 274–5, 293–4; attitude to Britain, 185, 288; asked to contest 1926 election, 187; compares Bennett and King, 188; on newspapers, 189; view of economic depression, 190–1, 199–200; election of 1930, 191–2; attitude to Bennett, 192, 195, 196, 198–9; on economic nationalism, 192; farm problems, 194; imperial preference, 195; Imperial Economic Conference, 196–7, 198; Canadian Pacific Railway, 198; Duff Commission, 198; Liberal-Conservative coalition (1931), 199; socialism, 199, 201; Keynes, 200–1; Aberhart, 201; U.S. New Deal, 201; on political leadership in thirties, 201; Cobdenism, 202; offers to resign from *Free Press* editorship, 202; western radicalism in thirties, 203; Liberal reforms, 203, 204–5, 206; losing touch with West, 204; Beauharnois scandal, 204; liberalism, 206, 208, 212–13, 287; Liberal-C.C.F. alliance, 207; C.C.F. 207–8, 271; Bennett New Deal, 209–11; *Sir Clifford Sifton in Relation to His Times*, 211, 285; refuses King's offer of cabinet or diplomatic post, 211, 216; trade with U.S., 212; Rowell-Sirois Commission, 216, 223–4, 226–7; British North America Act, 217–23; federal powers, 217, 225–6; Judicial Committee of the Privy Council, 217, 220; French-Canadian attitude to B.N.A. Act, 218; compact theory, 218–20, 221, 226; provincial rights, 220; constitutional amendment, 222; Dr. J. Sirois, 226–7; federal power of disallowance, 227; effect of war on federal system, 229–30; Dominion-Provincial Conference (1941), 231–2; continued advocacy of Rowell-Sirois principles, 232–4; wartime tax agreements, 233; Wilsonian faith, 235; public opinion, 235, 238–9, 285; determinants of Canadian foreign policy, 236; Canada, Commonwealth and League, 236–8, 240; League and democracy, 239;

League and Canadian status, 240; disarmament, 240–1; Treaty of Versailles, 241; causes of war, 241; Hitler, 242; appeasement, 243; Riddell incident, 244; imperial centralizers, 245, 258–9; King's foreign policy, 246–7; Canadian neutrality, 247, 252–3; national unity, 248; Imperial Conference (1937), 248–9; pessimism about peace, 249–50; on Shanghai, 250; Munich, 250–3; Cliveden Set, 250–1; Neville Chamberlain, 252; Polish crisis, 254–5; outbreak of war (1939), 255; internationalism, 256, 293, 294–5; critique of democracy, 256–7; power politics, 257–8; Canada and Second World War, 260–1; wartime election, 261–2; preparedness, 262; National Government, 262, 266–8; conscription (1917 and 1942), 262–3, 264–5; plebiscite, 263, 269–70; South York by-election, 266; Bill 80, 270; post-war politics, 271–2; John Bracken, 271–2; U.S. responsibility for Second World War, 273–5; *Canada Fights*, 273–5; U.S. entry into war, 275–6; post-war international organization, 276, 281–3; Luce publications, 277; Churchill, 277; wartime centralizers, 277–8; wartime relations with Britain and U.S., 278–9; Smuts' "third force," 279–80; journalism, 284–5; *Laurier: A Study in Canadian Politics*, 285; Westerner, 286–7; nationalist, 288; Commonwealth, 288–9; *Canada an American Nation*, 289–92; Canada's North Americanism, 289–92

Dafoe, Van, 259
Dafoe, Wallace, 211
Dale, Arch, vii, 209
Dawson, G., 170, 196, 250
Dawson, R. MacG., 119
Dexter, Grant, 196, 220
Dilke, Sir Charles, 38
Doherty, C. J., 279
Dominion-Provincial Conference: (1927), 219, 221; (1935), 222; (1941), 230–1
Dreadnoughts, 39, 61, 64
Drew, George, 262, 267
Drummond-Arthabaska by-election, 40
Drury, E. C., 113
Duff Commission, 198

Dunning, Charles, 104, 148, 152, 154, 155, 156, 162, 191
Dunning budget, 191
Duplessis, Maurice, 226, 261

ELCOMBE, MARY (J. W. D.'s mother), 4
Election: of 1896, 12–13; of 1911, 46–7; of 1917, 81–3; of 1921, 116; of 1925, 153–4; of 1926, 166–7, 168, 180; of 1930, 191–2; of 1935, 210; of 1940, 261–2
Ewart, J. S., 95, 129, 183

Family Herald and Weekly Star, 6, 12
Farmers' Advocate, 119
Fay, C. R., 200
Ferguson, G. Howard, 201, 219, 221, 222
Ferguson, G. V., 225, 251, 252, 255
Fielding, W. S., 33, 62, 104, 122
Fielding tariff, 33
Fitzpatrick, C., 32
Flavelle, Sir Joseph, 74, 97, 115
Forke, Robert, 124, 149, 156, 157
Forsey, E. A., 162, 164, 164–5n, 165
Foster, Sir George, 90
Fowler, R. M., 228
Freight rates, 42, 54–5, 126

GANDHI, 277
Garvin, A. L., 250
Geneva Protocol, 174, 257
George V, 161
George VI, 253, 254
"Ginger Group," 150, 194
Gouin, Sir Lomer, 103, 105, 109, 117, 120, 122, 123, 124, 147
Graham, George, 75, 78, 123, 143
Graham, Sir Hugh, 6, 12, 13, 62
Grain Growers' Guide, 49
Greenway, Thomas, 11
Greenwood, Hamar, 60
Gregory, W. D., 192

HALDANE, LORD, 218
Halibut Treaty, 138, 141, 267
Hankey, Sir Maurice, 142
Harris, H. Wilson, 245
Haydon, A., 118
Hepburn, M. F., 201, 222, 226, 229, 230, 231, 232, 262, 267
Herridge, William, 210
Hertzog, J. B. M., 181, 182

Hitler, Adolf, 239, 242, 244, 250, 251, 252, 253, 254, 255, 258, 259, 261, 262, 278
Hoare, Sir Samuel, 244
Hoare-Laval agreement, 244, 246
Hudson, A. B., 80, 148, 154
Hudson Bay Railway, 10, 30, 43, 148, 150, 163, 193

IMPERIAL CONFERENCE: (1911), 40; (1921), 134; (1923), 127, 140, 169, 267, 282; (1926), 180; (1930), 221; (1937), 248-9
Imperial Economic Conference (1932), 195-7
Imperial Press Conference: (1909), 37-9; (1920), 95; (1925), 153; (1930), 191, 195
Imperial War Cabinet, 129, 277
Imperial War Conference, 94, 128, 131
Innis, H. A., 291n
Irvine, William, 156

JOHNSON, M., 79
Jones, W. P., 226
Judicial Committee of the Privy Council, 217, 220

KERR, PHILIP, 58, 88, 210, 237, 249, 250
Keynes, J. M., 200, 201
King, W. L. M., 101, 104, 106, 107, 109, 122, 125, 148, 153, 156, 159, 162, 170, 188, 191, 201, 206, 207, 221, 222, 223, 225, 236, 239, 241, 253, 254, 255, 261, 262, 263, 265, 266, 267, 268, 269, 270, 271, 272, 279, 287; prospective Liberal leader, 87; weakness in West, 111, 152, 155, 204; leadership qualities, 113, 147, 202-3; and Progressives, 117, 118; forms Government (1921), 120; and ocean freight rates, 126; Imperial Conference (1923), 128, 138-9, 141-3; 1925 election, 154; in constitutional crisis of 1926, 165; on Lausanne Treaty, 174; Imperial Conference (1926), 180-2; offers Dafoe cabinet or diplomatic post, 211, 216; on Bennett New Deal, 215; Rowell-Sirois Commission, 230, 231; foreign policy, 246-7, 248; Imperial Conference (1937), 249; Munich, 251;
Imperial War Cabinet, 277; invites Dafoe to Peace Conference, 282
Kylie, Edward: describes Dafoe, 49

LABOUR TROUBLES (1919), 98
Lacombe, Father, 13
Lambert, R. S., 206
Langley, George, 104
Lapointe, Ernest, 103, 105, 120, 123, 180, 206, 219, 222, 230, 244, 255, 266, 269, 272
Lapointe Resolution, 71-2, 82, 84
Laurier, Sir Wilfrid, 8, 12, 13, 17, 24, 31, 47, 52, 79, 82, 131, 201, 224, 248, 264, 279; Manitoba school question, 13, 32, 33; on Lord Minto, 22; imperial policy, 25, 34; provincial status for Northwest, 32; on Western politics, 51; isolationist viewpoint, 59; election possibilities (1914), 68; bilingual schools, 69; Lapointe Resolution, 71; conscription, 75-6; fear of Bourassa, 76; Western Liberal convention, 78; on Dafoe, 83; view of Great War, 84-5
Lausanne Treaty, 174
League of Nations, 90-1, 210, 235, 240, 245, 249, 256, 257, 258, 281, 283, 294
Lemieux, R., 103, 105
Lippmann, Walter, 206
Litvinov, Maxim, 236
Lloyd George, David, 88, 136-7
Locarno Pact, 175, 244
Lothian, Lord. See Kerr, Philip
Luce, Henry, 275
Luxton, W. F., 11

MCCARTHY, D'ALTON, 11
McCullagh, G., 266, 267
Macdonald, E. M., 74
Macdonald, H. J., 15
Macdonald, Sir John A., 6, 7, 9, 11, 24, 26, 74, 131, 218, 224, 226
MacDonald, Ramsay, 161, 174
Macdonnell, J. M., 194
MacIver, R. M., 206
MacKay, R. A., 216
Mackenzie, Alexander, 201
Mackenzie, Ian, 254
Mackenzie and Mann, 54
Macklin, E. H., 15, 17, 45
MacRea, D. B., 180-1
Magurn, A. J., 15, 16

Manion, R. J., 262
Manitoba Act, 12
Manitoba Free Press: origin, 11; acquired by Sifton, 15–16; becomes *Winnipeg Free Press*, 202
Manitoba Grain Act, 30
Manitoba school question, 11–12, 31–2, 41–2. *See also* Bilingual schools
Maritime Rights, 155
Martin, Chester, 242
Martin, Joseph, 11, 14
Massey, Vincent, 204, 206
Mather, John, 15
Medicine Hat by-election, 113
Meighen, Arthur, 54, 77, 84, 107, 111, 113, 124, 134, 136, 143, 145, 152, 159, 160, 162, 163, 164, 166, 168, 169, 187, 271; imperial views, 131, 135; Chanak, 137; right to form Government, 154; danger to West, 157; 1926 Government, 162–3; Hamilton speech, 179; resumes Conservative leadership, 265; defeated in South York, 266
Military Voters' Act, 81
Milner, Lord, 21
Minto, Lord: Dafoe attacks, 21–2; protests to Laurier, 22, 23
Mitchell, Humphrey, 266
Moley, R., 201
Monk, F. D., 39, 56
Monroe Doctrine, 26
Mowat, Sir Oliver, 201
Muir, R., 206
Munich, 250–1, 252, 253, 254
Mussolini, Benito, 244, 247, 253

NANTEL, B., 56
Nanton, A., 74
National Liberal convention, 96, 105
National Policy, 8, 111, 286
Natural Resources Mobilization Act, 270
Naval aid bill, 63
Naval policy, 36–7, 39–41, 56, 57–8, 60–5
Naval Service Act (1910), 40
New National Policy, 98
Norris, T. C., 69, 158
North Atlantic shipping combine, 151
Northwest Rebellion, 8
Northwest school question, 31
Noseworthy, J. W., 265

O'CONNOR, E. G., 6, 7, 12
Ogdensburg agreement, 274
One Big Union, 98
Ottawa Evening Journal, 9–10
Over the Canadian Battlefields, 89–90

PACT OF PARIS, 241, 249, 257
Paris Peace Conference, 88, 282
Parmelee, Alice (Mrs. J. W. Dafoe), 13, 263
Pattullo, T. D., 229, 231, 233; attacks *Free Press*, 232
Pelletier, L.-P., 56
Peterson, Sir William, 151
Port Hope conference, 206
Preston, W. T. R., 151
Progressive party, 110, 116–17, 146–7, 148, 193–4; divisions, 109–10, 113, 119, 121; negotiations with Liberals, 119, 148, 152, 155, 168; freight rates, 122

QUEBEC NATIONALISTS, 40, 46, 60, 75–6
Queen, John, 101

RAILWAYS: public ownership, 30, 43, 54. *See also*: Canadian National Railways; Canadian Pacific Railway; Hudson Bay Railway
Ralston, J. L., 206, 255
Reciprocity (1911), 43–7
Regina Leader, 114
Regulation 17, 69
Reid, Escott, 243
Resolution IX, 94–5, 131
Richardson, R. L., 14
Riddell incident, 244
Riel, Louis, 8–9
Rinfret, T., 215, 224
Robb, J. A., 123, 126
Roblin, Sir R. P., 31, 33, 34, 39, 41, 55, 66, 68
Rogers, Norman McL., 220
Rogers, Robert, 33, 67, 68
Roosevelt, F. D., 201, 209, 254, 269, 275
Roosevelt, T., 20, 26
Round Table movement, 49, 58, 85, 93, 94, 130, 177, 178, 279
Rowell, N. W., 79, 81, 87, 88, 105, 106, 215
Rowell-Sirois Commission, 215, 250, 254, 259, 265; Dafoe's role, 228; recommendations, 228–9

Royal Commission on Dominion-Provincial Relations. *See* Rowell-Sirois Commission

ST. LAURENT, LOUIS S., 266, 267
Savard, A., 228
Sbaretti, Mgr, 33
Shanghai, Japanese attack, 250
Shaughnessy plan, 115
Shotwell, J. T., 201, 216, 223, 250
Sifton, Arthur, 87, 279
Sifton, Clifford, (1893-), 190
Sifton, Sir Clifford (1861-1929), 3, 4, 14, 21, 35, 36, 55, 81, 87, 98, 126; Manitoba school question, 12; acquires *M.F.P.*, 15-16; on journalism, 15-16; on Dafoe, 16-17; *Free Press* policy, 17; Alaska boundary dispute, 26-7; tariff, 29, 52, 110-11; resignation from Laurier Government, 32-3; conflict with Dafoe on reciprocity, 45-6; 1911 election, 45-7; naval policy, 61; Lapointe Resolution, 71; Western Liberal convention, 78; Union Government, 80; isolationism, 92, 172, 175; Winnipeg General Strike, 99; post-war politics (1919), 103; Liberals and Progressives, 118; Wheat board, 121; Imperial Conference (1923), 138-9; 1925 election, 154; Imperial Conference (1926), 181; death, 188-9
Sifton, Harry, 160, 190
Sifton, John, 190
Sifton, Victor, 190
Sirois, Joseph, 216, 226-7, 265
Skelton, Alex, 232
Skelton, O. D., 139, 141, 142, 143, 181
Smith, Goldwin, 38, 291
Smuts, J. C., 88, 136, 278, 288; Imperial Conference (1923), 143; suggests "third force," 279
Social Credit party, 205, 212, 287
South York by-election, 265-6, 271
Spanish Civil War, 244
Statute of Westminster, 221
Stevenson, John, 146, 148, 188, 265, 267, 268
Strachey, John, 201
Symington, H. J., 154

TACHÉ, ARCHBISHOP, 12

Taft, H., 43
Tarte, Joseph-Israël, 12
Taschereau, L. A., 219, 221
Tawney, R. H., 201, 206
Thompson, Sir John, 224
Toronto Electric Commissioners v. *Snider*, 217
Toronto Liberal convention, 78
Toynbee, A. J., 244
Treaty of Versailles, 241, 244
Tugwell, R., 201
Tupper, C. H., 7
Tupper, Sir Charles, 7, 36
Turriff, J. G., 79

UNION GOVERNMENT, 263, 279, 287; campaign for, 76-81; formation, 81; limitations, 86; disintegration, 97, 102; and labour unrest, 98; efforts to win Quebec support, 103
United Empire Loyalists, 4, 294

"VOICE OF CANADA," 273
Voters' lists, 42

WALKER, SIR EDMUND, 51, 58
Ward, Sir Joseph, 40
War-time Election Act, 81
Washington Conference, 136
Watson, Lord, 218
Western Liberal convention, 78-80
Western secessionism, 151
Wheat board, 121
Whitney, Sir James, 58, 60n
Whyte, Sir Frederick, 179
Willison, Sir John, 8, 95, 115, 134, 170
Wilson, Woodrow, 51, 89, 206, 250, 256, 275, 283
Winnipeg General Strike, 99-102
Winnipeg Grain Exchange, 19
Wood, Henry Wise, 80, 105, 113, 124, 287; group government, 108; on Crerar, 121
Woodburn, A. S., 9
Woodsworth, J. S., 105, 122-3, 149, 156, 209, 217
World Economic Conference, 242
Wrong, G. M., 74, 93, 201
Wrong, H. H., 177

ZIMMERN, SIR ALFRED, 240